SCOTTISH PRESBYTERIANISM RE-ESTABLISHED

Scottish Religious Cultures *Historical Perspectives*

Series Editors: Scott R. Spurlock and Crawford Gribben

Religion has played a key formational role in the development of Scottish society shaping cultural norms, defining individual and corporate identities, and underpinning legal and political institutions. This series presents the very best scholarship on the role of religion as a formative and yet divisive force in Scottish society and highlights its positive and negative functions in the development of the nation's culture. The impact of the Scots diaspora on the wider world means that the subject has major significance far outwith Scotland.

Available titles

George Mackay Brown and the Scottish Catholic Imagination
Linden Bicket

Poor Relief and the Church in Scotland, 1560–1650
John McCallum

Jewish Orthodoxy in Scotland: Rabbi Dr Salis Daiches and Religious Leadership
Hannah Holtschneider

Miracles of Healing: Psychotherapy and Religion in Twentieth-century Scotland
Gavin Miller

George Strachan of the Mearns: Seventeenth-century Orientalist
Tom McInally

Scottish Presbyterianism Re-established: The Case of Stirling and Dunblane, 1687–1710
Andrew T. N. Muirhead

The Scots Afrikaners: Identity Politics and Intertwined Religious Cultures in Southern and Central Africa
Retief Müller

Forthcoming titles

Dugald Semple and the Life Reform Movement
Steven Sutcliffe

William Guild and Moderate Divinity in Early Modern Scotland
Russell Newton

The Dynamics of Dissent: Politics, Religion and the Law in Restoration Scotland
Neil McIntyre

The Catholic Church in Scotland: Financial Development 1772–1930
Darren Tierney

edinburghuniversitypress.com/series/src

SCOTTISH PRESBYTERIANISM RE-ESTABLISHED

The Case of Stirling and Dunblane, 1687–1710

ANDREW T. N. MUIRHEAD

EDINBURGH
University Press

Edinburgh University Press is one of the leading university presses in the UK. We publish academic books and journals in our selected subject areas across the humanities and social sciences, combining cutting-edge scholarship with high editorial and production values to produce academic works of lasting importance. For more information visit our website: edinburghuniversitypress.com

© Andrew T. N. Muirhead, 2021

Edinburgh University Press Ltd
The Tun – Holyrood Road
12 (2f) Jackson's Entry
Edinburgh EH8 8PJ

Typeset in 10/12 ITC New Baskerville by
Servis Filmsetting Ltd, Stockport, Cheshire

A CIP record for this book is available from the British Library

ISBN 978 1 4744 4738 6 (hardback)
ISBN 978 1 4744 4740 9 (webready PDF)
ISBN 978 1 4744 4741 6 (epub)

The right of Andrew T. N. Muirhead to be identified as author of this work has been asserted in accordance with the Copyright, Designs and Patents Act 1988 and the Copyright and Related Rights Regulations 2003 (SI No. 2498).

Contents

	List of Tables	vii
	Acknowledgements	viii
	Detail from Ecclesiastical Map of Scotland, 1825	x
	Introduction: Post-Revolution Presbyterianism in Central Scotland	1
1	Scotland and its National Church in 1688	10
2	Ministering in the Presbyteries: Exiles and Antediluvians	32
3	Ensuring the Continuity of Ministry	46
4	The Courts of the Church and the Business of Presbytery	71
5	The Eldership and the Heritors	87
6	Celebrating the Sacraments	109
7	Preaching the Word, Week by Week	128
8	The Survival of Episcopacy	143
9	Church Discipline and the Law	158
10	Dunblane's Highland Parishes	179
11	The Church and the Union of Parliaments	195
	Conclusion: The New Ecclesiastical Regime	213
	Appendices	225
	Bibliography	232
	Index	251

Tables

1.1	Control of Parishes, 1689–1700	28
3.1	Average Collections when Probationers were Preaching in Alva, 1698–9	57
3.2	Average Collections when Probationers were Preaching in Dollar, 1700	58
4.1	Attendance of Ministers of Dunblane Presbytery	72
4.2	Attendance at Synod of Perth and Stirling, 1691–1709	81
6.1	Number of Baptisms Recorded, 1687–1710	120
7.1	Word Counts in Turnbull's Header Texts	140
9.1	Discipline Cases in St Ninians Kirk Session Records, 1667–93	159
11.1	Local Petitions against the Union of Parliaments, 1706	207

Acknowledgements

A book such is this is never written solely from the author's resources but relies to a great extent on the labours of others. This particular book owes a huge debt of gratitude to three first-class institutions, Stirling Council Archives, the Historical Search Room of the National Records of Scotland and the National Library of Scotland, and of course the staff who make them function.

The project originally grew out of indexing church records in Stirling Council Archives so my thanks go not only to Pam McNicol for her help and encouragement and for facilitating access to church records but to her colleague, Neil Dickson, and the Thursday morning volunteers whose chat, frequently rude but always entertaining, is sadly missed in the aftermath of Covid-19.

The staff of both the NRS and NLS are unfailingly courteous and helpful; the eResources available through the latter are a treasure beyond compare, especially as they gave access to material while the physical resources of the library were locked down. Thanks also go to John Harrison, a local historian with an encyclopaedic knowledge of Stirling and a generous spirit of sharing it, and the archivist at Blair Castle whose summary of relevant records obviated the need to go there.

Special thanks go to the anonymous compiler of Ecclegen.com, a website which indexes and links all the ministers listed in the *Fasti Ecclesiae Scoticanae* and in several other publications to the digitised versions of the works as well as exploring family relationships. A true labour of love, it saved considerable time in tracking down the ministers and probationers who appeared in my research.

To Scott Spurlock, series editor for EUP, I owe a debt of gratitude for encouraging me to submit my outline to EUP for consideration; his backing meant a lot. Other friends in academia have given considerable help; Alasdair Raffe and David Bebbington both read an early draft and gave me full and detailed suggestions for improvement, which I have tried, not necessarily successfully, to follow through. In a sense, David started my journey in academic history by supervising my MLitt thesis as his first postgraduate supervision in 1982; he has remained a friend and encouragement ever since. Others such as Karin Bowie and Alistair Mutch have commented usefully on small portions of the research while Tristram Clarke, Russell Newton and Michael Riordan have also brought light to bear on various aspects of the work, and some have generously lent books. EUP's copy editor, Jonathan Wadman, has done his work with an attention to detail which I can only marvel at and envy, so my thanks also go to him. All mistakes and shortcomings are, however, of my own making.

I am indebted, too, to the Strathmartine Trust for a grant which enabled me to buy books which I would otherwise have struggled to access as an independent researcher.

The illustration of a segment of Arrowsmith's 1825 *Ecclesiastical Map of Scotland* is reproduced courtesy of the NLS.

Closer to home, my thanks go to Tom Turner, whose unfailing encouragement and friendship has been so valuable in the writing of this, and to my wife Sheena, who has encouraged, prodded and tholed an enthusiasm (which she does not share) with exemplary patience and in the latter stages slaved over proofreading. Our children complained that they were not mentioned in my previous book; I therefore dedicate this book jointly to Gavin, Kirsty and Sandy, and to Sheena with love.

Detail from *Ecclesiastical Map of Scotland*, 1825, showing Stirling and Dunblane Presbytery bounds and location of parishes. © Mapping by Aaron Arrowsmith, Image supplied by National Library of Scotland

INTRODUCTION

Post-Revolution Presbyterianism in Central Scotland

Behold, I come quickly: hold that fast which thou hast, that no man take thy Crown.

In October 1706, the Reverend John Logan, minister of Alloa in the Presbytery of Stirling, preached from that text in the Book of Revelation[1] to the Duke of Queensberry, Queen Anne's high commissioner in Scotland, and to the Estates of the Scottish Parliament. It is one of a mere handful of printed sermons known by any member of either Stirling or Dunblane Presbytery in the twenty years following the accession of William as king.[2] The sermon was intended to encourage those charged with debating the terms of the Treaty of Union to be mindful of their responsibility to protect the Church of Scotland and particularly the Protestant succession. However, with its concentration on and concern for the rights and privileges of the church and the safety of the kingdom, it epitomises the priorities of the post-Revolution Church of Scotland.

Those two priorities, the rights and privileges of the church and the safety of the kingdom, are at the centre of much of the history written about the period. Several modern historians have concentrated both on the early years of William's reign and on the events surrounding the Union of the Parliaments in 1707. To a great extent these are 'top-down' histories, concentrating on affairs as they affected the nation as a whole or centred on events in Edinburgh. Monographs by Alasdair Raffe, Alistair Mann, Karin Bowie and Jeffrey Stephen,[3] and many shorter studies take a national view and although several of them have drawn widely on local sources, few of them have tried to show how events as a whole played out among the people in a restricted area. One exception to this is Bill Inglis's study of the parish of Dunblane, which covers much of the ground for an even smaller area than the current work.[4] The purpose of the present study is to examine the period from the opposite angle from the monograph authors, showing how events played out and the institution of the Church of Scotland developed in one restricted area of the country, the 'bounds' of the presbyteries of Dunblane and Stirling.

The core of the work is therefore to examine the way the two presbyteries responded locally to the opportunities and constraints of the reigns of William and Mary and of Anne. As a study of the institutions of the church, however, the book owes much to the 'national' work of Alistair Mutch, whose research on the system of governance of the church has been of significant influence.[5] Mutch's research on presbyterial visitations has made it unnecessary to consider these in any detail in the present work, although it is perhaps arguable that the systems he describes were much less uniform in the 1690s than in the later period.

The primary doctrine that Logan drew from his text was this: 'That a Church and people should hold fast their Priviledges and Attainments what they have received of the Lord, and what through him they do possess and enjoy.'[6] This motif and its exposition can be seen running through the recorded actions of the two presbyteries in the twenty or so years that followed the accession of William and Mary and the re-establishment of Presbyterianism as the mode of governance of the national church. For this reason, quotations from this sermon form the starting point of many of the chapters.

In one sense, from a national point of view, the accession of William and Mary forms a turning point in the nation's history, an attempt to put strife and particularly religious strife into the past. William's first letter to the newly re-Presbyterianised national church included this telling sentence: 'We never could be of the Mind that violence was suited to the advancing of True Religion . . . Moderation is what Religion Enjoynes, Neighbouring Churches expect from You, and We Recommend to You.'[7] Equally, though, the regime change was simply part of the ongoing continuum. As T. C. Smout wrote:

> After the wars were over the central plank of government was seen to be religious compromise; Charles II practised it in an Episcopalian frame: James VII failed to practise it at all, and lost his throne: William III [sic] practised it on a Presbyterian frame: Anne had to see that this frame was kept intact as a prerequisite for Union with England. It was still important to placate the nobles, but it was no longer so important as placating the other classes through an acceptable church polity.[8]

The crucial fulcrum of the Revolution for the church was that point when the Presbyterians changed from being dissenters, at odds with the government of the church and nation, to being in charge of the former and the partner of the latter. This work therefore examines how William's and later Anne's priorities were worked out in the life of two neighbouring presbyteries in central Scotland and considers the extent to which the people were indeed placated but also the extent to which local landowners and nobles continued to affect the life of the church.

The choice of Stirling and Dunblane presbyteries as the core of the study reflects a number of factors; the Presbytery of Stirling in particular has probably the best-preserved sequence of records of any presbytery in Scotland, although sadly there is a gap at the critical period of 1688–93. The Presbytery of Dunblane's records, though starting later, are equally complete thereafter. Prior to that date the register of the Diocesan Synod of Dunblane is a rare survival from the episcopal period. The two presbyteries are geographically tightly intertwined as can be seen from the map (see frontispiece), and form part of the boundary between Lowlands and Highlands, with some parishes showing the Highland proclivities of holding to Episcopalianism. They also functioned as a joint presbytery for eight years until there were enough Presbyterian ministers to let them separate.[9]

As in most areas, there is a variable survival of kirk session records (see Appendix 1) but there are enough to allow a detailed analysis of events in the parishes held by Presbyterian clergy. Some of these parishes were also Gaelic-speaking and so represent within the area a major concern for the Presbyterian establishment, the lack of Gaelic-speaking Presbyterian ministers. The area was also subject economically and politically to a number of the most powerful families of Scotland, the Campbells of Argyll, the Grahams of Montrose, the Erskines of Mar and the Murrays of Atholl. These families and their differing views of the role of the church had a distinct impact. Adding to that, the area included substantial ports in Kincardine-on-Forth (Tulliallan Parish), Alloa and Stirling, embryonic industry around Stirling, and an economically, militarily and politically important government institution in Stirling Castle. The area was physically the gateway to the Highlands with a resulting mixture of cultures, and had a history of Covenanting as well as Episcopalianism. All these factors combine to make the bounds of the joint presbytery representative of many of the issues which affected Scotland as a whole and a suitable case-study for examining the way these issues were played out at the most local of levels.

The chapters are organised as follows: Chapter 1 sets the scene locally, looking at how the Toleration of 1687 led to a small number of meeting-houses, and how the political and military activity impacted on the area. Chapters 2 and 3 then consider the provision of ministry locally. In the very rarity of its survival, Logan's sermon can be seen to represent one of the problems of the church of its period: that it lacked the spiritual leadership whose preaching could inspire the people. The major figures of the church of the time were not theologians, but rather politicians like William Carstares or polemicists like Gilbert Rule.[10] A new generation of theological thinkers was coming, Thomas Boston,[11] Thomas Halyburton[12] and others, but the old order had passed and there was no one clearly taking the lead in the final decade of the seventeenth century. Still less was leadership visible at a local level in the presbyteries of Stirling and Dunblane. Few of the ministers left any lasting impression on the parishes they ministered to and such folk memory attached to them was quirky rather than significant.[13] Nonetheless there was a fundamental issue that the thousand or so parishes of Scotland required filling with Presbyterian clergy and, although it took many years to complete, the processes by which the settlements progressed have not been examined in detail in the past. Chapter 2 considers the 'antediluvians'[14] and returned exiles who set up the joint presbytery and Chapter 3 covers the newly ordained ministers who became the next generation as well as the mechanism and tensions involved in filling the vacancies that occurred in the early years.

Thereafter Chapter 4 examines how the higher courts of the church functioned under the new regime, in particular suggesting that although a major difference between old and new organisations was that the eldership was once more involved in the higher courts, in practice not only was those elders' influence limited in the courts but also they failed to form the link back to their kirk sessions. Chapter 5 then looks at the elders and their roles within the kirk session, examining whether there was any significant difference between them and their episcopal predecessors. The place of the sacraments of Communion and baptism in the post-Revolution church forms the following chapter, considering the balance between the elements of public ceremony, healing ordinance and 'holy fair'.

The evidence regarding the week-to-week preaching and lecturing of the time is considered in Chapter 7. Based on the diaries of George Turnbull, this examines his header texts over a sixteen-year period which included both his ten years in Alloa and some years before and after. It will use the evidence of the diaries compared with the kirk session minutes to look at how local events influenced his choice of text, but also draw attention to some perhaps surprising gaps in the scripture from which he preached. A volume of his lectures and sermons of 1691 is then considered and the lectures shown to fill in some of the gaps of his sermons. No local comparison is possible from surviving evidence, but the records of Salton in East Lothian give comparable information for both Episcopalian and Presbyterian incumbents and are used for a comparison.

Chapter 8 considers the position of those Episcopalian sympathisers who did not accept the new regime, showing how a substantial resistance survived in Stirling at all levels of society. The four parishes which remained under episcopal incumbents until after the Treaty of Union are considered, and the reasons for the incumbents' control teased out. Meanwhile in the higher reaches of society the intertwining of Jacobitism and Episcopalianism was a factor. In Chapter 9 a discussion of discipline and the relationship between kirk sessions, presbyteries and the civil courts shows how the concept of church discipline was developing as the legal framework changed, but also varied in emphasis and strictness from parish to parish.

As Dunblane Presbytery had several Gaelic-speaking 'Highland' parishes within its bounds, Chapter 10 examines these, and the establishment's attitude to them, showing that where Presbyterian ministers were in place the undoubted prevalence of Gaelic was essentially ignored and the non-Anglophones left to fend for themselves, and local traditions were disapproved of. Finally, Chapter 11 looks at the specifically local aspects of the events leading up to the Treaty of Union. Although the 300th anniversary of the Union brought a plethora of writing about it, most is again about the national aspect with local reactions only quoted in passing.[15] Bowie's more recent work, a collection of addresses against the Union, does give local information about the signatories of the addresses[16] but lacks the close detail which can help evaluate the extent to which the petitions were influenced by the churches. The chapter ends with a brief summary of the issues which were coming into new prominence, even if they were not new issues.

At the centre of the work, then, is the question of how far the people in the area were engaged in the issues which exercised the church nationally and how stable Presbyterianism was in the area. Neither of the dual monarchs ever visited Scotland, leaving the administration to the king's trusted advisor, William Bentinck (successively Earl and Duke of Portland), who never visited the country either. Both Portland's and the new monarchs' information on Scotland came largely from one man, William Carstares, a Scottish Presbyterian minister and former exile, whose probity and integrity had come to William's attention in 1684, and who remained both Portland's and William's chief Scottish advisor until the king's death. As his great-nephew, Joseph McCormick, put it in his biography of Carstares, published in 1774:

> During the reign of King William, when he was the confidential minister of that great prince in all Scottish business, as he held no public office, and was a man of much discretion, as well as of real modesty, he was so far from thrusting himself forward, or making a display of the credit which he possessed, that his influence and operations were frequently unobserved, and he is seldom mentioned by the memoir-writers of the times.[17]

But that is to anticipate. The accession of Mary II and her husband William II (William III of England) to the throne of Scotland in May 1689 marks a watershed in Scottish history in many ways. Largely as a result of the influence of Carstares, helped by the honourable but politically and ecclesiastically disastrous loyalty of the bishops to James VII, the Church of Scotland, which had vacillated between Presbyterian and Episcopalian governance ever since the Reformation, became Presbyterian, at least for the next 330 years. William came from a Presbyterian country, albeit one which had a tolerant view of religious divisions. Portland was himself Presbyterian, but in all his time in England, never quite understood the deep-seated bitterness that Scottish Presbyterians felt for Scottish Episcopalians, let alone Roman Catholics. However, when the hierarchy of Scotland, led by Alexander Rose, Bishop of Edinburgh, rejected William as *de jure* king, William had no alternative but to place the governance of the Church of Scotland in the hands of the Presbyterians. Carstares manoeuvred the king towards a settlement.

The area covered by the post-Revolution presbyteries of Stirling and Dunblane is largely within the bounds of the present (2021) Presbytery of Stirling with the exception of five parishes. Historically, up until the union of the Church of Scotland and the United Free Church in 1929, Stirling Presbytery covered the Royal Burgh of Stirling and the nearby parishes, while Dunblane Presbytery almost surrounded it on the west, north and east sides. As well as having relatively well-preserved church and civil records, this area also gave rise to a number of diaries and memoirs covering the period and some voluminous family archives.

Availability of sources aside, the use of Stirling and Dunblane Presbyteries as the model has the advantage of considering an area that was partly in the central belt, relatively prosperous and essentially Lowland, but also partly Highland and Gaelic-speaking. The area was urban in places, but largely rural; it was inland, but with major ports. For its time it had reasonably good communications to Glasgow and Edinburgh, and was also seen as the gateway to the north. It was pro-Revolution in sympathy but with many Jacobite families. It was Presbyterian but had a significant number of Episcopalians and a remnant of conventicling spirit.

In August of 1702, the Presbytery of Dunblane considered the dispute between Mr James Forrester of Logie and Mr Alexander Douglas, minister of Logie. It was not a case of any great significance: the issue was whether the rent of the schoolmaster's house and yard was due to the laird or was part of the minister's emoluments. As the sum involved was £8 Scots per year,[18] it was not going to become a *cause célèbre*. But it makes an important point; the minister produced witnesses to show that the house had been built by a predecessor in episcopal times and therefore was part of his assets as minister. His witnesses included John Robb in Airthrey, who was ninety years of age and said he remembered a barn on the site owned by Mr Henry Schaw and did not know when James Forrester took possession. John Anderson in Blackgrange was a widower aged eighty-one. He said he remembered a barn on the site when he was at school, owned by Mr Henry Schaw.[19] These two witnesses had worshipped there in Logie since King James VI had been on the throne.

The previous year another case referred to the presbytery from Logie Parish had involved the mill at Bridge of Allan, owned and occupied by one James Stewart, who was called as a witness before the presbytery but died before he could appear.[20] According to a family history, based admittedly on family legend, James Stewart died in November 1701 at the age of 'not less than one hundred'.[21] An Episcopalian sympathiser, Stewart had been born before James VI joined the two kingdoms under one monarch; he died only six years before Queen Anne united the two parliaments. Stewart, too, had lived through a period of immense changes in Scotland. Both cases are a useful reminder of the continuum of memory within a community.

That tumultuous century had seen the governance of the Church of Scotland change and change again several times. In the previous fifty years alone, it had lost status and fragmented under Cromwell, only to be re-established as Episcopalian in 1661–2. In 1690 it had become

Presbyterian again. The permanence of that state of affairs was in doubt for a long time; no one knew then that that model would still be in place 330 years later.

In some ways the national Church of Scotland is like the legendary axe that has had four new handles and three new heads but is still the same axe. The analogy can perhaps be stretched a little further by suggesting that in 1690 both axe-head and handle were replaced at the same time. But the axe still remained the same axe. The crucial point is that, in the continuity of the lives of the people, the idea of the national church was indeed the same body in 1702 as it had been in 1602 or in 1560. That institutional continuity was validated by the continued involvement of the great majority the people of Scotland, despite strong and vociferous opposition from those outwith that church.

But a second continuity existed in 1690; in that case quoted above, Alexander Douglas produced the kirk session records which showed the income from the debated property in the reigns of Charles II and James VII.[22] A search of the kirk session register showed the history of the property and confirmed his case. That recognised continuity of records made the parish church of Logie in 1665 the same institution as the parish church of Logie in 1702 and indeed the same church today. Of course, that particular approach suited Douglas's and the presbytery's agenda. In another case over the ownership of a pew in Denny Church, Stirling's Presbyterian regime's minute of 3 May 1699 referred to a decision of the 'pretended session in Denny' showing the right of a Mr Wingate to his seat, a decision which the new kirk session did not uphold; the previous session's decisions were only binding if convenient.[23]

Thirdly, and perhaps indicating a different approach, the minister's case was that the Laird of Logie had appropriated the land in a 'sacrilegious act' (his words) at the Revolution. It would seem that the Revolution, both in its role of regime change in the monarchy and in its role of regime change in the church, was sometimes seen as a discontinuity and sometimes simply as a cleansing of long-standing blemishes.

That tension between continuity and discontinuity is a real one. Newly re-Presbyterianised, the national church emphasised the discontinuity by essentially writing the Episcopalian regime out of history and emphasised its continuity by inviting back all the ministers who had been deposed at the Restoration or during the reigns of Charles II and James VII to serve in the parishes from which they had been deposed (known as 'antediluvians'). At the same time individual kirk sessions and presbyteries were as keen to establish their legitimacy by taking possession of the old records, possibly because there was very limited continuity in the personnel of these courts under the two regimes.

As previously noted, the numbers of Presbyterian ministers in parishes was initially too small to sustain the existing structure of presbyteries in most areas, so temporary linkages were put in place until individual presbyteries were strong enough to sustain themselves. Thus Stirling and Dunblane presbyteries, together with part of Auchterarder Presbytery, initially worked as a unit so that the earliest surviving post-Revolution records were kept jointly. Within a few years the Auchterarder parishes quietly went their own way unnoticed in the records but Stirling and Dunblane remained united until 1698.

The earliest records of the joint Presbytery of Stirling and Dunblane are lost; the first surviving volume starts in 1693 although the presbytery was in existence from at least 1690. In that volume there is a continuing saga of an attempt to retrieve the previous volume, not from a recalcitrant Episcopalian, but from the antediluvian Presbyterian minister of Alva, who had been reappointed there before moving to Cockpen, taking the presbytery records with him. He died without returning them and subsequent attempts to retrieve them from the Presbytery of Dalkeith or his son-in-law were unsuccessful.[24]

Despite that loss, and the complete or partial loss of several sets of parish records, enough remains to piece together a picture of how presbyteries and kirk sessions worked together to 'possess and enjoy' their privileges and attainments within the new political circumstances brought in by the accession of William and Mary. Inevitably the heavy reliance on institutional records tends to make this an institutional history. Much of the underlying human narrative is missing. Records of decisions do not show the debate, decisions recorded as being by a 'pluralitie of votes' do not show the undoubted splits among those voting and it is only the rare recorded dissents that hint at differences in views. However, on rare occasions the people break through as individuals. Surviving letters, petitions to the General Assembly, even the periodic presbytery minutes recording ever-increasing exasperation at one or other of the brethren who has not fulfilled an instruction, all help to flesh out the bare decisions and remind the reader that these were real people attempting to rebuild their vision of the church. From those records unfolds the narrative of how Presbyterianism was re-established locally and how the church echoed or differed from the episcopal regime that had preceded it.

Sadly, while the writing of this work was in its final stages, it was decided that the Presbytery of Stirling would lose its 440-year-old identity and be subsumed into a much larger body (still to be defined) at the end of 2021.

Notes

1. Revelation 3: 11, Logan, *A Sermon Preached before His Grace James Duke of Queensberry*.
2. There are a handful of single published sermons such as Brisbane, *A Sermon Preached at Denny* and Hamiltoun, *A Sermon Explaining the Life of Faith*.
3. Raffe, *The Culture of Controversy*; Raffe, *Scotland in Revolution, 1685–1690*; Mann, *James VII*; Bowie, *Scottish Public Opinion and the Anglo-Scottish Union*; Stephen, *Defending the Revolution*.

4. Inglis, 'The Impact of Episcopacy and Presbyterianism'.
5. Mutch, *Religion and National Identity*.
6. Logan, *A Sermon Preached before His Grace James Duke of Queensberry*, p. 5.
7. His Majesty's Gracious Letter to the Assembly: see 'Acts: 1690', in Church of Scotland, *Acts of the General Assembly of the Church of Scotland, 1638–1842*.
8. Smout, *A History of the Scottish People, 1560–1830*, p. 107.
9. A part of Auchterarder Presbytery also was part of the joint presbytery but for a much shorter period.
10. Brother of Robert Rule, Minister of Stirling, 1693–1703. For brief biographies of these men see *Fasti Ecclesiae Scoticanae*; where references to ministers are unannotated it can be assumed that *Fasti* is the source.
11. Sometime probationer within the bounds of Stirling Presbytery.
12. Born in St Ninians parish.
13. For example John Gray, minister of Dollar 1700–1745, made a fortune acting as a local banker and was nicknamed 'The Baron'.
14. 'Antediluvians' was a term coined at the time to describe those Presbyterian ministers who had been deprived of their charges from 1661 onwards. See for example Wodrow, *Analecta*, vol. 2, p. 276: 'This moneth Mr Heu Campbell . . . dyed, he was ane antediluvian minister, ordained before the flood . . .' This was originally written around 1721 and the term appears also in his letters. The original ones were therefore elderly. Later in the period, some who had been ordained under the episcopacy were deprived after being convinced by Presbyterian views. These men were younger but were still considered to be antediluvians.
15. Stephen, *Scottish Presbyterians and the Act of Union 1707*; Bowie, *Scottish Public Opinion and the Anglo-Scottish Union, 1699–1707*.
16. Bowie, *Addresses against Incorporating Union, 1706–07*.
17. McCormick, *State-papers and letters addressed to William Carstares*, p. vi.
18. As there were twelve pounds Scots to the pound sterling, this is equivalent to 13*s*. 4*d*.
19. Stirling Council Archives (hereafter SCA) CH2/723/5 18/8/1702.
20. SCA CH2/723/5 17/12/1701. Called as a witness, Stewart was reported to have died.
21. Steuart, *By Allan Water*, p. 66.
22. SCA CH2/723/5 18/8/1702.
23 SCA CH2/722/8 3/5/1699.
24. SCA CH2/722/8 24/1/1700, 20/6/1700 and 17/8/1700.

CHAPTER ONE

Scotland and its National Church in 1688

> Consider what intestine Broils and Confusions this Land was under, while deprived of some of these things, and what Peace and Tranquility it hath enjoyed under the possession of them since the late happy Revolution.[1]

Looking back in 1706, and speaking with a view to tact, John Logan, minister of Alloa, referred to 'the late happy Revolution'. The terms 'Glorious Revolution' or 'Bloodless Revolution' may be widely used in English history to describe the events of 1688–9, but in Scotland it was neither glorious nor bloodless and 'happy' only perhaps from the viewpoint of Presbyterians.

This chapter therefore examines three aspects of the background to the Williamite Revolution in the area surrounding Stirling. It looks briefly at the background to the events of 1688–90 in the area, the effect of the Toleration of 1687 and the role of the area in the period before William's rule and the re-establishment of Presbyterianism as the mode of governance of the national church were consolidated.

At the Reformation, Scottish Protestantism had taken on a model of governance where the human rule of the church was vested in the supreme court, the General Assembly (comprising both clergy and laymen), and not in the supreme rule of a monarch. Despite the word 'Presbyterian' being used to define its mode of governance, it was a later innovation. Kirk sessions ruled individual parishes with their membership of several elders and one or more ministers. The General Assembly ruled the church nationally. Synods came next, fulfilling the role of bishops in governing a region of Scotland, and meeting normally twice a year, but by 1580 the need for smaller groups of parish ministers to meet for their mutual support and control led to the gradual introduction of presbyteries.

When the young King James VI tried to impose bishops of his choosing over the whole country in 1572, the Church of Scotland determined that bishops were in fact contrary to the law of God and generally a bad idea.[2] The whole course of the next century became a battleground, often literally, between church and king. Bishops, royal appointees, held sway at some times; at other times the church had the power and the king was forced to accept his lack of control. It was in this context that the two covenants were written and very widely signed, the National Covenant of 1638 and the Solemn League and Covenant of 1643. These documents defined Presbyterian aspirations of 'preventing the ruin of the true reformed religion'[3] and while they supported the king made it clear that he should have no power over the church. The Solemn League and Covenant went further, with the intention of establishing Presbyterian government over England, Wales and Ireland.

The restoration of power to the Presbyterians in in the 1640s led, by the end of the decade, to the first serious schism in the national church between those who were prepared to reconcile with those who had worked with Charles I and those who were not, the 'Resolutioners' and the 'Protesters' respectively. This schism was serious enough for the latter to form a breakaway presbytery in 1651, led by James Guthrie, minister of the 1st Charge of Stirling. With the local community split between the two factions, Guthrie's attempt to import an ally, the young Robert Rule, into the 2nd Charge, ended with Rule expelled from the burgh and the calling of a colleague in the 2nd Charge who was a 'Resolutioner'. Another result was the physical splitting of the Burgh Kirk into West and East kirks by the erection of a wall between chancel and nave.[4] Religious partisanship was a feature in the town from an early stage. Guthrie was also instrumental in persuading the young King Charles II to sign the two covenants.

Despite his having thus sworn to uphold the covenants of 1638 and 1643 when he accepted the throne of Scotland in 1650, or more likely because he was made to swear under substantial duress, Charles had a hatred of the covenants which very quickly manifested itself in an attack on those who pressed for their implementation. James Guthrie became the first Covenanting martyr of the new regime. Like the Marquess of Argyll, who was also implicated in 'persuading' the king to subscribe to the covenants, he was arrested on a charge of treason and executed in 1661.

The Restoration of Charles II ushered in yet another period of upheaval in the Scottish Church, including the restoration of the bishoprics which the General Assembly of 1638 had abolished. Two dioceses were filled by lifelong Episcopalian supporters, while the others were filled by a variety of Presbyterians of the former Resolutioner party.[5]

The Presbytery of Dunblane fell under the hand of the new Bishop of Dunblane, Robert Leighton, a former Presbyterian. This see was the poorest in Scotland and comprised the presbyteries of Dunblane, Perth, Dunkeld and Auchterarder. The other prominent Presbyterian minister who became a bishop was James Sharp. Ordained as a Presbyterian in 1648, he has the unenviable distinction of being one of the most loathed figures in Presbyterian history. He soon made his allegiance to the restored Charles II clear and was rewarded by being appointed Archbishop of St Andrews, being consecrated by the English hierarchy in London. He took up his new role with enthusiasm and supported the Earl of Lauderdale in his efforts to extirpate recalcitrant Presbyterians.

Both Leighton and Sharp were former Presbyterians, but there the resemblance ended. Leighton was widely regarded as a peacemaker and worked both in Dunblane and later in Glasgow, where he was appointed archbishop in 1671, to try to reconcile the national church by his widely admired piety and personal faith. Just after being consecrated as Bishop of Dunblane in 1661, he wrote in a letter of his intention 'to use all the little skill and strength I have to recall their zeal from all the little questions about rites and discipline to the great things of religion, and of their souls, which in these debats are litle or nothing concern'd'.[6] Sharp, on the other hand, seemed to be motivated largely by his dislike of his former opponents in the Protester party and set out to mould Scotland into a truly Episcopalian state.

While the Restoration had been received with enthusiasm in Scotland, those of a Presbyterian bent were concerned, and rightly so. Those in the north-east of the country were quite content; Episcopalianism generally was fairly popular there. Those in the south-west were incensed; as a stronghold of the Protester party, they saw the new regime as a disaster. In Stirling and Dunblane presbyteries, despite the death of Guthrie, reaction was more muted. Some Presbyterian ministers were forced out while others quietly conformed.

Worship remained essentially similar if not quite the same. The courts of the church, too, remained. Kirk sessions still ruled in parishes in much the same way as they had done since the 1580s. Presbyteries, now tending to revert to their old name of 'exercises', and synods still met, although with a bishop-appointed moderator and no elders present. The General Assembly was theoretically replaced by a national synod including bishops, deans and moderators of presbyteries together with an additional member of each presbytery and representatives of the universities. This last was be called at the king's pleasure; it never met.[7]

Those ministers serving in a parish in 1662 faced a choice: conform to the new regime or leave their charges. In Dunblane, the gentle touch of Leighton allowed conformity to flourish. At the inaugural meeting of the diocesan synod he declared that 'each member of it hath now as full and free libertie and declaring their assent and dissent in all things that occur as ever they had in the former tymes'.[8] In the event, while some 270 ministers throughout Scotland had been deprived by 1663,[9] when Parliament and the Privy Council deposed those ministers who did not accept the new regime, only three ministers from Dunblane Presbytery together with two from Auchterarder left their charges.[10] Within Stirling Presbytery, aside from James Guthrie, already executed, and James Simson, another Protester minister who left Scotland for Ireland at the Restoration but was arrested and imprisoned on his way to the coast, three ministers were deprived. After that a period of stability followed, punctuated by the natural deaths of a substantial number of the clergy and their replacement by patron-presented and episcopally collated successors. Latterly, many of them were also ordained by the bishop.

The Pentland Rising of 1666, a rebellion against the arbitrary fining of persistent Presbyterians, led to a reining back of the aggressive policy of the more doctrinaire Episcopalian supporters, for a few years. Following a policy of toleration first in 1669 and again in 1672, many Presbyterian ministers were offered an indulgence to preach in particular parishes (not necessarily their own) on condition of not leaving them; Alva's minister, Richard Howieson, and Tulliallan's John Forrest were among them. Most declined and of those who accepted, few remained for any length of time and all were deprived by 1684 when the indulgences were cancelled. Those who accepted the role functioned essentially as independent dissenting ministers outwith the episcopal machinery and were disparaged as 'king's curates' by the more committed Presbyterians.[11] The Presbyterian party being thus split, the less amenable portion was soon identified as the target of the government's efforts to retain control.

Soon there came a fiercer campaign against those who stood out against all forms of episcopacy and persisted in holding conventicles illegally. As reaction follows action, there was a steady escalation. Despite ever more draconian penalties, conventicling increased and in response the 'Highland Host' was unleashed by the government. A correspondent of the Duke of Hamilton writing from near Stirling clearly knew the extent of the threat; as well as rearming and provisioning Stirling Castle and strengthening its defences,

> The wholl nobilety who hay any interest in the Hylands, as Huntly, Atholl, Argyll, Marshall, Moray, Mar, Kintoir, Caithness, etc., are ordered instently to hav all the Hylanders in reddines upon a call to march to Stirling, wher they shall receiv arms and amunition for all that went, and itt appears ther ar non invyted hether, militia or Lolanders, bott Hylanders only . . . Itt wes talkt in plain tearms, that if the Hyland men wer forst to march to the west to suppress a rebelleion of the Uigs [Whigs], they should not only have frie quarter bott liberty of plundering, and if they pleased to settell themselves ther as a new plantation and possess the countrey for a reward.[12]

In January 1678 over 5,000 troops were mustered in Stirling; the whole Highland Host numbered about 8,000. Highlanders were preferred because of their lack of historic attachment to Presbyterianism (although there were certainly dissident Presbyterians in south Perthshire) but also because they were looked on by the Lowlanders as alien in dress, tongue and manners, and most greatly to be feared. Although the host was initially billeted on the various towns of Stirlingshire, that area was not its target. They were being gathered to deal with the more radically Presbyterian south-west, but nonetheless their presence must have affected Stirling and around.

One Presbyterian commentator described the passage of the host in these terms: 'After they past [sic] Stirling, they [the Highlanders] carried as if they had been in ane enemie's countrey, living upon free quarter, where ever they came.'[13] Indeed the depredations in the south-west were considerable and though the sojourn of the Highland Host lasted only three months, it left its mark.

The Highland Host incursion was then followed by an agreement by a Convention of the Estates for a tax to raise regular troops to hunt out and suppress conventicles. Three events the following year go much of the way to define the happenings of the following ten years: the murder of Archbishop Sharp, the skirmish at Drumclog and the Battle of Bothwell Bridge. Part of the problem for the Covenanter[14] side at the Battle of Bothwell Bridge was that the leaders were in the throes of a serious debate as to exactly how far they should go in opposing the king. Some went so far as disowning all allegiance to him on account of his actions in attacking Presbyterianism, roundly condemning the indulgences and those ministers who accepted them. The following year, at a meeting in Torwood, on the southern side of Stirlingshire, Donald Cargill took the lead in excommunicating both Charles and his brother and condoning their 'preventive murder'.[15] Some were more moderate in their opposition. James Ure of Shirgarton,[16] a minor landowner in Kippen parish in the Presbytery of Stirling, was one of those who fought and he left his memoirs of the rising. Ure had been drawn to the Covenanter cause by the actions of his minister, who was reputed to have acted as an 'intelligencer' for the government. Several Presbyterian ministers in the area had been arrested at a conventicle at Lochlegan in Kippen parish and Ure felt that if he stayed put, he too would be facing arrest. Ure's account describes how he acted as captain to a troop of Stirlingshire men detailed to guard the bridge end at Bothwell. Several were killed and he narrowly escaped. Many of those taken at the battle were lodged in Greyfriars Kirkyard in Edinburgh until they could be tried. Ure himself was tried in his absence, the first name of twenty-two so treated. Found guilty and sentenced to death and to the forfeiture of his estate, Ure managed to escape to Ireland.

Those three events, Sharp's murder, Drumclog and Bothwell Bridge, were the harbingers of the 'Killing Times'. Legislation was enacted to ensure Protestantism, the royal supremacy and the succession. Ostensibly, as in England, intended to weed out Roman Catholics from public office, it was actually used to identify those whose loyalty was suspect because of their Presbyterian views, for in signing the Oath of Abjuration one acknowledged the king as supreme 'in all causes, as well ecclesiastical as civil' and also abjured the covenants. All those in public office in Scotland had to subscribe; those who did not lost their offices. In the countryside, however, it took on a more sinister tinge. The newly appointed circuit court meeting in Stirling in February 1683 had the task of enforcing the Test Act. Some of those summoned to attend were suspected of involvement at Bothwell Bridge, others were simply the landowners who might have been expected to be commissioners of supply or other office holders. The young John Erskine observed how 'Mr Gordon, the clerk, asked at some if they thought Bothwell a rebellion, and the Bishop's death a murther? If they were either silent or answered negative, it was crime enough.'[17]

Many of those called to take the act did not attend the court, 120 of them from Stirlingshire alone. When some of them did turn up to the court in Stirling ready to take the oath a day or two later, they were made to do so on their knees. Ecclesiastically, the imposition of the Test Act and the Oath of Abjuration cleared most 'indulged' Presbyterian ministers from their parishes; it even cleared some Episcopalian ones. It also led into the peak of the 'Killing Times' in 1684–5. Tacit passive resistance by moderate Presbyterians ceased to be an option. Attendance at the services held by Episcopalian ministers was enforced and absence taken as a sign of political rebellion.

In February 1685, Charles II died. With ever-growing concern in England about the prospect of a Roman Catholic king, rebellion exploded. On the accession of James, Duke of York and Albany, as James II of England, the Duke of Monmouth proclaimed himself king. The rebellion was speedily and bloodily suppressed. In Scotland the Earl of Argyll had been primed to lead a rising prior to Monmouth's arrival in England in order to tie up government forces in the north. It was a complete failure and a disaster for Argyll and his supporters. Argyll was captured and his army disintegrated without a pitched battle. As a result, having defeated Monmouth's and Argyll's rebellions, James successfully took up his crown as King James VII. He never returned to Scotland.

It is widely, but not universally, recognised that high on James's agenda was the propagation of Roman Catholicism in his kingdoms.[18] Having lived through the turmoil of his own conversion and the obstacles that were put in his way, he had the personal triumph of securing his brother's deathbed conversion and saw his accession as an opportunity to work for his faith. In Scotland, James had early success in the conversion of various nobles in south Perthshire. The Earl of Moray in particular, converted privately but not publicly, was appointed high commissioner to James's first parliament. Despite the warfare between Episcopalian and Presbyterian factions during Charles's reign, there was one thing that they agreed on. Both factions were equally anti-Catholic. Politicians such as the Duke of Queensberry made it clear to James that any thoughts of changing the established (Episcopalian) religion would meet great resistance.

Shortly after his accession, James abolished the Test Acts, primarily to relieve his co-religionists, but this had the collateral effect of relieving Presbyterians. This motive was certainly recognised by most of the Presbyterians of the time but many took advantage of it despite their misgivings. John Willison, a native of Bannockburn and later a minister in Angus, writing some decades later referred to the Toleration of 1687 having 'proceeded from a vile spring, to wit the King's absolute dispensing power'.[19] It might be noted, however, that Willison was only seven years old then so his view was hindsight rather than experience.

James's first priority was to strengthen his own power base. A longer-term aim was to consolidate that power by a widespread placing of suitable men into positions of influence at every possible level of administration in the burghs and counties, leading to appropriate people being elected to Parliament when that should meet again. He therefore embarked on a programme of planting potential allies in burgh councils and elsewhere. In September 1686 Stirling Council was forbidden to hold elections until the king's pleasure should be known, and on 19 October, under the eye of Lord Livingstone, one of the Privy Council and a committed supporter of James, Stirling was allocated its new council:

> His Majestie being now resolved to nominat and appoynt the persones underwrittin magistrats, cownsellers, and clerk, for the burgh of Strevling, as such whom he judges most loyall and readie to promott his service and most forward to support the good and interest of the said burgh; wherfor the lords of his Majesties privie cownsell, in persueance of his Majesties commands aforsaid, doe heirby nominat and appoynt Hugh Kennedye of Schelloch to be proveist of the said burgh of Striveling.[20]

All the other positions were duly nominated and filled as well, and the government of the Royal Burgh of Stirling, together with that of all the other burghs, was safely in the hands of the king. The process did not run entirely smoothly; Kennedy, who had previously been provost, was in fact barred from involvement in the town's affairs for disobeying the burgh council's commands in March 1684. The first act of the new council, with appropriate condemnation of its predecessor, was to restore to him the privileges of a burgess to allow him to take office. Kennedy himself also became the parliamentary commissioner for the burgh, although in due course he changed allegiance and took the oath of loyalty to King William.

James, it is clear, had no particular grudge against Presbyterians provided, and it is a big 'provided', that they were loyal to him as king and did not let their views affect how they served him. Early attempts to pass an Act of Toleration to promote this cause foundered. The Declaration of Indulgence finally came into force in Scotland in February 1687, with a revised version in June spelling out a less restricted toleration as it applied to Presbyterians.[21] In the first version Presbyterian ministers were allowed to worship in their own house, under the second they were able to hold services in barns and meeting-houses as well. As was perhaps intended, this proclamation divided the Presbyterians. It specifically excluded the activities of the field-preachers and Cameronians from its toleration, and indeed, the last of the Covenanter martyrs, James Renwick, was captured and executed after the proclamation came into force. Not surprisingly those who had followed Renwick and Cameron were hostile to the Toleration. Most less militant Presbyterians, on the other hand, seem to have accepted it gratefully. In July 1687 'The Humble Address of the Presbyterian Ministers in His Majesties Kingdom of Scotland' expressed their gratitude for his 'gracious and surprizing favour' and pledged their loyalty to him as king, disowning those who 'promote any disloyal practices'.[22] A similar effusion was offered by Presbyterians in Edinburgh and Canongate, referring to the 'many sad and grievous burthens we have long groaned under', and professing a loyalty and duty to the king 'that no difference in Religion can dissolve'.[23] In the exile community, the response was more mixed, particularly among those who were already plotting the overthrow of James.[24] Nonetheless many exiles returned from the Netherlands and from Ireland and soon Presbyterian meeting-houses were to be found throughout the Lowlands.

Several meeting-houses appeared within the bounds of Stirling and Dunblane presbyteries, including those erected in the parishes of St Ninians, Logie and Gargunnock. There was an expectation, though, that people would travel from other parishes. The Gargunnock meeting-house was deliberately placed to be accessible from several neighbouring parishes.

What then was the response to the new meeting-houses locally? Alasdair Raffe has pointed out the substantial fall-off in attendance and decrease, in some cases virtual collapse, in collections in (episcopal) parish churches in a number of areas of Scotland.[25] In Logie Parish, the meeting-house opened in 1688, and there was an immediate and measurable dip in the collections in neighbouring Alva (see Appendix 3). The Alva collections can be seen to be a bellwether of local opinion throughout the following decade.

Toleration was not enough, particularly when Mary of Modena gave birth to a male heir for James VII; William of Orange put his planning into action. James made preparations: Stirling Castle's fortifications were boosted and supplies laid in, the Scottish standing army was sent south to reinforce his English regiments, militias were set up in its place to 'defend' Scotland. Elections took place to a promised new parliament, but though James managed to have his supporters elected in burghs such as Perth and Stirling and in some counties, many commissioners known to be supporters of the coming revolution were also elected in places such as Ayrshire and Linlithgow.[26]

In Stirling, with rumours already rife about William's plans, on 16 October the council met and confirmed a new council described as 'such whom his Majestie judges most loyeall and readie to promote his service and most forward to promote the good and interest of the said burgh'.[27] Nonetheless, the new council was essentially the same men running Stirling, it may be assumed, in their own interest.

For the next few months it went about its business quietly: electing its provost to the Convention of Royal Burghs, setting the local customs rates, approving accounts, and so far as the minutes are concerned, keeping out of political controversy. If Stirling was still vowing loyalty to James in late October 1688, it was not alone in holding to the old regime in the days leading to William's invasion.

William arrived in England with his army on 5 November 1688 and news of his landing clearly reached Scotland not long after the event. The Convention of Royal Burghs knew it was imminent if not actually happening by 8 November. With the burghs, including Stirling, all represented by men chosen by James or his advisors, the Convention of Royal Burghs still had its colours nailed to James's mast even as William landed. Meeting for a 'Particular Convention' in Edinburgh in November,[28] the commissioners of the twenty-five burghs wrote a letter to James, dated five days after the arrival of William in England, including this statement of loyalty:

> Having at this our meeting been informed of a most unjust and unnaturall invasion designed against your Majestie and your kingdomes wee doe find ourselves concerned by our allegiance and gratitud to assure your Majestie, and let all your other subjects see, that the former professions wee have made of adhering to your royall interest upon all occasions wer not meer and emptie complements but that the same sincerity from which they proceided then shall still animat us to hazard all for your Majestie, his royall highnes the Prince of Scotland, and the royall lyne, being fully convinced that whatever tends to shak the thron must necessarly overturn the liberty and property of all your subjects.[29]

By late December 1688, James had fled to France. Anti-James riots in Edinburgh in early December were followed in the south-west by an outbreak of 'rabbling' where episcopally placed ministers were ousted from parish and manse with scarcely more than they stood up in, and sometimes not even that, by mobs variably described as hill-people, Cameronians and malcontents from other parishes.

The news had reached Stirling too; despite its not being recorded in the burgh minutes, William's declaration of intent of 10 October 1688 was read at the Cross of Stirling on the first Saturday of 1689.[30]

England declared that James had abdicated and that the joint monarchs William and Mary were legal rulers in February 1689. In Scotland, a Convention of the Estates was called for March. By that stage the Cameronians had reputedly driven out around 200 ministers with the process spreading north through Ayr to Glasgow. There was still the threat of military action in Scotland; John Graham of Claverhouse, newly elevated to the peerage as Viscount Dundee, remained at large with the forces which he had used to keep the Covenanting areas subdued. When the convention gathered in March of 1689, the Cameronians were given official recognition by being charged with the protection of the convention under the nominal command of the Earl of Leven. Among these forces were also men from Menteith and Kippen forming a company led by James Ure of Shirgarton.

Even at this point it was far from clear what the outcome of the convention would be. Some of James's office holders might have followed him into exile, but his supporters attended the convention in numbers. As well as the bishops and some of the nobility, the commissioners from the burghs included many whom James had placed in positions of power in the councils, who were then able to be elected as his men on the convention as he reckoned. Thus Hugh Kennedy of Shelloch, provost of Stirling, attended the convention as commissioner for the Royal Burgh. Others were clearly waiting to see which side would prevail before making sure they joined it.

Despite this the convention voted decisively to depose James and accept the English *fait accompli* that was the accession of William and Mary. Two men stood out on James's side. The Earl of Balcarres had already told William of his allegiance to James, and although he returned to Scotland in February 1689, he was quickly arrested, jailed and exiled. Viscount Dundee, on the other hand, loathed by the Presbyterian faction for his role in extirpating Covenanters, took physical action. It was the threat of the troops available under Dundee's command that made the arrival of the 'Cameronians' from the west so welcome to William's party.

On 4 April the Convention resolved that James VII was no longer king. Unlike England, which held that James had abdicated, the Scots actively deposed him. William, Prince of Orange, king of England, was offered the joint monarchy of Scotland with his wife and in due course accepted on 11 May. The conditions were laid down in the Claim of Right, passed by the Convention on 11 April, which formed the basis of Scottish constitutional law thereafter. For the Presbyterians, a crucial difference from the English Bill of Rights, which fulfilled the same purpose south of the border, was that it described prelacy, the rule of bishops, as a 'great and unsupportable grievance and trouble to this nation'.[31]

The statement also hints at the single event which placed Presbyterian governance back in control of the national church, and relegated the Episcopalian tradition to nonconformity. Prior to the Convention's meeting, Alexander Rose, Bishop of Edinburgh, had been sent by his fellow bishops to London to watch over the interests of the church. His interview with William was disastrous. With the widely quoted comment that he would serve William 'so far as law, reason or conscience shall allow me', he sealed the fate of episcopal rule in Scotland. William, despite being all too happy to rule over an episcopal Church of England, was persuaded that the Presbyterian party in Scotland would be the more loyal and a year later Presbyterianism was re-established. When the Convention of the Estates had opened in March 1689, two archbishops and seven bishops had their seats; when it formally sat again as the parliament of the nation three months later, the prelates were gone.

Dundee left the Convention to raise support for James, his first intention being to summon a rival Jacobite convention in Stirling. The burgh was, like so many others, in the hands of those whom James had thought loyal. The provost whom he had put in place was also the commissioner from the burgh to the Convention and later to Parliament. As late as October 1688, burgh records show that the provost's son was reimbursed expenses in Edinburgh for his outlay for the king's gift in electing the Stirling magistrates. Nonetheless his father had no difficulty in switching allegiance to William when he saw how the wind was blowing.

Back in Edinburgh, a large proportion of the men who had come from the south-west were enrolled into the national army as the Earl of Leven's Regiment and the Earl of Angus's Regiment, both having long and distinguished records in the service of the country. The latter contained the more radical of the former Covenanters, the regiment retaining the title 'The Cameronians' and many of its Covenanting traditions until its disbanding in 1968.[32]

Not all the former Covenanters were enrolled in the regular army. The Kippen and Menteith men led by James Ure of Shirgarton had taken on the role of blockading Edinburgh Castle, where the Duke of Gordon still held out for James, if rather ineffectively.[33] The Kippen company was not absorbed into the army, but instead sent home to help form a militia, together with many of Shirgarton's neighbours, to protect Stirlingshire and south-western Perthshire from Dundee and a potential new Highland Host. As a result of Shirgarton's support for the new regime he was restored to the possessions forfeited by the government after Argyll's rebellion. It was a feature of attempts to establish the legitimacy of the Revolution that legal sentences dating from the previous regime were still held to be in place unless formally taken off. This was true both of civil and ecclesiastical sentences and various men, including some of the local ministers, had to wait to have sentences of banishment or deposition removed.

At around the time of the meeting of the Convention in March 1689, it is clear that the Stirling area was in a state of flux. As noted above, William's proclamation had been read publicly at the start of the year. But the new regime was first mentioned in the local records only on 15 April, when the council appointed Their Majesties King William and Queen Mary to be proclaimed at the Cross the following day, four days after the proclamation in Edinburgh. The same day the dean of the Guildry and the deacon convener of the trades were respectively commissioned as lieutenant and ensign of the militia raised to protect the town, presumably but not necessarily, from Dundee's troops.

The Convention was turned into a parliament by William on 5 June. Perhaps not surprisingly, the next scheduled General Convention in July 1689 tacitly and pragmatically acknowledged the rule of William and Mary, but even at that stage the final outcome of Dundee's efforts to retain the throne for James was not known: Dundee raised his standard in April, by which time Parliament and most of the south of the country had officially accepted the new regime. His army had marched north, passing through Stirling on 19 March, but had taken control of Perth on 11 May. The proclamation of 16 April had been followed next day by the arrival of seven companies of soldiers to add to the garrison already in Stirling Castle. These soldiers, the Cameronians from the south-west, were from the Earl of Angus's regiment and they were billeted in various places in the Stirling area, some as far away as Dunblane and Doune, while Lord Kenmure's Regiment was quartered in Stirling itself. They were untrained as soldiers and one of the early tasks on their arrival in the Stirling area was to equip them properly, with gunpowder, pikes and muskets being supplied from Stirling Castle and elsewhere in late May 1689.

Stirling Castle itself was also to be strengthened and the counties of Stirlingshire and Clackmannanshire were assessed for providing transport and labour for the task, but it was recognised that the presence of so many troops was a huge extra burden on the area, and arrangements were made to pay for the services.[34] Arrangements had also to be made to pay the soldiers. Looting seems to have been widespread and the only way to stop it was for the local authorities to lend money to the government to pay the soldiers so that they could, in their turn, pay for their subsistence.

Despite their sometimes problematic behaviour, the arrival of so many Presbyterian soldiers strengthened the hand of the Presbyterian inhabitants of the Burgh of Stirling, who had been trying to gain access to the unused half of the parish church (divided during the Commonwealth). An act of the Privy Council of 16 July 1689 granted access as no house could contain them, and they were 'tender to take it at their own hand without lawful warrand'.[35] According to the anonymous author of 'Episcopacy in Stirling', however, the council had already allowed the take-over, which took effect on 21 July.[36] When John Monro, Episcopalian minister of the 1st Charge of Stirling, was informed of the decision that the Presbyterians should have access to the other half of the church, he was said to have stamped his foot, thrown his cape on the floor and said, 'This is all I have got for following you all these years.'[37] On 19 August a considerable number of men from Angus's Regiment invaded the Episcopalian half of the church prior to the minister's arrival and forbade the service from being carried on. A group of officers from the regiment then went to the home of the minister of the 2nd Charge, James Hunter, and instructed him and his senior colleague Monro never to preach there again.

This intervention in Stirling was not the only case of Angus's Regiment taking a hand in ecclesiastical affairs. In late June two companies based in Dunblane had taken possession of the manse in Logie and helped themselves at the ministers' expense for several days.[38] The following Sunday,

> the parish Presbyterians brought their minr Mr Alexander Douglas from his meeting-house in the parish and possest him in the kirk and on Wednesday thereafter being the 26th day of June 1689 the parish Presbyterians have sermon in the church & in the meantyme the Presbyterian minr was preaching, 20 or 30 presbyt women being guarded by the companies of shoulldiers then in arms entered in the minrs house violently breaching down all the coffers and whole plenishing of the house, throwing all to the doors and during all the time

of this invasion they kept the minrs thir prisoners with a guard of musqueteers threatening and menacing Mr Schaw, ane old gray haired man of 70 years of age. Having committed Mr Elphinstone, ane young man, to the mercy of the women, they most barbarously like savage wild tigers fell upon him & rent the whoall clothes from his body, One Elspet Campbell ripping up back of his coat with a knife & all the time the sholdiers were holding his hands that the foresaid Mr Elphinstone might make no resistance. All this being done, both shouldiers and women returned to the kirk to hear the rest of the sermon.[39]

The same Elspet Campbell was also involved in further attacks on the two Episcopalian ministers of Logie. Hearing that a mob was threatening to burn the manse, Elphinstone prevailed on Colonel Graham, then commanding the garrison of Stirling Castle, to provide an escort to challenge them. Elphinstone asked the mob to desist and was pelted with stones for his pains, being pursued back to Stirling, his escort having, it is claimed, been bribed not to take action.

The women involved were part of the congregation of the Logie Presbyterian Meeting-House. This constitutes a rare occasion when there are more women identifiable in a congregation than men. Four of them can be identified as the wives of elders in the congregation. Several were unmarried and all but two resided in the parish, but they came from all corners of the parish and seem, from incomplete hearth tax returns, to have been of the 'middling' sort.

But if William's forces had control in Stirling and the parish of Logie, Dundee's troops were never far away and the long-term outcome was far from clear. In Alva, the next parish to Logie, Sir Charles Erskine, petitioning the government for the renewal of his commission in Stirling Castle, mentioned in passing in a letter of 15 June 1689 that 'the hillanders ... yeasternight have plundered my wholl hills and tennants to a considerable vallow'.[40] This is indeed borne out in the collection record of Alva Kirk, which shows a sum of four shillings for 9 June 1689 sandwiched between a more typical nine shillings and eleven shillings.[41]

Nationally, matters moved on: both armies moved north and Dundee came to battle with William's forces at Killiecrankie on 27 July. Dundee had the victory, but lost his life. Had he lived, Scotland would certainly have had a much bloodier transition to William's rule. The Earl of Angus's Regiment was not involved in the debacle at Killiecrankie, but was sent north to intercept the victorious Jacobites who fell on them at Dunkeld on 21 August.

The action at Dunkeld was almost an accidental battle. The Earl of Angus's Regiment had been detailed there not by General Mackay but by the Privy Council, who ordered them to move from their quarters in Dunblane and Doune. When the troops arrived in Dunkeld[42] they were met by a hostile populace who believed they were there to destroy and plunder. There is a little evidence to suggest that this fear was unfounded. Early skirmishes with local people were inconclusive, but part of William's force, including a party of dragoons led by Lord Cardross, was recalled to Perth, leaving the regiment on its own. The Jacobite forces then arrived and joined up with the local men of Atholl and battle was engaged. The Cameronians' Colonel Cleland was killed early on in the engagement, as was his major. The command fell on Captain George Monro of Auchenbowie, a Stirlingshire laird, and it was he who consolidated a crushing and unexpected victory, ending the immediate threat of James's forces retaking central Scotland. A final skirmish completed the work at the Haughs of Cromdale in the following spring.

The same week, Schaw and Elphinstone were able to retake possession of Logie Kirk, perhaps because there were no troops to enforce the Presbyterians' possession, although further actions to discourage Elphinstone followed in December 1689 and the following year.

The military action had been uncomfortably close to the presbytery bounds of Dunblane and Stirling. Soldiers fleeing from either battle and released from military discipline were a threat to peace and safety throughout Perthshire and Stirlingshire. Stirling, as the hub through which traffic went, was particularly vulnerable. On 30 August 1689 Viscount Kenmure was asking for weapons and munitions to be released to him from Edinburgh or Stirling Castle so that his regiment might defend itself from being 'attacqued by the Highlanders in that disaffected town of Stirling wher they now lye', a clear indication that local loyalties were divided in the town.[43] Meanwhile, such was the continuing uncertainty that in 1690 the Privy Council ordered the transfer of Archbishop Leighton's Library, a bequest to the Diocese of Dunblane, to Stirling Castle for its safety.[44]

Other military events continued to cast their shadow. Colonel Graham was confirmed as lieutenant-governor of Stirling Castle. There was protest; Lord Cardross complained, with the implication that Graham's loyalty could not be assured. It is perhaps no coincidence that within two years Cardross's half-brother John Erskine, later of Carnock,[45] took Graham's place when the latter was sent to serve in the Low Countries. From that position both Erskine and his successor, another Lieutenant-Colonel John Erskine, were to exert ecclesiastical influence as elders of Stirling Kirk Session and within Stirling Presbytery.

The real power in Scotland throughout the confused transition from James to William lay with the Privy Council. They decreed that all ministers should acknowledge the new dual monarchy and pray for King William and Queen Mary by name. Failure to do so timeously was to result in the defaulting ministers' deposition. Protected by the Earl of Angus's Regiment, the Presbyterians were able to send a long list of cases to the Privy Council from the newly restored Presbyterian Presbytery of Stirling and Dunblane, with six from the former and eight from the latter.[46] Only one of these fourteen was acquitted: John Monro, minister of the 1st Charge of Stirling, who told the Privy Council that he had prayed for

William and Mary but was prevented from reading the proclamation because he had not had a copy sent to him, nor could he get hold of the copy that he saw in the possession of someone else. His colleague in the 2nd Charge of Stirling was, however, deprived on the grounds that he had prayed for the restoration of James VII and tried to alienate his congregation from Their Majesties.

Some of the others to be deprived had been accused of more than failing to pray for their new majesties. Under an act of James VI, Robert Young, minister of Kippen, was accused of drunkenness, profaning the Sabbath by baiting his fish-hooks, assaulting his neighbours, speaking bawdy and profane language, using the art of magic with his Bible and a key, and making use of the poor's money. To these crimes were added those of not praying for William and Mary and rejoicing at the news from Killiecrankie.[47] Young was a special target of the Presbyterians because he had been assiduous in trying to root out the Covenanters and had been instrumental in informing James's forces of the activities of James Ure of Shirgarton, one of his parishioners. In 1680 Young had also seized a field belonging to Ure as church property set aside for the upkeep of the beddal (beadle). Ure's claim to the hereditary beddalship of Kippen was to resurface in Presbyterian times.[48]

Similarly, in Gargunnock, the evidence against John Edmonstone stated that he was

> a persone most scandelous in his lyfe and being frequentlie guiltie of drunkenness so that with reverence he pished his breaches and at other tymes he was holden upon his horse, and never gave communion these twentie four years nor visited the sick, and if accidentlie came to ane house where a sick person was, he neither exorted them nor prayed over them, neither ever keeped exercise in his own family, as alsoe he never hade the face of the congregatione sometymes having three or four people and sometymes ten or twelve as hearers, except when forced by law, and those who have heard this considerable tyme bygone being but a family or to at most are knowen to be disaffected to the government.[49]

Gargunnock was one of those parishes which had a Presbyterian meeting-house immediately after the Declaration of Indulgence, but it also had heritors who were firmly in the Presbyterian camp, specifically William Cunninghame of Boquhan and Robert Gourley of Kepdarroch. Cunninghame was the brother-in-law of Lord Cardross and of Erskine of Carnock. The question of who brought forward the cases against the Episcopalian incumbents has some relevance. In some parishes it was claimed to be the whole parish, in some a number of the heritors, in others specific named men. John Sage, the most influential Episcopalian historian of the time, described the complainants against Paul Gellie in Airth as 'two or three rash insignificant persons',[50] while the *Register of the Privy Council of*

Scotland simply describes them as 'the Presbyterian partie in the parochin of Airth'.[51]

Of the eleven occupied parishes of Dunblane Presbytery (Tillicoultry being recently vacant), nine were deprived of their minister by the Privy Council by the end of 1689. Two more ministers may have been deprived, but do not appear in the *Register* and may simply have been rabbled. That said, the Highland parishes of Balquhidder and Callander essentially ignored the deprivation. Despite one minister, Robert Stewart, having actively served with Dundee at Killiecrankie and being deprived as a result, Balquhidder already had the services of another, William Campbell, who was able to remain there under the protection of the Murrays of Atholl until he moved in 1710. The circumstances are unclear, but both men were in the parish prior to the Revolution. Aberfoyle, another parish to escape the deprivation of its minister, lost Robert Kirk by death in 1692; he was replaced by another Episcopalian 'intruder' in 1696. What unites all three parishes is that the ministers were protected by powerful landowners and they were all Gaelic-speaking at that time. Although Gaelic still survived in Kilmadock and Port of Menteith parishes, the remainder of the presbytery was largely English-speaking.

In the case of Stirling Presbytery there were eleven parishes but twelve ministers. Eight were tried by the Privy Council although one, John Monro, was assoilzed (acquitted) and another remained on appeal, to be deprived the following year. Those deprived included another active Jacobite, Alexander Sutherland in Larbert. Four parishes remained under episcopal care, the ministers having presumably been seen to pray for William and Mary. None of the ministers was deprived on doctrinal grounds; the core charge was the refusal to pray for the new monarchs or read their proclamations, but this was very much reinforced by a campaign to show how unsuitable the clergymen were morally, with a long litany of offences to aggravate their political shortcomings.

In 1690, Parliament turned its attention to ecclesiastical affairs. The Westminster Confession was confirmed as the main secondary standard of faith after the Bible, and the whole gamut of church courts from kirk session to General Assembly was restored, each with its allocated proportion of ruling elders alongside the teaching elders (ministers). Ministers previously deprived of their livings were restored to their churches and stipends. But it was not a return to the church of the 1640s or 1650s. There was no statement that the National Covenant and the Solemn League and Covenant were to have any legal standing within the kingdom. Some Presbyterians were quick to point this out as a 'betrayal'; others took the view that it was implicit in Presbyterianism and that the heirs and descendants of those who had signed them were equally bound by them.[52] The National Covenant in particular remained at the heart of Presbyterian thinking, sometimes tacitly, sometimes explicitly. William, however, made it clear in 1690 with the letter to the first General Assembly of his reign, already quoted, that 'Moderation is what Religion Enjoynes, Neighbouring Churches expect from You, and We Recommend to You. And We assure You of Our constant Favour and Protection, in your following of these Methods, which shall be for the real advantage of True Piety, and the Peace of Our Kingdoms.'[53]

In Stirling Presbytery, the act restoring deprived Presbyterian ministers led to the deprivation of William Lindsay, minister of Alva. He was deprived in order to allow the return of the antediluvian Richard Howieson in June 1690. Unusually the session minute records a dignified and formal handover:

> The quhich day after prayer the minr acquainted the elders that by virtue of ane act of parliament he was now to leave his ministry in this place & that therefore he had called them together to order the affairs of God's house in this place and particularly to clear the accompts from the intromission of the present treasurers, that the poor's money might be presented and employed for the use it was given . . .
>
> These things being digested in their order and the accompts faithfully and conscientiously cleared, he did desire Mr Richard Howieson accidentally present (who by virtue of the act of parliament was to enter immediately on the actual exercise of his ministry here) to take notice of and bear witness of them. As also he desired Mr Alexr Rosse and Mr John Fergusone, both servants to the family of Alva being accidentally present to bear witnesse thereof.
>
> The minister having recommended the elders and the whole parish to the blessing of God and the influences of his grace, dismist them &c.[54]

Just as the opening of the Logie meeting-house had had an impact on Alva's weekly collections in 1688, Howieson's return was marked by an immediate increase in the average weekly figure (see Appendix 3).

But this seeming resolution of 1690 anticipates matters. William may have arrived in England and taken control there quickly enough. In Scotland the situation was much more doubtful and his throne less secure.

The unhappy post-Restoration years had underlined deep divisions in Scottish society. The heirs of the conventicling tradition were used to protecting themselves with arms and might be expected to continue thus. Equally those thirled to the Jacobean dynasty had a belief that William's reign would be a mere interruption. Both sides were expected to take up arms, but the crucial factor was that Scotland was largely governed by the power of the magnates and so a final resolution of the conflict lay in the hands of men whose commitment to any cause was likely to depend on the pursuit of their own interests. In military terms the country was a partial vacuum; James's removal of the Scottish army to England had left Scotland under the control of relatively small contingents but in the restricted areas in which they operated, they were forces to be feared or welcomed. Even in 1690, the area of Stirling and Dunblane presbyteries was in a real state of uncertainty as to the future and the inhabitants divided as to what result they hoped for.

Christian Russell, a Presbyterian supporter writing from Stirling in October 1690 to her uncle in Rotterdam, surely spoke for many when she wrote: 'This pleas is lyk to be mor sade to be in it then when percicoution was in its full power for we are not like to get a gospel minister to it . . . God loke on us in mercy and deal not with us as we deserff.'[55] Fear of a very unsettled future was widespread.

The gradual transfer of control of individual parishes took place over the next decade, but not without some setbacks. Having given up his pulpit in Alva to allow the return of Howieson, Lindsay asserted his perceived right to return when Howieson was translated to Cockpen in November 1691, claiming his deprivation was solely dependent on the rights of Howieson to the charge, and not any other Presbyterian minister. He moved back into the manse and remained there for several years as minister of Alva once more although the kirk session accounts suggest that support for him was limited.[56] Clackmannan and Dollar parishes held on to their Episcopalians until later in the decade, while Bothkennar, despite attempts to deprive him in 1701 and 1717, remained in John Skinner's hands until about 1722. In this case his survival seems to have relied on a group of minor lairds rather than a single powerful patron as in Aberfoyle or Balquhidder. Table 1.1 summarises the position in the early years of the 1690s.

The other factor in considering the fortunes of the Episcopalian ministers is their own actions. The bishops, of Dunblane for Dunblane Presbytery and Edinburgh for Stirling, seem effectively to have abdicated all responsibility for their dioceses. Bishop Douglas remained in Dunblane only long enough to ensconce his son, an Episcopal minister rabbled from his charge in Lanarkshire, as the second librarian of the recently founded Leighton Library in Dunblane before retiring to Dundee. No evidence survives of the Episcopalian clergy receiving advice or support from the hierarchy. What does survive are two letters implying that some of them were in correspondence and assembling in 1690. Eight of them wrote to a group meeting in Edinburgh saying that they were 'very sensible how necessary such attempts are and what obligations lie on us to continue heartily for the strengthening and advancement of them'.[57] These were attempts to secure those ministers in their parishes and the names involved, which included George Schaw in Logie, George Monro in Dollar, William Urquhart in Clackmannan and John Monro in Stirling, together with William Lindsay in Alva, who was named as another member of the group in a second letter, are all those of Episcopalian ministers who were able to hold on to their parishes for several years after the Revolution. Lindsay and Schaw, of course, were in slightly different circumstances, having left and returned. As far as the evidence goes, it seems likely that this was a group of episcopal incumbents who would have been prepared to support William, praying for

Table 1.1 Control of Parishes, 1689–1700

Dunblane Presbytery	1689	1690	1691	1692	1693	1694	1695	1696	1697	1698	1699	1700	1701	1702	1703	1704	1705	1706	1707	1708	1709	1710
Aberfoyle	E	E	E	E	E	E	E	E	E	E	E	E	E	E	E	E	E	E	E	E	E	E
Balquhidder	E	E	E	E	E	E	E	E	E	E	E	E	E	E	E	E	E	E	E	E	E	P P
Callander	E	E	E	E	E	E	E	E	E	E	E	E	E	E	E	E	E	E	E	E	E	P P
Dunblane	E	d	d	d	d	P	P	P	P	P	P	P	P	P	P	P	P	P	P	P	P	P
Kilmadock	E	p	d	d	d	d	d	P	P	P	P	P	P	P	P	P	P	v v	P	P	P	P
Kincardine	E	p	d	d	d	d	d	d	P	P	P	P	P	P	P	P	P	P	P	P	P	P
Kippen	E	E	p	p	p	p	P	P	P	P	P	P	P	v v v	P	P	P	P	P	P	P	P
Lecropt	E	?	?	?	?	?	?	p	P	P	v v v	P	P	P	P	P	P	P	P	P	P	P
Logie	E	p	p	P	P	P	P	P	P	P	P	P	P	P	P	P	P	P	P	P	P	P
Port	E	E	d	d	d	d	d	d	d	d	d	P	P	P	P	P	P	P	P	P	P	P
Tillicoultry	E	p	p	p	p	P	P	P	P	P	P	P	P	P	P	P	P	P	P	P	P	P
Tulliallan	E	p	p	P	P	p	P	P	P	P	P	P	P	P	P	P	P	P	P	P	P	P

Stirling Presbytery	1689	1690	1691	1692	1693	1694	1695	1696	1697	1698	1699	1700	1701	1702	1703	1704	1705	1706	1707	1708	1709	1710
Airth	E	d	d	d	d	d	d	d	p	p	p	p	p	p	p	P	P	P	P	P	P	P
Alloa	E	p	p	p	P	P	P	P	P	P	P	P	P	P	P	v	v v v v v v v	P	P	P	P	P
Alva	E	d	P	P	P	E	E	E	E	E	E	E	p	p	p	p	P	P	P	P	P	P
Bothkennar	E	E	E	E	E	E	E	E	E	E	E	E	E	E	E	E	E	E	E	E	E	E
Clackmannan	E	E	E	E	E	E	E	E	E	E	E	E	d	d	p	p	p	P	P	P	P	P
Denny	E	p	p	p	P	P	P	P	P	P	P	P	P	P	P	P	P	P	P	P	P	P
Dollar	E	E	E	E	E	E	E	E	E	E	E	E	E	E	E	p	p	p	P	P	P	P
Gargunnock	E	P	P	P	P	P	P	P	P	d	d	p	p	p	P	P	P	P	P	P	P	P
Larbert	E	p	p	P	P	P	P	P	P	P	P	P	P	P	P	P	P	P	P	P	P	P
St Ninians	E	P	P	P	P	P	p	p	p	p	P	P	P	P	P	P	P	P	P	P	P	P
Stirling 1st	E	E	E	E	E	E	E	p	p	P	P	P	P	P	P	P	P	v v v v	P	P	P	P
Stirling 2nd	E	d	d	d	d	d	d	p	P	v v v v	P	P	P	P	P	P	v v v	P	P	v v	P	P

| Episcopalian | E | Disputed | d | Presb. Control | p | Vacant | v | Presb. Minister | P |

the new king and queen, and those who had already been deprived, mainly for not praying for them, were noticeably absent from both the correspondence and any meeting.[58]

The question does arise whether the people of the two presbyteries supported the return of Presbyterian governance to their church. Nationally there has been considerable debate over the extent of popular support from the time of the very events themselves. Locally, there is no evidence that those Episcopalian ministers who hung on did so in defiance of the wishes of the population, although there were known Presbyterian supporters in both Bothkennar and Balquhidder. Equally, St Ninians and Stirling both showed signs of a split population with Episcopalian congregations having a continuous existence up until 1715 and later. Nonetheless, in some parishes where the records might appear to be silent, evidence does exist.

The financial accounts of both Tulliallan and Alva provide some kind of statement as to the reception of returning antediluvians. In the case of the former, the account book has the following introduction: 'A particular account of collections received by Walter Brown since the return of our Minister. September 28 anno 1690' and the first entry shows a highly impressive collection of £11 10s. Scots against a normal weekly collection of between £2 and £4. Added to that there is the evidence of the baptismal roll, which shows that two children were baptised on 28 September and a further eleven baptised by the end of the year. This figure of thirteen baptisms can be compared to the total of nineteen baptised in the first nine months prior to John Forrest's return.[59] Clearly for much of the parish, this was a welcome restoration.

In the case of Alva, the account book already quoted shows evidence of how the local congregation responded to change. As shown in Appendix 3, the average collection under Lindsay's pastorate had already declined when the Presbyterian meeting-house opened in Logie in August 1688. After Howieson's departure in the autumn of 1691, there was a two-month hiatus before Lindsay returned and then the collections were significantly less than they had been the previous year. Lindsay claimed the support of local landowners for his return, which may well have been half-true as the laird was abroad and the estate run by his mother. Lady Erskine did repay her late husband's bond to the church after Lindsay returned so may have been sympathetic to him.

The transition from James's rule to William's therefore played out in a number of different ways in the two presbyteries: it is clear that the population was left divided and that there was a considerable degree of uncertainty as to how events would develop in the future. There were parishes which were settled in the new regime, others that quietly resisted it, others too which were heavily influenced by the presence of troops and the threat of war at least in the earliest years. Nonetheless, despite the ever-present shadow of a possible Jacobite return, the newly restored Presbyterian Church of Scotland began to consolidate in the two presbyteries of Stirling and Dunblane.

Notes

1. Logan, *A Sermon Preached before His Grace James Duke of Queensberry*, p. 13.
2. Burleigh, *A Church History of Scotland*, p. 194.
3. Quoted ibid., p. 218.
4. *Fasti Ecclesiae Scoticanae*, vol. 4, pp. 317, 319.
5. Burleigh, *A Church History of Scotland*, pp. 238–9.
6. Quoted in Allan, 'Reconciliation and Retirement in the Restoration Scottish Church', p. 270.
7. Burleigh, *A Church History of Scotland*, pp. 244–6.
8. *Register of the Diocesan Synod of Dunblane*, p. 7.
9. Burleigh, *A Church History of Scotland*, p. 246. The figure of depositions varying between 330 and 450 refers to the total throughout the period and includes many deprived after the Battle of Bothwell Bridge and the Test Acts of 1681–4.
10. *Register of the Diocesan Synod of Dunblane*, p. 13. It should be noted that two of the three were from Culross, later not part of the presbytery.
11. The term 'curate' in a Scottish context is almost always a pejorative term for

an Episcopalian clergyman, a usage that seems to have started in Presbyterian writings of the Restoration period.
12. Historical Manuscripts Commission (hereafter HMC), 'The Manuscripts of His Grace the Duke of Buccleuch and Queensberry', Appendix 8, p. 230.
13. Kirkton, *The Secret and True History of the Church of Scotland*, pp. 386–8.
14. The term 'Covenanter' as shorthand for those in opposition to the Stuart regime has been challenged, particularly by Alasdair Raffe, on the grounds that all Presbyterians were bound by the covenants even if few remained who had signed them. The author's feeling is that conspicuous mention of the covenants on the surviving banners associated with the Battle of Bothwell Bridge justifies the term at this period. There is less justification to use it for those Presbyterians who remained dissident after the Revolution.
15. Mann, *James VII*, p. 149.
16. Shirgarton is variously spelled Shergarton and Shurgurton in the records.
17. Erskine, *Journal of the Hon. John Erskine of Carnock, 1683–1687*, p. 23.
18. Stephen, *Defending the Revolution*, p. 2 summarises some of the differing attitudes.
19. Quoted ibid., pp. 14–15.
20. Stirling Burgh Council, *Extracts of the Records of the Royal Burgh of Stirling*, A.D. 1667–1752, p. 50.
21. *By the King a proclamation*.
22. 'To the King's Most Excellent Majesty, James, the VII, the Humble Address of the Presbyterian Ministers in His Majesties Kingdom of Scotland'.
23. 'To the King's Most Excellent Majesty, the Humble Address of the Cittizens And Inhabitants That Are of the presbyterian Perswasion in the City of Edinburgh and the Cannongate'.
24. Gardner, *The Scottish Exile Community in the Netherlands, 1660–1690*, p. 158.
25. Raffe, *Scotland in Revolution, 1685–1690*, pp. 53–4.
26. Mann, *James VII*, p. 208.
27. Stirling Burgh Council, *Extracts of the Records of the Royal Burgh of Stirling*, A.D. 1667–1752, p. 54.
28. As distinct from the general convention of all burghs, held in July. This extra meeting was scheduled at the general convention for particular purposes and was not in response to the unfolding events.
29. *Extracts from the Records of the Convention of the Royal Burghs of Scotland, 1677–1711*, p. 86.
30. 'Episcopacy in Stirling', p. 214. This is a transcription of a transcription of a near-contemporary manuscript, both now lost. The Stirling historian John Harrison believes this may have been written by James Hunter, one of the local episcopal ministers.
31. Parliament of Scotland, Claim of Right Act, 1689 c.28, http://www.legislation.gov.uk/aosp/1689/28/paragraph/p40 (last accessed 8 February 2021).
32. These included a regimental kirk session, marching to church with side arms and posting armed sentries around their services, which were referred to as 'conventicles'.
33. Begg, *The Kingdom of Kippen*, p. 78.
34. *Register of the Privy Council of Scotland, 3rd Series* (hereafter RPCS), vol. 14, p. 544.
35. RPCS, vol. 14, p. 520.
36. 'Episcopacy in Stirling', p. 215.

37. RPCS, vol. 14, p. 184.
38. Logie's elderly and long-serving minister, George Schaw, had an assistant and successor, William Elphinstone, who was also his son-in-law.
39. NLS MS 7593 has two very similar versions of the proceedings, both signed by Schaw and Elphinstone, possibly with a view to publication. There is also an unexplained list of twenty-seven women's names, headed by Elspet Campbell. The implication is that these were the women who rabbled.
40. NRS GD26/9/104 Charles Erskine to Lord Melville? 15/6/1689.
41. SCA CH2/10/4 9/6/1689.
42. Dunkeld is of course the smallest city in Britain, but demographically a village.
43. RPCS, vol. 14, p. 152.
44. RPCS, vol. 15, pp. 341–2.
45. Referred to subsequently as Erskine of Carnock to differentiate him from the various other John Erskines.
46. There are many instances of temporary conjunction of presbyteries due to the small number of Presbyterian ministers available. Twelve ministers was generally seen as a desirable number. Stirling and Dunblane met as one from the Revolution until 1698. A portion of Auchterarder Presbytery was also part for the first four years. Other conjoint presbyteries remained together much longer. The constituent presbyteries, however, still sent their commissioners separately to the General Assembly.
47. RPCS, vol. 14, pp. 372–3.
48. Begg, *The Kingdom of Kippen*, p. 72.
49. RPCS, vol. 14, p. 376.
50. Sage, *The Case of the Present Afflicted Clergy in Scotland*, p. 73.
51. RPCS, vol. 14, p. 182.
52. Stephen, *Defending the Revolution*, pp. 82–4.
53. His Majesty's Gracious Letter to the Assembly: see 'Acts: 1690', in Church of Scotland, *Acts of the General Assembly of the Church of Scotland, 1638–1842*.
54. SCA CH2/10/1 6/6/1690.
55. NRS RH15/106/709/10 Christian Russell to Andrew Russell 13/10/1690.
56. SCA CH2/10/4.
57. NRS CH12/12/467.
58. Clarke, 'The Scottish Episcopalians, 1688–1720', pp. 30–32.
59. SCA CH2/710/1 (accounts) and NRS OPR 397/10 (baptisms).

CHAPTER TWO

Ministering in the Presbyteries: Exiles and Antediluvians

In 1686, Quintin Dick, an Ayrshire farmer, wrote in his 'Brief account of some signall passages of God's Good Providence . . .':

> [I saw] the Presbyterian cause brought to such a period, that not one minister of that persuasion could be seen or heard to administer any of these ordinances in October and November 1684, either in private or in publick within all Scotland, presbytrie and the professors thereof being thus overthrown and prelacie violently introduct in its place.[1]

It might therefore be said that institutional Presbyterianism, from this low point in 1684, owed its new beginning to those who returned to Scotland or otherwise reappeared to open up tolerated meeting-houses in 1687, and in many ways it was the people of these congregations, rather than the antediluvians restored in 1690, who laid the foundations for the re-establishment of Presbyterianism under William.

Given the wealth of detail which Robert Wodrow provided in his *History of the Sufferings*, it was perhaps inevitable that many historians looked no further for information and hence concentrated largely on Edinburgh and Glasgow, as Alasdair Raffe has commented.[2] Raffe has extended the examination of Presbyterian resurgence wider than that and given detail outwith the two cities, but no historian has taken on a systematic examination of how a limited area recruited its Presbyterian clergy over the period in question, and that is what this chapter and the next seek to do.

These ministers who returned during the reign of James VII quickly realised that they had to combine into presbyteries for the sake of the orderly presentation of their faith. The Presbytery of Linlithgow was one of the first to be refounded, with four ministers meeting in Bo'ness on 30 November 1687. Robert Stiedman, William Weir, William Crighton and Michael Potter thus met together in presbytery while the Episcopalian presbytery was still meeting in Linlithgow and elsewhere, continuing until July of the following year.[3]

At around this time several meeting-houses appeared within the bounds of what became the joint Presbytery of Stirling and Dunblane. Although no pre-1690 records survive, their ministers too met as a presbytery, with its existence noted in the synod record of Glasgow and Ayr.[4] Meeting-houses were formed in St Ninians, Logie and Gargunnock. The buildings are long lost but Logie's was in the village of Blairlogie, a quarter of a mile from the parish church, while that in Gargunnock was at Glentirran, close to the parish border with Kippen and to the Cardross lands of the Erskines. Both Logie's and Gargunnock's meeting-houses were easily accessible to neighbouring parishes.

George Barclay, who ministered at Glentirran, had been a Covenanter; pursued throughout Scotland and imprisoned on more than one occasion, he was exiled to the Low Countries where he also managed to amass a small fortune. Barclay was very much on the moderate wing of the pre-Revolution Presbyterians and opposed to the activities of Richard Cameron and James Renwick. In 1690 he transferred to Uphall in West Lothian. In moving, he transferred to a parish which was under the control of Lord Cardross. Once there he was in the fortunate position of being able to build himself a country house and later give up his stipend to his colleague and successor.[5]

Another meeting-house minister who did not stay long was Patrick Couper. He had been licensed to preach while in exile in 1684 and was ordained and appointed to the meeting-house in Bannockburn, in St Ninians Parish, in August 1687, only to be transported to Pittenweem in 1692. Couper had been imprisoned on more than one occasion for his Covenanting activities and like Barclay had been part of the exile community in the Netherlands. He had returned to Scotland after the Act of Toleration came into force, but quickly went back to Holland, returning to Bo'ness the following year and being called to Bannockburn.

After being called to the parish kirk in 1690, it is clear that Couper was not acceptable to everyone in St Ninians. As early as March 1691, records show the depth of the schism. Referred by the joint presbytery after the Commission of Assembly had also considered it, the synod record shows that the elders who had been confirmed as the kirk session of St Ninians Parish were keen to retain Couper's services; however, the heritors were a different matter. At the following meeting of the synod,[6] they made it clear that nothing would satisfy them other than 'a loosing of Mr Patrick Couper from St Ninians and a declaring of the church vacant'. The elders meanwhile were 'earnestly insisting to have [him] continued amongst them at least until the Heritors, elders and people of St Ninians give a Call to another minister to the Presbyteries satisfaction'. The matter was sent back to the Commission of Assembly, but the synod bowed to the heritors' pressure and in the meantime used Couper as peripatetic pulpit supply. Clearly the congregation was split. Couper himself was quite clear that he wanted to leave; his elders, led by William Livingstone of Greenyards and John Forrest of Thirtieacres, were equally keen to retain him. The synod wanted him at least to stay within the bounds so that he could be used elsewhere. The heritors meanwhile expressed their willingness to accept any minister whom the presbytery might recommend, 'Mr Patrick Couper only excepted'. In the event the synod bowed to the inevitable and Couper took his departure to Pittenweem, although his arrival there was resisted by some of the local Jacobites.[7]

The same month as Couper had been ordained in Bannockburn, Alexander Douglas was ordained in the meeting-house in Logie. Alone of the three meeting-house incumbents, he stayed on after being confirmed as parish minister, preaching in the meeting-house at Blairlogie until the Episcopalian incumbent, George Schaw, was finally persuaded to vacate the church, with Schaw giving up his pulpit in 1690 but retaining the manse until 1693.[8]

Douglas was an older man, middle-aged by the time of his ordination. He was the son of Robert Douglas, one of the outstanding ministers of the previous generation, who had preached at the coronation of Charles II. Douglas remained in Logie for the remainder of his life. His problems with gaining access to the manse were made the worse by the unwillingness of the heritors to make the manse habitable and he finally had to repair it at his own expense, hoping to reclaim the outlay at a later stage. The advantage that these meeting-house congregations had when Presbyterianism was re-established was that they came with a functioning Presbyterian kirk session and this gave those parishes the basis for Presbyterianism that a parish which only had the old Episcopalian session might not have.

If Douglas had a settled kirk session and no great issue with his heritors other than their unwillingness to fulfil their legal obligations to the church, he did find himself at variance with his presbytery. Like many other presbyteries in 1690, Stirling and Dunblane presbyteries had been working as one due to lack of numbers. In 1698, the ministers of Dunblane Presbytery, to which Logie belonged, decided unilaterally to sever the connection with Stirling Presbytery. Douglas dissented strongly from this decision, to the extent that he continued attending Stirling Presbytery. When the decision of the synod supported Dunblane, Stirling merely recorded Douglas's attendance as a visitor. He then volunteered to join a three-month visitation with the Commission for the North and when he returned, he quietly complied with the *fait accompli* and remained a member of Dunblane Presbytery until his death.

To these three men can be added two other ministers who had been involved in meeting-houses elsewhere, Michael Potter and George Turnbull. Potter, admitted to the meeting-house in Bo'ness in 1687, had a well-known background as one of the younger dissident Presbyterians. He had been ordained by Presbyterian ministers to look after the meeting-house in St Ninians in 1673 but had to leave that parish. He was then appointed as schoolmaster in Culross before being subjected to a legal process that saw him imprisoned on the Bass Rock, before being exiled for a second time to the Netherlands. Coming back in 1687 under the Toleration must have been a significant risk. After five years in Bo'ness, where he had been a founding member of the new presbytery, he moved to Dunblane and took his place as a senior member of the Presbytery of Dunblane.

Also an exile in the Low Countries, Turnbull was ordained by expatriate Scots in London in 1688, moving northwards over the next few months to a meeting-house in Dalmeny near Edinburgh, where he was admitted in the November of that year. Alexander Hamilton, the antediluvian previous minister of the charge, had apparently no wish to return to it and Turnbull looked set to move to the parish church. However, a few months later, Turnbull found himself summarily dismissed from the parish and, after preaching in a number of places, was called to Alloa. Just what the grounds were for his dismissal are unclear; but Hamilton returned to Dalmeny in 1690 for all of eleven weeks before moving to Edinburgh. Meanwhile Turnbull's diary shows him as taking legal action against the heritors of Dalmeny in 1702 and as late as 1709.[9] Court of Session papers show that his case for payment of the stipend of Dalmeny for two years finally came to court and was contested by the heritors. Unfortunately the outcome is not clear due to the loss of the end of the document.[10]

Not all exiles had been in the Low Countries, though. Hugh Whyte, minister of Larbert & Dunipace, had spent some years in Ireland after being declared a fugitive in 1684. He was licensed as a preacher in Ireland in 1688 but was only ordained when he came to Larbert in 1690. One factor that seems to draw these men together is the strength of networking in bringing former exiles to their new charges. Other than Douglas, most had moved in the same circles in the Low Countries; in St Ninians, one of the leading members of the kirk session had been a known Covenanter who had suffered imprisonment, so it seems reasonable to believe that his enthusiasm for Couper stemmed from previous connection. Barclay in Gargunnock was geographically in the Cardross estates, and although Lord Cardross himself served his exile elsewhere, his brother, John Erskine of Carnock, was well known as one of the younger exiles and returned to Scotland with William, being appointed lieutenant-governor of Stirling Castle. Turnbull was very much in the same network, having taught Erskine the French language during their exile. His ordination in London was witnessed by Cardross. One of the ministers taking part in the service was Robert Traill, former exile and brother of James Traill, another exile, whose reward under the new regime was to be appointed as ensign in Stirling Castle, where he became one of most assiduous elders in the Stirling Kirk Session.

The brevity of ministry in the early days of re-establishment seems to be a feature of the lives of the meeting-house incumbents, with two of them leaving the area shortly after 1690 and two others moving into the area after equally brief incumbencies. That said, there were two other ministers who came to the area shortly after 1690 and did stay there. These men, John Watson in Denny and Robert Gourlaw in Tillicoultry, followed a rather different career path. Gourlaw was newly inducted into his parish of Tillicoultry. He had come from a ministry elsewhere but nothing is known of his previous activities. Alone of the local ministers he achieved the doubtful accolade, and that within a few months of ordination, of a satirical reference in *The Scotch Presbyterian Eloquence Display'd*:

> One Mr. *Robert Gourly* preaching on the Woman of Canaan, how our Saviour called her a Dog, told, Sirs, some of you may think that our Saviour spake very improperly, for he should have called her a Bitch; but to this I answer, a Dog is the Masculine or Feminine Gender, there is a He-dog and a She-dog. But you will ask why did he miscall the poor Woman, and call her a Dog? There are God's Dogs and the Devil's Dogs, she was God's Dog, not the Devil's Dog.[11]

Of Watson nothing is known at all except that he was admitted at Denny sometime prior to March 1691, presumably having been ordained elsewhere, and that he was a minor laird with the appendage of 'Knowhead'. He was in his early thirties when he went to Denny.

With a statistical sample too small to be meaningful, it is nevertheless worth noting that those who were ordained into the area from 1689 onwards tended to remain in their parishes, while those who came to the area as ordained ministers moved on. The reasons for this difference are not entirely clear, but there is some evidence, especially in St Ninians but also in Gargunnock and Logie, that the heritors were not entirely at one with the minister. For all that the right of patronage had been removed, as holders of the parish purse strings, the heritors were still in a position of strength locally and it would be very hard for any minister to gainsay them for an extended period of time. There is also a question as to who exactly had called the exiles to specific parishes and therefore some doubt as to the ministers' right to be there.

If the small number of meeting-house preachers laid the foundation for the new presbyteries after the Revolution, the clearest indication of the resurgence of Presbyterianism was the symbolic restoration of the oldest Presbyterian ministers to their previous charges, enshrined in an act of Parliament of 1690.[12] Much has been made of the return of the antediluvians to the pulpits of Scotland after 1690, and particularly of their control of the General Assembly of 1690.[13] It was, of course, a symbolic act. By limiting membership of the assembly to those who had been deprived under Charles II and those ordained under their hands, the newly established Presbyterian church was essentially saying that it was the legal and actual successor to the church of the 1640s/1650s and that the intervening period was a mere aberration.

General meetings of the Presbyterians in 1687–9 had laid the foundations of the restored court and authorised the meetings of synods and of presbyteries which sent commissioners to the newly reconstituted General Assembly in 1690. The first session of the first General Assembly of the new regime was initially moderated by the same man, Gabriel Cunningham, who had been moderator at the last General Assembly before the hiatus caused first by Cromwell in 1653 and then by the reintroduction of prelacy by Charles, a clear statement of continuity.

That first General Assembly of the newly re-established church included sixty 'antediluvians', a further fifty-six ministers who had been ordained under them in the intervening years together with forty-seven elders.[14] The records of the Synod of Glasgow and Ayr show that the last general meeting of the Presbyterians prior to the General Assembly had decreed that all the ministers of the new synods, and especially the 'aged brethren', were expected to attend as far as they were able.[15] To the Presbyterians of the day, that first General Assembly was a triumph and a vindication. To the Episcopalians of the day it was a gross miscarriage of justice and left an abiding opinion that, because it was an entirely self-selected group representing only one element of the church, that assembly and its successors were not representative of the Church of Scotland. Those sixty antediluvians were not the sole survivors from the days before the Carolean flood; a list compiled by Wodrow thirty years later gives eighty-six names of ministers who were still alive when William crossed the English Channel, together with a note of the parishes to which they returned, showing their territorial spread. Not all, however, returned and some were very elderly and probably too frail to play much of a part in events.

The act of Parliament of 7 June 1690 placed back in their pulpits all 'Presbyterian ministers who were outed since . . . 1661 for non-conformity to prelacie, or not complying with the courses of the tyme, and are now restored by the late act of parliament'.[16] In his *History of the Sufferings of the Church of Scotland from the Restauration to the Revolution*, published in 1721-2, Robert Wodrow identified 411 who had been outed, including those eighty-six survivors.[17] The list of survivors was not entirely accurate, however: it included some who had not lived to see the new regime, and it missed a few out whose careers had been somewhat atypical.

There is a tendency to regard the returning ministers as a 'block vote' dedicated to turning the clock back. Gordon Donaldson referred to the direction of the Church's affairs being 'committed initially to sixty "antediluvians" as they were called, aged ministers who had been deprived in the early 1660s, . . . along with a number of other Presbyterians who had not conformed, at least in full, to the pre-Revolution Episcopalian establishment.'[18] However, the antediluvians were not a homogeneous group by any manner of means. Reference has been made to the Protester/Resolutioner controversy of around 1650, with the Protesters being much more hard-line in their attitude to the Covenants than the Resolutioners. The former had been much less likely to conform to Charles's episcopal regime than the latter but both groups were represented among those purged from the church in 1661-2 and among those who returned in 1690. A further group had accepted the various indulgences offered by Charles II before being deprived at a later stage. They too were included in the sixty. While they were functioning as 'indulged' ministers, there had been a mixture of attitudes to them from those Presbyterians who did not accept indulgence, with many refusing to recognise them as any different from the Episcopalian clergy, but a few declining to hold conventicles in parishes where an indulged Presbyterian officiated.[19] Even within the Scottish exile community in the Netherlands, the splits were apparent between the two groups, those who had never accepted an indulgence and those who had accepted and then been deprived at a later stage.

It is perhaps stating the obvious to point out that no one coming back to Scotland in 1687 knew that Presbyterianism would be re-established three years later. But a smooth transition from tolerated meeting-houses to established kirk was not realistically on the horizon for them. The accession of William changed that, and most of the more radically minded Presbyterians who had remained furth of Scotland returned by 1690, leaving behind only a few to minister to the Scottish community in the Netherlands. A clear difference can therefore be seen between those who served within Scotland prior to William's arrival in England and those who did not return until William and Mary were on the throne and reasonably safely ensconced. In addition, there were the three surviving field preachers who were excluded from any toleration that James VII was likely to enact and who had prices on their heads until the end of his reign.

The potential Presbyterian Church of 1690 therefore included ministers from any or several of these groupings:

- Pre-1660 Protester
- Pre-1660 Resolutioner
- Post-1660 Conformist later turning to Presbyterianism and deposed
- Post-1660 Episcopalian later turning to Presbyterianism and deposed
- Presbyterian accepting one of the earlier indulgences (scornfully referred to as 'king's curates')
- Presbyterian or Episcopalian deposed for refusing the Test Act of 1682
- Presbyterian exile returning under the Toleration
- Presbyterian exile returning only when William was in control
- Field preacher still operating in Scotland in defiance of James.

In a rare moment of non-doctrinaire common sense, the General Assembly of 1690 decided that the Protester/Resolutioner controversy was actually an old wound that should be allowed to heal rather than being reopened. It effectively admitted that the differences in opinion in the past were 'not managed with due charity and love, but with too much heat and bitterness, injurious reflections used against pious and worthy men on all hands and scandalous divisions occasioned'.[20] There does seem to have been an effort to integrate the various groups. However, it did take the Assembly of 1690 considerable thought to decide that the three surviving free field preachers could be absorbed back into the established church despite their having made 'several peremptory and gross mistakes, unseasonable and impracticable proposals and uncharitable and injurious reflections'.[21]

The whole question of the power and influence of the antediluvians, though, is coloured by two other factors. Both were demographic. Firstly, there was a geographical imbalance so that the antediluvians were over-represented in some presbyteries and absent in others. Stirling and Dunblane presbyteries lay somewhere in the middle. The second factor was age. By definition the youngest of the antediluvians were in late middle age and many were downright elderly. Their influence was always going to be temporary.

As the Assembly had not met since 1653, there was no need for the equivalent of the Rescissory Act of 1661, by which the Scottish Parliament wiped out all decisions taken by any court in the land since 1640 and in effect from 1633.[22] Among other effects, that act had effectively denied that any of the ministers who had been appointed to parishes between 1649 and 1661 were legally appointed, thus leading to the great deprivation of so many ministers. However, the Assembly of 1690 overrode any sentence of deprivation passed as a result of the Protester/Resolutioner controversy in the 1650s and restored any ministers still alive.[23] Acts of Synod and acts of Parliament referring to religious matters in the Restoration period were also acknowledged and dealt with.

As mentioned above, the Assembly of 1690 was not the first meeting of the resurgent national Presbyterianism. Although allowed for under the mixed episcopal system which kept presbyteries and synods, albeit in a different form, no national synod or assembly was held after the Restoration, but as soon as exiles had returned to Scotland after the Indulgences of 1687, a national 'meeting' was held. After it adjourned on 5 July 1687, one immediate result was the reconstitution of presbyterian (as distinct from diocesan) synods. The Synod of Lothian and Tweeddale therefore met the very next day. The 'General Meeting' had only included 'ministers from the severall Provinces of the Kingdom' and the synod's first meeting also included 'Ministers of this Province and such other ministers as for the tyme are residenters within the bounds'. No elders at that stage were included, although apparently probationers were given membership. The early meetings were entirely devoted to filling pulpits, ordering the transportation of ministers and assessing the doctrine and competence of the probationers, the process being largely facilitated by regularly meeting committees. Only in May 1688 did elders appear on the sederunt list,[24] five attending together with fourteen ministers. The probationers had disappeared from membership. On the other side of the country, the Synod of Glasgow and Ayr similarly assembled without elders until its meeting of April 1688.[25]

The earliest surviving record of the Synod of Perth and Stirling dates only from March 1691. It is clear from the Glasgow record, though, that it had been in existence longer for in April 1688 the synod was trying to show that Thomas Forrester was one of their members by virtue of his deposition from Alva in 1674.

What then was the situation in the presbyteries of Stirling and Dunblane? In 1661, the twenty-four charges had sixteen ministers who had conformed, and seven who had been deposed; one charge was vacant.[26] In addition, Robert Rule had been deposed from the 2nd Charge of Stirling during the Protester/Resolutioner controversy and had moved to Kirkcaldy from whence he was deprived in 1661.

Of the seven men who were deposed, one lost his life: James Guthrie, minister of the 1st Charge of Stirling, as previously noted, became the first martyr to the Covenanting cause in the reign of Charles II. The remaining six had less dramatic and longer subsequent careers. Four were in the Presbytery of Stirling: James Simson in Airth, who left in 1660 to go to a new charge, but was later arrested before being sent into exile in the Netherlands where he died; Richard Howieson in Alva, who was deprived in 1662 and later indulged in Logie; John Blair in Bothkennar, who was deprived in 1660 and died in 1703 in Edinburgh; and Thomas Hog in Larbert, who was deprived in 1662 and died in 1681, and so did not see the restoration of Presbyterianism. The other two, in the Presbytery of Dunblane, were John Forrest in Tulliallan, who was deprived of his living in 1662, then served as an indulged minister in Tillicoultry and later in Carmichael where he served until readmitted to Tulliallan briefly in 1690; and Thomas Forrester, minister of Kincardine, who had conformed but demitted in 1682, probably as a result of the Test Act, and whose subsequent fate is unknown. Of these, Guthrie, Simson and Hog had previously withdrawn from Stirling Presbytery and formed their own Protester presbytery.

To these candidates for restoration in 1690 can be added another Thomas Forrester, who was episcopally appointed to Alva in succession to Richard Howieson before being himself deposed in 1674. A further minister who enters the records of the presbyteries of Stirling and Dunblane was William Spence. Episcopally appointed to the parish of Glendevon in the Presbytery of Kinross in 1664, he was converted to the Presbyterian cause and was deprived in 1679. He became the Earl of Argyll's secretary and suffered torture after Argyll's rebellion in 1685.

History has tended to present the restoration of the antediluvians in rather violent terms, but away from the south-west of the country, the process could be carried out with a certain degree of decorum. As quoted in Chapter 1, the Episcopalian incumbent of Alva, William Lindsay, called together the four elders who comprised his kirk session on Friday 6 June 1690 and handed over his charge to the antediluvian Richard Howieson in an orderly and dignified fashion.

John Blair, who had been minister of Bothkennar in the 1650s, was strongly resisted when he was originally inducted there. Certainly he returned to the bounds after the Toleration. He had a cameo role as a member of Stirling Presbytery in 1687 when he was mentioned in the

Glasgow and Ayr Synod minutes, being advised to take notice of Larbert & Dunipace and Airth parishes so that their inhabitants might cease from importuning Glasgow for pulpit supply.[27] However, that was apparently the last mention of him functioning as a minister in Stirling Presbytery and he disappeared from locally recorded history.

The other locally restored antediluvian was John Forrest, former minister of Tulliallan, deprived of his living in 1662 and 'indulged' in two other parishes in the meantime. He returned to Tulliallan in 1690. A letter from Forrest to Andrew Russell in Rotterdam suggests the sort of pressure that the returned antediluvians were under: '[Mr Fleming, a Scottish minister in Rotterdam] would not have thought that either I would be so destitute here or so desyrous to be there or my bretheren so content to want mee, that upon his simple letter to one single minister I would be loosed or suffer myself to be loosed from my charge here.'[28] The following year he was called to Falkland in Fife before moving to Prestonkirk a year later, dying there in 1704.

Thomas Forrester, who had been ordained into Alva during the Restoration period but saw the Presbyterian light and was deposed, became a well-known polemicist on behalf of the Presbyterians. He was later an indulged minister in Killearn in Dumbarton Presbytery. Stirling Presbytery did its best to bring him back to its bounds, but shortly afterwards he was confirmed in Killearn, where he had returned to open a meeting-house in 1688. He later moved to the University of St Andrews, where he became one of the major theologians of the period.

The fifth antediluvian with local links was William Spence, included only because part of Auchterarder Presbytery was added to the joint Presbytery of Stirling and Dunblane in the early 1690s. Like Forrester, Spence had come back to open a meeting-house. In the parish of Kinross, it served four parishes but early attempts to place him in Kinross after the Revolution failed when he, in a like manner to Episcopalians in the south-west, was rabbled and not allowed to settle there. The views of the local landowners were also important in persuading him that Kinross was not to be his parish. He was therefore resettled in Glendevon, from which he had been ejected in 1679, and consequently came under the care of the joint presbytery.

These men, Howieson, Forrest, Forrester and Spence, and perhaps even more so John Blair, all demonstrate one common characteristic of the returned ministers. When reinstated to their old parishes, they only remained there for a few months before moving on. This was a widespread pattern throughout the country. At least seventeen returning ministers had moved to new parishes within two years of reinstatement.

This was a matter of comment at the time. That notably polemical *Scotch Presbyterian Eloquence Display'd* remarks both on the propensity of Presbyterian ministers to hold two appointments at once, a criticism chiefly levelled at those who combined university posts with parish ministry, and on those who reclaimed their old parishes very briefly in order to claim their stipends before moving on to somewhere more profitable. The author's chief target in this was James Kirton (Kirkton), who,

> out of Malice against the episcopal Minister, and covetousness to get the Stipend of the Place, comes from Edinburgh and preaches one sermon in the parish of St Martins, and returning some days after, left the Church without a minister, by which means he obtained to himself the Stipend of the Parish though he lived and preached in the City of Edinburgh ever since.[29]

It therefore follows that the restored antediluvians made little or no impact on their old parishes and presbyteries after the Revolution. Howieson served briefly in Stirling Presbytery as clerk, and in the Synod of Perth and Stirling as moderator, but as noted, his chief reason to be remembered was that when he was called to Cockpen in 1691 (where, incidentally, he only remained three years) he took the presbytery records with him, never to be seen again. Forrester made it clear he would not return to the bounds and Forrest is invisible in the records that remain. Spence was the one partial exception, for his quick move from the meeting-house in Kinross to Glendevon and then to Fossoway left him still in the Presbytery of Auchterarder.

One other antediluvian remains to be considered. Robert Rule had been called to the 2nd Charge of Stirling in the unhappy days of the Protester controversy, but his admission had been declared illegal by the synod and he soon left. He then went to Kirkcaldy, from which he was deprived shortly after arriving in 1662. He was reinstated to Kirkcaldy, as was his legal right, in 1690, having been serving in the meeting-house there since 1688. In 1693 he was recalled to the 2nd Charge of Stirling by Stirling Presbytery. He served there until his death in 1703, transferring from the 2nd to the 1st Charge in the course of the decade.

Although nothing seems to have been said at the time, the implication is that his arrival was symbolic of the old Protester regime in Stirling and a statement of continuity from the time of the martyred James Guthrie. His arrival in 1693 coincided with the final days of John Monro's Episcopalian incumbency of the 1st Charge, when Monro was absent for several weeks. On Monro's return they reached a compromise for two or three weeks whereby Monro preached in the morning and Rule in the afternoon. It was noted that neither went to listen to the other and the two diets of worship had largely different congregations. Monro was soon barred from preaching in Stirling by the Privy Council, his final sermon, on 2 Corinthians 13:11,[30] being preached on 9 July 1693. Rule's own formal induction to the 2nd Charge of Stirling was thereafter delayed until November due to negotiations with the Presbytery of Kirkcaldy.[31] A surviving sermon of Rule's preached in Edinburgh in 1688, quoted by Raffe, shows how he upheld the old orthodoxy in opposition to those who were already moving towards a new moralistic approach.[32]

Quite irregularly, though, Rule had already been functioning as a member of Stirling Presbytery for several months, even to the extent of interviewing those under scandal. On his induction, he was immediately also elected as moderator, continuing to complete a second six-month term. However, when he conformed to the practice of the outgoing moderator by offering a leet of two for the election of his successor, the presbytery selected neither John Watson in Denny nor Alexander Douglas in Logie, preferring instead George Turnbull in Alloa. Clearly Rule was not going to be allowed to have things his own way. He was again elected moderator in 1698 and 1701, but failed to be elected in 1700. Rule's attendance throughout the period was sporadic; he had long spells of absence and was, like the other ministers, periodically challenged for his absences, although usually excused for reasons of health.

His attendance at presbytery meetings and visitations outwith Stirling was particularly occasional, but then he was over seventy years old when he returned. His contribution was therefore restricted largely to writing letters and occasionally interviewing people under scandal or candidates for the ministry. As brother of Gilbert Rule, principal of Edinburgh University and one of the more polemical Presbyterian writers, he might have been expected to have a wider influence than just in Stirling, but this was not the case. His contact with his brother seems to have been slim, limited to being instructed to write to him on one occasion, the instruction later being withdrawn. He attended the General Assembly on occasion and served on the Commission for the North, but left no record of any contribution to proceedings. The one minor sign of distinction that he gained was in being nominated as one of the six clergy to revise the *Scriptural Songs* of Patrick Simpson 'that so they might be the fitter for private and publick use'.[33]

Rule seems to have been a fairly undistinguished parish minister. The words of George Turnbull are at best a muted compliment after he preached at the thanksgiving for the Sacrament in Alloa in 1699: 'On moonday did Mr Rule, aged eighty, preach near thrie hours, neither memory or strength failing.'[34] Locally too, he had his detractors: a day or two after his death one Thomas Blackburn was brought before the burgh court in Stirling for 'venting most base and calumnious expressions in a furious and raging manner Saying that old Rogue Mr Robert Rule late minister of this burgh lately deceast his soul was frying in hell for the ill-done deeds he had done in this place'.[35] As epitaphs go, it was less than fulsome.

Coming from a Protester background, Rule had not gone into exile in the Low Countries during the Restoration period. Rather he went to Derry in the north of Ireland, where he sat out the reigns of Charles and James in an ever more difficult set of conditions until he fled, as one Irish source has it, back to Scotland after the Toleration. The very fact that despite the consistent targeting of his brother in *The Scotch Presbyterian Eloquence Display'd*, Robert Rule escaped without any mention at all seems to suggest that the pseudonymous Jakob Curate did not think him worth attacking.

William Spence, on the other hand, had the full Covenanter credentials, including suffering a well-documented period of torture described by John Erskine of Carnock in his diary.[36] Like Rule, he attended presbytery meetings only sporadically and he too was challenged over his record. There is little evidence of his activity at presbytery or parish level, but long after his departure from the joint presbytery, his actions regarding a probationer minister from Dollar brought him criticism from the Synod of Perth and Stirling, of which he was a member albeit generally an absentee one. The case itself will be dealt with in Chapter 4, but the committee detailed to examine the case had this to say of Spence, whom they did not name but referred to as 'the reverend Minister of Fossoway': 'If in this we shall be found to condemn the deed of a reverend brother whom we do honour and respect we cannot help it since we are obliged to give a greater regard to the credit of the Gospel.'[37] Spence was by this time an old man, excused attendance at the synod on grounds of age, and it looks as though his influence on his younger colleagues had passed.

Nationally, the influence of the returning antediluvians was by and large limited. The old order passed quickly. Many died within two or three years of their return. Of those who survived, probably the most influential were those who, like Forrester of Alva and Killearn, Gilbert Rule and James Wodrow, taught the next generation at Scotland's universities. For the rest, they served their parishes to the best of their ability and passed on.

Notes

1. Mullan (ed.), *Protestant Piety in Early-Modern Scotland*, p. 182.
2. Wodrow, *The History of the Sufferings of the Church of Scotland*, vol. 2, pp. 606ff.; Raffe, *Scotland in Revolution*, pp. 32–3.
3. NRS CH2/242/7 30/11/1687; NRS CH2/242/6 4/7/1688.
4. NRS CH2/464/1 30/8/1687. Published as 'Register of the Provincial Synod of Glasgow and Air'.
5. Primrose, *Strathbrock*, p. 56.
6. NRS CH2/449/3 7/4/1691.
7. In 1704 Couper was involved in the Fife witchcraft trials.
8. Fergusson, *Logie*, vol. 1, pp. 153–68.
9. Turnbull, 'The Diary of George Turnbull', p. 410.
10. NRS CS140/244.
11. Curate, *The Scotch Presbyterian Eloquence Display'd*, p. 107. The *Fasti* ascribes the authorship of this, at least in part, to John Monro in Stirling. There seems little if any evidence to back this up.
12. Records of the Parliaments of Scotland to 1707 (hereafter RPS), Act Restoring the Presbyterian Ministers Who Were Thrust from Their Churches since 1 January 1661 (1690), www.rps.ac.uk/mss/1690/4/13 (last accessed 9/2/2021).
13. See for example Donaldson, *The Faith of the Scots*, p. 104.
14. Drummond and Bulloch, *The Scottish Church, 1688–1843*, p. 9.
15. 'Register of the Provincial Synod of Glasgow and Air', p. 274.

16. RPS, Act Ratifieing the Confession of Faith and Settleing Presbeterian Church Government (1690), www.rps.ac.uk/mss/1690/4/43 (last accessed 9/2/2021).
17. Wodrow, *History of the Sufferings of the Church of Scotland*, vol. 1, Appendix 37, pp. 72–8.
18. Donaldson, *The Faith of the Scots*, p. 104.
19. Gardner, *The Scottish Exile Community in the Netherlands, 1660–1690*, p. 52.
20. Act anent a Solemn National Fast and Humiliation, with the Causes Thereof (1690); see Church of Scotland, *Acts of the General Assembly of the Church of Scotland*, p. 229.
21. Church of Scotland, *Acts of the General Assembly of the Church of Scotland*, p. 224.
22. RPS, Act Rescinding and Annulling the Pretendit Parliaments in the Yeers 1640, 1641 etc. (1661), www.rps.ac.uk/mss/1661/1/158 (last accessed 9/2/2021).
23. Act anent Sentences Past against Ministers from the Year 1650 (1690); see Church of Scotland, *Acts of the General Assembly of the Church of Scotland*, p. 230.
24. Register of attendance, one of a handful of Latin words and phrases still in use in Scottish church courts.
25. 'Register of the Provincial Synod of Glasgow and Air', p. 224.
26. *Fasti Ecclesiae Scoticanae*, vol. 4.
27. 'Register of the Provincial Synod of Glasgow and Air', p. 200.
28. NRS RH15/106/709/4 John Forrest to Mr Andrew Russell.
29. Curate, *The Scotch Presbyterian Eloquence Display'd*, pp. 32–3.
30. 'Episcopacy in Stirling', p. 220 mistakenly gives 2 Cor. 13:22.
31. 'Episcopacy in Stirling', pp. 219–20.
32. Raffe, 'Presbyterians and Episcopalians', pp. 587–8; NLS MS5770, sermon notebook 1688.
33. 'Register of the Provincial Synod of Glasgow and Air', p. 250.
34. Turnbull, 'The Diary of George Turnbull', p. 385.
35. SCA B66/25/779/1. I am grateful to John Harrison for drawing my attention to this.
36. Erskine, *Journal of the Hon. John Erskine of Carnock, 1683–1687*, pp. 78–9.
37. NRS CH2/449/5 14/10/1708.

CHAPTER THREE

Ensuring the Continuity of Ministry

The New Ministers

> These young converts were exhorted with purpose of heart to cleave unto the Lord, come Prosperity or Adversity, they were to stand by Christ and the Profession of his ways.[1]

Visiting in 1702, Thomas Morer estimated the number of parishes in Scotland at about 900, with collegiate charges raising the number of ministers required still further. In the wake of the re-establishment, the numbers of available antediluvians and meeting-house preachers was clearly limited. Even allowing that some episcopally ordained ministers would conform to the new regime and that a rather greater number would sit tight in the parishes and ignore it altogether, there was a significant shortfall of trained orthodox, Presbyterian-minded ministers available.

Within Stirling and Dunblane presbyteries, there were no conforming 'curates', and only four long-term recalcitrant ones out of a total number of twenty-four possible charges. By 1693, when the joint presbytery record begins, there were eight ministers in parishes, two others having demitted without so far being replaced. Although there were attempts to recruit existing ministers from elsewhere, the shortfall had to be made up by training and ordaining new men. As the 1690s progressed, too, a number of parishes lost their episcopal incumbents to be replaced by Presbyterians, several of whom were newly minted from the, now Presbyterian, universities.

As already described, some of those arriving up until 1692 were newly ordained, trained in the Low Countries or in England. Others had been trained less formally by the Presbyterian community in Scotland. Some had been able to acquire the non-theological elements of their training at the episcopally controlled universities of Scotland. One, Thomas Buchanan, had had to apologise for his compliance with the Episcopalian regime before he could be ordained. Buchanan, ordained minister of Tulliallan in 1691, had committed the sin of subscribing to the Test Act. In March of 1690 he presented a paper to the Presbytery of Dumbarton asking that he might be received. Two months later the presbytery appointed him to 'declare his sorrow both in word and wryt before them for his taking the Test that the scandal thereof may be removed'. That written apology, together with a testificat from the ministers of Edinburgh, proved sufficient and he was able to embark on his trials for licence, the process to establish his fitness to be a minister of the Church of Scotland.[2]

Education for the ministry and call to the ministry are two different things. Whytock's study, *An Educated Clergy*, takes a broad and chronological view of the education of ministers over three centuries, but does not consider the question of 'call'. Some of the documents in Mullan's *Protestant Piety in Early Modern Scotland* do mention motivation, but it is given much less prominence than the authors' conversion experiences. Gabriel Semple, for example, ordained in 1657, simply described his call as follows: 'Since I was a child, I had a great respect for that tribe [that is, ministers], and could never incline to another employment myself.'[3] Alexander Hamilton, successively minister at Ecclesmachen, Airth and Stirling, had a more unusual route: drawn to the ministry from an early age, he was forced to go to London by his father to pursue a career in business. However, hearing of a challenge to any comers by a famous pugilist, he took him on and won in somewhat under thirty-five rounds and the prize money, supplemented by gifts from the onlookers, financed his return to Scotland and his training for the ministry.[4]

The actual factors which drew men to train for the ministry are not always easy to ascertain. Those who have left the most articulate accounts are also those who were atypical, those whose service as ministers led to their prominence, usually on the evangelical wing of the church, men like Thomas Boston[5] or Thomas Halyburton.[6] John Willison, born near Stirling and later a noted evangelical preacher, left no autobiography, but his biographer described how 'his parents devoted him, from a very early period of his life, to the service of the church, and in this determination young Willison cordially acquiesced'.[7] Woodruff has shown, however, how important the concept of 'call' was at the time.[8]

What is lacking is detail of what might be termed the 'journeyman ministers', those who quietly served their parishes to the best of their abilities without ever being noticed elsewhere. One such was George Turnbull, minister of Alloa, whose published diaries present a humdrum picture of his life without ever describing his motivation to enter the ministry.[9] There also survive some accounts from men who did not become ministers, such as John Erskine of Carnock, which discuss briefly reasons for not pursuing that route.

The whole education system, as run by the church, was intended towards a Christian education, at the very least aimed at allowing people to read the Bible themselves. Much rural education virtually stopped there, but sometimes a schoolmaster or minister would take a promising student and push him further. Presbyteries were also quickly attuned to identifying and supporting financially those who showed potential to go further, not necessarily with a view to the ministry. Those in, or close to, the bigger burghs were in a more privileged position in that university entrance was more easily achieved by someone who had succeeded at a burgh school. This also tended to favour students of a particular class. Although there were always students from less prosperous backgrounds, a significant number were the sons of ministers, shopkeepers and minor lairds. Scotland's middle class was small, but it dominated the ranks of the church.

John Erskine was atypical, though not unique, in being the younger son of a peer, and as a Covenanter deeply steeped in the theology of his day. His articulation of the call he felt in 1685 is clearer than some. He had intended to become a lawyer, which was a common destination for those of his background, but he also felt some tug towards ministry:

> I sought of God that he would give me to know his mind to . . . my will going much contrary to my inclination in that which I had been following, being inclined when abroad not to make law my only study, but to join it with the study of Divinity, which I was now fully resolved to study if I were at a colledge abroad, or where the Lord should tryst me to be, and wait upon God for further direction as to what I should follow. Thow knows O Lord I have dedicated myself to thee and thy service for ever, be thow therefore pleased to direct and let me know what service thou calls me to, and how upon earth I may most advance thy glory.[10]

With this in mind Erskine attended both divinity and law classes in his exile in Utrecht, adding in anatomy for good measure. His final career choice took none of these routes as the accession of William led him into the army. As an army officer, however, Erskine was still able to serve his church as an elder while his legal and theological training made him a useful contributor to the courts of the church.

George Turnbull also had his theological training in Utrecht. Although he was not a particular friend of Erskine, they moved in the same circles.[11] Turnbull had started along the more conventional path of taking an arts degree at Edinburgh before circumstances forced him into an Irish and then a Dutch exile. In Ireland he lived in the family of his uncle, Robert Tailyour, a minister, and it is perhaps here that he had some inclination towards the ministry. Turnbull's diary is not introspective or particularly spiritual and he makes no reference to the processes by which he settled on the ministry. After two years in Ireland, he spent a further four looking after his father's affairs in Scotland before following him into Dutch exile.

Thereafter, like Erskine, he attended the University of Utrecht, almost immediately starting the study of divinity. No other details of his activities that led him into ministry survive until in mid-1687 he found himself in London where he and another exile, Robert Fleming, were licensed as preachers by a group of Scottish Presbyterians in London. Thereafter Turnbull returned to the Low Countries and began a career of preaching before starting his trials for ordination back in London in early 1688. Ordained without any idea of his sphere of ministry, an irregular procedure later forbidden, Turnbull makes no reference to any form of mentoring or pastoral training or even conversation with other ministers along the way.

After the Revolution such casualness died out. The curriculum was still very heavily book-based, but Robert Wodrow's life of his father James Wodrow outlines how it was to be put into practice, at least to some extent.[12] James Wodrow had been appointed to train Presbyterian ministers after the Toleration of 1687, and in the wake of the purging of Glasgow University in 1692, was appointed professor there with a more formal position. Wodrow stressed the value of the pre-divinity education in 'humanity and philosophy' as a basis for future study and thought but also warned against the confusion caused by studying several systems of divinity without mastering one to use as a basis of the studying the others. Above all else, though, he stressed that knowledge of the Old and New Testaments was absolutely paramount: 'I know not how any Christian scholar can have peace, or how a minister can be conscientious about his work, that is ignorant of these.'[13]

At the same time, part of Wodrow's teaching was aimed specifically at the trials for licence that a student would have to undergo prior to being allowed to preach unsupervised. The normal Tuesday in Glasgow University was spent in rehearsing the kind of exercises that made up the trials: a lecture, a homily, an 'exercise and addition'[14] and either a 'popular sermon' or a 'catechetical sermon'. On Wednesdays, the students were expected to attend whatever courts of the church were available to them. This included presbytery meetings, which were public, but also, by an act of the General Session of Glasgow, it included kirk session meetings, which were not. By this means the students were enabled to learn what they could of the discipline cases which would they would meet as parish ministers.[15] While probationers were certainly present at meetings of Stirling and Dunblane presbyteries (although their presence is rather shadowy and shown mainly in their immediate availability to take on pulpit supply), there is no evidence to suggest that they attended meetings of the kirk sessions or were given any role other than preaching.

Away from their studies, however, the students were advised to visit ministers frequently and also to 'endeavour to have fellowship with some soul-exercised private Christians, where you will learn many things which you will neither find in books nor from learned men'.[16] This advice accords completely with Boston's experience while he was in the Borders and later in Clackmannan.[17] In the former he 'had the advantage off converse with Mr Murray, a learned and holy man, the meeting of which two in a character was not very frequent there, as also of Janet Maclaunie, an old, exercised, godly woman'.[18] On Boston's moving to Clackmannan, Thomas Brown in Ferrytown provided a similar role, as well as being the means by which Boston was to meet his future wife. Otherwise, he 'kept a correspondence with his neighbouring ministers . . . and conversed much with some serious Christians about the place'.[19]

From this it would appear that Wodrow's teaching and Boston's learning was all done without exposure to opposition. This was not necessarily the case; the teaching on a Monday included a paper given by a student on a topic given to him some weeks before. This was then critiqued by his fellow students at considerable length before the professor gave his views. Although presumably a supportive environment, it was one where the student was expected to learn how to stand up for his belief. This might well be put to the test if, as so many did, the aspirant found himself as tutor or chaplain in a household. Boston certainly found it so; on arrival at Kennet in Clackmannan in 1696, he was ostensibly only tutor to the son of his absent employers, but he took it upon himself to act as chaplain, keeping up family worship, catechising the servants, encouraging prayer and trying to reform the 'vicious'. To this activity he ascribed growing confidence in having, in his words, 'the charge of souls', surely a core skill for any minister.[20] Whether Boston was unusual in having at least a little experience of pastoral care prior to ordination is not clear, but one of those opposed to his going to Clackmannan permanently gave as his reason that Boston was young and still a probationer, and that was someone who was known to be in broad theological agreement with him.[21]

Boston's contemporary Thomas Halyburton gave no space in his memoirs for his growth into ministry. For Halyburton prayer and internal preparation were all that was needed and there is little sense of him seeking other guidance from anyone for the means of carrying out his ministry.[22] Surviving accounts from other ministers tell the same story. All in all, education for the ministry can be seen at this time to be almost entirely based around the various forms of preaching and teaching rather than any pastoral concerns. James Wodrow left copious notes on preparing both lectures and sermons; these were published long after his death.

What then of the 'new men' who entered the ministry of the presbyteries of Dunblane and Stirling after the re-establishment of Presbyterianism? The records of the presbyteries of Dunblane and Stirling show around eighty names of students and probationers. Only ten of these were to remain there as parish ministers. Of the remainder, most were called to parishes elsewhere and some disappeared without trace. This chapter will identify issues which they faced and look at individuals' experiences where they are set down in church records, diaries and memoirs. It will also consider the role of former patrons, heritors and the presbytery in influencing congregations in their choice of a new minister.

About sixty probationers appear in the records of the two presbyteries, with an additional twenty or so students who never acted as probationers within the bounds. Some of these were students receiving support for their studies, some possibly with no link to the area. The latter can be ignored but where they can be identified, many do not seem to have become ministers anywhere. They may have become schoolmasters or indeed died before the completion of their studies.

The names of some of those sixty probationers who flit across the pages of the records are mentioned once, or appear for a few weeks and are never seen again. Even the Christian names of some of them were not recorded.

Others became part of the life of the presbyteries but had to take themselves off to find a charge elsewhere, while others remained to be called, ordained and inducted locally.

Fifty-two can be identified as becoming ministers in charges, although in some cases the identification is assumed rather than firm. Ten of these were ordained into Stirling or Dunblane presbyteries, five into each. Not all were preaching within the bounds as potential candidates for charges; in a few cases the probationers providing pulpit supply were simply filling in time before an ordination that was already scheduled.

These ten men were around the presbyteries as probationers for an average of eleven months prior to their ordination, with the period ranging from three to twenty months. Leaving out those who are assumed to have been already committed to another charge, the remaining probationers seem to have taken an average of slightly over three years to be settled. Even allowing for uncertainty in some of the identifications, finding a parish willing to call could be a long process.

This length of time without a charge can, however, be understood when it is realised that while a probationer was within the bounds of a presbytery, he was theoretically bound to it and barred from consideration of a call from elsewhere without the presbytery's permission. Even allowing a year in each presbytery, the period mounts up. One probationer, William Reid, came to Stirling with testimonials from four presbyteries, Wigtown, Stranraer, Glasgow and Biggar, but appears never to have been called to a charge.[23]

There were various routes to becoming accepted as a probationer in a presbytery. One was to go as a tutor or a chaplain to a laird's family after leaving university. This had the multiple purpose of bringing the former student into an area where he could become known, giving him practice in expounding his faith in the context of family worship, and giving an education in manners that would make him acceptable in the society of his time, hence the young Thomas Boston's appointment as tutor to the family of the Laird of Kennet. Others had similar posts in the Erskine family. Such an appointment was not necessarily a passport to the ministry. Thomas Todd, appointed to the household of the Earl of Mar in November 1691, having already been chaplain to the Earl of Lothian, was dismissed within a scant five weeks.[24] He may have been the Thomas Todd who was ordained to Durisdeer in Dumfriesshire in 1700; if so, it had taken him thirteen years from graduating before he was called to a parish.

Other names emerged from personal networks. In some cases, someone in a parish may have had a name to recommend. The young Thomas Halyburton was recommended for Airth while still a student, but nothing came of it. A year or two later, after he was minister of Ceres, there was another attempt to call him, this time to Alloa. Sometimes, the commissioners going to the General Assembly were asked to keep their eyes open for possible recruits to the area. Family and local links also played their part, with Michael Potter, called to be minister of Kippen, being the son of the minister of Dunblane. One unsuccessful probationer, George Mair, was son-in-law of a previous minister in the parish of Airth.

Some came straight from university, but others had been probationers in other presbyteries and came with licences to preach and with testimonials. All were retested for knowledge and orthodoxy by undergoing trials for licence. This was an extended process and well documented. In the case of the exercise and addition, it might be that two probationers shared the task, but each would also have to provide a popular sermon, a homily, a theological thesis in Latin to be defended, a discourse on church history and a test of Greek and Hebrew, all designed to make sure standards did not fall and orthodoxy was defended. Success was not a foregone conclusion, although few were given as candid a response as John Clow, a St Andrews student with testimonials from Stranraer Presbytery who was interviewed in 1695 and told to go away and do more studying.[25] He may be the same John Clow dismissed as a schoolmaster by the Society in Scotland for Propagating Christian Knowledge (SSPCK) after the 1715 rising.[26]

Occasionally the system worked well. Kilmadock became vacant in 1704 when its minister, John Logan, was transported to Alloa. Initial attempts to transport Thomas Buchanan from Tulliallan parish failed. Buchanan's appeal against being transported was rejected by the presbytery, which set the date for his induction in March 1705, but he simply declined to attend. He appealed to the General Assembly and had his appeal sustained. It took only a further three months to find the right man. Although we do not know how he was found, George Campbell, a probationer from the Presbytery of Irvine in Ayrshire, appeared before the presbytery on 13 June 1705, produced his licence and testificat and was promptly appointed to provide pulpit supply in Kilmadock. He started fresh trials for licence in Dunblane Presbytery by preaching to it the following month, completing these fresh trials on 4 September. Meanwhile the people of Kilmadock had called him to be their new minister in August, and he accepted the call, being ordained and inducted on 20 September.[27] The only real fly in the appointment was that the previous minister had left because after ten years he still had no manse, and Campbell was in the same situation, faced with heritors who were Episcopalian at heart and a parish which had a considerable number of Jacobites in it.

If George Campbell had a fairly easy route into his parish, others had a different experience. The first probationer mentioned in the earliest surviving presbytery minute book was George Mair, providing supply in Airth, south-east of Stirling. He was summoned to appear before the presbytery in August 1693 for preaching a sermon inveighing against ministers for taking the Oath of Allegiance, which had become a legal requirement for ministers in June. He did not obey the summons, but when he did attend a month later, he handed in a letter explaining his objection to the oath and met with two ministers to discuss it.[28] His letter, to Alexander Douglas, shows both the depth of his sense of call to Airth and his hurt at rejection by Stirling Presbytery. He was told that he was not expected to stand in the way of a settlement at Airth, but the following month the people of Airth called him to be their minister. Stalemate followed for several months with his case unusually being considered in Mr Crighton's chambers in Falkirk, in a different presbytery. Finally he was admonished and required to attend the presbytery, which he failed to do, and as a result the case was referred to the synod and then to the General Assembly for his divisive doctrine and disorderly practices. By May of 1694 he was still preaching in Airth, asserting that Airth was his charge and he had a call from God to preach there. The Commission of Assembly delayed a decision but told him to behave as a probationer and attend the Presbytery of Stirling, which he declined to do until the Commission had decided his case. He was then further charged in December 1696 with preaching without a licence and continuing to preach in Airth without authority of the presbytery and in defiance of church law. His faults were compounded by the fact that he had persuaded John Hepburn, a suspended minister of non-juring Presbyterian views,[29] formerly in Urr in Kirkcudbrightshire, to baptise his child in Airth the same month. Finally, in 1698, Mair was called, ordained and inducted to the 2nd Charge in Culross in Fife, where his colleague was James Fraser of Brea, a famous but ageing former Covenanter. Airth itself was not settled until 1700. Mair himself would join Dunblane Presbytery as minister of Tulliallan in 1714.

The issues in this case seem to have been twofold. Mair represented a tradition in the national church that it was trying to shake off, the successors of the United Societies. Some had come into the Church of Scotland, including all the surviving ministers, but some were uncomfortable with the national church's willingness to make commitment to the Covenants implicit rather than explicit. Hepburn was prominent in this resistance movement, was suspended, accepted back in and finally deposed again, forming a dissenting neo-Covenanter sect known as the Hebronites. It is perhaps significant that after he settled in Culross, Mair acted as intermediary between the Commission of Assembly and Hepburn as they tried to patch up their differences. However, their friendship did not necessarily survive. Mair also became a friend of Thomas Boston, who refers in his memoirs to being pestered by Hepburn as he tried to hold rival intruding services in Boston's parish of Ettrick some years later.[30]

The other aspect of the Airth saga is the splits which were apparent in the congregation. A large part of the congregation clearly supported Mair. The fact of the call and the appearance of elders to prosecute it are evidence of that, but it was a parish where passions ran high. In the 1680s it had had a part to play in that very strange group the Gibbites, or 'Sweet Singers', whose leader, John Gib, had publicly burned a copy of the Bible on Airth Muir.[31] At the same time, two of the parishioners were being excommunicated on the grounds of relapse in adultery, and other ministers were sent to Airth to investigate another scandal, essentially the bullying of the precentor by two of the elders. Even after Mair's settlement in Culross, it was clear that the parishioners and heritors were split and such calls to ministers as they produced proved unsuccessful. The unhappy parish was further disturbed when the young Laird of Airth was murdered by one of his neighbours in a drunken brawl.[32]

If the case of George Mair showed the presbytery trying to obstruct the calling of a minister of whom it was wary, the influence of heritors was more widespread and usually more destructive. The case of Kilmadock, whose lack of a manse was a crucial hindrance, has been mentioned. But more direct obstruction was also found. Patronage, the right of a particular person or institution to call a minister to the parish, was abolished in 1690. Nonetheless, the old patrons were still recognised as having a major say in calls and were consulted as a matter of course. In several cases this had a substantial effect even if they were not resident in the parish.

Thomas Boston was one of the kenspeckle figures of the early eighteenth-century church and a hero of what became the evangelical wing of the church, his sermons remaining in print for 150 years. As an impoverished young man of twenty, he had left university after only two years but nevertheless, a short time after moving to Kennet, he was invited by George Turnbull to preach before the presbytery, although he had no intention at that time of starting his trials for licence. The following year he was almost persuaded to start his trials by the neighbouring ministers, Turnbull and Thomas Buchanan, with a hint that the elders of Clackmannan were unwilling that he should leave the area. At the same time the Presbytery of Penpont in the Borders was trying to persuade him to take his trials there, closely followed by the Presbytery of Duns. In the event, it was the combined Presbytery of Duns and Chirnside which finally licensed him to preach and he spent a year there before returning to the Presbytery of Stirling. There he was directed by the presbytery to Clackmannan, but never really wanted to settle there. The decision was made for him by the laird's factor, who objected to Boston's refusal to bow to him from the pulpit or go back with the heritors after the service. If Boston did not want to go to Clackmannan, the neighbouring parish of Dollar was another matter. He had been tempted to ask for his testificat and move on but was persuaded to stay. In December 1698 some of the elders told him they were inclined to call him to the charge. However, it soon appeared that eight or ten of the parish wrote to the patron, the Earl of Argyll, objecting to the call, and it also transpired that some of the local ministers, including two in neighbouring parishes to Dollar, were against his settlement there. Finally, it became clear that Argyll had in fact a candidate of his own to press and in due course John Gray was ordained and inducted. Boston then was persuaded to consider Airth as a possibility at the suggestion of George Mair, but this was quickly ruled out. His own verdict on the whole episode was that 'perhaps the trouble they had by Mr George Mair, in Airth, on the strict side, made them the more wary of me, though I never entertained separating principles'. As soon as the induction date was set for Gray in Dollar, Boston took his leave and left the area for the Borders with a heavy heart. He later heard that all but six of the elders and heritors had been of a mind to call him, but that 'the Presbytery had still some dependence on Argyle in the matter' and Argyll had his way.[33]

A later case presented a different set of circumstances leading to rejection, but again with the hand of the former patron firmly on the tiller. Balquhidder was one of Dunblane's 'highland' parishes, and Gaelic-speaking. The episcopal incumbent had remained in possession of the church, applied to join the presbytery, been rejected and then deprived. Efforts to find a Gaelic-speaking probationer were obstructed by the lack of numbers, by the unwillingness of presbyteries to let them go, and by a national imperative which saw Gaelic speakers sent to fulfil a perceived greater need further north. In the case of Balquhidder, this meant that when they were close to finding an acceptable candidate, he could very easily be lost to the north. One such was Alexander Shaw, who was no sooner ready to take on a charge than he was sent to the province of Moray. Another was John Robertson, a native of Argyll, who preached regularly in Balquhidder, despite the obstacles put in his way which meant that sometimes he had to preach in the churchyard. During the course of his service there, the synod first of all sent him to Caputh for three months. On his return he went back to Argyll to 'improve his knowledge of the Irish language'. Returning from there, he was finally sent to the Presbytery of Ross for a year and lost to Balquhidder completely. Further efforts at settlement there were prevented by the Duke of Atholl, who was reluctant to remove the deposed incumbent but promised to concur in the settlement of anyone with Gaelic whom the presbytery approved. That said, though, he showed great displeasure at not being consulted when it looked as though a candidate might be found, insisted on visits to him in Dunkeld by both representatives of the presbytery and the potential minister, and produced red herrings such as a letter purporting to show the candidate was unworthy to be a minister, before taking on himself to tell the presbytery that he would consult the parishioners to decide if the candidate was acceptable or not. Not surprisingly he was apparently not acceptable and Balquhidder remained without a Presbyterian minister until 1710. But if Robertson was reduced to preaching in the kirkyard because William Campbell had occupancy of the church, he fared better than some of the English-speaking ministers sent to intimate presbytery decisions. The previous incumbent would hide in the pulpit early in the morning and when the church was opened up to the congregation, he was already in place and no visitor could get access to the pulpit. Nor would any of the congregation listen to a minister whose language they could understand barely, if at all. As a result, visiting preachers had no hearers when they tried to speak in the kirkyard and came home without having preached. The Duke of Atholl was a Presbyterian elder in Dunkeld at this point, but in a letter of 1706 he gave as his philosophy that he thought it reasonable to keep on episcopal ministers 'who are good men'.[34] For Atholl, though, the imperative of having a minister who could preach to the people of Balquhidder in their own language was paramount.[35]

If these cases of Mair, Boston and the parish of Balquhidder show the influences at work in rejecting probationers, influence in appointing was also to be found. James Mitchell and Michael Potter (the younger) both came into the bounds of the presbytery as students in September 1698. Potter was the son of the minister of Dunblane and therefore local. Mitchell preached in several of the vacant churches for some months but finally was given his testificat and was ordained in Auchterarder in 1700. Potter also asked for an extract of his licence in August 1699 so that he could move on, but in what looks like a contrived series of events, at the same meeting, both he and his father were instructed to provide supply at Kippen. Visits from other ministers followed when it appeared that there was a dispute over who to call within the parish. Permission to allow Potter to provide supply in Auchterarder Presbytery was refused as he was making progress towards a call. Finally in December, the younger Michael Potter was called to Kippen.

From a parish or presbytery's point of view, calling a probationer had one huge advantage. Calling a minister from another charge was a long-drawn-out process if the charge or presbytery was unwilling to release him, and the records are full of disputed calls, some of which took several years to settle. Probationers tended to come much more easily. They could also be got rid of, at least unofficially. The minister was, it is true, inducted *ad vitam aut culpam*, for life or until deposed. But the heritors had two weapons for persuading him to leave. Not paying his stipend was the obvious one, rarely used for legal reasons. More subtle was burdening the charge with a ruinous and uninhabitable manse. A year or two down the line either the minister was so frustrated that he told the presbytery he laboured under 'insufferable grievances' and wished to be made transportable, or the heritors were satisfied and rebuilt the manse. The third option, of the minister rebuilding the manse at his own expense and seeking to recover the costs, as at Logie, was unlikely to be open to probationers. It goes without saying that in some parishes of Dunblane Presbytery, the heritors were Jacobite, and Episcopalian in their sympathies, hence not too eager to make their new Presbyterian minister too comfortable.

The process by which a congregation came to its decision to call a particular probationer is unclear. After 1690 and the abolition of patronage, it was in theory in the hands of heritors, elders and the (male) heads of families. The previous patrons' writ still ran, however, and approval was virtually always sought. So far as the rest of the congregation was concerned, however, some hint as to how the land lay can be gleaned from records of the weekly collection.

Table 3.1 Average Collections when Probationers were Preaching in Alva, 1698–9

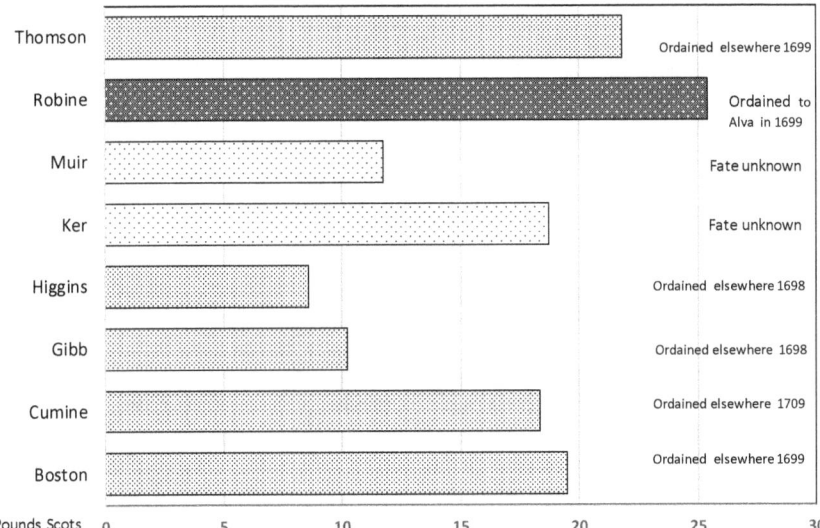

Source: SCA CH2/10/4.

Alva's financial records have been referred to already as evidence of congregational opinion. Table 3.1 shows that during the vacancy caused by the final deposition of William Lindsay the collections gathered at services taken by Harie Robine were greater than those taken when other probationers were preaching.[36] Dollar's records start part way through the vacancy;[37] the parish had already been split over the possible call to Thomas Boston, but the accounts show a solidification of support for John Gray as represented by the monies collected at each service. Throughout 1700 preaching was supplied to the vacant parish by any of four probationers or by a minister from the presbytery. Many Sundays are missing from the record, and some have no preacher specified. When Gray was preaching the collection averaged £1 0s. 8d. When it was a different probationer in the pulpit, it averaged 16s. 4d., if a local minister was sent to preach, 15s., while if no preacher was specified an average of 13s. was collected (see Table 3.2).

John Gray was ordained on 18 September; on the following Sunday the collection was an impressive £1 10s., a clear indication of the support, or least curiosity, of the parishioners of Dollar.

In both cases the collections show that the successful candidate was the one at whose services the collection was highest. These figures cannot be taken as showing a reaction to the preaching as the collection was generally taken on the way in, but as a sign that a greater proportion of the parishioners was present if Gray or Robine were to be preaching and hence a sign of support for their being called. Sadly the Dollar records only begin after Boston ceased from preaching there but his memoirs do tell us that while Clackmannan was a possibility for him, there were those who would not hear him.

Table 3.2 Average Collections when Probationers were Preaching in Dollar, 1700

Probationer	Average Collection (Pounds Scots)	Fate
Young	~18	Fate unknown
Sands	~14	Ordained elsewhere 1701
Ker	~19	Fate unknown
Gray	~22	Ordained to Dollar 1700

Source: SCA CH2/763/7.

The financial side of being a probationer remains shrouded in mystery. There was certainly not a guaranteed stipend, still less a fixed supply fee. Some students received bursaries from presbyteries or elsewhere but probationers did not have that resource. Those supplying pulpits north of the Forth were meant to receive payment from the funds accrued by vacant charges; Thomas Boston mentions a fee of 18 merks (£12 Scots, £1 sterling) paid to him for services in Clackmannan.[38] The Presbytery of Dunblane had an officially appointed collector to go around the heritors collecting the money, but Thomas Hunter was still waiting in 1707 for monies earned in Kilmadock in 1703, having been told by the collector of stipend to approach the heritors himself. South of the Forth, financial rewards seem to have been even more uncertain; Thomas Boston records in his memoirs that he received two dollars (£6 Scots) from Airth, the first income he ever received from them.[39] There is certainly no mention in the Alva accounts of payments or expenses for visiting probationers in the 1690s but in 1715, when Alva was once more vacant, the accounts do show sums expended on the 'entertainment' of visiting preachers, ministers and probationers.[40]

The other uncertainty faced by the probationer was the likelihood of being sent for an extended period, or permanently, to the Highlands. The Commission for the North, charged with establishing Presbyterian polity beyond the Highland line, demanded that southern presbyteries provide ministers for up to three months to preach in the north, and several of the Stirling and Dunblane ones did. It also could demand that any probationer who spoke Gaelic be placed in a Gaelic-speaking parish for a year or permanently, and part of the battle that Dunblane Presbytery had was in convincing the commission that its need for Gaelic-speaking ministers was as great as that of any more northerly parish. The settling of both Balquhidder and Callander parishes, and hence their adoption of Presbyterianism, was hampered by this policy. Thomas Boston left the bounds of Stirling Presbytery because, having lost his opportunity in Dollar, he thought it likely that, even without a knowledge of Gaelic, he would be sent to the Highlands, a prospect that terrified him.[41]

The life of a probationer was hard, financially insecure, uncertain of future, at the beck and call of presbytery and General Assembly alike, still influenced by patrons, and dependent on the goodwill of heritors. A call to a parish, however poor the manse, must have been a substantial relief. For the congregations calling a probationer, the down side of calling a man with no proven record was counter-balanced by the knowledge that the call could be fulfilled quickly without the delays and expenses involved in appeals to the Assembly.

Filling the Pulpits

As time went on those three groups of ministers, the former exiles, the antediluvians and the newly ordained, were supplemented in their presbyteries by another group: those who were transported from other parishes, willingly or otherwise.

Of course, this had always happened. Re-established antediluvians had moved on with remarkable alacrity and meeting-house ministers sought fresh fields. But as the presbyteries matured in their new role, and as congregations settled into a Presbyterian regime, newly emerging vacancies put another dimension into keeping the pulpits filled.

The concept of 'transportation' was one which was perhaps peculiar to Presbyterianism. Ministers were called to a charge and ordained with the expectation that as God had called them, they were there until He released them.[42] Ministers could not normally unilaterally resign their charge for another, nor could congregations dispense with their minister's services. Movement to another parish was therefore only to be done by order, or at least permission, of the presbytery and was subject to possible appeal to the higher courts. Walter Steuart of Pardovan defined 'transportation' thus in his *Collections*, a compendium of church law and practice published in 1709:

> Transportation or translation is an authoritative loosing of a minister's relation to one charge, and a making up of that same relation betwixt him and another, done for the greater good of the church. This act hath no resemblance to the dissolving of the relation itself betwixt a minister and the church, as in the censure of deposition; but it only resembles a master's taking one from labouring in such a part of his vineyard, to continue the same work in another part thereof.[43]

However, there have always been good reasons for ministers to move to different parishes, from the days of John Knox. The reintroduction of

Presbyterianism in the new meeting-houses of 1687 brought with it a document which specifically mentioned the needs of Edinburgh being paramount over other parishes in calling for the transportation of ministers 'and in the meantime while ministers can be got to them [Edinburgh meeting-houses] in an orderlie way by transporting or otherwayes the respective ministers of the bounds usefully provide them with the most able of those'.[44]

Various other reasons for transportation existed: in the early years of the new regime, ministers were effectively driven out by the heritors making life untenable by virtue of an uninhabitable manse, or none at all. The case of Patrick Couper, minister of the meeting-house in St Ninians, has already been quoted as being unacceptable to the heritors. One of their arguments was that he was not legally called there. Even in the meeting-house, it was said by some of the local heritors, he preached only 'to two of the meanest heritors and some tenants and cotters'.[45] The congregation's and Couper's views were different from the complainants'. In part of the legal process within the church, it was said that 'daily persons were joining the congregation until they came to the number of 1500' and that 'fourteen or fifteen of the existing elders had concurred in Mr Couper going to the meeting-house and made session'.[46]

Nonetheless, the presbytery pragmatically took the view that St Ninians parish was better off without Couper, who was willing to go. St Ninians was seen as a problematic charge not only because of its awkward heritors but also because of its size and large population. Despite that, its new minister, John Logan, was not particularly experienced, having been ordained to the nearby parish of Lecropt a mere ten months previously.

Others of the newly placed ministers also found their position difficult: Robert Campbell in Gargunnock finally simply deserted his charge. Made 'transportable' but told to remain within presbytery bounds, he disappeared only to turn up many months later in a parish in the south-west of the country. The other John Logan, minister of Kilmadock, also found the unwillingness of the heritors to house him adequately a great grievance. In 1696 the joint presbytery warned them that he would be made transportable if they did not address the issue, and indeed he was mooted as a possible incumbent for the 2nd Charge in Stirling.[47]

There is no doubt that there was an order of priority in calling potential ministers. As a royal burgh, Stirling, like Edinburgh, saw itself as entitled to an experienced minister, but Dunblane and Alloa also saw themselves as important charges and therefore also entitled to have an incumbent of proven worth. It was recognised too that certain smaller parishes were also in need of experience: Airth in particular, with its mix of radicals supporting the rejected probationer George Mair and of Episcopalians as well, was clearly potentially difficult and had a long vacancy before being allowed to transport Alexander Hamilton from Ecclesmachen in 1699. In this case, the choice was made from a leet of three names, all of them ordained.

Even so, Hamilton too found himself targeted by Stirling in 1703[48] and was finally transported there at a later vacancy in 1726.

Parishes which had ministers, however, were inclined to keep them, or at least fight hard so to do. Stirling had found this in 1694–6 when attempts to fill the 2nd Charge met with resistance, resulting in expense and long delays. In May of 1694, a draft call was prepared for Thomas Ramsay, minister of Calder, but a month later, the presbytery decided not to prosecute the call because of a legal process between the elders and Stirling Burgh Council.[49] Two leets of three names were then offered to the council for consideration. The first in August comprised three ordained men from Dalmeny, Cambuslang and Cleish. The second, in October, comprised two local men, Robert Campbell, mentioned above as being anxious to leave Gargunnock, and John Logan, recently ordained to Kilmadock, along with Alexander Orr, minister of Beith in Ayrshire. This last being the preferred candidate, he was called by the burgh council and the kirk session to be second minister, the call being sustained by the presbytery.[50] Thereafter a flurry of activity involved representatives from the kirk session and the presbytery going to Ayrshire in January 1695 to attend the Presbytery of Irvine, which referred the matter to the synod. Robert Rule then attended the Synod of Glasgow and Ayr in the March. Orr never did come to Stirling, but the session records for November 1696 show that that abortive journey to Irvine had cost the congregation of Stirling £100.[51]

The attempts continued. A call to John Logan, minister of Kilmadock, from the same leet was not sustained because the needs of Kilmadock were felt to be greater,[52] while another favoured candidate, John Adie, in fact died before the process was complete. Finally, in September 1696, John Forrester in Edinburgh was invited to visit Stirling, preached and was found acceptable. On the 28th the magistrates and council,

> being resolved that ane call be given to Mr John Forrester, minister of the Gospell, who preached here yesterday, doe recommend to the dean of gild to conveene the gildrie, the deacon conveener to conveen the trades, and the baillies to conveen the maltmen, mechanicks, and omnigatherum, ... in order to the giving of their severall assents to the said call, and report to the councill against ten aclock in the foirnoon the said day.[53]

In November he was admitted, the burgh council paying £200 to transport 'his books and other necessaris'. Forrester, who had been ministering in Ware in Hertfordshire, was apparently back in Scotland, and not being in a Scottish charge, his call was a much simpler process.

By 1699, the first tranche of movement had finished. All the parishes which were likely to be planted by the Presbyterians in the two presbyteries had been planted, and while efforts continued to gain the remaining four, realistically that was not going to be achieved soon. A second generation of vacancies began to arise, however. Alloa became vacant in 1699 with the transportation of George Turnbull to Tyninghame in East Lothian, followed by the deaths of John Forrester, minister of the 2nd Charge in Stirling, in June 1702, and his colleague Robert Rule in September 1703. In their wake came a vacancy in Kilmadock and a potential one in Tulliallan.

With the immediate pressure of the early Williamite years past, other reasons for transportation began to appear. It might be the minister who wished to make a fresh start elsewhere. While some elderly ministers stayed put in onerous charges, like Robert Rule in Stirling, George Turnbull, only forty-two years old but plagued with gout among other ailments and believing that Alloa was too big to be a single charge, applied to be made transportable. The presbytery 'out of pity and compassion . . . granted it upon the matter, though not in express terms'.[54] It then told the elders and heritors of his wish on 30 June, and a month later, despite the parish's appearance at the meeting, which was held in Alloa, 'the pbitry made me transportable upon the first call'.[55] This was somewhat disingenuous on Turnbull's part, as he had actually already been told that a call from Tyninghame was in preparation. He was meant to meet with a committee of presbytery before he committed himself, however, and that did not happen. The presbytery therefore took the view that he had left without permission and took his case to the synod after he left. Due to mistakes in paperwork the synod did not pursue it.[56] Tyninghame had about a tenth of the population of Alloa, so clearly it fitted Turnbull's wish for a less arduous field of activity. Turnbull did, however, have some second thoughts. In his diary entry for the day of his induction his 'mind was in great perplexity, my spirit in bonds, rackt to know what was sin or diuty; the desolation of poor Alloway paroch was grievous to me'.[57] Unusually, after his admission to Tyninghame, he preached there the following Sunday and then left for a month during which he returned to Alloa to preach his farewell sermon and spent the rest of the time with relatives in Edinburgh and elsewhere before moving with his family on 1 November.

In the ensuing vacancy, the congregation of Alloa looked to the possibility of calling John Logan from Kilmadock. He was known to be dissatisfied there and he had already been mooted as a possible minister of the 2nd Charge in Stirling and of South Leith. Despite this, he declared his earnest desire to remain at Kilmadock. The Presbytery of Dunblane, under which Kilmadock fell, voted unanimously for him to remain. This vote, however, was challenged robustly by Stirling Presbytery in its appeal to the synod. 'The sentence contains a manifest falsehood,' it wrote, challenging the written record of proceedings.[58] It continued:

> The presbyterie [of Dunblane] was most arbitrary in their proceedings in so far as they delayed to give their sentence when the process was fully before them and fresh in their memorie att their former meeting when there was all Calmness in the proceeding of both parties and

no appearance of force, violence or threatenings till this day where industriuouslie and designedly there was a rabble of a great multitude of men and women who not only obstructed the free ish and entrie [i.e. access] of the pursuers before the said presbyterie but also threatened the said pursuers that if their minister should be transported the pursuers should not go home in safety and thereby the pursuers have ground to suspect that the Presbyterie of Dunblane was overawed in their sentence.[59]

It is perhaps worth noting that the minister sent by Stirling Presbytery to present the call at Dunblane was the other John Logan, minister of St Ninians, who had, prior to his ordination to Lecropt in 1694, been schoolmaster and session clerk in Kilmadock[60] and so was well known to the 'rabble'.

The appeal was heard by the synod and went all the way to the Commission of Assembly, where Logan presented himself as manifestly unsuited to take on the parish of Alloa. 'A third reason', he wrote after commenting that he had been 'wonderfully supported by the Lord' in his work in Kilmadock, 'may be draun from my weakness and inability of body' which allowed him to function in Kilmadock but not in a parish 'the inhabitants whereof are very numerous and the Kirk larger and capacious'.[61] A second call to Alloa was presented to Logan a year later, backed up by a letter from the Earl of Mar.[62] This time Dunblane did not oppose the transportation, the heritors did not attend the meeting, sending no written objections, and Logan himself no longer protested about leaving Kilmadock. He moved to Alloa in May 1704, after a vacancy there of some four and a half years. The phrasing of the record suggests strongly that it was the intervention of Mar, who dominated the town, which made the difference.[63]

The ensuing vacancy in Kilmadock did not proceed smoothly. Having lost their minister to replace George Turnbull in Alloa, the parish fixed on his brother-in-law, Thomas Buchanan, in Tulliallan as the preferred candidate. As this move only involved the Presbytery of Dunblane, the process was potentially simpler than when a neighbouring presbytery was involved. The process took on a farcical tinge however, when the presbytery officer was sent to summon Tulliallan parish to attend:

The Moderator [Robert Gourlaw] reported that conform to the presbytery's appointment upon Friday last the 15 of September current he [the presbytery officer] was going to Tulliallan to deliver the call from the parish of Kilmadock to Mr Thomas Buchanan minister at Tulliallan with the reasons of transportation, he was intercepted by a great rabble before he got near Mr Thomas Buchanan's house, who laid violent hands upon him and ryped his pockets and robbed him of his commission and searched him further for the call which with great difficulty he got preserved and by no means would they suffer him to go near Mr Thomas Buchanan's house but forced him to return home. And therefore he had called the presbytery to consider what was proper to be done in the circumstances, which the presbytery considering they approved the moderator's calling the presbytery *pro re nata*.[64]

After which John Guild, officer to the presbytery reported that upon the said day he was going along with the moderator to cite Mr Thomas Buchanan to compeer before the next presbytery to answer to the call from Kilmadock to him and reasons of transportation and he had a copie of the saids reasons upon to him to affix on the kirk door of Tulliallan upon the sabbath thereafter when he was to cite the parish and a great number of people fell upon him and searched him to the skin and took the coppie of the said reasons from him and after they had read them they interrogated him whither he was going and what his business at Tulliallan, and when before a great number of people he told there was a call from the parish of Kilmadock to Mr Thomas Buchanan, their minister at Tulliallan presented before the presbytery and sustained which the presbytery had ordered to be transmitted to Mr Buchanan and that he was sent to cite Mr Thomas Buchanan and the parish of Tulliallan to answer to the said call and reasons for transportation they had taken violently from him at Dunblane the 2nd day of October anixt. They stopped him and would not suffer him to proceed but conveyed him by force out of the bounds of the parish of Tulliallan.[65]

The presbytery decided that because the paperwork was in the hands of the parish of Tulliallan, the parish had been lawfully cited. It therefore proceeded to sustain the call, setting a date for Buchanan's induction. The presbytery duly attended and constituted at Kilmadock, complete with designated preacher, but Buchanan simply never turned up and the presbytery went home without attending to any business. Buchanan then lodged an appeal against the transportation which went to the Commission of Assembly, and so his non-attendance was not seen as a disciplinary offence.

Buchanan's grounds for non-transportation were various and shed some light on relationships in the presbytery. Firstly the size of the parish, both geographically and demographically, made it one fit for a young man, and Buchanan was well known to be a 'valetudinarian' and would never be able to cover the visiting and catechising. Secondly the proximity of other settled parishes made Kilmadock less of a priority. Thirdly he was unwelcome to the heritors as he had been involved in previous cases before the Privy Council and in fact the call was signed by only three heritors. As Buchanan said, 'Whoever is Minister of Kilmadock may lay accompt in all probability to meet with such difficulties and discouragements as would wholie lay me bye, whose natural disposition is not ordered out for struggling.'[66] A further grievance was that Buchanan had been a day early for the presbytery meeting and the previous day had asked the moderator what was happening about Kilmadock. Being essentially told to 'wait and see', he was then presented with the call at the meeting the following day and so started off feeling aggrieved.

Buchanan's congregation also petitioned the synod against his removal from them, pointing out the difficulties they had in appearing personally:

> That most of us being coalhewars and salters to our occupation cannot attend the reverend Synod for discussing our appeal made from the sentence forsaid without manifest injuring our master in leaving his work, do therefore most earnestly obtest and beseech the rev synod for the Lord's sake (in whose name we act) to reverse the sentence of the presbytery forsaid and continue our minister with us as you tender the salvation of our immortal souls and the preventing of much sin and depravity.[67]

The appeal was sustained and Buchanan remained at Tulliallan for a few more years while a probationer was successfully called to Kilmadock, once more to do battle to be furnished with a habitable manse.

There is no doubt that some parishes saw an attempt to call their minister as a move to be resisted at all costs. While perhaps few went to the physical extremes of Kilmadock in threatening those who came to present the call, or those in Tulliallan who ambushed the presbytery officer, the relationship between minister and parish was seen as close and God-given. It was perhaps exaggerated in the response of the heritors of Kilmacolm in Renfrewshire to Stirling's call to James Brisbane in 1703:

> We cannot but say that it has been a matter of surprise to some very thinking persons who have been witnesses to the ordination of a minister and have heard the nature of that ... near relation held forth with all solemnity and seriousness upon the part both of ministers and people, to find notwithstanding that relation dissolved and broken upon very small (not to say trivial) accounts.[68]

Later in the same document, the relationship is described in even stronger terms: 'The people who have an affection for their minister, doe justlie look upon him as a piece of their propertie, and to be deprived of him as no less than robbery and oppression.'[69] The heritors went on to suggest that the early church 'when it was in its greatest purity' was entirely a stranger to the concept of transportation, 'except one from Antioch to Jerusalem'.

Kilmacolm's 'Answers for the heritors and whole inhabitants' is an outstanding example of the special pleading that such cases incurred, but few matched them for invective:

> It seems most unaccountable that when there is such a fair access of planting vacancies in the ordinary way with young men in abundance,

> ... that people should be so much in love with that invidious way, by transportations, and when there is bread enough in our Father's house and to spare, some should be like pettish children, whom no food can please, but what they can see on their neighbours plates.[70]

The authors then go on to answer each point directly with more or less conviction, decrying Stirling's eminence as a royal burgh and sometime seat of the Court and quoting their own eminence as the site of the first Protestant Communion in Scotland. They also raise doubts as to the validity of the call by pointing out that men had signed it several times in different capacities, as elders, burgh councillors and heads of families.[71]

Like all such reasons for appeal, and there are many both prosecuting and opposing transportation, the core motive is the desire to avoid the 'desolation' of a congregation and parish. This is a word which was used over and over again, with the result that its force was substantially weakened, but it does signify the fear that every congregation had of a long and divisive vacancy.

Kilmacolm's reasons do raise another question, though. They had a jibe at Stirling's recent failure to call Alexander Hamilton from Airth, who was obviously well known in the burgh but whose role in Airth was seen to be important enough not to remove him. They wondered how the fitness of Brisbane to be minister in Stirling could be known to the people there. 'They have given a call, and such a call, to a person whom they have never heard or saw and their zeal had been commendable had it been according to knowledge.'

When John Forrester had come to Stirling in 1696, the people had had the opportunity to hear him, although what mechanism drew him from Ware is not known. Brisbane's connection to Stirling can at least be surmised. Ordained in Kilmacolm in 1693, he was one of two ministers involved closely in the Bargarran witch trials of 1697, which led to the deaths of seven people. The contemporary account of the case, 'True Narrative of the Sufferings and Relief of a Young Girle; Strangely Molested, by Evil Spirits and Their Instruments, in the West', which was published in Edinburgh, may have been written by him.[72] Nor was that the only case in which he was involved. A further witch hunt led to the arrest of thirty people, although the case was abandoned by the judge. In the 1697 case, Brisbane was appointed to investigate on behalf of Paisley Presbytery, but equally involved, appointed by the courts, was Matthew Brisbane, the official physician to the city of Glasgow. The two were certainly kin, possibly uncle and nephew, but Matthew Brisbane was also the grandson of John Napier of Merchiston, the mathematician.[73] Another of Napier's grandsons was Francis Napier of Craiganet, provost of Stirling in 1700–1702 and again in 1703–5. As Stirling Council had considerable influence in the choice of minister, it is hard to imagine that its members were not aware of James Brisbane and his history.

This question of how ministers were 'targeted' for transportation is one that would benefit from a wider study. One possibility was calling a minister from a neighbouring parish. The abortive call of Alexander Hamilton from Airth was one of several examples within the presbyteries of Stirling and Dunblane. Others include the two John Logans' moves to Alloa and St Ninians and the unsuccessful attempts on John Logan in Kilmadock to Stirling and Thomas Buchanan to Kilmadock.

When a minister was moving further, it must largely have been a matter of contacts and reputation. George Turnbull was certainly looking for a move to a smaller parish, but his move to Tyninghame in East Lothian was facilitated by John Forrest, minister of Prestonkirk and former minister of Tulliallan, where he had been succeeded by Turnbull's brother-in-law. On top of this, Turnbull's other ministerial brother-in-law, Adam Glass, was incumbent of Aberlady in the neighbouring presbytery of Haddington.[74] Turnbull's diary at around the time of his move shows the extent to which he had contact with other gentlemen of the area as well as preaching to the people of Tyninghame and showing himself to be acceptable.[75]

The interconnectedness of middle- and upper-class society, not to mention clerical society, in Lowland Scotland should not be underestimated, but through all the calls to ministers comes a clear message that, although patronage had been abolished, at least temporarily, in the 1690s, the rights and influence of the heritors were very much to the fore in any call to a parish. Yet also the flexing of congregational muscle, which was behind the rabbling of some of the Episcopalian clergy in 1689–90, was likely to be experienced when Presbyterian congregations were subjected to decisions of which they did not approve.

Presbyteries' decisions, sustained or overturned by synod or Commission of Assembly, were usually based on what each judicatory recognised as 'the greater good of the church', a phrase which appears regularly to justify putting ministers into burgh churches, parishes at risk from Episcopalian heritors, parishes where there was a significant amount of Gaelic spoken and various other sets of circumstances. To the average parishioner 'the greater good of the church' applied first of all at home, and 'what I have I hold' was a much more cogent mantra.

Notes

1. Logan, *A Sermon Preached before His Grace James Duke of Queensberry*, p. 9.
2. NRS CH2/546/4 25/2/1690, 17/6/1690, 15/8/1690.
3. Mullan (ed.), *Protestant Piety in Early-Modern Scotland*, p. 142.
4. Undated transcription (c.1863) of an article in the *Stirling Observer* in a manuscript notebook compiled by James Shirra, 'Nips and Rips No. 1', in Stirling Central Library.
5. Thomas Boston, minister of Simprin and later of Ettrick, had spent some time in Clackmannanshire as a tutor and a probationer without being called to any church there. He later was identified as an evangelical by his espousal of *The*

Marrow of Modern Divinity. This was a mid-17th-century English Puritan work which was rediscovered by Boston and made a great impression on him. It was reprinted in Scotland and led to the 'Marrow Controversy', where a dozen or so ministers on the evangelical wing of the church were roundly condemned for their support of it, as it was claimed to promote antinomian views. Several of the Marrowmen, as they became known, became the nucleus of the Secession in the 1730s, although the actual cause was patronage, not theology. Boston's sermons are among the most influential of the eighteenth century and his memoirs a major source of information.

6. Minister of Ceres and later professor of divinity at St Andrews, the author of a highly influential autobiography which described his spiritual life.
7. Chambers (ed.), *A Biographical Dictionary of Eminent Scotsmen*, vol. 2, p. 467.
8. Woodruff, 'The Pastoral Ministry in the Church of Scotland in the 18th Century'.
9. Turnbull, 'The Diary of George Turnbull'.
10. Erskine, *Journal of the Hon. John Erskine of Carnock, 1683–1687*, pp. 149–50.
11. Turnbull, 'The Diary of George Turnbull', p. 319.
12. Robert Wodrow, minister of Eastwood, was the author of several works of history which give the Presbyterian view of seventeenth-century Scottish church history. He also left voluminous collections of sermons and other material which are a major resource for the history of the time.
13. Wodrow, *Life of James Wodrow A.M.*, pp. 134–7.
14. The 'exercise' was an exposition of scripture giving context and interpretation, while the 'addition' was an explanation of how the passage could be applied to contemporary daily life.
15. Wodrow, *Life of James Wodrow A.M.*, pp. 123–4.
16. Ibid., p. 138.
17. Boston was a student at Edinburgh University and therefore not a student of James Wodrow. The details of teaching there are less clear but probably not dissimilar to Glasgow.
18. Boston, *Memoirs*, p. 23.
19. Ibid., pp. 29, 43.
20. Ibid., pp. 25, 29.
21. Ibid., p. 45.
22. Halyburton, *An Abstract of the Life and Death of the Reverend Learned and Pious Mr Tho. Halyburton*, pp. 37–78.
23. SCA CH2/722/8 29/8/1694.
24. Turnbull, 'The Diary of George Turnbull', p. 348.
25. SCA CH2/722/8 29/4/1695.
26. Atkinson, 'The Society in Scotland for Propagating Christian Knowledge', p. 173.
27. SCA CH2/723/5 15/5/1705 etc.
28. NLS Wod. Qu.LXXIII fo. 50–51, Mair to Douglas 2/2/1694.
29. Non-juring Presbyterians declined to take the Oath of Abjuration on the grounds that William and Mary had not sworn to uphold the covenants. They were therefore barred from the established church.
30. Boston, *Memoirs*, p. 24.
31. Somerset, 'Walter Ker and the "Sweet Singers"'.

32. Turnbull, 'The Diary of George Turnbull', pp. 360, 381; SCA CH2/722/8 multiple dates 1693–4.
33. Boston, *Memoirs*, pp. 56–69.
34. Leneman, *Living in Atholl*, p. 89.
35. SCA CH2/723/5 23/10/1703.
36. SCA CH2/10/4.
37. SCA CH2/763/7.
38. Boston, *Memoirs*, p. 52.
39. Ibid., p. 52.
40. SCA CH2/10/4.
41. Boston, *Memoirs*, p. 47.
42. John Warden, minister of Gargunnock, remained in post from his ordination in 1698 until his death in 1751, but was outdone by Archibald Lundie, who was minister of Saltoun parish from 1696 until 1759.
43. Steuart of Pardovan, *Collections and Observations Methodiz'd*, p. 14.
44. NRS CH1/2/1/1–2, Overtures for making the liberty practicable, July 1687.
45. RPCS, vol. 16, pp. 617–19.
46. NRS CH1/2/1/46.
47. SCA CH2/722/8 26/9/1694, 11/11/1696.
48. SCA CH2/722/9 20/1/1703.
49. SCA CH2/722/8 23/5/1694, 20/6/1694.
50. SCA CH2/722/8 29/10/1694, 3/12/1694.
51. SCA CH2/1026/5 28/10/1696.
52. SCA CH2/722/8 26/8/1696.
53. Stirling Burgh Council, *Extracts of the Records of the Royal Burgh of Stirling A.D. 1667–1752*, pp. 82–3.
54. Turnbull, 'The Diary of George Turnbull', p. 382.
55. Ibid., p. 385.
56. SCA CH2/722/8 28/2/1700.
57. Turnbull, 'The Diary of George Turnbull', p. 388.
58. SCA CH2/723/5 13/1/1703.
59. Ibid.
60. SCA CH2/212/2 23/1/1694 (in 19th-century transcription) Kilmadock KS.
61. NRS CH1/2/4/1/10.
62. SCA CH2/723/5 4/1/1704.
63. Ibid.
64. A meeting called '*pro re nata*' was a special meeting to discuss one specific newly arising issue. The moderator called it but his calling of it had to be homologated by the presbytery. It is a practice and phraseology which is still used in the Church of Scotland.
65. SCA CH2/723/5 20/9/1704.
66. NRS CH1/2/5/1/80.
67. NRS CH1/2/5/1/79.
68. NRS CH1/2/4/1/91 Answers for the heritors and whole inhabitants of the Parish of Kilmacolm, Reason I.
69. Ibid., Reason III.
70. Ibid., Reason V.
71. This practice seems to have been widespread as a means to show the strength of the call in the various segments of the community.

72. Earlier authors have ascribed it to the judge, Lord Cullen, but Hugh McLachlan has placed it at the door of one of the two ministers, Brisbane or Turner. See McLachlan (ed.), *The Kirk, Satan and Salem*.
73. McLachlan (ed.), *The Kirk, Satan and Salem*, p. 476.
74. Glass was later to be deposed from his charge and his status as a minister. He afterwards joined and was ordained in the Church of England.
75. Turnbull, 'The Diary of George Turnbull', pp. 381, 386–7.

CHAPTER FOUR

The Courts of the Church and the Business of Presbytery

True Discipline and Government, that which is conform to and founded upon the Word of God is to be held fast . . . and that is presbyterial in its mould this Nation generally seemeth to be confirmed.[1]

Despite giving its name to the system of governance of the Church of Scotland, the presbytery was the last of the church courts to be established, some twenty years after the Reformation. Stirling was one of thirteen centres selected as pioneers for this new form of government and its records, dating from 1581, are the earliest surviving of any presbytery.[2] That first meeting in 1581 had representatives, either ministers or elders or both, from twelve churches, with others gradually being added later. From the earliest time, one of the ministers of Dunblane had resisted the call to join Stirling Presbytery and attempted, ultimately successfully, to have a separate presbytery erected for the town and its neighbours by 1588. The Presbytery of Dunblane has records dating from 1616 to 1688 but suffers the same lacuna for the period 1688–93 when it was held jointly with Stirling.

The institution of the presbytery had partly grown out of the 'exercise', which was a local meeting of ministers to share scriptural knowledge. It was a public gathering which anyone could attend and in 1579 it was recognised that these meetings should form the basis of the new court, with the addition of elders. Hence Stirling's being set up as one of the 'exemplars to the rest'. As well as providing spiritual nourishment for the ministers who shared scriptural exegesis, the exercise also became a way of monitoring the orthodoxy of ministers and of testing the suitability of men who were being considered for local churches, whether as ordained ministers or as trainees looking for ordination. Consequently the exercise became part of the regular agenda of the new court.

Alistair Mutch has made a systematic study of the workings of Presbyterianism nationally in the eighteenth century, sampling five specific presbyteries.[3] The present study examines the institutions of the church within a different area, but also concentrates on the setting up of the renewed courts before Mutch's timeframe. Mutch's study therefore provides a useful background and comparator.

The original constituent churches of the embryonic joint presbytery contained the churches around Stirling, but also a few which later were hived off to presbyteries that were more local. Despite this they retained some residual connection to Stirling, for when Presbyterianism was re-established in the area in 1690, ministers from Glendevon and Fossoway had brief membership until they were able once again to operate in their local presbyteries. In the years following 1581 the presbytery took on the roles which it was to have through the remainder of its early history, roles that involved discipline not only over the ministers and elders who were members, but also over the morals of the whole local population, acting as a higher court with greater authority than the kirk sessions, which had primary responsibility.

One of the prime duties of any minister was, as it still is, to play a part in the courts of the church. Having been set up on 8 August 1581, it took only until 5 October for the Presbytery of Stirling to be taking action against one of its number for his absence and negligence. Attendance was an issue and remained so permanently. Of course, part of the reason for ministers' reluctance to attend was simply the logistics involved in a country that was singularly lacking in good roads in the seventeenth century. The two presbyteries met in Stirling and Dunblane respectively, but with some meetings held elsewhere for visitations or other purposes. Attendance at meetings involved several hours' travelling for many, and as the area controlled became greater a day's journey was required each way from Balquhidder in the north-west or Tulliallan in the south-east for the minister to attend a meeting in Dunblane. The attendance record of those ministers attending the joint Presbytery of Stirling and Dunblane from 1693 to 1698 and the individual presbyteries thereafter shows the effect that distance might have (see Table 4.1).

Leaving aside those parishes which were technically constituents of the presbyteries but whose ministers did not recognise presbyterial authority, there was an average attendance of 72.3 per cent. When the two presbyteries split, the attendance patterns of those attending Dunblane instead of Stirling changed, in some cases quite dramatically. Without exception, the attendance of those for whom Dunblane was closer improved, while the attendance of those for whom Dunblane meant a longer journey deterio-

Table 4.1 Attendance of Ministers of Dunblane Presbytery

Minister	Parish	% attendance at Stirling (1694–8)	% attendance at Dunblane (1698–1705)	Miles from Stirling	Miles from Dunblane
Michael Potter (elder)	Dunblane	54.3	96.2	6.6	0.0
Hew Walker	Lecropt	62.5	95.0	4.0	2.8
Alexander Douglas	Logie	73.2	69.4	3.4	5.6
John Logan	Kilmadock	70.0	86.8	9.9	5.8
Matthew Wallace	Kincardine	82.0	91.2	6.0	5.8
John McLaren	Kippen until 1699	68.7	61.5	9.4	9.3
Michael Potter (younger)	Kippen	-	85.6	9.4	9.3
Robert Gourlaw	Tillicoultry	62.3	51.0	11.0	11.8
Arthur Forbes	Port of Menteith	72.7	69.2	15.3	14.2
Thomas Buchanan	Tulliallan	68.4	54.4	12.3	16.7

rated. Other factors may have come into play; perhaps there were health issues involved. Some of the absences were excused because of illness, the minister being 'indisposed' or 'valetudinary'. In the Stirling portion of the joint presbytery, George Turnbull, minister of Alloa from 1689 to 1699, was one of those with a poor record (63 per cent attendance), but it is clear from his diary that he was often in considerable pain from gout, so that the prospect of riding from Alloa to Stirling and back must have been a real barrier to his attendance.

One acceptable excuse for non-attendance was attendance on more pressing business. The presbytery might meet while the General Assembly was in session so that the commissioners were automatically absent at the higher court.[4] The Commission of Assembly and the Commission for the North also regularly prevented the attendance of those commissioned to attend. The age of the ministers might also come into play. It is noticeable that the septuagenarian Robert Rule of Stirling ceased attending visitations and attended only the regular meetings held in his own church across the road from his manse. With rather less excuse, Michael Potter, minister of Dunblane, had an attendance of a mere 54 per cent when he had to travel the six miles to Stirling; but when he only had to cross to his own church after 1698, his attendance record shot up to an impressive 96 per cent.

The lack of attendance was acknowledged as a problem. It is clear in the presbytery record that when ministers were needed to supply a service at a vacant church, absentees were likely to be chosen, sometimes with a note as to the reason. In November 1694, Thomas Buchanan, minister of Tulliallan, was required to go to ordain new elders in St Ninians as a censure for his non-attendance.[5] The records of the Synod of Perth and Stirling show this to an even greater, more formalised, extent. It decreed in 1705 that Arthur Forbes, minister of Port of Menteith, 'for his absence and sending no excuse should be sent to correspond with the Synod of Glasgow and Air'. Several others drew similar action, being sent to preach in various churches around the presbyteries.[6]

Church courts are chaired by a 'moderator', who 'moderates' or chairs the discussion in kirk session, presbytery or General Assembly. He has no intrinsic powers other than those involved in chairing the meetings, but he is recognised as 'the mouth of the meeting'.[7] Surviving through the episcopal times of Charles II and James VII, the kirk session's role continued to take the oversight of 'discipline' in the parish. The moderator of the kirk session, then as now, was the minister. In the case of collegiate charges, charges of a size to need more than one minister, the role of moderator alternated or rotated round the ministers in turn. This arrangement was retained through the period of episcopacy and after. The practice in vacant parishes was for the other ministers in the presbytery to preach and 'hold session' on an *ad hoc* basis.

The episcopal regime of Charles II and his brother was by definition based on the appointment of bishops, but it retained the Presbyterian structure of kirk sessions, presbyteries, synods and, in theory, a National Synod (which never met). All but one of those structures, however, were changed radically in their composition. The kirk session remained as it was; moderated by the minister of the parish, it contained also a variable number of elders. However, under Charles's regime the old practice of sending elders to sit in the higher courts ceased. Presbytery and synod were composed only of ministers, with the moderator appointed by the bishop. Thus Stirling Presbytery, which had welcomed nine elders to its first recorded meeting on 8 August 1581,[8] was reduced to a ministers' fraternal after Charles took control.

The end of episcopal governance brought elders back into the presbytery, and the selection of the moderator reverted to election by the court itself, with candidacy still being restricted to ministers. Looking at the three sets of records under consideration, the joint presbytery and the separate presbyteries of Stirling and Dunblane, it can be seen that the role of moderator changed hands twice a year, being appointed from the date of one half-yearly synod to the next. Thus, in a small presbytery, ministers had several spells of office. Since the minutes survive only from 1693 for the joint Presbytery of Stirling and Dunblane, until then there is no detail of moderatorial elections, although some individual moderators can be identified from other sources. In the period 1693–7 inclusive, the existing records identify eight ministers, with one, Robert Rule, serving two successive terms, and another, Michael Potter, serving two discrete terms. Most elections were contested and the outcomes recorded as being 'by a plurality of votes'; the numbers were never reported.

Robert Rule's election in November 1693, referred to in Chapter 2, seems to have been a symbolic statement of continuity, a clear statement that the presbytery of the 1690s was the direct successor to that of the 1650s. In those first few months, several others moderated meetings in Rule's absence on a fairly regular basis, the reason is lost, but Rule was elected in May of 1693 for a second term, this time after an election in which he defeated the presbytery clerk, Hugh Whyte. Thereafter moderators served single terms: in all, five from Stirling Presbytery and three from Dunblane. There was a custom of the retiring moderator offering to the presbytery a leet of two names from which his successor would be chosen. In some years, however, the brethren were not satisfied with that choice, for whatever reason, and added two further names to the contest.

In almost every case, the newly appointed moderator was one of those whose names had been put forward unsuccessfully six months previously. Also clear is that those early moderators were ministers of at least six years' experience. None of those elected moderator within the lifetime of the joint presbytery had been ordained by it.

This pattern continued in Stirling Presbytery after the split, and indeed the first four moderators after 1697 had all served previous terms, with Rule, now almost eighty, being the first. The pattern changed radically in 1700, however, with three moderators in a row being 'new men'. John Logan, ordained to Lecropt in January 1694 and then translated to St Ninians in July 1695, was elected in May 1700; John Wylie, translated from Saline in Fife to Clackmannan in April 1700, became moderator in November 1700; and Alexander Hamilton, inducted to Airth also in April 1700, succeeded Wylie in 1701. A fourth 'new man', John Warden, ordained and inducted to Gargunnock in 1698, had stood unsuccessfully in each of these three elections, but from his ordination had acted as presbytery clerk. It seemed that a new group had taken its place at the heart of presbytery life, a group that was to be at the centre of Stirling Presbytery for the next thirty-five years or more.[9]

The disjunct Presbytery of Dunblane also followed the practice of changing moderator every six months. But Michael Potter, minister of Dunblane and senior member of that presbytery, was recalled to be moderator of Dunblane in 1698, having served the joint presbytery as moderator in 1693 and 1695. The other senior members took their turns behind him, despite two of them being less than satisfactory in their attendance and commitment.[10] The other John Logan, minister of Kilmadock, was the first of the recently ordained men to serve in the role, again some six years after ordination. The others followed fairly speedily. Arthur Forbes and Hugh Walker, both ordained in the early months of 1697, were elected as moderator in the first halves of 1700 and 1701 respectively, Forbes unusually serving a double term. Walker was the unsuccessful candidate three times in a row before his final election and served as presbytery clerk while Forbes was moderator. The younger Michael Potter, son of his namesake, the minister of Dunblane, was ordained and inducted to Kippen in May 1700 and elected moderator of the presbytery a mere two years later. Every minister of Dunblane Presbytery, except one who left in early 1699, had served as moderator by 1706, almost in order of seniority through the period although one or two of the more senior men occasionally appeared out of order. In the case of Dunblane there was always a leet of two and again a tendency, although a less strong tendency, that the unsuccessful candidate should be selected at the next election.

Election as moderator of the presbytery, or even of the synod, does not seem to have been regarded as a great honour. George Turnbull, minister of Alloa from 1690 to 1699, never mentioned the role in his diary, despite being moderator of the Synod of Perth and Stirling in early 1694 and being elected moderator of the joint presbytery at the end of 1694. Yet he must have valued it enough to allow his name to be put forward unsuccessfully on a further five occasions.

The other major elected role was that of presbytery clerk. Here, though, a much smaller group of men dominated. The post did not have to be held by a minister, or indeed an elder, and on two occasions it was held by a schoolmaster, who was not necessarily a member of the presbytery. Adam Wardon, schoolmaster of Larbert, held the post in Stirling Presbytery in

1700[11] and James McEchny, schoolmaster of Dunblane, was employed briefly as clerk in Dunblane Presbytery immediately after the split in 1698.[12] Continuity seems to have been more important for the clerk than for the moderator, though. Hugh Whyte, minister of Larbert & Dunipace, served as clerk to the joint presbyteries and then in Stirling for eight years, while Matthew Wallace served Dunblane in the role for about ten years.

Other than the obvious ones of respectively chairing the meetings and recording them, the duties of the posts of moderator and clerk remain slightly vague. The moderator, it would appear, was first choice in the election to be commissioner to the General Assembly, although almost always elected by a majority rather than unanimously. He wrote some of the letters that went out on the presbytery's behalf, but the clerk wrote more and gave out the legal extracts that were required in dealings with other presbyteries, with petitioners and with malefactors.

The other presbytery functionary was the presbytery officer. Employed to deliver citations and enforce decisions of presbytery, his role in contested settlements has already been referred to. Like the presbytery clerk, he was paid by contributions from each parish.

One item that does not appear in either presbytery or kirk session minutes is the approval of previous minutes. This practice seems to have been restricted to synod-level courts at the time. Inspection of the minutes was therefore done by the superior court, the presbytery attesting session minutes annually, the synod attesting presbytery ones at each six-monthly diet. That indeed was the theory. The presbytery records in particular are full of ongoing efforts to persuade ministers to produce session minutes for 'revision' and equally full of excuses as to why it had not happened. None of them quite achieved the 'dog ate my homework' standard, but there is a similarity. On occasion minutes were ordered to be rewritten and from that it can be adduced that the surviving fair copies were not in fact written until many months after the meetings they record. This probably explains why names are sometimes left blank in the record, the clerk having forgotten them in the meantime, and why on one occasion in Stirling the clerk apparently referred to 'Her Majesty' while William was still on the throne. Presumably the session clerk had forgotten that the king had still been alive at the date of the meeting. Most egregious of all, and a sign that the attestation regime did not work, was the case of Port of Menteith Kirk Session, which in 1719 sacked its clerk, schoolmaster and precentor on a variety of grounds among which was that he had not written up the session record for seven years. He completed the task before he left, signing his final entry with a flourish.[13] Mutch has pointed out several similar cases throughout the eighteenth century.[14]

Some presbytery work was delegated to small committees. Depending on the seriousness of the topic a committee might be of ministers in one area who could conveniently meet, or it might be of ministers of some seniority where the problem was thornier. Other committees seem to have been randomly assigned. With occasional exceptions, committees were usually largely ministerial, although the involvement of a Court of Session judge, Sir Colin Campbell of Aberuchill, in presbytery meant that he was often drafted in to help.

Harking back to its earliest origins, the first item in almost every presbytery meeting was the 'exercise and addition', where one minister would give a theological exposition of a passage of scripture, the 'exercise', and a second would explain how the passage related to the circumstances of the time, the 'addition'. On occasion both elements would be given by the same man. The expositors would leave the meeting and their work would be considered by the rest before being formally approved. There were no cases locally of approval being withheld, but it was a mechanism by which theological orthodoxy could be maintained. Where the designated minister was absent, another minister would normally preach, often from his 'ordinary', the normal sequence of sermons which he was giving his own church. The normal practice was for the ministers to take their turn in a set order, but this might be broken because of absence or because of the need to hear those undergoing trials for licence.

The testing of candidates for the ministry filled a considerable part of a presbytery's time, particularly in the 1690s when the imperative to fill pulpits brought many students and probationers into the bounds. This was made more time-consuming by the fact that a student licensed by one presbytery still had to undergo trials in any successive one in which he was based, and a probationer called to a charge had also to undergo a fresh inquisition, as described in Chapter 2. Again, few failed. Students were given an easier passage, but those whom the presbytery supported as bursars were expected to give proof of their attainments. Bursars were generally allocated to groups of parishes for their financial support.

Immediately associated with the approval of students was the allocation of pulpit supply to vacant churches, or to churches whose minister was absent on church business. For the vacant churches in the 1690s, this might mean one Sunday in the month or two, with occasional visits from ministers to allow session meetings to be held. It did not always run smoothly, with preachers being left stranded by the non-arrival of horse or boat to enable their attendance.

More time-consuming, but leaving little trace on the local record other than the fact of the discussion taking place, was the presbyteries' responses to questions coming from higher courts.[15] The 'Barrier Act', which still prevents a General Assembly from taking too hasty a decision on contentious issues, was introduced in 1697 and decreed that any decision made by the Assembly regarding the substance of faith should be considered by presbyteries and a vote taken. If the matter was passed by a majority of presbyteries the matter would be reconsidered at the following meeting and a further vote taken.[16]

Taking sittings of presbytery away from Stirling or Dunblane was the practice of holding 'visitations' to individual parishes. These might happen at the behest of the local minister if there were an issue, particularly with the heritors, or possibly just in the run of events. The research of Alistair Mutch into this aspect need not be repeated as his work analyses the practice in considerable detail.[17] Local records confirm his view that visitation lapsed into virtual desuetude early in the eighteenth century but it was a regular feature in the preceding decade. As Mutch has shown, the proceedings took a regular course with heritors, elders and heads of families summoned and asked for their views on their minister. Those heritors opposed to Presbyterianism rarely attended. If all was well the minister was exhorted to continue to do his duty; he was then asked how the heritors, elders and heads of families behaved and they too were exhorted. But it was an opportunity to deal with issues over manses, upkeep of the kirk, glebes, attendance and many other subjects. For property matters tradesmen were in attendance to give estimates for work required and sometimes the heritors gave permission for work to go ahead. For some issues local 'honest men' or 'burliemen' were in attendance to give an impartial but local verdict on issues.

Even if the bulk of the meeting was concerned with property and the secular affairs of the parish, education and spiritual matters were also explored. Questions would be asked about local schooling and the competence of the schoolmaster, who was required to attend and the need for schools to be set up in remoter areas of the parish discussed. Private schools were also enquired about, and the existence of schools under episcopal schoolmasters was a matter for concern in many parishes. For his part the minister might be asked the extent and efficacy of his work. At the visitation to Larbert & Dunipace on 26 June 1695, the minister, Hugh Whyte, was 'interrogat if he had sermon weekly; answered that he had ordinarily but not always, being discouraged by the people's not resorting frequentlie to the weekdays sermon, the most of them living at so great a distance from both kirks'.[18] The elders were also asked if the minister were 'diligent and painful in his preaching and visitation', to which they replied that he was. Whatever the trigger for a visitation, it must have been anticipated with a degree of trepidation by the ministers as any shortcomings might become apparent. Robert Gourlaw in Tillicoultry was visited by the Presbytery of Dunblane soon after its disjunction from Stirling in 1698 and must have felt somewhat under fire by the end of it:

> The elders being again called, the minr removed they were interrogate by the Moderator whether their minister was faitfhfull and diligent in the Lord's work among them particularly in preaching, administrating the sacraments, visiting families and the like, catechizing. They gave him a good testimony . . .
>
> It being found on enquiry that the minister had not administered the Sacrament of the Lord's Supper since his entrance there [March 1692], the Moderator recommended to him to go about the work as soon as possible.

It being found on enquiry that the minister had not weekdays sermon it was also recommended to him to preach on the weekday. The Visitation finding that the session wanted the Acts of the General Assembly did recommend it to the session to have them forthwith.

In respect the session book was not ready when called for the minister appointed to have it ready on demand.[19]

It would appear that Gourlaw's kirk session was more easily satisfied than the presbytery and indeed in a follow-up visitation in December 1699, the elders and deacons were instructed to attend the weekday sermon once Gourlaw had started it. Gourlaw was not the only minister failing to provide weekday sermons, for the younger Michael Potter was also found wanting in Kippen in 1703. His excuse was that no one would attend.[20] It is very easy to over-estimate the zeal of the people for attending sermons, and in certain parishes, such as St Ninians and Alloa, it is recorded that attendance was problematic in some quarters.

In the case of St Ninians this led to a long-running campaign from 1698 to have a new church erected at Sauchenford. In theory everyone agreed. Sir John Shaw of Greenock seemed prepared to give up land for the church, but none of the other landowners was prepared to give up their share of land for manse or glebe, all arguing that the real need was elsewhere in the parish. Despite all efforts which were still continuing in 1708, the church was not erected and the parish remained entire until the nineteenth century.

Mutch has commented upon the distinction made between 'ordinary' visitations, with the full gamut of questions for everyone with any responsibility in the congregation, and 'extraordinary' ones, set up for a particular purpose. An 'overture' (a proposal sent to the presbytery for discussion by the General Assembly or the Commission of Assembly) of 1704 stated that the former should take place preferably once a year, but if not, in order until all parishes were visited.[21] This is only imperfectly reflected in the practice of Dunblane and Stirling Presbyteries. Thirty visitations took place between 1693 and 1708 with a maximum of five in 1703. Several churches, among them Alloa, Dollar and Clackmannan, never underwent visitation at all. In Alloa's case one was arranged in 1696 but cancelled because both the Earl of Mar and the Laird of Tullibody were out of the country. It was never rescheduled.[22] It is clear that the full visitations did not happen after 1700; the thirteen between 1700 and 1708 (five in Stirling, eight in Dunblane) were all entirely concerned with the secular affairs of the church, manses, repairs, glebes, allocation of desks. This was, however, temporary, for by 1715 Dunblane Presbytery had returned to the full scheme, with visitations on successive days in Tulliallan and Tillicoultry in April. Within the period of this work, however, there is no sign of either presbytery taking significant steps to restore the system.

One regular event in presbyteries was the meeting for prayer and privy censure. The privy censure element entailed each minister being 'exhorted' and examined one by one then leaving the meeting while a discussion about him took place.[23] In the meetings of this period, the record shows only a blanket approval; no issues are recorded. These meetings, however, took place without the elders present. Their privy censure took place similarly at kirk session level, although not frequently. This did give the ministers the opportunity to meet as a presbytery without elders, and on occasion they did make use of this despite its being entirely against church law. The preliminary discussions about the church's response to the Act of Union was one area where it is clear that elders were not welcome. In Dunblane the crucial meetings were held without their presence, while in Stirling there is evidence of ministers meeting together outwith presbytery and taking unofficial decisions.[24]

Also within the presbyteries' aegis, although shared with synods and the General Assembly, was the task of calling for special collections for non-local and local causes. International causes might include support for the Protestant church in Koenigsberg, the French church in London or the Presbyterian congregation in Newcastle, or ransoms for sailors held as slaves by Algerian or Turkish pirates. National causes might include pleas for the building or repair of harbours and bridges as far away as Eyemouth or Irvine as well as support for the victims of fire in Edinburgh or Leith. As McCallum has shown, this very wide interpretation of Christian charity had its roots in mediaeval practice and was well represented through all periods of the Church of Scotland's history.[25]

As kirk sessions were responsible to presbyteries, so presbyteries answered to synods, an area which Mutch's book does not cover. The Synod of Perth and Stirling encompassed Dunblane and Stirling as well as Perth, Dunkeld and Auchterarder, meeting for several days in April and October.[26] With each charge supposed to be represented by its minister and an elder, these meetings rotated round the seats of each presbytery in turn.[27] It is clear from the sederunt lists that attendance very much depended on location with the 'home' presbytery dominating in terms of numbers. It is also clear that where a minister did not attend, no elder from that charge attended either.

At the meeting of 13 April 1708, held in Stirling, ten of Stirling's eleven ministers were present with eight elders, while of the nine ministers in Dunblane Presbytery, seven were present accompanied by six elders. At the same meeting, a mere two elders accompanied ten ministers (out of nineteen) from the Presbytery of Perth and no elders at all accompanied the two ministers (out of twelve) from the Presbytery of Dunkeld. The reciprocal proportions would tend to apply at synod meetings elsewhere, with Stirling and Dunblane being under-represented in their turn (see Table 4.2). Because of the time and expense involved, such elders as were involved tended to be the more prestigious landowners, and in many cases elders who rarely if ever attended their home kirk sessions. This does raise

Table 4.2 Attendance at Synod of Perth and Stirling, 1691–1709

Presbytery	Mar. 1691	Meeting in Perth	
	Settled ministers	Ministers present	Elders present
Auchterarder	2	1	
Perth & Dunkeld	5	3	2
Stirling & Dunblane	6	5	1

Presbytery	Oct. 1691	Meeting in Stirling	
	Settled ministers	Ministers present	Elders present
Auchterarder	no record	1	1
Perth & Dunkeld	no record	3	1
Stirling & Dunblane	no record	6	7

Presbytery	Apr. 1699	Meeting in Perth	
	Settled ministers	Ministers present	Elders present
Auchterarder	8	6	
Dunblane	9	6	
Perth & Dunkeld	22	22	15
Stirling	7	3	

Presbytery	Oct. 1699	Meeting in Auchterarder	
	Settled ministers	Ministers present	Elders present
Auchterarder	no record	9	3
Dunblane	no record	6	3
Perth & Dunkeld	no record	15	4
Stirling	no record	4	3

Presbytery	Apr. 1700	Meeting in Stirling	
	Settled ministers	Ministers present	Elders present
Auchterarder	9	6	
Dunblane	8	8	1
Perth & Dunkeld	23	17	
Stirling	7	7	2
Unidentified			2

Presbytery	Oct. 1700	Meeting in Dunblane	
	Settled ministers	Ministers present	Elders present
Auchterarder	11	5	2
Dunblane	9	9	7
Perth & Dunkeld	26	16	
Stirling	10	10	7

Presbytery	Apr. 1708	Meeting in Stirling	
	Settled ministers	Ministers present	Elders present
Auchterarder	13	10	3
Dunblane	9	7	6
Dunkeld	12	2	
Perth	19	10	2
Stirling	11	10	7

Presbytery	Oct. 1708	Meeting in Perth	
	Settled ministers	Ministers present	Elders present
Auchterarder	13	8	6
Dunblane	9	3	
Dunkeld	12	6	4
Perth	19	18	14
Stirling	11	5	

Presbytery	Mar. 1709	Meeting in Stirling	
	Settled ministers	Ministers present	Elders present
Auchterarder	14	9	4
Dunblane	9	7	6
Dunkeld	12	6	
Perth	19	10	1
Stirling	11	10	9

Presbytery	Oct. 1709	Meeting in Perth	
	Settled ministers	Ministers present	Elders present
Auchterarder	13	9	8
Dunblane	9	4	
Dunkeld	12	9	2
Perth	21	17	14
Stirling	11	8	1

Source: NRS CH2/449/3, NRS CH2/449/5 (Apr.1708).

the question of how representative any individual synod meeting was of its membership.

Synod proceedings seem to have been more robust than presbyteries in their discussions. The case of John Geddes, a probationer from Dollar, who, in 1706, confessed to ante-nuptial fornication in Fossoway, brought a chorus of disapproval from the synod meeting in Perth. Geddes had appeared before the congregation of Fossoway just once to do his penance 'as a private individual' and was referred back to Stirling Presbytery for further sanction on him as a probationer. The presbytery referred the matter to the synod in April 1707 but the resulting case was a mess. Geddes did not comply with the sanction of the synod and was recalled but the General Assembly disputed the synod record as bad clerkship and demanded it be rewritten. The synod then voted on the revised record but a group of members led by Harie Robine, minister of Alva, dissented, favouring leniency. Robine gave detailed reasons for his dissent and as a result was given very rough treatment by the committee of the synod appointed to answer them. The committee gave its reasons at some length as to why the minister of Fossoway had been wrong in his first actions against Geddes. The said minister was William Spence, one of the last antediluvians still in a charge and a man who had suffered torture and imprisonment as a Covenanter, so this was embarrassing. The committee blamed Robine: 'Mr Robine and his adherents have by their dissent forced us to lay open this matter more plainly than otherwise we were willing to have done.'[28]

The committee also showed its disdain of the lower courts in its description of the kirk session of Fossoway as 'a minister with two or three of his elders occasionally met together'. The treatment of Robine showed a considerable degree of sarcasm:

> Our brother's fourth reason is such that it seems very odd how any man proposing himself Presbyterian in his principles can own it.
>
> However by this means our brother has the honour of appearing on the head of a dissenting partie and that in the records of the Synod, because of their zeal against fornication in a probationer.[29]

Further reasons for censure on Stirling Presbytery included comments on other discipline cases including criticising it for absolving a woman from public appearance because she 'continued ignorant and hardened'.

Although Robine's actual reasons for dissent seem thin, he was leading a group of at least fifteen like-minded ministers including Geddes's own minister in Dollar and others from Stirling Presbytery. The incident also shed light on the practice of recording votes. In the records of the courts of the church, votes are always shown as unanimous or 'by a pluralitie of votes'. In this case, while the synod record shows that the decision from which Robine was dissenting was 'by a pluralitie', his dissent shows it was tied and decided on the casting vote of the moderator, an interesting sidelight on the recording practice of the court.

It took until April 1710 for the synod finally to write off the case as completed when the 'brethren' involved reported that they had fulfilled the court's instructions.[30] Harie Robine was left bruised and hurt by the encounter. In a letter to the Earl of Mar in November he wrote:

> I have had often struggles in my mind about this [seeking transportation from Alva], for on the one hand I have had discouragements in this parish more than I expected and also from some ministers

and others in this country, because I would not fall in with their rigid measures, nor go to such a length as they would have had me to go.[31]

The whole episode makes it plain that the rigidity of the seventeenth century was giving way to a more urbane atmosphere in the early years of the eighteenth, at least for some. Whether Spence's over-lenient treatment of Geddes was a sign that even the old order was mellowing is perhaps open for discussion, but there is no doubt that there was a core of the men ordained since the Revolution who had a less doctrinaire view of the discipline of the church courts.

Reference has been made to two other bodies, the Commission of Assembly and the Commission for the North. The General Assembly commissions were the ongoing agents of the General Assembly between its meetings. It was the duty of each presbytery to elect ministers and elders to sit in the General Assembly, although here the elders were elected at half or one third of the number of ministers dependent on the size of the presbytery. The planned proportion was 180 ministers and 68 elders, but the numbers of elders were to be made up by a further sixty-seven elders appointed by the royal burghs.

The commissions of the Assembly acted with the authority of the Assembly and their decisions had the same weight as those of the parent body. Quite large groups, they met two or three times a year sending out overtures and instructions, receiving petitions and appeals, and taking decisions. The two geographical ones were particularly concerned with the transition to Presbyterianism and the filling of pulpits. The Commission for the South barely had an effect on the two presbyteries of Stirling and Dunblane, but that for the North will be dealt with in Chapter 10.

If the presbytery was responsible to the synod and the commissions, it also had relationships with the other presbyteries and synods. The synods had a standing arrangement whereby each was represented at its neighbours' meetings by 'correspondents'. Presbyteries had no such arrangements, and even two so closely connected geographically as Stirling and Dunblane only had one formal link after the disjunction of 1698, and that was where they jointly sponsored a bursar studying at one of the universities. Stirling Presbytery was aggrieved with its neighbour over the disjunction, accusing Dunblane of deserting it because the latter had supplied all the pulpits it was likely to fill and wanted to avoid responsibility for supplying the several vacancies in Stirling's bounds.

Friction with neighbours was not new. As early as 1687, the Synod of Glasgow and Ayr felt that requests from Dunipace, Airth and Larbert for Presbyterian pulpit supply were unreasonable, although it did supply a single Sunday:

> The Synod considering that the saids parochs were not within the bounds of this Synod, appointed the commissioners therefrom to

have recourse to the brethren of the Presbytrie of Strivling for their direction and supply ... It was appointed also that a letter be sent from this Synod to Mrs John Blair and Richard Huison, that they take special notice of the forenamed parochs, in order to their being supplied in the future.[32]

Contact between presbyteries was generally either about students and probationers or about parishioners fleeing from discipline. In the former there was a mixture of co-operation, where a probationer unlikely to receive a call was passed on with testificats as to his character, and blank refusal, where the presbytery was all too keen to retain the services of its ministers, especially if they were Gaelic-speaking. In the case of fugitives from discipline, so many seem to have gone to Edinburgh or its suburbs that it is hard not to feel sympathy for the kirk session or minister there who was constantly being asked for help in tracing them. Letters often took a long time to receive a reply.

It is quite difficult to gauge the effect which the synod had on the average church-goer. It was remote; such elders as went, and they were not many, were from a limited group and rarely reported on proceedings. If an appeal was made to it, it was unlikely that ordinary people would be able to fight their own case. This is made clear in a letter, already quoted, from the elders and heads of families of Tulliallan appealing against the decision of Dunblane Presbytery in 1704: 'Also that most of us being coalhewars and salters to our occupation cannot attend the reverend Synod for discussing our appeal made from the sentence forsaid without manifest injuring our master in leaving his work.'[33]

The issue of the accessibility of the church courts which this quotation highlights was true of presbyteries as well as synods: attendance at presbytery, synod or General Assembly for an elder meant a considerable commitment of time. Presbytery meetings generally started at 10 a.m. and went on all day, with a second session starting at 2, 3 or 4 p.m. For those coming from a distance, arrival the previous day might be necessary, and possibly staying overnight after the meeting as well. Synods were worse, meetings lasting for several days, while General Assemblies were even longer. Ordinary elders, of the kind ordained in ordinary parishes, simply could not afford take the time to devote several days to this work.

So it transpired: each parish might have elected an elder to attend the presbytery and synod, but very few actually attended. In many cases those who did were the ones known to be free of daily work such as Lord Aberuchill, Lieutenant-Colonel Erskine or Ensign Traill, men of consequence untrammelled by the necessity of earning a daily living. Where the ordinary elder might attend the presbytery was when there was a 'visitation' to his or a neighbouring parish. Even when elders were present, they were almost invisible in the written record. Rarely set tasks to perform, they are shadowy figures on sederunt lists without even an identification of what parish they came from or any means of knowing if they participated in the debates or votes.

The sederunt lists show the numbers clearly. Dunblane Presbytery might have two elders attending, sometimes three, rarely more and frequently one or even none. Stirling Presbytery was little better, especially if those employed at Stirling Castle or members of Stirling Burgh Council are ignored.

It is clear, too, that the expectations of elder participation in presbytery were limited. Ministers' absence was recorded, with excuses sometimes or with absence challenged at the next meeting if no excuse had been received. Ministers' failure to attend sometimes had consequences; for elders, no such sanction was enforced. Those who were there were noted, the gaps ignored and no attempt was ever made to encourage kirk sessions to send elders to the higher court.

The higher courts of the church, perhaps more than kirk sessions, had to reinvent their role after 1690. Despite that, it is clear that attendance was not seen as a privilege hard won, but as somewhat of a chore. In the area under consideration, presbyteries rarely criticised sessions, but synods had fewer qualms and put both sessions and presbyteries under examination. However, the geographical considerations affecting attendance at synod meetings make it clear that their decisions could be considered if not partial, at least not representative of the whole area and inconsistent from meeting to meeting. It is also hard to avoid the conclusion that despite paying lip-service to the value of lay input in the higher courts of the church, those courts really were not interested in lay input from anyone other than those already in authority in other spheres.

Notes

1. Logan, *A Sermon Preached before His Grace James Duke of Queensberry*, p. 10.
2. Kirk (ed.), *Stirling Presbytery Records, 1581–1587*.
3. Mutch, *Religion and National Identity*.
4. Contrary to present church law.
5. SCA CH2/722/8 21/11/1694.
6. NRS CH2/449/3 25/4/1705.
7. Steuart of Pardovan, *Collections and Observations Methodiz'd*, p. 38. It is a role which some moderators over the years have taken more literally than others.
8. Kirk (ed.), *Stirling Presbytery Records, 1581–1587*, p. 1.
9. Warden remained minister of Gargunnock from 1698 to 1751, Hamilton served in Airth from 1700 to 1726, when he was translated to Stirling, Wylie was in Clackmannan from 1700 until 1728 and Logan remained in St Ninians from 1695 to 1727. See *Fasti Ecclesiae Scoticanae*.
10. Robert Gourlaw, minister of Tillicoultry, and Thomas Buchanan, minister of Tulliallan, were both admonished about their attendance and pursued over neglected instructions from the presbytery at various times.
11. SCA CH2/722/8 22/4/1700.
12. SCA CH2/723/5 26/4/1698.

13. SCA CH2/1300/1 4/10/1719.
14. Mutch, *Religion and National Identity*, p. 21.
15. Some presbytery responses are preserved among General Assembly papers. Those prior to 1701 were lost in a fire.
16. Act anent the Method of passing Acts of Assembly of general concern to the Church, and for preventing of Innovations: see 'Acts: 1697', in Church of Scotland, *Acts of the General Assembly of the Church of Scotland, 1638–1842*.
17. Mutch, *Religion and National Identity*, pp. 56–66.
18. SCA CH2/722/8 20/6/1695.
19. SCA CH2/723/5 19/5/1698.
20. SCA CH2/723/5 30/11/1703.
21. Mutch, *Religion and National Identity*, p. 59.
22. SCA CH2/722/8 17/6/1696.
23. SCA CH2/722/8 25/9/1695.
24. SCA CH2/723/5 28/10/1706, 3/12/1706. NRS GD124/15/457/2 23/12/1706 John Logan to Mar.
25. McCallum, *Poor Relief and the Church in Scotland, 1560–1650*, pp. 28, 126–7.
26. NRS CH2/449/3, NRS CH2/449/5.
27. Mutch, *Religion and National Identity*, p. 28, states incorrectly that presbyteries selected members of synods; in fact all ministers were members and the elders were elected by the kirk sessions.
28. NRS CH2/449/5 14/10/1708.
29. Ibid.
30. NRS CH2/449/5 11/4/1710. Geddes's later history shows that he took up a place as schoolmaster in Saline in Fife and was finally ordained to Culross in 1718.
31. NRS GD124/15/922 29/11/1708 Harie Robine to Mar.
32. 'Register of the Provincial Synod of Glasgow and Air', p. 200.
33. NRS CH1/2/5/1, p. 79.

CHAPTER FIVE

The Eldership and the Heritors

The Eldership

> Besides Ministers do nothing alone, but with the Peoples Representatives the Elders, who may be of the best quality, if they are qualified for that work and chosen by the church.[1]

Those words from David Williamson, minister of the West Kirk in Edinburgh, were preached to the 1703 General Assembly and reminded that body that ministers had limits to their powers and responsibilities. It was a reminder that was, perhaps, well timed, because if the role of the elder had been severely curtailed by the Presbyterian episcopacy of Restoration Scotland, it was in perpetual danger of being relegated to the side-lines by the fully Presbyterian Kirk of post-Revolution Scotland.

Bill Inglis's study of Dunblane Kirk Session[2] examined the session's social status before and after the Revolution and showed how the status of members had perceptibly diminished. Prior to the Revolution, Dunblane Kirk Session had an unspecified number of landowners together with five lawyers. Not all of these attended regularly, but there was a constant presence of some. After the Revolution the only landowner was Sir Colin Campbell, a lawyer who sat in the Court of Session as Lord Aberuchill. His attendance at the kirk session was almost non-existent, but he did represent it at the presbytery and was assiduous in working for the church in general. Non-landowning, non-lawyer members of the Dunblane Kirk Session from the burgh itself tended both before and after 1693 to be relatively high-status artisans, but those from the landward area of the parish tended to be of a lower status after that time.[3]

A similar change in the rural make-up of post-1690 kirk sessions can be clearly seen in the parish of Port of Menteith. Although most pre-Revolution records are lost, some were transcribed by William MacGregor Stirling and published in 1815.[4] His transcript shows eighteen elders being added to the session in 1668. Of the eighteen, of whom he believed six were already elders, one was an earl, one a lord, one the younger son of an earl, one a knight and at least four others were lairds (described as 'of' an estate). One of the lairds, Lord Cardross, was later to be pursued as a conventicler but at this point he was involved in his parish church. No fewer than seven of the eighteen shared the surname Graham, the dominant family locally.

By contrast, the kirk session as assembled in Port in 1697 had only one Graham in its fifteen members. While the earlier session was filled with landowners, thirty years later the elders were almost entirely tenants. It is impossible to identify with certainty people of the same name in the hearth tax records and the kirk session, but thirteen of the fifteen new elders shared names with men on the hearth tax records of 1694.[5] In some cases there were more than one of the same name, but whatever the identification, the overarching impression is that they were all at a similar level socially, being named as co-occupants of houses with either two or three hearths.[6]

Three shared the surname Ure, two were called McAlpine and two Sands, with another member married to a Sands. Five would appear to have been tenants of the new Lord Cardross. Given the history of the Cardross family and their tenants as Covenanters at the Battle of Bothwell Bridge, it is tempting to see these as men of the same stamp but there is no evidence to confirm this. The 1697 session presents a quite different demographic from that of 1668, albeit still with strong influences from particular families. The record shows that despite the potential of fifteen attending, the numbers had dwindled significantly by 1703 when three were added to the number, making the session up to nine. This included Henry Dow of Wester Polder, and it was he who was usually detailed to attend the presbytery or synod. As a heritor and landowner, he was of higher status than most of his fellow elders, but in fact the hearth tax records suggest that he was of much the same economic class, being the co-owner of three hearths. Confirming Inglis's findings about Dunblane landowners, Dow had the poorest attendance record at session meetings. Although the meetings were usually held on a Sunday after morning sermon, Port of Menteith Kirk Session records show a poor attendance generally. At some meetings only three or four were present, two on one occasion, and this must imply that the elders themselves were not assiduous in attending church.

Aside from the differences in status between the sessions of the two periods, a question needs to be asked about how they functioned. It is tempting to assume that the presence of the more powerful men on the session in the earlier period is symptomatic of the economic and political establishment making sure it had control of the ecclesiastical one as well. After all, these were the men charged with almost all other responsibilities locally: roads and bridges, law and order, taxes. However, lest it be thought that the 1668 elders took office for power or prestige, the Carolean record in Port goes on to state that the new session, 'considering the necessitie of reforming their own lives and manners befor they endeavour any such things among others, hath ordained, that none of their number shall, after both sermons endit, goe into any ell [ale] house except in case of real necessitie'.[7]

The elders were still seen as very much under the supervision of the church. Even attendance at session meetings was insisted upon, with a fine of £10 being levied on any elder failing to provide a cogent excuse for non-attendance. At a time when a recipient of session assistance might receive 13s. 4d., it is clear that an elder had to have a considerable income to risk the penalties for non-attendance. The record does not show how effective this policy was in encouraging good attendance, although one elder was excused on account of 'pain of leg' and one meeting is described as having all members present except one.

Such a regime, though, was not necessarily found throughout Scotland, or even throughout Dunblane Presbytery. Inglis has shown how the Dunblane Kirk Session was twice taken to task for poor attendance during the period of episcopacy and interprets the fact that 60 per cent of session meetings during the period do not even list those attending as implying a casualness as to attendance.[8] Contrariwise, while Inglis found that attendance in Dunblane after 1690 was strictly enforced, the Port records from 1697 show that the attendance of some elders was decidedly sporadic.

Port's post-Revolution kirk session was entirely made up of new elders, and this was a pattern followed by many parishes. Of those with surviving records, whether at session level or via the presbytery, only Alva, St Ninians, Stirling and Logie showed significant numbers with continuous service, although there were undoubtedly other long-serving individuals such as Lord Aberuchill in Dunblane parish. Logie and St Ninians had sessions ruling the post-1687 meeting-houses, so it may be assumed that there was continuity from them with additional members added after re-establishment as the parish kirk. In a kirk session with a minister in place, nominations to the eldership came from within. Notice was given of the need for new members, names were given in, they were discussed by the session and the nominees examined for their suitability both theological and moral. Then the list was made public and objections invited. If all was well the ordinations went ahead. If there was no existing session, or if there was a session but no minister, the presbytery took responsibility. It would consult any existing kirk session or if there was none, the heritors and heads of families, possibly even asking the congregation as a whole for names of men of suitable calibre. The call given to be an elder was expected to be obeyed, although there were exceptions.

The new St Ninians meeting-house had a session of eighteen elders ordained in 1688. This included two minor lairds, William Livingston of Greenyards and John Forrest of Thirtieacres. Both of these had to acknowledge their guilt in signing the Test Oath, while two others also had to acknowledge their guilt for having signed a bond before the Circuit Court of Glasgow. They were all men who had been potentially or in fact associated with attending conventicles. That number compares with the fifteen or so who served in the pre-Revolution parish kirk session.[9]

After his deposition as minister in October 1689, the Episcopalian James Forsyth carried on meeting with his session for some months, but at some stage the minister of the Presbyterian meeting-house, Patrick Couper, took over the parish church. Six months later, in May 1690, there was a substantial augmentation by a further eighteen elders, the 'spaciousness' of the parish being cited as the reason. This group was clearly selected with geography in mind for almost all were from communities away from the main centre of population at St Ninians itself and the nearby Bannockburn. In 1694, a further six were ordained but as sixteen existing elders were also named in the presbytery record, it would seem that there had been some diminution of the session. This being prior to the induction of John Logan as minister, it was also the occasion when Thomas Buchanan, minister of Tulliallan, was charged with responsibility for the admission of the new elders as a censure for his non-attendance in presbytery.[10] In the absence of a parish minister, the presbytery took on responsibility for examining the potential new elders for suitability, but the addition of Livingston of Greenyards to the committee of three ministers charged with the task was a rare example of a presbytery commissioning an elder to do this.

Little can be made of a comparison in the two sessions of St Ninians. Each had two lairds, the Episcopalian one having Torbrex and Cornton to balance the Presbyterian Greenyards and Thirtieacres. The parish was characterised by a large number of small landowners rather than a single magnate, but most of them, though heritors, did not function as elders. As it had one of the largest parishes by population in Lowland Scotland, it is particularly hard to identify individuals of lower status. Both sessions had members called William Buchan at the same time, but they cannot be the same person.

The one rural kirk session which stands out on its own is Alva, possibly reflecting the congregation's different route through the decade. With William Lindsay formally handing control of the church to Richard Howieson at the behest of the Privy Council, there was no impetus to change or augment the session. Although the session minutes from that point no longer exist, the financial accounts show that the pre-1689 session of four elders, William Rob, Alex Young, John Duncanson and Patrick Mores, continued to uplift the weekly collections under Howieson, who saw no reason to augment their number. They still continued when Lindsay returned in 1691. When Lindsay finally left in 1696 and the presbytery took control, they added another seven to the session, but the accounting record continues to show three of the old Episcopalian elders still serving at the plate after the arrival of Harie Robine as minister. Only Duncanson was missing, possibly having died. Again, the perils of identification are evident. In the minute discussing the appointment of new elders, the name of 'John Dason, litster' is found alongside 'the other John Dason'. Both were in due course ordained.[11]

The kirk session of Stirling itself was quite different from those in the other parishes. As previously mentioned, the presbytery had a battle on its hands when the burgh council tried to impose its own choice of potential elders, with one of the issues being the presbytery's wish to include elders from Stirling Castle, outwith the burgh boundary. This was essentially a political squabble with ecclesiastical overtones. Until the Privy Council took a hand, the burgh council had been packed with supporters of the previous regime, and with the nominees from the castle being clearly William's men, they would clearly affect the ethos of the kirk session. In 1693, at a time when the Episcopalians and the Presbyterians were still in contention over possession of the Burgh Kirk, the matter was the subject of a good deal of controversy.

The new session of the burgh council insisted on presenting a list of potential elders; the presbytery thought otherwise and produced another list. One of the debating points was the presence on the presbytery's list of three men who were stationed in Stirling Castle: the lieutenant-governor, John Erskine (later of Carnock), Captain (later Lieutenant-Colonel) John Erskine and Ensign James Traill.[12] The first and last of these had been exiles in the Netherlands, returning to Scotland in the wake of William's invasion. They were not likely to sit comfortably with elders representing a council which was still sympathetic to the old regime and Episcopalianism.

The presbytery won the argument, just as the Privy Council had won the argument over the burgh council. New men, favourable to William and Presbyterian principles, controlled the council. To a substantial extent the same men came on to the session and this group became the centre of power in the burgh, with the three from Stirling Castle adding an extra conduit to the centre of power in Edinburgh. In fact, it would appear that the town council, now entirely loyal to William, may have sent men to be elders *ex officio* as the church records show bailies and provosts as elders, but with relatively short periods of activity.

From the point of view of the church, the huge advantage of a link to the burgh council was that it assured civil support in the session's pursuance of ecclesiastical order. In discipline cases recalcitrant sinners could be handed over to the civil power in the knowledge that they would be consigned to the tolbooth to consider their sins, in addition to the possibly less uncomfortable stool of repentance. In the case of financial issues such as persuading those who had borrowed money as a bond from the poor-box to repay it when required, letters of horning were easily procured and frequently resorted to. In the matter of poor relief itself, the burgh had its own resources in the form of Cowane's Hospital. The fact that the controllers of Cowane's Hospital were the same people as those responsible for the church's poor relief made a concerted provision possible. The immediacy of the kirk session's access to the burgh power base can be seen in the number of times a reference to the councillor who was also an elder resulted in a decision the same day.

Not that all was entirely rosy, for individual councillors produced their own complications. Bailie Burd, one of the elders, was in front of his co-elders in August 1697 on a charge of wife beating. Burd's defence was that his wife was drunk at the time, which sounds a rather unconvincing defence to modern ears, but the two ministers and three of the elders were duly sent to interview Mrs Burd, thus obviating the need for her to face the embarrassment of a formal appearance before the session. One of the three was a fellow bailie but the other two elders were not from the highest status on the session. The upshot was that Bailie Burd was suspended from the eldership for some time. Two more bailies were in trouble in 1699–1700 with Bailies Miller and Wilson being removed from the congregation and put to the horn.[13] The interests of session and council were not necessarily in harmony.[14]

The elite of the Royal Burgh included the families that regularly provided the councillors over several decades. Of these the highest status were the merchants, from whom the provost, dean of the guildry and bailies were recruited. The lower status comprised those who served as deacons of the Seven Incorporated Trades. Both groups were regularly represented on the kirk session through the eighteenth century and in this early period the former group, bailies and provosts, were among those who attended the presbytery and the synod. But this elite also included men such as James Forrester of Logie, a heritor in Logie but an elder in Stirling as well as a lawyer. Perhaps involvement in church affairs in Stirling rather than his home parish saved embarrassment, for as a heritor in Logie he was sometimes at odds with the kirk session there. The other elite grouping consisted of the officers in the castle, particularly Erskine of Carnock and Ensign Traill. Despite his seemingly low rank in the army, Traill was middle-aged and essentially the administrator in the castle. The son of a Covenanter minister, the brother of another and former brother-in-law of the Lord Advocate of Scotland, he was well connected and a man of influence.

The advantage of having this group on the session is that they were available to take on some of the more sensitive duties such as taking landowners to task for their morals, pursuing debts, and generally showing the parish church as part of the establishment of the town. Possibly as the other side of this arrangement, some of the elite elders seem to have been exempt from some of the more mundane duties. They were not expected, as some others were, to patrol the streets looking for Sabbath breakers, neither were they in a position to identify those in need of relief, as were elders who lived within the burgh. The one action that all were expected to undertake was to inspect the various accounts, and unusually the inspecting committees might have up to eight members. Unlike in some of the more rural parishes, Stirling's accounts might only be inspected several years in arrears. The reason for this is not clear.

The kirk sessions did tackle attendance, although perhaps not with the assiduity of the presbytery nor with the strictness of the Episcopalian session in Port. Two elders of Stirling Session were pursued at length for non-attendance in August 1698: John Chrystie and John Cairns were cited more than once to answer to their peers for non-attendance, leading in time to Cairns 'refusing peremptorily to attend'.[15] Both disappear from the record shortly thereafter; the outcome was not recorded.

This general lack of continuity between pre- and post-Revolution kirk sessions, combined with the lack of continuity in the ministry, must have meant that very few elders knew the protocols of session business. Inevitably it is likely that very few had any experience of formal meetings. This, combined with the inexperience of newly ordained ministers, may have made for some unconventional meetings in the early stages, but sadly no evidence remains and of course the men were chosen for their moral stature, sobriety and faithful behaviour. Although, as noted, the elder of the post-Revolution church was likely to have been of a lower social status than his pre-Revolution counterpart, there were limits, and by 1704 it was affirmed that potential elders should not be 'menial servants'. It is not clear whether any such had already been ordained.[16] Indeed, the men chosen were almost without exception, as Mutch has noted, 'men who had a stake in the parish and knowledge of those who they would be watching over'.[17]

This is not to say that no mistakes were ever made. The presbytery made concerted attempts to dislodge continuing episcopal ministers and in two cases went as far as ordaining Presbyterian kirk sessions as part of the campaign. The events in Balquhidder will be discussed more fully in a later chapter, but the new kirk session of Bothkennar showed the presbytery's weakness in trying to implement such an institution when it had only very partial knowledge of local circumstances. In 1701 six names were suggested as a potential Presbyterian session in rivalry to the Episcopalian one in Bothkennar. One nominee was a local landowner, Gabriel Ranken of Orchardhead. Almost all of the other landowners were strongly Episcopalian in their views. Bothkennar was a small parish and a session of six would probably have been adequate given the size of the population so the six were duly ordained on 13 August 1701. In May of the following year it became clear that Orchardhead had since married clandestinely and irregularly. He was temporarily suspended from the eldership, rebuked privately and absolved. By September, his fellow elders were petitioning the presbytery to restore him to the eldership, which was granted.[18] Orchardhead's bride, with whom he eloped in February 1702, was Sophia Clerk, daughter of Sir John Clerk of Penicuik. Clerk's correspondence shows that even prior to the marriage, Orchardhead had hit Sophia in Clerk's own house and Clerk refers to him as 'a beggar and a mad man', the latter description being backed by correspondence from Orchardhead's brother. It was 1707 before Clerk finally received his daughter and 1711 before he agreed a marriage settlement, when Orchardhead's brother told him he had cleared his debts. It can be assumed that Orchardhead's contribution to church matters was limited, but the very fact of his ordination as elder shows an attempt to raise the social profile of the eldership in that parish, despite the lack of financial and behavioural respectability which was normally required.[19] No further record of that session's activities has survived.

Writing in the first decade of the eighteenth century, Sir Walter Steuart of Pardovan declared as a matter of regret, 'especially about the beginning of our Happy Revolution in the year One Thousand Six Hundred and eighty-nine, that the judicatories of this church, very much wanted fix'd and established rules, for directing their proceedings'.[20] An attempt to codify church law in 1697 was considered by the General Assembly:

> The General Assembly, having heard the Report of a Committee of their own number for overtures anent the Overtures concerning the Discipline and Method of proceeding in Ecclesiastic Judicatories in the Church of Scotland, now produced in their own presence, appoints the same to be sent as overtures, from private hands, to the several presbyteries within this National Church; and ordains the said presbyteries to send their animadversions and observations thereupon to the commission to be appointed by this Assembly.[21]

It may well be that Pardovan was one of the 'private hands' involved. A committee set up to consider the overtures included both Gilbert Rule, brother of the minister of Stirling, and the previously mentioned Lord Aberuchill. It may be surmised that Aberuchill's experience of Dunblane Presbytery gave him insight into the procedures outlined by the overtures. The matter was considered by the Assembly several times in the intervening years without any real progress but finally Pardovan set to and codified such regulations as existed with the intention of their being part of the education of future ministers. The *Collections* of 1709 were the result, a volume that was reprinted and republished into the nineteenth century.

It was, to some extent, a counsel of perfection. Some matters were never ordered in actual practice as Pardovan thought they should be. But the fact that the *Collections* were not published until nineteen years after the re-establishment of Presbyterianism and were never actually endorsed by the General Assembly but simply tacitly accepted perhaps explains why there was considerable latitude and variance in the practice of kirk sessions. Despite this variety of practice, but perhaps to some extent because of this, record keeping was central to the life of the session. Mutch has commented on three crucial elements of responsibility that depended on record keeping: the exercise of discipline, the proper administration of the sacraments and the provision of poor relief. Part of the presbytery's role in the supervision of its constituent parishes was to make sure that kirk sessions did record their decisions correctly and fully.[22]

In tandem with concern in Pardovan's text for the current record came an insistence on gathering in the previous session records. In one sense this can be seen as a statement of authority and an assertion of the continuity of the parish through all its vicissitudes. In another sense, though, it is simply the provision of the new session with the tools it needed to do its appointed tasks. Presbyteries had the responsibility to examine and order the revision of records which did not attain a high enough standard of recording while their own records were equally open to scrutiny and criticism by the synod.

Pardovan saw elders as occupying one of the two ordained roles, but a role with limitations. 'He is called a Ruling elder, because to rule and govern the church is the chief part of his Charge and Imployment therein . . . his principal Business is to rule well, and it belongs not to him to Preach or teach.'[23] A summary of elders' duties follows: as the pastors were to be diligent in teaching and sowing the Word of God, the elders were to look for the fruit of that teaching in people's lives. They were to assist in the examination of potential communicants, visit the sick, cause church law to be obeyed, admonish men of their duty. An elder would have a specific part of the parish, a 'quarter' (although there might be more than four of them), and visit it at least once a month, reporting to the session what scandals and abuses he found. He should keep a list of 'examinable persons' within his quarter and annotate it with details of their moral status and need for poor relief. Elders were to assist the minister at the serving of Communion and, in the absence of deacons, look after the collections and the distribution thereof. What an elder could never do is replace the minister in any of his duties from the pulpit, whether preaching, intimating sentences, pronouncing sentences or absolving the penitent, nor could he ever moderate (chair) kirk session meetings. The minister was permanently the chairman of the session and it was not a session meeting without him.

The second non-clerical role described by Pardovan was that of the deacon, and he thought it an 'unwarrantable omission in some congregations' that they neglected to appoint any. Specifically, their task was to be responsible for collections and their distribution to the poor. However, despite his strictures, in the presbyteries of Stirling and Dunblane only Tillicoultry appointed deacons, as far as can be ascertained from existing records. In February 1699, the minister and kirk session there ordained eight new elders and eight new deacons. It is clear from the record that they attended kirk session meetings and took their full part. Pardovan suggests that they had a vote only when the matters under discussion referred to the financial affairs of the congregation or poor relief, but whether this was so at Tillicoultry cannot be ascertained. They also had a role within the heavily formalised Communion service as described in Tillicoultry.[24]

Of the various roles of the elder, the one which would have been new was the theoretical lay involvement in the higher courts. As shown in the previous chapter, for most of the elders, their duties and influence were almost entirely restricted to their own parish and session and were not intrinsically different from those of their predecessors in episcopal times.

Assuming the absence of deacons to look after the collections, the elders had four roles. Three of these were those noted by Mutch of administering poor relief (receiving the collections at the church door), adjudicating on discipline and helping to administer the sacrament of Communion. To them can be added the administration of the church fabric, although some aspects of this last were the responsibility of the heritors. Discipline and the sacrament of Communion will be dealt with in later chapters.

Poor Relief

Alms for the poor had always been a responsibility of the church, and the reformed church took the concept seriously. The desire for accountability of those responsible for gathering and distributing them thus made the recording of such alms an early priority of the kirk session. As such there have been several detailed studies made of the topic nationally, Rosalind Mitchison's covers the period under review, while those of John McCallum and R. A. Cage cover periods before and after.[25] Karen Cullen's work on the reign of William also covers the subject within a narrower timeframe but broader context, giving particular attention to Tayside.[26]

In general, account books for the two presbyteries under consideration have not survived as well as minutes, but in the case of Alva, the accounts have survived where the minutes have not. In other parishes, such as Port of Menteith and Tulliallan, the minutes and accounts are in the same volume, neatly separated in the former case and mixed through in a mixter-maxter of later binding in the latter. The case of Alva is unusual in that the same volume covers fifty years of charge and discharge through the later episcopal period, the period of turmoil, and long enough to record that on 13 November 1715 'no coll: upon the accompt of the battell of Sherramoor'.[27]

Accountancy practice was very far from standardised at the time. Alastair Mutch has tracked the development nationally in his study of Presbyterian administration in the eighteenth century,[28] showing in the process that Stirling Presbytery in particular had the most advanced accounting in the country. As he points out, neither the overtures of 1696 nor Sir Walter Steuart of Pardovan's recommendations of 1704 actually laid down a standard practice. Some sessions approved the accounts annually, others when the boxmaster's tenure was ended.[29] At the very least they had to be presented at presbyterial visitations. Tulliallan's accounts noted meticulously the date and amount of each collection, together with the elder responsible. The disbursements follow on but the book fails to record dates. The charge and discharge then refer simply to the totals on the different pages.[30]

In contrast, in an account book which started only with the ordination of Arthur Forbes in October 1697, the charge and discharge accounts of Port of Menteith are prepared on facing pages, with a page to a year being the norm so it is almost possible to track the fluctuations in the amount held in the box from week to week. Unfortunately, the crucial word here is 'almost', for while the income from collections is expressed from week to week, other income was added only at the end of the accounting period, which happened to be at the end of November. For Port, this other income included fines from errant parishioners and the collections from midweek marriages and baptisms.

Other forms of income are included in other parishes' accounts. Alva included annual payments of interest on loans or bonds while Tulliallan included annual figures for 'bell and mortcloth'.[31] Mortcloth fees, however, might appear in separate accounts for some parishes with different governance arrangements. Indeed, they might belong not to the parish church but to a mortcloth society or even an individual who might garner the profits from funerals.

Every few months there would be a special collection for a particular purpose in place of the normal one. This was a practice that carried on from pre-Revolution times. Sometimes it might be purely local to help a parishioner in particular straits. Alex Nicoll, a chapman or pedlar in Alloa, had 'a child cut of the gravell and had not the money to satisfy the doctor for his pains'. In this case a house-to-house collection by the elders was organised after intimation from the pulpit. The result was an outstanding £48 14s.[32] The collections ordered by presbytery, synod or General Assembly for national or even international causes have already been noted. What is noticeable and unexplained is that such causes always brought a return higher than the usual week-to-week average.

The 1690s saw the 'ill years', a succession of bad harvests which caused widespread distress and starvation through the whole country over a five-year period. Different areas suffered worse at different times but between 1695 and 1701, there was scarcely any part of the country that did not suffer prolonged destitution at some point. Cullen has suggested that the designation, echoing Genesis 41:30, suited both Jacobites, who saw it as a judgement on the nation for deposing James VII, and Presbyterians, who saw it as a judgement on the shortcomings of the people.[33] Incidentally, George Turnbull never preached from that particular chapter nor commented on anything other than the fact of the dearth.

Living in Alloa parish, Francis Masterton described the 1695 harvest in these terms: 'Cropt this year ane bad dry summer til July, a late harvest.' As a result, he records that the price of grain rose from £8 a boll to £20 during the course of the year.[34] This is significantly higher than any price which Cullen recorded for Tayside.[35] Masterton's response, to build another barn, suggests that he had profiteering on his mind. Rosalind Mitchison has noted the Stirling experience in her *The Old Poor Law in Scotland*,[36] with Stirling Kirk Session commenting on the number of unknown dead on the street in 1699. Other parishes had their own crises, and records show payments to strangers, payments to bury strangers or requests to the heritors to play their part. In December 1698, the kirk session of Port tried to arrange a meeting with the heritors with the intention of persuading them to be responsible for the maintenance of 'their own' poor.[37]

The system of parish relief was struggling; sixteenth- and earlier seventeenth-century legislation had allowed for a voluntary stent (tax) on heritors, but it had rarely been invoked. It was perhaps a relief to many congregations that acts of Parliament of 1695, 1696 and 1698 gave jurisdiction over poor relief jointly to heritors and kirk sessions and indeed gave the possibility of the session not being formally involved at all. Although this last scenario may not actually have happened, it does reinforce the idea that the Sunday collection was not the only source of money for the relief of the poor. The Burgh of Stirling was in a special case locally in that it had Spittal's and Cowane's hospitals as a resource for the relief of tradesmen and guild brethren, which may have taken some pressure off parish relief, though as McCallum notes, this kind of funding tended to benefit men more than women or families.[38] Nonetheless, the churches' collections were the main, the most visible and the most demographically comprehensive source of relief.

Tulliallan was a relatively prosperous parish, and because much of its wealth depended on trade and industry, it was perhaps slightly protected from agricultural dearth. There the kirk session recorded special measures in February 1698:

> Which day session mett. After prayer the session, considering the great strait the poor are in, the meal being at 16s or 18s per peck, have resolved to give the double allowance unto all the poor of the parioch until the Lord be pleased to send plenty; and for that end allows the thesaurer [treasurer] to give to the poor of the parioch according as he understands their straits, in the intervalls between sessions, and to lay his depursements every day before the session to be judged by them.[39]

The thesaurer's first list was approved on 13 March, as was another on 5 April, and individuals were helped on an almost weekly basis.

The kirk session of Stirling had considerable cash reserves lent out as bonds, but sometimes they must have seemed more trouble than they were worth. They usually represented a capital sum acquired, sometimes by legacy, and put to a trustworthy recipient to hold and pay interest upon. That was the theory, but in practice things were not quite so simple. The holders often were laggard in paying the annual interest,[40] but if they were tardy in paying the interest, persuading them to repay the principal could be a long-drawn-out affair. Stirling Kirk Session was probably one of the richest parishes in the area and had been the recipient of various legacies. The exigencies of the bad harvests of 1697 led to the session calling in all its debts except the Earl of Mar's bond for £1,000 in January 1698. At the same time the elders were charged with going around their quarters making lists of those in need of support.

The calling in of debts was one thing; actually receiving the money was another. In a time of national dearth, those who had borrowed from the church were not likely to be able to find the means of repaying their debt. By September 1699, two of those involved, James Millar and the Laird of Broich, were threatened with being put to the horn for their refusal or inability to pay. Broich paid up in early October, Millar was put to the horn by January 1700, but his bond was still being listed as one of the assets of the congregation a year later. The other large bond, that to the Laird of Clackmannan, had been transferred by the laird to one Thomas Ridge, who had since died. After an unsuccessful attempt by Lieutenant-Colonel Erskine, it was left to Robert Rule, the senior minister, to approach Ridge's heirs for repayment, which he successfully did. However, the laird had a second bond which was not repaid and the session took him to the civil courts. The process was finally abandoned when it became clear that Clackmannan had so many debts that payment of any of them was unlikely.[41]

A session entry from Stirling in July 1699 lists thirty-two recipients of relief, each receiving 9s. 9d.[42] A fortnight later the Earl of Mar was being asked to pay the 'annual rent' on his bond. At the same meeting £1 was paid to Alexander Droper 'for burying several persons'. It may be assumed that reasons of geography and demography drew the desperate into the town, but the smaller parishes had their share of transient poor. Port paid five shillings and two shillings in September 1700 to unknown strangers; Tulliallan, too, paid for a coffin for a beggar in 1698. The situation within the Stirling/Dunblane area is very much in line with what was outlined nationally by Cullen,[43] although the lack of burial records from the area precludes comparisons with Cullen's findings about the demographic results. Another indicator of demographic change, the number of baptisms, will be considered in the next chapter.

Port of Menteith was a poor parish: with a population figure of about 1,865, its average weekly collection in 1698 had been 10s. 6d. Alva, equally rural and with a population of around 436, gave an average of £1 4s. each week it had a service in 1697.[44] Tulliallan, a parish which included a small port and some industry, had a population of only about 1,321, but in 1696–8 had regular collections of £3 6s. 8d. per week, excluding collections from two Communion seasons.[45] Why there should be such a huge discrepancy in the givings per head is not entirely clear. Local poverty may be one answer, the lack of actual coinage another. Fortunately for the poor of Port, the misdemeanours of some of its more prosperous inhabitants gave it an income from fines which in 1698 far exceeded the offerings of the people, although the proportion of £28 collections to £48 in fines was not repeated in other years. Essentially Port, as a largely Gaelic-speaking parish on the fringes of the southern Highlands, may have functioned as a virtually cashless economy and other forms of local aid in kind would be unrecorded.

As a side issue regarding the availability of coin, a significant part of the money in any particular poor-box was in fact 'doyts', bad copper coin worth only about half of its face value which was periodically sold on and recorded as a loss to the poor. As an example from Port in 1708, James Hardie, the schoolmaster, was 'delivered to sell £4/6/8d of doyts and lettered turners, an insufficient thripence, a 3/- piece and a six pennie piece'.[46]

In theory, it was the responsibility of the kirk session to use the collections for the relief of the poor, but it was recognised that there were many other costs which had to be met, especially wherever the heritors were unwilling to agree to expenditure. In many cases this might be paid out of the income the session gleaned from selling burial places or renting space for 'desks' in the church, and in other cases mortcloth income would pay, at least for the costs associated with death and burial.

Mutch has quantified the proportion of collection income spent in various categories in five presbyteries in the final decade of the eighteenth century, showing that poor relief took up between 65 per cent and 93 per cent of the spending of kirk sessions, with part of the discrepancy being because fees to be paid at a fixed level took up a higher proportion of the resources of lower-income parishes.[47] Looking at the equivalent figures for Port and Tulliallan during the lean years, the former was paying out a mere 59 per cent while the latter paid out 85 per cent. The actual amounts paid out on poor relief were on average £35 and £18 respectively but on the other hand, Port paid out nearly £16 in fees against Tulliallan's £9. It was not just a matter of proportion, then, because Tulliallan really did have fewer calls on the poor-box. It can only be assumed that the fees paid to synod and presbytery clerks and the presbytery officer, together with the salaries paid to the session clerk and session officer, were met in some other way in Tulliallan, perhaps by heritors or from a separate unrecorded mortcloth fund.

Other expenses met in Port, but apparently not in Tulliallan, included the purchase of books for the session, purchase of a new sackcloth gown for the use of penitents, building works (which should have been a call on the heritors) and so on. Even the ordination of their new minister in 1697 led to substantial expense in Port in the provision of horses for conveying ministers from elsewhere.

Taking a longer look at poor relief than simply the ill years, it is clear that there was wide variation in the way sessions dealt with their poor, although most seem to have maintained a standard list of people in need of help. Alloa seems to have been particularly organised, with a list of monthly 'pensioners'. In October 1690, nine were named with the follow-up a fortnight later that they were summoned to the church to receive their pensions and be reminded of their duty to God.[48]

Extraordinary circumstances also brought the need for occasional poor relief, and that might be awarded at a higher or a lower level than the regular awards. On the whole, strangers and beggars received small amounts, although there is the occasional exception. On the other hand, a father coping with new twins and a sick wife, a woman caring for six children, or men who had lost their means of livelihood with the death of their horse all received relatively generous treatment. Also in the case of Port, those who had suffered as Covenanters were among those helped.

One overarching principle does seem to govern the administration of poor relief and that is that the debit side of the accounts was made to balance the income. Thus a meeting of the kirk session in Port in November or early December paid the year's salaries and any outstanding debts and then what was left was split among the poor to leave only a small sum in the box to meet emergencies. The session then approved the accounts and a new boxmaster was elected or the existing one continued.

The collection, however, cannot be seen to be a response to preaching, being taken at the door of the church before the service, so there must have been some notice of the special collections.[49] This point as to the lack of connection between the collection accrued and the message offered by the minister applies also to the collections at the Communion season. However, the routine of fast day, preparation day, sacramental day and thanksgiving day leaves the possibility that the effect of the previous days bore fruit at the later services. Be that as it may, the income available for the benefit of the poor from a Communion season could be substantial: that at Tulliallan from 2 to 6 June 1698 brought in over £100 compared to a weekly average of £5 17s.; that in Alva in 1702 brought in £64 compared to the average Sunday sum of £1 10s.[50]

Parts of these substantial collections were generally disbursed immediately. Tulliallan gave £30 'to the poor of the paroch after the Sacrament' and £4 to 'the poor folk att the Kirk yatte [gate] at the Sacrament'. As the account was closed immediately after, this meant that unlike in Port the box had a substantial sum in it for future calls, but it was soon needed. Shortly into the new accounting period, a further £6 was sent to 'heads of families' and then in a sequence of undated entries to eighteen poor persons £30, for the poor in their straits by order of the session £10 2s., and again £5 10s., and then £16 and then £30, together with £9 for 'several sad chists', presumably coffins, and £1 4s. to the beddal 'for making poor folks graves'. The year 1698 was a challenging one even if Masterton's summary of it was 'a late rainy harvest but ye vitail in end all weil won' (the victuals in the end well won). The following year brought some respite, but 1700 was again a year of dearth, if not quite so bad.[51]

The church's role in poor relief, while clearly major, cannot have been the whole story. Neighbourly assistance is largely unrecorded, but Thomas Boston, by this stage looking for a call in the Borders, recorded: 'I had but three pence left that morning, of which I gave two pence halfpenny to buy bread for the poor ... So all my money was now gone, save a half-penny reserved for the Sabbath's collection.'[52] But that role was always high in the priorities of minister and session, and in intimating the forthcoming Communion season to his parishioners in Port, Arthur Forbes's words clearly were deeply meant: 'Mr Forbes having publickly read the grounds & causes thereof ... exhorted them earnestly to the religious observation of the said day, and for this end to attend upon the publick ordinances. Moreover the minister exhorted the people to extend their bowels of charity to the poor.'[53]

Leaving aside the matter of poor relief, one question that needs to be addressed is that of possible conflicts of interest within the session. This could happen in a variety of ways, but mainly in three contexts. One was when the elder or members of his family fell on hard times and so needed poor relief, another was when surpluses in the poor-box became available to be disbursed as loans and the third was when contracts for church work were awarded to members of the session. All of these scenarios seem to have happened, although there is no evidence of wrongdoing in any of those cases seen and the use of burliemen at visitations suggests that efforts were made to keep transactions open and honest. In Alva, for example, one of the last minutes before the return of Richard Howieson records:

> The sd day the minr, knowing the straits of Alexander Young elder, & withal his modesty that he would not take any out of the box by way of charity, ordered the Treasurer to convey 40ss Scots as his necessities by way of loan, forbidding the Treasurer to seeke it back except it should please God to put him in a capacity to repay it.[54]

The designation 'elder' probably implies that he may have been the father of the 'other' Alexander Young, who was in fact the treasurer mentioned. Another elder was himself in receipt of a loan which was never repaid: 'By ticket by John Duncanson £12/7/8d which is concluded to be lost, the man having died in poverty.' John Duncanson was the one elder who did not continue under Howieson, but his handwriting at an earlier checking of the accounts suggests frailty.[55]

Meanwhile in Port of Menteith, and elsewhere, there are many instances of small payments to tradesmen who were also members of the session. In a rural community with a limited number of artisans in the parish, it would be natural to have recourse to those easily available. In April 1703, Robert Sands, an elder who was also a wright, was paid £28 for making Communion tables and seats and a desk for the minister's family, the money coming from both the mortcloth account and the poors' fund.[56] Three years later, in May 1706, James Turner was to 'be paid 12/- for nails for the black stool, for helping the chain of the bell and the slot of the kirk doors'.[57] Turner had served both as collector of the mortcloth money and as boxmaster of the session, so it must have been a severe blow to his pride when he had to confess to having been shoeing horses on the fast day in 1709 and told that he would not be allowed to take Communion at the upcoming sacrament nor attend session meetings unless he consented to be rebuked before the congregation on that very 'black stool' which he had been instrumental in making. He refused and was duly barred and deposed as an elder.[58]

Heritors and Patrons

As well as the kirk session, there was another group with a formal connection to the church, and that was the heritors, those who owned or leased land in the parish. Although they might sit in a formal meeting, and heritors' minutes do survive, none survive for Stirling or Dunblane presbyteries for the period under consideration. There was, naturally, a wide variation in the number of heritors in any given parish. A valuation roll of 1709 for Stirlingshire identifies 545 estates (there are some minor ones are alluded to but not identified) with numbers in each parish ranging from 118 in St Ninians to 3 in Alva with an average of 25.[59] Heritors might reside in the parish or not, according to individual circumstances. Many major landowners might have estates in many different areas of the country. The Earl of Mar, for example, had his home in Alloa, but also estates elsewhere in Clackmannanshire, as well as in Stirlingshire and Aberdeenshire, all of which would have given him a legal interest in the parishes involved.

The patron, who had had the right to nominate the minister, was sometimes the chief among the heritors but could be the crown or an institution such as a university or burgh council. Although an act of 1690 had removed the rights of nomination from patrons, this was looked on by many of them as a temporary aberration and the right was to be restored in 1712, outwith the timespan of this study but the source of much secession and schism over the next centuries.[60] However, even though the right of patronage had been removed, most of the parishes looking for a new minister paid at least lip-service to the previous arrangement, even still referring to the former patron by that term and consulting him or, more rarely, her as to their choice of minister.[61] Patrons and heritors were not necessarily sympathetic to the new regime and the support some of them provided to Episcopalians remaining, or indeed arriving, in their parishes after 1690 was crucial. Locally, Aberfoyle and Balquhidder in particular remained in Episcopalian hands due to the patrons' support of individuals despite the dukes of both Montrose and Atholl being Presbyterian, at least on paper.

It was the duty of the heritors to pay the minister's stipend, maintain the church and manse and provide the minister with a glebe and pasture for his horse. This was done via the payment of teinds (tithes), which were in turn raised from the tenants. As alluded to elsewhere, this meant that a minister or kirk session at odds with the heritors would have difficulty in having the church or manse repaired, or in some cases even built. The fact that many lairds were impecunious, particularly after the debacle of the Darien scheme,[62] did not help. Heritors also had legal rights and responsibilities such as being commissioners of supply, but in addition many had their own courts presided over by their own appointed bailie. As a result, a sympathetic heritor could be a real asset to the kirk session in backing up its discipline with civil penalties.[63]

However, while heritors had their responsibilities they also had rights, and competing claims of heritors who were not necessarily friends filled much of the time of sessions, who were called on to adjudicate on the allocation of space within churches. Each heritor would want his own 'loft' or 'desk' for himself, his family, his tenants and his servants. The potential for friction was substantial and in a parish like St Ninians, with its 118 heritors, the problems were virtually insoluble, especially when the lairds wanted their lofts embellished with additions which impeded the views of others. Diplomacy was a useful skill in sorting out allocations.

At the other end of the scale, Alva's reliance on only three heritors meant that nothing could be done while the chief heritor, who owned three quarters of the parish, was absent with the army for several years. Despite William Lindsay having left in 1696, no minister could be appointed until Sir John Erskine could be consulted, which did not happen until 1699.[64]

Presbytery visitations had to consult heritors as well as elders and, to a lesser extent, male heads of families. Almost the first item of business was to confirm with the minister that intimation had been made to resident heritors and letters of intimation sent to non-resident heritors. This was a considerable task in larger parishes and not one which would encourage frequent repetition. The heritors themselves might come in person, or send a representative such as their factor. As well as being asked the same questions as the elders about the minister, the meeting gave a chance for minister and session to complain about the lack of support given by the heritors and for the presbytery to try to resolve some of the issues. Similarly, when the time came to call a minister, the call would be signed by elders, heritors and heads of families, preserving the heritors' official status as a crucial part of the infrastructure of the church. Thus it was that the majority of the heritors in St Ninians in 1689, who loathed Patrick Couper and refused to countenance his moving from his meeting-house to the parish church, were able to say that they would accept a different Presbyterian minister even if they had no intention of supporting him.

As shown, some heritors, although not many, were elders too, but they might also have a role in some places as joint administrators of the mortcloth. Thus in St Ninians, the mortcloth committee included both the minister and several heritors who were firm supporters of the episcopal regime and they seem to have found a way to work together. Likewise the assent of the heritors was required for the appointment of a parish schoolmaster. James Hardie's appointment as schoolmaster of Port of Menteith in 1701 was resisted by four of the heritors but the majority view prevailed after the minister contacted all the heritors individually and finally he was appointed with the assent of the heritors as a whole.[65]

As quoted, at a national level, in the depths of the famine of the 1690s, the heritors were called upon to take at least some responsibility for poor relief. Acts of Parliament throughout the 1690s made assessment of heritors for poor relief at least an option, although Mitchison and Cullen suggest it was not universally enforced.[66] The church records locally do not show the extent to which this happened, but the kirk session of Port of Menteith met with the heritors to decide on methods for the maintenance of the poor and agreed that each heritor should maintain his own poor.[67]

After his removal to Tyninghame in East Lothian in 1699, one of George Turnbull's first acts in his new kirk session was to put poor relief on to a sustainable footing with a list of weekly pensioners (later made monthly). On 17 December he intimated a meeting of elders and heritors: 'The elders were appointed to meet with the minister 1 hour before the heritors that they may prepare matters for them.' The meeting duly decided that the pensioners would be given relief at various levels between 2s. and £1 and that the costs would be borne by tenants and householders equally.[68] Clearly there were limits as to what the parish could bear, but in this the church was still seen to play a paramount role, and to be in a position both to gauge need and act as a co-ordinator of relief available. It seems fair to suggest that Turnbull's actions reflected on his experiences in Alloa.

In conclusion, Walter Steuart of Pardovan summarised the role of the eldership in the following words:

> The power of their particular elderships is to use diligent labours in the bounds committed to their charge, that the kirks be kept in good order, to inquire diligently in naughtie and unruly persons, and travel to bring them in the way agine, either by admonition or threatning of God's judgements; or by correction.
>
> It pertains to the eldership to take heed that the word of God be purely preached within their bounds, that sacraments rightly ministred, the discipline rightly maintained, and the ecclesiastical goods uncorruptedly distributed.[69]

In essence that role had not been changed by the Revolution. Elders took their place in the higher courts of the church once more but the evidence is slight that the ordinary elder, who attended his kirk session week in, week out, had any meaningful impact on the wider life of the church. The role of the elders in the General Assembly was negligible unless they were landowners or lawyers. Most of these did not otherwise attend their local kirk session. Elders' attendance at synods was sporadic to say the least, attending only when the meeting was held locally. Even in presbytery their attendance was largely token, with many congregations being represented only at meetings concerning visitations or vacancies.

The influence of the elder was essentially local and remained so. Only at visitations did they have a chance to comment on how their minister functioned and whether the Word of God was being purely preached, and visitations were an early feature of the presbyteries which did not carry on long.[70] Within the parish their role was in serving on sacramental occasions, maintaining discipline and disbursing relief, and that did not change significantly for the next century.

Notes

1. Williamson, *A Sermon Preached in Edinburgh*, p. 57.
2. Inglis, 'The Impact of Episcopacy and Presbyterianism'.
3. Ibid., pp. 41–9.
4. Stirling, *Notes, Historical and Descriptive, on the Priory of Inchmahome*, Appendix 8.
5. NRS E69/19/1/78.
6. Ibid.
7. Stirling, *Notes, Historical and Descriptive, on the Priory of Inchmahome*, p. 171.
8. Inglis, *A Scottish Town*, pp. 36–7.
9. The clerks of both St Ninians sessions were irritatingly vague about the attendance of meetings, regularly giving about five names and adding 'etc.'. The Presbyterian session can be identified by the elders' ordination records, although presumably some were lost by death over the years.
10. SCA CH2/722/8 21/11/1694.
11. SCA CH2/722/8 27/12/1697.
12. In due course confusion was created by the service of the two Colonel Erskines not only as successive lieutenant-governors of Stirling Castle but as successive provosts of Stirling.
13. 'Putting to the horn' or 'horning' was a civil process involving publicity and a threat of outlawry if the issue were not resolved.
14. SCA CH2/1026/5 11/8/1697, 3/1/1700.
15. SCA CH2/1026/5 16/3/1698.
16. Mutch, 'To Bring the Work to Greater Perfection', p. 250.
17. Mutch, *Religion and National Identity*, p. 87.
18. SCA CH/722/9 28/5/1701, 16/9/1701.
19. Barclay, *Love, Intimacy and Power*, pp. 181–2.
20. Steuart of Pardovan, *Collections and Observations Methodiz'd*, p. 2.
21. Act anent Overtures concerning the Discipline and Method of proceeding in Ecclesiastic Judicatories, offered to the Assembly by a private hand: see 'Acts: 1697', in Church of Scotland, *Acts of the General Assembly of the Church of Scotland, 1638–1842*, pp. 256–67.
22. A discussion of the history of this topic can be found in Mutch, 'To Bring the Work to Greater Perfection', pp. 240–61.
23. Steuart of Pardovan, *Collections and Observations Methodiz'd*, p. 41.
24. SCA CH2/726/1 27/2/1699.
25. Mitchison, *The Old Poor Law in Scotland*; Cage, *The Scottish Poor Law, 1745–1845*; McCallum, *Poor Relief and the Church in Scotland, 1560–1650*.
26. Cullen, *Famine in Scotland*; Cullen, Whatley and Young, 'King William's Ill Years'.
27. SCA CH2/10/4 13/11/1715. A similar note is found in the Port of Menteith accounts SCA CH2/1300/1 13/11/1715.
28. Mutch, *Religion and National Identity*, pp. 106–30.
29. The boxmaster was the official responsible for the poor-box or other specific funds. Essentially it was a synonym for 'treasurer'.

30. NRS CH2/710/1, pp. 12–32.
31. That is, the ringing of the bell for funerals, and the use of a black velvet drape or pall to cover the coffin on its way to the graveyard. The rental of the latter could be a useful source of funds.
32. SCA CH2/942/6 21/11/1698.
33. Cullen, *Famine in Scotland*, pp. 28–9.
34. Paton (ed.), 'The Masterton Papers, 1660–1719', p. 471.
35. Cullen, Whatley and Young, 'King William's Ill Years', p. 260.
36. Mitchison, *The Old Poor Law in Scotland*, p. 41.
37. SCA CH2/1300/1 25/12/1698.
38. McCallum, *Poor Relief and the Church in Scotland, 1560–1650*, p. 236.
39. NRS CH2/710/2 15/2/1698.
40. '@rent' as it is described in the records.
41. SCA CH2/1026/5 21/9/1698, 16/3/1699, 16/8/1699.
42. SCA CH2/1026/5 12/7/1699.
43. Cullen, *Famine in Scotland*, p. 120.
44. An analysis of Alva's rather volatile collection records relating mainly to the vagaries of Episcopalian/Presbyterian control can be found in Appendix 3.
45. Kyd (ed.), *Scottish Population Statistics*, pp. 36, 45–6. These population figures do not reflect any demographic changes in the fifty-seven years between the period and Alexander Webster's census but are indicative of the relative populations of the parishes.
46. SCA CH2/1300/1 6/2/1708.
47. Mutch, *Religion and National Identity*, p. 119.
48. SCA CH2/942/6 26/10/1690, 9/11/1690, 19/11/1690.
49. Steuart of Pardovan, *Collections and Observations Methodiz'd*, p. 126 lays down that collections should either be taken at the church door coming in, or within the church at the end of the service before the blessing. The evidence seems to be that the former method was the more common in this period.
50. NRS CH2/710/1, p. 18.
51. Paton (ed.), 'Masterton Papers', p. 475.
52. Boston, *Memoirs*, p. 74.
53. SCA CH2/1300/1 26/6/1709.
54. SCA CH2/10/1 6/4/1690.
55. SCA CH2/10/4 1/11/1702.
56. SCA CH2/1300/1 13/4/1703.
57. SCA CH2/1300/1 5/5/1706.
58. SCA CH2/1300/1 12/6/1709.
59. Davies, 'Law and Order in Stirlingshire, 1637–1747', Appendix 4 analyses the numbers and valuations of each estate. The roll includes fourteen parishes not in Stirling Presbytery and excludes the Burgh of Stirling and three parishes in Clackmannanshire which were in the presbytery. It also includes the Stirlingshire portions of two parishes split between counties and within Dunblane Presbytery.
60. Whitley, *A Great Grievance*, p. 96.
61. Lady Alva and Lady Cardross were both consulted by Stirling Presbytery. SCA CH2/722/8 2/2/1693, 10/3/1697, 1/1/1699.
62. The ill-judged and ill-fated attempt to plant a Scottish colony in Darien in Panama was both an economic and a human catastrophe, leading to the loss of

about 30 per cent of Scottish wealth. Many people and institutions in the area of this study lost significant amounts.

63. For a full discussion of the rights and responsibilities of heritors and patrons see Whitley, *A Great Grievance*, particularly Chapter 5.
64. SCA CH2/722/8 1/3/1699. Sir John Erskine of Alva asked for settlement of the parish to be delayed until his return from Paris.
65. SCA CH2/1300/1 30/11/1701, 8/12/1701.
66. Mitchison, *The Old Poor Law in Scotland*, pp. 35–43; Cullen, *Famine in Scotland*, p. 121.
67. SCA CH2/1300/1 25/12/1698.
68. NRS CH2/359/3 23/11/1699.
69. Steuart of Pardovan, *Collections and Observations Methodiz'd*, p. 273.
70. Mutch, *Religion and National Identity*, pp. 62–3.

CHAPTER SIX

Celebrating the Sacraments

The Sacrament of Communion: An 'Occasion' and its Impact

These [privileges] which the Church and People of God enjoy, are indeed Precious and Valuable in their native excellency and worth, in their Divine Original, in the Puritie of their Purchase, and in their blessed and glorious Effects; on which Accounts they are preferable to all the gold of Ophir.[1]

There are two regular narratives regarding the celebration of the sacrament of Communion in eighteenth-century Scotland. One is that of the 'sealing' or 'converting' ordinance, a sacrament crucially important in the life of the church which brings those involved, or some of them, to a surer knowledge of God and of their own inadequacy, leading if not to an expectation, at least to a hope, for their own salvation. The second narrative is that of the 'Holy Fair', an event which has its religious significance accompanied, and sometimes overwhelmed, by its place in popular, secular entertainment. However, a third, possibly overlapping, narrative is also possible, that of a public ritual performance, and it is to this narrative that at least some of the post-Revolution occasions belong.

Under the episcopal regime, the annual celebration of Communion was encouraged. The diocesan synod book of Dunblane has many references to the ministers being asked whether they had celebrated the sacrament, or giving excuses for their failure to do so. The common excuse, as George Schaw explained to the Bishop of Dunblane in 1683, was that 'they had not all administered the sacrament to their people this year, because the maist pairt of them were not in a capacitie to give it, neither the people to receive it'.[2] Among the many shortcomings ascribed to Episcopalian ministers in the post-1689 Privy Council registers is the failure to celebrate the sacrament of Communion.[3]

It cannot be said with certainty that the Presbyterian churches did not celebrate Communion within the bounds of Dunblane or Stirling presbyteries in the years between the Toleration and the re-establishment of Presbyterianism after the Revolution. The records are too piecemeal to be sure, but where records do exist, it was often several years before preparations for the service are mentioned.[4]

Even nationally there was a marked reluctance to celebrate the sacrament. Elisabeth West records in her memoirs that August 1694 saw 'the sacrament in Edinburgh, which was the first after the Revolution, and the first ever I was partaker of'.[5] This reluctance to hold Communion services was not universal, and West's statement may be true only for Edinburgh itself. In neighbouring South Leith, on the other hand, the Presbyterian meeting-house celebrated Communion in 1692, having also had a celebration the month before the Revolution.[6]

George Turnbull's diary records that he had previously received the sacrament in Rotterdam in 1684, in London in 1687 prior to his ordination and again in March of 1688, six weeks after his ordination as a minister. The first time he helped to officiate was a year later when he was minister of the meeting-house at Dalmeny and served two tables in neighbouring Queensferry, probably assisting John Dalgleish. Having been inducted to Alloa in the autumn of 1690, Turnbull twice undertook the visitation of his parish before he added four new elders to his session and announced the sacrament day to be on 23 October 1692.[7] His diary only records the fact and the names of those assisting him, not any comment about the occasion.

Turnbull was relatively prompt in his arrangements. As already mentioned, Dunblane Presbytery's visitation to Tillicoultry in May 1698 recommended that the minister should administer the sacrament within the year as he had not done so since his arrival in March 1692.[8] Similarly, Arthur Forbes in Port of Menteith waited six years before he first suggested celebrating Communion in 1703. In Port's case, preparations had been in hand for a year as a new Communion table was ordered in July 1702,[9] a full year before the actual celebration.

Among the most meticulously recorded preparations were in the Burgh Kirk of Stirling. Here, Communion did not take place until 1699 and was the first in the church since the episcopal days of 1687. There had, however, been an Episcopalian celebration locally in 1698. Unusually, and even more scandalously, it was reported that 'Mr George Brown, a stranger, hath resided in this congregation for a considerable tyme without any testimonial that he setts up the English liturgy here and administers the sacraments after the manner of the Church of England'.[10]

This may have been the spur for the kirk session; certainly, there is an implication that the decision to hold the service in 1699 was hurried. The session meeting which outlined the procedure was held *pro re nata*, in other words to deal with a matter that was newly arisen outwith the normal sequence of meetings. However, the approaching Communion season was expected, for one of the elders, John Burd, a former bailie whose suspension from the eldership for drunkenness and wife beating in August 1697 was noted in Chapter 5, petitioned the session successfully in early April 1699 to be restored to its membership in time for Communion.[11] The session record is a detailed action plan:

> The session having determined that God willing the sacrament of the Lord's supper will be celebrated in this place the last

Sabbath of May being twentie eight instant, Do hereby order Bailie Allan one of their own number to represent to the magistrates and town Council the necessity of having the Elements timeously provided.

It is also recommended to the Boxmasters to see the Communion tables and formes repaired fixed and in good order, the Cups and basons cleansed as also the table cloth. It is intrusted to Baylie Don to cause to make fifteen hundred tokens and have them ready in due time. John Chrystie and Henry Fogo are nominat to view the lofts in the Church and report against the next.[12]

A further meeting filled in more detail:

Ordered that the seats in the body of the church be removed to give way for the sacrament table.

Appointed ruling elders the Lieutenant Governour at one end of the table and Provost Napier at the other to receive in the communicants and keep the people from thronging in upon the table or any other disorder.

For the Bread, Baylie Burd and Thomas Gillespie.

For the Cups, Ensign Traill, Baylie Chrystie, Logie[13] and James Willison. For the four flagons with the wine are nominat John Stivenson to wait on Ensign Traill, Walter Allan to attend Baylie Chrystie, Harie Fogo to wait on Logie, and William Allan to attend James Willison which four serving with the flagons are likewise appointed to receive the tokens from the communicants.

For the drawing of the wine the Church and Town thesaurers.

Collection of the Oblation are nominat Baylie Allan, Baylie Don, Baylie Chrystie and Baylie Burd to assist the Dean of Guild and the Convener. The Basons for the collection being to stand, the one on the highway opposite to Mr Rule's door, the other at the head of the steps which lyeth towards the Backraw.

Thomas Gillespie, John Anderson, Patrick Stevenson and John Stivenson are nominat for the Easter Church door, John Chrystie and William Murray for Argyle's loft and are so to admit persons into the church as prudently and discreetly as is possible that all disorder and confusion may be evited.

Intimation to be made on Thursday next that sermon will begin on Saturday before the Sacrament at one of the clock in the afternoon. On Sunday morning the Work beginneth at eight. On Monday sermon begins at nine in the forenoon.

All that have a mind to communicate are to wait upon the ministers on Thursday next immediately after sermon to receive their tokens. Those of the third and fourth quarter with the elders thereof are to attend Mr Rule[14] at the Session house, those of the first and second quarter, with Mr Forrester[15] in the Church.

> Any in the neighbouring paroches who are to be partakers are to repair to their Ministers who may receive the tokens from them or bring a Certificate or ane elder or two to the Minister of the Congregation and they shall be waited upon.
>
> To be intimated that these in this Congregation Entertain Strangers kindly.
>
> Also considering the present necessitous state of the poor, all are to be put in mind to extend their charity.[16]

Clearly a hierarchy of the eldership was in place and adhered to. The places of greatest honour and authority were occupied by Provost Napier and Lieutenant-Colonel Erskine, representing burgh and crown. The next most prestigious roles, those of administering the elements of bread and wine, were assigned to the other army officer, two bailies, magistrates of the town, and the one laird who served on the session. It should be noted that the titles of provost and bailie do not necessarily refer to the current holders of these roles but to men who had filled them in the recent past.[17] The actual pouring of the wine was shared between the burgh treasurer and the kirk session's treasurer, the burgh council, as chief heritor of the parish, having paid for its purchase.

Similar status-defined arrangements were a feature of Communion both before and after the revolution. An example in Montrose in 1687 shows town bailies at the head of the tables, with one responsible also for the collection at the kirk door.[18] The Stirling arrangements can be interpreted as showing a symbolic partnership of the two kingdoms: the earthly kingdom, represented by the army and the magistrates, working together in balance and harmony with God's kingdom as represented by the church.

If this highly stage-managed event was a feature of a clearly hierarchical structure like a burgh, it was not necessarily so in a less structured non-urban parish. Logie was a country parish contiguous to Stirling. Alone of the churches in the presbyteries of Dunblane and Stirling, its minister had come to a pre-Revolution meeting-house in 1688 and stayed, taking over the parish church three years later on the deposition of George Schaw. Here too there was a substantial gap before the sacrament was celebrated in the parish.

In the summer of 1696, eight years after the induction of Alexander Douglas into Logie meeting-house the session minutes read as follows:

> 22nd June; The session condescended that the Sacrament of the Lord's Supper should be administered in the congregation (if the Lord wishes) on the first Lord's Day of August nixt to come and appropriate intimation hereof to be made by the Minister from the pulpit upon Sabbath next.
>
> 22nd July; It being represented to the session that there was visible differences and jars betwixt several families and persons in the congregation, the session judged it fit that these be taken up before the

Communion. Therefore it is recommended to the elders in their respective quarters to take seriously variance, difference or jars that [may] be betwixt families or persons and to endeavour through the Lord's strength to reconcile them one to another and to exhort them to live as brethren in peace and amity and to report to the session if there be any families or persons in the congregation that refused to be reconciled one to another.[19]

As in the Burgh Kirk three years later, part of this reconciliation process included a suspended elder, John Henderson, who was readmitted as an elder having acknowledged his previous guilt for drunkenness and fighting. It does seem to have been crucial that the sacrament only be celebrated in a spirit of local harmony.

The elements to be ordered were carefully calculated. Sixteen double loaves were ordered from James Alexander, a baker in Dunblane, and twenty-one pints and a chopin of claret from Stirling.[20]

By 28 July, the roles for the actual administration were allocated. Elders reported that all 'variance, differences and jars' were resolved among those who intended to communicate. Four elders were allocated to ingather the collections on the Fast Day (Thursday), Saturday and Monday, and eight on the Sunday of the actual sacrament. As in Stirling specific roles were allocated to each of the elders, a one-way system instituted for communicants, times agreed for the various services and John Henderson and the beddall deputed to go to Stirling for the wine after the sermons on Saturday.[21]

In this case, it has not been possible to analyse the social status of the various elders to see whether their responsibilities were proportionate to their importance, but it is clear that importance was laid on each man knowing his own role, and on the orderly distribution of the elements. Oddly there is no reference to the sacrament actually having been administered within the minutes, the only reference being to the disbursement to 108 poor people of the collection of £60 4s. 6d. collected at the time.[22] The following year the arrangements show a smaller number of elders designated to gather in the collection, presumably as a result of the previous year's experience.[23]

Leaving aside the idea of the sacrament of Communion as ritual, two other narratives have to be considered: Communion as a healing or converting process, and Communion as public entertainment. Leigh Schmidt's *Holy Fairs; Scotland and the Making of American Revivalism* refers to 'the quickness with which this eucharistic festival became an established feature of evangelical life after 1688' and adduces as evidence John Sage's savage and sarcastic attack in his 'Fundamental Charter':[24]

> It stands fair to be a Scare-crow to the weak Christian; He dares not approach, where there is so much frightening Address; It stands as fair for being a scandal to the strong and understanding Christian, when

he sees so much vain shew, so much needless ostentation, so much odd, external tricking about it; And the Hypocrite can hardly wish anything more useful for him; For who should doubt of his being a Saint, when he approaches, amidst so much solemnity?[25]

There were contemporary concerns about 'the great confluence of people'. Despite Schmidt's quoting Turnbull and Thomas Boston as evidence, there are few signs at this early stage of the unruliness which was to become common later, but the arrangements do show that the fear of disturbance was there. As well as this, the size of the collections compared to the normal Sunday offering may suggest greater numbers. Additionally there was a degree of moving round the various celebrations as there would be no preaching in those churches whose ministers were participating in neighbouring parishes.

Neither is there evidence for large-scale conversion or revival at this stage. Boston himself described how the ninety-nine people attending his first Communion in Ettrick had increased to 770 at his final one in 1731. This latter figure is twice the population of the parish as enumerated twenty years later by Webster. On the other hand, at the sacramental occasion of 1699 in Stirling, 1,500 tokens were made for the communicants in a burgh which Webster identified as having 3,951 examinable persons, which suggests that there was not a large-scale influx.[26] There was, however, sufficient concern about disorder that the elders were commissioned to stop it, and a few years later two of the ministers of Stirling Presbytery were detailed to draw up an overture for preventing disorder at the distribution of Communion tokens.[27]

There is no doubt that taking, or even simply observing, the sacrament could have a huge effect on the individual. This was not a period for the mass conversion/revival experiences of the 1740s, but many writers describe the effect on themselves as individuals. Turnbull himself tended to be sparing in his emotional engagement: at his first celebration in Alloa, in 1692 he simply noted that 'there were eight tables served'.[28] Three years later, however, he noted 'a good day of the gospel here' and in growing enthusiasm, his 1697 occasion he described as 'a great day of the gospel here; the Lord follow it with lasting blessing'.[29] Nonetheless, there is nothing in his diary or in his session minutes to suggest any sort of revival as a result. It would appear that it was still an individual response.

Two women of the time, and lower-class women at that, have left their testimonies about their spiritual experiences. One, Elisabeth West, spent much of her free time following the Communion season round Edinburgh and its environs looking for 'gospel light' and it is to her testimony that much present knowledge is indebted. To what extent this was encouraged is unclear, but even in 1688 Robert Rule seemed to support West's view. Preaching at a preparatory service in Edinburgh, he said: 'Ye must be like the bee that goes from flower to flower seeking honey, so ye must go from one ordinance to another and your design must be this, the great thing that ye seek is Jesus.'[30]

West did not visit the Stirling area, although she did visit Tyninghame twice later in Turnbull's ministry there, having two different responses.[31] Elizabeth Cairns, on the other hand, was local to Stirling in as much as she was brought up just outside the presbytery bounds, in Blackford in Perthshire, and moved to Stirling as a young woman in about 1708. Her memoirs, posthumously published in 1762, show, like West's, the very real effect that the combination of preaching and the taking of the sacrament had on her. The first Communion service which she attended was at an unspecified place in 1702 when she was seventeen years of age:

> The place where the Lord's supper was to be celebrated was a good way off. On the preparation day, the two texts were wonderfully ordered for me, the one was for my trial, the other for my consolation. The one was on Jeremiah 30; 21 'Who is he that changeth his heart'. The other was in John 3; 16; 'For God so loved the world . . .' This was a sweet day to me, but on the Sabbath morning I was sore straitned for I could neither pray nor meditate. In the first sermon I was again revived; the text was Prov 8; 4 The whole of the sermon was good. There was a word in the close of the sermon with which, I hope, power came, Take Christ in the arms of the love, and thou shalt have him.
>
> With this word there shined a light in my soul and immediately I arose and went to the table, believing it would be as the Minister said. And while I was partaking, there shined a light into my soul more brighter than the former and continued in less or more for the space of half a year.[32]

A few years later Cairns moved to Stirling and again described her almost mystical experiences at the sacrament: 'On the Sabbath Morning and through the Day it was like a Day of Heaven to me. And at the Table, my glorious Redeemer revealed himself to my Soul, and brought me near, and filled me full with the Sense of his Love . . .' The Thanksgiving service on the Monday was as effective for her. The minister preached on a text from Habakkuk: 'This was a remarkable sermon to me, from which I was sent home rejoicing.'[33]

Cairns in particular stresses that the whole sacramental experience – services on Thursday (Fast), Saturday (Preparation), Sunday (Sacrament), Monday (Thanksgiving) – was a single event, and that the multiple sermons were as important to her as the actual receiving of the elements. But as with West, hers was also an entirely private response, and not necessarily visible even to the minister.

It is clear both from bibliographies of published sermons and from Turnbull's diary that sacramental sermons tended to use texts not taken at other times. Not only did Turnbull break the sequence of his ordinary when the Communion season came round, but of the fifty-eight Communion texts listed, only seven were used at other times. Nine were from the Psalms, but five of those were from Psalms he never otherwise used as header texts. Only two sermons came from a book not otherwise preached from: The Song of Solomon. This book was somewhat of a shibboleth as it was a favourite of Presbyterians and shunned by Episcopalians. Turnbull's use of it twice, six years apart and neither time in his own church, is nonetheless a statement of his faithfulness to Covenanting tradition, but not perhaps of an overriding attachment.[34]

Practical arrangements for holding the sacrament are sprinkled liberally through church records and show that such an event had an economic impact for the local population. As well as the supply of the elements, the provision of linen and its sewing into cloths of the right size, the removal and replacement of pews which were in the way and the casting of lead Communion tokens all brought benefit to local merchants or tradesmen. On the other hand, the hospitality required to be given to visitors could be a serious drain on local resources in bad times. Though rarely mentioned as an issue, the influx of strangers must have been a challenge, and the lack of Communion services in the 1690s may in part be a reflection of the poor economic circumstances. A generation later, in 1729, Thomas Boston was constrained to cancel a Communion season in Ettrick:

> the people being withal straitened for victual to maintain their families, that I could not find it in my heart to burden them with the strangers resorting to them on such occasions in great numbers . . . It would be hard to get as much hay or straw in the parish as to make beds for strangers.[35]

One crucial arrangement for the Sacrament which has left little record in the minutes was the sharing of the work with other ministers. The number of people participating in the sacrament was usually much greater than the normal population of the parish, and as the numbers were physically limited by the size of the table which all sat round, the process had to be repeated many times through the day. The 'home' minister would preach the 'action sermon' but others would preach in the churchyard for the edification of those waiting their turn or not communicating. The additional services on the Thursday, Saturday and Monday would also have guest preachers taking part. This might in itself have implications for the minister's home economy as he might be expected to entertain the visitors. Some session minutes do mention wine being provided, and on occasion transport for visiting ministers.[36] There can be no doubt that, stressful as it was, the Communion season gave ministers opportunities to have fellowship with their brethren, exchange ideas and recharge their batteries from the isolation of conducting services week by week on their own.

Turnbull's diary lists those with whom he celebrated the sacrament both in his own parish and as a visitor and it is possible to build up a picture of ministerial networks through that. It was expected to invite neighbours, but also friends and those of a like mind. Turnbull regularly worked with Thomas Buchanan, his brother-in-law in Tulliallan, even after his move to Tyninghame; he rarely co-operated with his other brother-in-law, Adam Glass, minister of Aberlady and a close neighbour to Tyninghame, who was later to be deposed for deserting his charge and ultimately became a Church of England curate. Turnbull often seems to have made a point of inviting the most recent local addition to his presbytery to join with him in Tyninghame. Similarly, Arthur Forbes, minister of Port of Menteith, assisted his brother-in-law at Communion occasions in Bathgate as well as assisting in local parishes such as Balfron or Kilmadock. By intimating such to his congregation, he gave them the opportunity to attend the sacrament at nearby churches.

Aside from the mundane organisational elements of the sacramental season, a more important preparation was to make the people ready, and this also partly explains the infrequency of celebration. Mention has been made of the 'jars' between people in Logie in 1688 which inhibited Alexander Douglas there. The need for a congregation to be at peace with itself was important. So too was the need for the people to understand the import of the sacrament, and this was achieved by the minister visiting and catechising the people to determine the level of their understanding. Just before the Communion season the minister and the local elders would visit the various quarters and districts of the parish to distribute the tokens to those deemed worthy. Those under discipline were excluded but so also were those who were under suspicion. John Spalding, minister in Dundee, left his script for the administration of Communion, which was published in 1703. He 'fenced the table' (barred the unworthy) in a long address which included these words: 'I am by virtue of the Keys of the Kingdom committed to us Ministers, to shut the Door of this Ordinance upon those whom Christ hath judged unworthy thereof, and to exclude Swine from these pearls.'[37]

In Port in 1709, the session not only barred the elder who had refused to accept discipline for shoeing horses on a fast day, but,

> being informed that several of the tenants of the Barronie of Port had openly and contemptuously prophaned the fast day late by past, ... by filling their meal sacks upon Tuesday morning and transported the same openly from Milling upon the said day. The Session judged that none of those persons who were that guilty should be allowed access to the Table of the Lord on the following Occasion.[38]

It is interesting that Spalding saw it as the minister's prerogative to bar the unworthy, while Forbes in Port allowed the kirk session to take responsibility.

Perhaps because of the precautions taken, the unruly tradition of the 'Holy Fair' does not seem to have had any appearance in Stirling or Dunblane presbyteries at this time. Elsewhere, the effect of the Communion season on public order was evident by 1711, when John Wilson, minister of North Leith, brought a report to his kirk session which alluded to 'the great profanation of the Lord's day by the flocking of Multitudes of idle People to the West Kirk, Cannongate [*sic*] and Leith Churches when the Sacrament of the Lord's Supper is administrate there upon pretence to hear Sermon in the Churchyard'.[39]

One hundred years after the events described in this chapter, some of the ministers of the period were memorialised by John Brown, Secession minister of Whitburn, in his *Gospel Truth Stated and Illustrated*, a biographical volume devoted to evangelical ministers. In it there were brief notices of John Warden, 'a man well seen in the doctrines of free grace', and John McLaren, who 'had a most fertile imagination, which abounded with instructive similes in his sermons, by which he both instructed and delighted his hearers'. To celebrate Alexander Hamilton, minister of Airth, Brown was inspired to quote Ralph Erskine's verse elegy:

> At Airth this silver trumpet long did sound,
> To solemn feasts convening thousands round.
> . . .
> Laid in the word, insured by Jesus death . . .
> He shone 'bove others with superior light,
> The Gospel warrants, and the grounds of faith.

But again, the eulogy for Hamilton is centred on his sacramental occasions in almost revivalist fashion. Alone of the local ministers covered, James Brisbane was initially described in critical terms: 'For some time after he came to that place, his views of the gospel were dark and incorrect, but soon becoming acquainted and intimate with Mr Hamilton of Airth, he obtained clear and accurate views of gospel truth.'[40] The whole tenor of Brown's description, though, is clearly coloured by his view of his subjects' attitude to the Marrow Controversy and their role as early presagers of the Secession of the 1730s led by one of the Stirling ministers, Ebenezer Erskine. Nonetheless his descriptions of their effect on their listeners, particularly at Communion services, serve to emphasise the centrality that was held by the sacrament of Communion.

Even an account of the celebration in St Ninians a generation later, in 1725, by an anonymous and rather disapproving English visitor refers to the great numbers attending. Alluding to the reputation for trouble, he qualified it by recording:

> I am told there are frequent disorders amongst those poor people . . . who being to make a whole day of it at the place where they meet cannot be supposed wholly to abstain from meat and drink and sometimes go to an excess in the latter. But as I saw nothing of this kind, I cannot charge them with it.[41]

And again: 'It was a rainy day, but they sat or stood it out with great patience and attention to what the twentieth part of them could not possibly hear one word of.'

The sacrament of Communion was central to the Presbyterian Church of Scotland as it had been during Episcopalian times, despite the apparent reluctance of many ministers to celebrate it. Its significance was different for different people: for those steeped in the Covenanter tradition there was a deep spiritual and personal resonance which nonetheless was seen as dangerous and enthusiastic by those of a different view; for those organising it and involved in the celebration and distribution it was a symbolic ritual highlighting the central position of the church in society; for the ministers it had elements of both aspects and their reluctance to celebrate it can be put down to an unwillingness to devalue the occasion by embarking upon it before they were convinced of the readiness and worthiness of their congregation to take part in it.

Baptism

Compared to the meticulous arrangements which some churches recorded making for the sacrament of Communion, the sacrament of baptism seems to have been approached more casually. Perhaps this is because it was celebrated far more often, but its impact on participants and observers seems to have been much less. While the literature of revivalism and evangelicalism is firmly rooted in the sacrament of Communion, baptism is rarely, if ever, mentioned.

It was however, celebrated far more often than Communion. In the largest parish in this study, St Ninians, there was an average of 186 baptisms per year through the period, equating to one for every thirty-five inhabitants. The figures from the other parishes whose records survive average out at about one baptism to forty inhabitants, ranging from a peculiarly fecund figure of one to twenty-nine in Alva to a very low one to eighty-five in Kilmadock (see Table 6.1). It should, however, be recognised that baptismal records have a very uneven survival rate.

The turmoil of the Revolution clearly shows in the variation in numbers. In a curious reversal, Episcopalian St Ninians had 63 baptisms recorded in 1687 against 133 in the neighbouring Burgh of Stirling, a proportion which almost reversed the following year to 143 and 85 respectively. This latter proportion then persisted for the next twenty years, but with the burgh figures dropping very significantly in 1693 and 1694, when the Presbyterians were finally consolidating their hold on the burgh. The lowness of the numbers may well be connected with the fact that Stirling Presbytery was engaged through 1694 in trying to wrest the records and Communion utensils back from the council.[42]

The same challenge of retrieving the record books is recorded for several other parishes in the two presbyteries, Clackmannan, Dunblane and Kilmadock among them.[43] The low figures for many of the parishes, for example Kilmadock and Tillicoultry, in those early years may suggest that many of the children were being baptised elsewhere than in the parish

Table 6.1 Number of Baptisms Recorded, 1687–1710

Parish	Presb.	1687	1688	1689	1690	1691	1692	1693	1694	1695	1696	1697	1698	1699	1700	1701	1702	1703	1704	1705	1706	1707	1708	1709	1710
Aberfoyle	Dun	x	x	x	x	x	32	26	x	x	x	x	x	6	18	38	36	45	33	37	54	32	35	34	27
Airth	Sti	74	78	63	37	22	42	30	55	49	37	37	49	34	38	83	80	89	67	95	65	75	91	76	75
Alloa	Sti	106	106	107	100	127	96	120	133	132	116	95	112	95	78	93	123	111	113	100	112	102	110	101	107
Alva	Sti	14	21	17	17	12	13	18	13	9	15	5	9	14	19	13	30	24	26	28	38	19	17	18	17
Balquhidder	Dun	x	x	x	x	x	x	x	x	x	11	18	12	25	24	13	14	16	10	5	31	30	31	5	10
Bothkennar	Sti	x	x	x	x	x	x	x	x	x	x	x	x	x	x	x	x	x	x	x	x	x	x	x	x
Callander	Dun	x	x	x	x	x	x	x	x	x	x	x	x	x	x	x	x	x	x	x	x	x	x	x	22
Clackmannan	Sti	68	76	77	65	73	89	32	67	66	62	32	38	34	29	82	91	81	93	82	87	85	98	75	65
Denny	Sti	40	52	39	10	7	40	46	43	71	36	24	50	29	30	46	16	27	27	28	49	24	37	20	54
Dollar	Sti	x	x	x	x	x	x	x	x	x	x	x	x	x	x	14	33	21	18	16	22	21	26	22	19
Dunblane	Dun	72	73	41	19	31	18	99	114	82	101	83	89	72	59	84	69	82	84	66	73	68	72	70	72
Dunipace	Sti	x	x	x	x	x	x	x	x	x	x	x	x	x	x	x	x	x	x	x	x	x	3	14	17
Gargunnock	Sti	22	3	1	33	10	29	28	18	13	10	11	9	0	14	30	16	31	28	21	41	31	37	33	28
Kilmadock	Dun	37	96	64	18	25	6	0	46	65	70	50	64	6	36	41	11	22	9	30	32	19	8	50	17
Kincardine	Dun	x	x	x	x	19	14	15	6	29	41	32	41	35	25	28	41	31	42	25	35	40	41	52	40
Kippen	Sti	x	x	x	x	x	x	x	x	x	x	x	x	x	32	36	49	47	47	46	44	56	19	50	36
Larbert	Sti	x	x	x	x	x	x	x	x	x	x	x	x	x	x	x	x	x	x	x	x	x	x	x	x
Lecropt	Dun	x	x	x	x	x	x	x	x	x	x	x	x	x	x	x	x	x	x	x	x	x	x	x	x
Logie	Dun	x	26	54	26	83	74	65	42	43	42	36	58	51	42	55	41	46	44	49	49	45	43	53	40
Port of Menteith	Dun	x	x	x	x	x	x	x	x	x	x	18	35	31	27	50	56	54	41	51	71	50	66	55	49
St Ninians	Sti	63	143	210	175	176	178	96	150	188	170	151	194	148	141	203	225	223	201	201	228	206	216	232	178
Stirling	Sti	133	85	63	52	72	85	35	41	90	100	88	110	89	105	101	138	107	118	61	119	x	x	x	x
Tillicoultry	Sti	26	26	23	3	0	31	46	29	32	42	34	38	31	15	23	31	22	30	8	18	15	30	15	19

Note 1: Dunipace was linked with Larbert throughout the period: it seems to have had a separate kirk session and separate baptismal register.
Note 2: 'x' denotes no surviving records.
Source: ScotlandsPeople, https://www.scotlandspeople.gov.uk/

church, that parallel registers were kept which have not survived, or that children were not baptised until the situation became clearer.

Even where the records do survive, there was a wide range of diligence in keeping them. The standard of recording probably reached its nadir in the parish of Balquhidder: 'Patrick Ferguson in Glenogle, 3 Dec 1696 had a child baptised.'[44] At the opposite end of the spectrum, in 1702 Stirling Burgh Kirk recorded both parents' names, sometimes the father's occupation, the child's name, the names of the witnesses with designation where appropriate, and the date.[45] Many of the parishes were less than consistent in recording the mother's name. Occasionally the name of the minister officiating is also added where he was not the parish minister. Stirling was also quite rare at this time in naming the witnesses, as very often the formula was simply 'in the presence of the congregation'.

When a church was vacant it was normal for the number of baptisms to drop. Baptism can only be carried out by an ordained minister, and so if pulpit supply was provided by probationers, as was usually the case, baptisms were postponed until a minister was available. This was one of the reasons that a vacant charge was normally supplied once a month by a neighbouring minister. The records of Airth show the names of the various ministers who took their turn.[46] In the years of vacancy prior to Alexander Hamilton's arrival in 1700 there was an average of forty baptisms per year; from his first full year, Hamilton averaged eighty per year.

Not only the local church circumstances influenced the figures, however. Any discussion of the 'ill years' of William's reign will quote the drop in the birth-rate as evidenced in the parish records. Karen Cullen's *Famine in Scotland* examines a sampled set of baptism records to show regional differences, but with every area having a significant drop in the birth-rate.[47] Only one of Stirling and Dunblane presbyteries' parishes is included in Cullen's analysis, but consideration of all the surviving records confirms that although the picture changed from parish to parish, virtually every one showed a drop in numbers in 1697 (see Table 6.1). Evidence from other years is less clear, but the period 1699–1700 also shows widespread decreases. Cullen's analysis suggests that, as represented by the birth-rate, the 'east lowlands' had a higher resilience than other areas of Scotland. Within the two presbyteries, the numbers of baptisms do seem to show a 25 per cent increase between the two seven-year periods 1694–1700 and 1701–7 but there are many issues with the figures and it is not probably safe to make too dogmatic an assertion, especially as parishes as different as Denny and Kilmadock seemed to show significant reductions in the birth-rate in the post-famine period. As a side issue, it is curious that while the birth-rate may have dropped, the number of marriages taking place in the bad years seem, if anything, to have risen. Sadly no burial records survive for the period in any of the parishes.

Having looked at the figures, what can be gleaned about the actual process? Turnbull's diary records his participation, frequently mentioning the numbers of children involved, but not mentioning any impact on those present, even when it was his own child being baptised, usually by a neighbouring minister. The entry for his eldest son, William, baptised on 19 April 1696, shows that Thomas Buchanan, minister of Tulliallan, baptised the child, but Turnbull preached as usual. Buchanan's name is also given in the baptismal register, the whole entry being in a different hand from the rest of the register. When his third son, George, was born in July 1698, it was Mr Gourlaw, minister of Tillicoultry, who baptised him. This time it was on the Friday, the child having been born on the Monday. The situation was perhaps complicated by Turnbull's ill-health. Gourlaw had preached for him the previous Sunday and there was no sermon the Sunday after the baptism. In this instance the entry in the register is in the same hand as the rest and there is no mention of a different minister having been the celebrant.[48]

Perhaps because of the frequency of baptisms, there is little if any trace of the occasion of a baptism being reflected in the sermon preached. The surviving sermons of George Turnbull from 1691 include two when children were baptised but the sermon bears no specific relevance to them.[49]

A different pattern can be found in Alva. When Harie Robine, minister of Alva, had his child baptised in 1709, the record simply says he 'had a daughter baptised as Jean' with 'George John Wylie [sic] minister of Clackmannan' as witness, so it is not clear whether Wylie might have performed the baptism. Incidentally, the next entry is the baptism of the laird's son, where one of the witnesses was 'Mr Alexr. Ross (Chaplain)'.[50]

According to the *Westminster Directory* of 1645, which was loosely followed as the only official guidance on the conduct of worship, baptism had to take place in the face of the congregation, and not in private. Both baptismal records and indeed Turnbull's diary show that it was frequently performed on weekdays, but as most parishes had midweek services this may be a reflection of that, and certainly Turnbull was preaching on the occasions that he baptised midweek. The other possibility is the children were baptised while the minister was doing his rounds catechising his flock as he was meant to do each year. It would only be a small stretch of the rules to gather a group of neighbours for the purpose and treat them as a congregation. Such an occasion would also have the added bonus of letting the minister gauge whether the father of the child was sufficiently aware of the purpose of the sacrament to be allowed to sponsor his child.

The question of the baptism of children 'born under scandal' was one which exercised Stirling Presbytery in particular, though Dunblane less so. The rule was normally that the parties should 'give satisfaction' before the child could be baptised or alternatively some other person, perhaps a grandfather, could stand as sponsor. In 1695, Hugh Whyte, minister of Larbert, was authorised by the presbytery to baptise the child of Margaret Richardson and George Williamson (born in adultery) if a person free from scandal would present the child and take responsibility for its education.[51] On other occasions, if the father was not known, the kirk session itself could stand as sponsor.

There does seem to have been a strong imperative on parents to have their children baptised, an imperative that may well have been the factor that made them submit to the discipline of the kirk session. Another adulterer who wanted his child baptised was the Laird of Clackmannan, one of whose mistresses gave birth to his child in Edinburgh in 1693. The laird had his servant take the child to a local celebrant, Mr Naughty, residing in Cowgate,[52] to be baptised. With only the servant and a nurse present, it is hard to see just why the laird took this course of action, especially when he did not attend in person.[53]

Like clandestine and irregular marriages, irregular baptisms took place in some numbers, especially among those who declined to accept Presbyterianism. Unlike marriages, which had to be acknowledged in order that the couple might live openly, baptisms were more easily concealed. The presbytery did not take action in the parishes where an Episcopalian remained as incumbent, but if an episcopal minister acted in any other parish attempts were made to stop the practice. Action against James Hunter, former minister of Stirling, was stopped when it was made clear that the irregular baptisms and marriages had in fact been celebrated in St Ninians rather than Stirling Burgh. On the other hand, the schoolmaster of Doune, James Wingate, was charged with acting as an agent bringing together clients for both baptism and marriage, facilitating arrangements with Episcopalian ministers for his own profit.[54]

One other source of irregular baptisms was from the other end of the theological spectrum, the former conventiclers and their sympathisers. As previously described, George Mair was a probationer in the Church of Scotland with a conviction that he was called to be minister of Airth. His father-in-law had been minister there prior to deposition in the time of Charles II. Firmly thirled to the more radical edge of the church, Mair was not wanted by the presbytery, which declined to sustain his call. The action which finally prevented his ordination there, as quoted in Chapter 3, was that he had persuaded John Hepburn, a suspended non-juring Presbyterian minister, to baptise his child in Airth, the act being recorded in the register.[55] Airth itself was rather an uncomfortable place for other members of the presbytery: a year later George Turnbull 'met with some opposition on Mr Mair's acct'[56] when he went to preach and to baptise children. His colleagues Hugh Whyte and John Watson both reported being subjected to abuse while in Airth to baptise children.[57]

George Mair was not the only parent to be looking to maverick Presbyterians to conduct irregular baptisms. The baptismal register of John Macmillan, former minister of Balmaghie and later founder of the Reformed Presbytery, shows that he travelled round the country baptising children of families in the praying societies which had remained outwith the established Church of Scotland in 1690. He periodically came into the Stirling and Dunblane bounds, baptising children from the parishes of Logie, Kincardine, Kilmadock, Airth and Kippen.[58] The numbers locally seem to have been small, and the fact that the children might be several years old underlines both the infrequency of his visits and the concern for the parents to have their children baptised by a minister of whom they approved.

Yet it was not just irregular baptisms which undermined the church. An incident on 1 April 1705 seemed to attack the very sanctity of the sacrament, when a group of drunken inhabitants of Cardross in Port of Menteith carried out a mock baptism in a barnyard:

> The which day the Minister informed the Session that Mungo Haldan in Dykehead of Cardross hade comed to him, desiring baptism to a child which his wife hade brought forth to him; the Session considering that the said Mungo hade been guilty of a scandalous profanation of the sacrament of baptism in conjunction with Mr Robert Drummond & some other profane persones, who after they had been drinking in the said Mungo's house in the Dykehead, did immediately resort to John Keer's house in Lochenwan, where there was a child begotten in fornication, and brought forth by the said John his wife's sister. And because they could not get access to the house they sent in Mungo Haldan who brought forth the child to the open fields contrar to the mother's inclination and the said Mr Drummond baptized the child in the barn-yeard in a most scandalous and disorderly manner after they had been at their cups.[59]

The kirk session decided that Haldan should be sessionally rebuked before his own child could be baptised, but it was over a year before he came back again asking for his child to be baptised. The delay and lack of submission to the rebuke led to a charge of contumacy (obstinate disobedience) and baptism was made conditional on his appearance before the congregation for confession and public penance. Both the original offence and the contumacy seem to have been dealt with in a surprisingly lenient fashion; a charge of blasphemy could easily have been brought in the circumstances, so there must have been some influence at work in mitigating the offence given. Whether the date of the original offence, 'April Fools' Day' or 'Hunt the Gowk Day', had any bearing on it is unclear. It is, however, a shocking incident, and the lack of follow-up from either the kirk session or the Presbytery of Dunblane equally surprising.

The surviving records from the presbyteries of Dunblane and Stirling show the baptisms of just over 20,000 children between 1689 and 1710. Baptism was an important, indeed crucial, part of the work of the ministry, yet it seems very understated in the recorded impressions of the time. Whether because the very number of celebrations of the sacrament made it commonplace, or because it was essentially an intimate occasion, it does not seem to have garnered the enthusiasm of the people in the same way as Communion did.

The Church of Scotland, both before and after the Revolution, was adamant that there were only two sacraments to be observed. Other special additions to services were observed – ordination and induction of ministers, ordination of elders, absolution of penitents – but these, although no doubt deeply meaningful to the participants, were not sacraments. It is clear that the sacraments, especially that of Communion, were central to the life of the parish. The rarity and perhaps even reluctance with which Communion was celebrated made its significance the greater but it is a significance which was not necessarily of the same order for each participant. Nonetheless, once the initial hesitation in celebration was overcome, the Communion season became part of the annual life of most parishes with both the good and ill results that such a confluence of people was to bring.

Notes

1. Logan, *A Sermon Preached before His Grace James Duke of Queensberry*, p. 6.
2. *Register of the Diocesan Synod of Dunblane, 1662–1688*, pp. 202, 205.
3. As noted in Chapter 1, RPCS, vol. 14, p. 376 charges that John Edmonstone, minister of Gargunnock 'never gave the communion these twentie four years nor visited the sick'.
4. NLS MS 5770 shows that two antediluvians who later returned to Stirling Presbytery, Robert Rule and Richard Howieson, participated in a celebration of Communion in an Edinburgh meeting-house in 1688.
5. West, *Memoirs*, p. 6.
6. Marshall, *The Church in the Midst*, pp. 92–3.
7. Turnbull, 'The Diary of George Turnbull', pp. 313, 324, 328, 335, 354.
8. SCA CH2/723/5 19/5/1698.
9. SCA CH2/1300/1 5/7/1702.
10. SCA CH2/1026/5 31/8/1698.
11. SCA CH2/1026/5 6/4/1699.
12. SCA CH2/1026/5 4/5/1699.
13. Mr James Forrester of Logie. He was an elder in the Burgh Kirk of Stirling and a major heritor in the neighbouring parish of Logie.
14. Mr Robert Rule, minister of the 1st Charge of Stirling.
15. Mr John Forrester, minister of the 2nd Charge of Stirling.
16. SCA CH2/1026/5 22/5/1699.
17. The provost of a Scottish burgh was (and is) the equivalent of the mayor elsewhere in Britain. In the seventeenth and eighteenth centuries he was the figurehead of the council but in the case of Stirling had no power and did not even chair the council, that role being assigned to the dean of the Guildry. The bailies, of whom there were four in Stirling at any one time, were the burgh's magistrates. They were always elected by the council from among the councillors who were members of the Merchant Guildry. Both roles would be elected annually, but a second consecutive election was allowed and further periods of office after gaps. They were the real positions of power in the burgh.

18. Burns, *Old Scottish Communion Plate*, p. 604.
19. SCA CH2/1001/1 22/7/1696.
20. A chopin was a Scots measure of volume, equal to half a Scots pint or 1½ imperial pints. Twenty-one Scots pints and a chopin would therefore amount to about 60 imperial pints.
21. SCA CH2/1001/1 28/7/1696.
22. SCA CH2/1001/1 26/8/1696.
23. SCA CH2/1001/1 15/6/1697.
24. Schmidt, *Holy Fairs*, p. 44; Sage, *The Fundamental Charter of Presbytery*, pp. 370–1.
25. Sage, *The Fundamental Charter of Presbytery*, p. 374.
26. Kyd (ed.), *Scottish Population Statistics*, pp. 18, 37.
27. SCA CH2/722/9 16/5/1705.
28. Turnbull, 'The Diary of George Turnbull', p. 354.
29. Ibid., pp. 364, 373.
30. NLS MS 5770 fol. 13.
31. West, *Memoirs*, pp. 124, 151.
32. Cairns, *Memoirs of the Life of Elizabeth Cairns*, pp. 19–21.
33. Ibid., pp. 101–3.
34. The Song of Solomon is quoted several times by Rule and Howieson at the Communion services in Edinburgh in 1688. NLS MS 5770.
35. Boston, *Memoirs*, p. 421.
36. Marshal, *The Church in the Midst*, p. 93 shows a charge of £8 for sack for 'the ministers and preachers and such as were with them' in South Leith meeting-house in October 1688, in addition to the £23 for 'wyne to the communion'.
37. Spalding, *Synaxis Sacra*, p. 173.
38. SCA CH2/1300/1 12/6/1709.
39. Quoted in Marshall, *North Leith Parish Church*, p. 41.
40. Brown, *Gospel Truth Accurately Stated and Illustrated*, pp. 440–45.
41. HMC, 'The Manuscripts of His Grace the Duke of Portland', vol. 4, pp. 122–4; Muirhead, 'Eighteenth Century Occasions'.
42. SCA CH2/722/8 28/2/1694 onwards.
43. For example, Clackmannan, SCA CH2/722/8 9/9/1696; Dunblane, SCA CH2/722/8 31/5/1693, CH2/723/5 9/9/1698; Kilmadock, SCA CH2/212/2 29/5/1693.
44. NRS OPR 331/10/6 Balquhidder.
45. E.g. NRS OPR 490/20/331 Stirling.
46. E.g. NRS OPR 469/10/345 Airth.
47. Cullen, *Famine in Scotland*, pp. 133–5.
48. Turnbull, 'The Diary of George Turnbull', pp. 367, 376; NRS OPR 465/20/37 Alloa; NRS OPR 465/20/49 Alloa.
49. Turnbull, 'The Diary of George Turnbull', p. 346; NRS CH12/21/7 Sermons on Jer. 3:12.
50. NRS OPR 470/10/164 Alva.
51. SCA CH2/722/8 31/5/1693.
52. Believed to be the deprived Episcopalian minister of Stow.
53. NRS CC8/6/62 21/8/1694 Process of Divorce: Lady Margaret Mackenzie *v.* David Bruce.
54. SCA CH2/722/8 31/5/1693.
55. NRS OPR 469/10/345 Airth.

56. Turnbull, 'The Diary of George Turnbull', p. 360.
57. SCA CH2/722/8 23/5/1694.
58. Macmillan, *Register of the Rev. John Macmillan*, pp. 4, 9, 12.
59. SCA CH2/1300/1 1/4/1705, 28/4/1706.

CHAPTER SEVEN

Preaching the Word, Week by Week

> Pure Worship as agreable to the pattern delivered in the Mount, without corruption or mixture of human Invention ... and the true simplicity thereof held fast and adhered to.[1]

Preaching of the Word was absolutely central to the practice of religion in seventeenth- and eighteenth-century Scotland, as evidenced by John Logan's words to Parliament in 1706, quoted above, and yet the actual week-to-week provision of preaching is not so easy to define. One of the problems about any consideration of week-by-week post-Revolution preaching is that a significant proportion of printed sermons were written for special occasions, either internal, such as for fast days or sacramental days, or external, such as preaching before Parliament, a synod or the General Assembly. Even those which have survived in only manuscript form were often preserved because they were 'special', perhaps preached at a sacramental occasion,[2] while where 'ordinary' sermons are collected and printed, there is every reason to believe that they were rewritten and polished for publication and have lost the local context.

The second issue is that the preaching of the final decade of the seventeenth century has not been recognised as of notably high standard; perhaps the ministers' best efforts were devoted to polemic. Although John Macleod pays tribute to a number of the preachers quoted by Elisabeth West, few preachers retained the reputation enjoyed by the outstanding men of the next generation such as Thomas Boston, John Willison or Thomas Halyburton.[3] Carrying on into the following century, this view is reinforced more recently by John McIntosh: 'One of the striking features of evangelical publication in the eighteenth century is the relative sparsity of theological work. Apart from the notable figure of Thomas Boston there are only about eight writers who made a contribution of any great substance to theological publication.'[4]

Post-revolution worship had several constituent parts. Preceding the morning sermon there would be the singing of psalms and a lecture on some part of scripture. A second sermon without a lecture would follow in the afternoon. To this was added the offering up of extempore prayers.[5] Early in the morning service (but rarely in the afternoon diet) would be the formal entrance of those undergoing penance and at the end of the service the formal rebukes and exhortations. Intimations of fasts and the reasons for them or of collections for special purposes the following week would also be included. But in all of this, the lectures and sermons were central and to be given their due place. Just how long they lasted is a matter for some doubt. George Turnbull commented that Robert Rule in Stirling could lecture and preach for three hours despite being eighty years of age.[6] On the other hand the English Dissenting minister Edmund Calamy, travelling to Edinburgh in 1709, described the Edinburgh ministers' 'usual way to expound some portion of Scripture, during half an hour, which they called lecturing. After a short prayer, a sermon followed of the same length.'[7]

The lecture was a peculiarly Scottish practice. As described by the 1645 *Westminster Directory*, this was originally a means of reading the whole Bible in order, one chapter each of Old and New Testaments at each service. To this could be added an exposition by the minister after the reading was completed: 'regard is always to be had unto the time, that neither preaching, nor other ordinances be straitened or rendered tedious'.[8] Soon this developed into a lecture where the reading was interspersed with explanation.[9] The Episcopal church of between 1660 and 1688 used very much the same form of service as the Presbyterians, but the lecture was banned by the Privy Council in 1670, and further discouraged by Robert Leighton, then Bishop of Dunblane, who saw it as a barrier to providing simple access to scripture without commentary. It was replaced by unadorned reading of the Bible. The Presbyterian field preachers made a much more extended form of lecture a characteristic of their worship. At the Toleration, and even more so on the re-establishment of the Presbyterian Church of Scotland, the lecture became an integral part of the service and from 1694 was determined to be mandatory.[10]

The preservation of lectures among the printed works or surviving manuscripts of the late seventeenth and early eighteenth centuries is not widespread although a number can be found. Having outlined the difficulties in examining the regular fare of a parish kirk, there is some evidence from the parish of Alloa, within Stirling Presbytery. George Turnbull was minister there from 1690 to 1699 and in Tyninghame in East Lothian from 1699 until his death in 1731. Turnbull seems essentially to have been a fairly typical parish minister. But for one factor, he would have left almost no trace on the history of the church in Scotland, being involved in no controversies, under no investigation for heresy, and holding no notable positions. At most he has a cameo role in the *Memoirs of Life, Time and Writings of the Reverend and Learned Thomas Boston* as a friend to the young theologian.[11] What sets him apart is that he left a detailed diary of his ministry. It was published in 1893 and covers the period from August 1687 until December 1704. In it he notes the subject of his 'lecture' and the text of his sermon almost without exception for sixteen years, a grand total of 684 lectures and 975 sermons. This listing therefore makes the core of this chapter.[12] Although Turnbull's is unusual for its presence in a diary, listings of sermon texts are occasionally found within the context of kirk session minutes. One such listing is found in the records of Saltoun Kirk in East Lothian, which records texts week by week throughout the episcopal period and well into the eighteenth century.[13] This therefore gives a means of comparison with Turnbull.

There are effectively three discrete periods in the diary, incumbencies in Dundas, Alloa and Tyninghame, with two shorter periods of non-settled ministry before and after his time in Dundas. The sermons were preached on 435 different texts (there are a scatter for which the text cannot be identified) while his lectures covered 378 chapters of the Bible.

Inevitably Turnbull's early lectures stood alone, as he travelled from meeting-house to meeting-house. When he was settled in Dundas, though, and also during a brief incumbency at Dalmeny, he embarked on the study of complete books, starting with the epistle of James, lecturing on the five chapters for a total of seventeen weeks from September 1688 to February 1689. This was immediately followed by ten lectures on the first epistle of Peter.

Once formally inducted to Alloa, Turnbull lectured for two Sundays on 2 Corinthians 5 and then embarked on a series on the gospel of Luke on 12 October 1690, completing it on 24 April 1692, fifty-nine lectures and eighteen months later. After a few weeks when he lectured on a wide range of individual portions of scripture, Turnbull then turned his attention to Genesis in June 1692, giving a series of sixty-seven lectures on that, immediately followed by fifty-eight on Exodus, taking him to December 1696. He then had several series on individual psalms, not in order, before moving on to the book of Numbers with thirty-five lectures lasting nine months, and so the pattern continued, with a similar sequence in Tyninghame, where he once again started with lectures on the epistles of Peter as he had at Dundas twelve years previously, giving forty-five on the first epistle followed by sixteen on the second epistle. This was followed by a group of five on John 6, and then sixty lectures going through the whole of the Acts of the Apostles.

So what significance has this pattern of lectures? It clearly gave a structure to his weekly services. His sixteen years of record shows that he lectured on just under one third of the entire Bible, whether by going through books sequentially, or by picking and choosing books or individual chapters. We will presumably never know how much more was covered in the twenty-seven years of his ministry that followed the end of the diary. The other question is the extent to which lecture and sermon formed a unified service. In the weekly services there were a few occasions when the preaching was taken from the book being lectured upon, sometimes even from the chapter, but it was not a regular occurrence.

There is little or no information about the content of the lectures in Turnbull's diary. Boston was slightly more forthcoming, reflecting sometimes on the difficulty of lecturing without commentaries. Boston was extremely poor when he started his ministry, and had few books to aid him, as he records, but he also refers periodically to his acquisition of a new book and the help given by it. Like Turnbull, Boston found the Psalms a ready stopping place. Early on in his ministry at Simprin he 'determined to begin with the book of Psalms for lecture and for the exercise on the Sabbath-evenings, to explain a question of the catechism'.[14] A few months later he reported, 'This kept me above the world, led me to a text, Job 23: 3, and helped me to understand my lecture, John 20: 11 et seqq., for I had no commentary.'[15] Unfortunately Turnbull never referred to possession or use of books in his diary, nor is there any external record of what he possessed.

The details of Turnbull's lecture themes and sermon header texts can, however, be augmented, for one manuscript volume survives containing twelve sermons and six lectures from a six-week period in July and August 1691.[16] Dating from the earliest part of Turnbull's ministry in Alloa, the sermons now share a binding with a more substantial set of sermons by the contemporary Edinburgh minister George Campbell. The volume bears signs of the ownership of the Dowager Countess of Mar and the two parts may have been bound together from different sources. Turnbull's part throws up some issues, not least the brevity of the eighteen items. With a word count of around 1,200 each, each sermon or lecture would have lasted eight to ten minutes, and yet they show no sign of omission or summarising. The volume comprises a series of five Sunday lectures from the series on the gospel of Luke together with ten sermons on chapter 3 of Jeremiah. The sixth set comprises a lecture on Psalm 111 and two sermons on chapter 6 of Hosea from the Wednesday fast day for 'the success of the King's arms'.[17]

Unlike the published lectures of field preachers such as Richard Cameron, the lectures show no sign of specific local and contemporary context.[18] Cameron's directness owes much to the context of conventicles and the extreme danger that he and his hearers were in. By contrast, Turnbull's approach is cool and analytical. James Wodrow, a professor at Glasgow University at this period, gave guidance to his students on the structure of lectures and sermons. Although this was not published until over a century later, and although Turnbull never studied under Wodrow, it is clear that he followed the same conventions which Wodrow had codified.[19] This included the copious use of bullet points:

> 4th, Let not the number of your notes be above ten or twelve at most, for that would overwhelm the memory of your hearers, but let them be as few as can be, with dependence one upon another.
> 5th, Apply one of your most useful and seasonable notes in the several usual six uses . . .[20]

Turnbull and Wodrow shared a passion for numbered notes and subdivisions of numbered sub-divisions, which must have made following the gist rather a challenge. Alasdair Raffe has related this practice to the influence of 'Ramist logic' and has suggested that it made the gist easier for the listener to follow, but also gave the preacher a useful technique for helping to preach from memory.[21]

On the whole the lectures concentrate on the relationship between his hearers and God in fairly general terms:

> The psalm layes doune many general grounds wherby to magnify the Lord and then in the v[erse] following ther are more general grounds of praise concerning the Church of God of old. We are to praise because he is glorious and honorabill & 3 because of the equitie of all his providences, for his righteousness endures for ever. 4 to praise him, because of his mercie and compassion, he discovers himself to his people, by his works of providence in the 4 v[erse] he is gracious and full of compassione. The 1 ground I say of praising the Lord is because of his works. Are not the Lordes works of creation and providence towards the world and his owne people great, and are sought out of all of them that have pleasure in them. We may sit and observe that the works of providence in relation to his church is speciallie great. We learn that it is the exercise of godliness to take pleasure in the wayes and works of God.[22]

As Wodrow advised, Turnbull starts with a brief explanation of context and an analysis of the structure of the psalm, draws out the message and significance of it and finishes with a summarised conclusion:

> In the last v[erse] he shuts up all with a remarkable conclusion; the fear of the Lord is the beginning of wisdom. Is it so with many in the world, are not they compted the wisest of people that can trample on God's lawes and regard the comandments of man, more than the comandments of god. Yea they are but foolish are they in the eyes and sight of God. They are such whom the Lord will severelie punish in his wraith. Therfore learn to fear the Lord and to depart from iniquity, as thow may become wise into Salvatione.[23]

Turning to his lectures on Luke 12:15 given in the same summer, what comes over is essentially a straightforward unpicking of the text to give a simple interpretation to his people:

> Covetousness appears by these two marcks. 1 In that he makes no scruple to make a purchase, for all things and all methods are alike unto him. 2 It appears by unwarrantable omissions, it is a necessary dutie to help the sterving brother in his neid. This dutie the covetous man passeth by and omits.
>
> I go forward; Christ to inforce this doct. Layes out a notable parable from the 16 to the 29. The ground of a certain rich man brought forth fruitfullie & wealth becomes to tumble on this man, my barns, he sayes will not hold, I will make bigger barns & will lay up my store for many

yeirs and for rest unto his soul; but in comes the messenger of death, Thou must part with all, and thy soul must go with me. The ground of a certain rich man brought furth plentifullie & whereby we may observe that the righteous judge makes the sun to shine also weill on the wicked as on the godlie, and by all the things of the world we may never guess the hatred of God, or the love of God for all is alike in the world, and in the 17th and he thought within himself saying, what shall I doe for I have no roume to store my fruits, we may notice from this that the increase of wealth increaseth care; in this respect there is no great difference betwixt the beggar and the rich man for the one is over craving and the other his care is not only sett upon what he has but is still anxius after more. His mynd is never at rest till Death deprives him of all.[24]

In those fifteen years of lecturing, Turnbull tackled four fifths of the Pentateuch, Joshua and Judges, all in order over the years, but he totally ignored Leviticus both in lectures and in his sermons. There were many other substantial books which never figured either. There is almost no attention to the histories of Samuel, Kings and Chronicles. The books of Daniel, Ezra and Nehemiah too are conspicuous by their absence. In fact, considerable swathes of the Old Testament were entirely ignored both in lecture and in sermon. The absence of Daniel from his lectures and sermons does seem to underline that he had not the apocalyptic zeal of his contemporary Robert Fleming.

The story is slightly different in the New Testament, where several of Paul's epistles, including 1 Corinthians, Galatians and Colossians, never figured in lectures but were frequently used in sermons, so there is clearly a difference in his practice between Old and New Testaments. One feature of the latter was Turnbull's fascination with some of the smallest books of the New Testament for his lectures. Most of his series of lectures cover a complete book at an average of about one to two lectures per chapter. The five chapters of Peter's first epistle and the three of his second were covered in fifty-five and sixteen lectures respectively, followed by the epistle of James with twelve lectures on its five chapters.

Clearly, with only six examples out of 473 lectures by one minister out of Scotland's 900 or so, this small volume cannot be taken as typical of anything other than one minister's theology at one limited period in his life. Nonetheless it does cast light on an obscure part of the early modern minister's activities.

Attention having been drawn to the Episcopalians' rejection of the 'lecture' as a part of the morning service, it appears that the matter is not quite as simple as that, for the episcopal minister of Saltoun in East Lothian, Archibald Douglas, habitually preached on one series of texts at his morning service, allowing one or more sermons to consider a single verse of scripture, while in the afternoon he preached on a different series covering between six and thirty verses and thus worked his way through the Bible at very much the same rate as Turnbull did in his lectures.[25]

Obscurity was a charge sometimes levelled against the post-Revolution Presbyterian ministry. In his satirical squib *The Scotch Presbyterian Eloquence Display'd*, the author says of the Presbyterian preachers that 'their Texts are generally out of the obscurest Places of the Old Testament'.[26] This can be tested against the repertoire of Turnbull. Among his sermons, the 973 texts quoted represent 435 passages of scripture.[27] Looking closer at the figures, of those 435 texts, 231 were preached from only once and a further 91 twice. At the other end of the scale, twenty-one texts were used six times or more, with the overall favourite being 1 Corinthians 1:30, 'But of him are ye in Christ Jesus, who of God is made unto us wisdom, and righteousness, and sanctification, and redemption', which he used eighteen times, representing a mixture of one series of six sermons, one of five, one of two and five individual sermons, in eight different churches.

This practice of looking for more than one sermon from an individual text was common and is alluded to by Boston perhaps even as the norm:

> At last, thinking on my own unworthiness, I was made to say within myself, 'It is of the Lord's mercy I am not consumed.' This was the text I was thus led to, and determined after prayer to take. But so few things presented themselves to me, that I feared I would not get two sermons on it.[28]

Looking at the general balance of the sermons, we find that Old Testament texts form about 35 per cent of the whole, with a variation between 28 per cent in Alloa and 40 per cent in Tyninghame (see Appendix 5). As a visiting preacher through the whole period, Turnbull used the Old Testament 43 per cent of the time. It is noticeable, though, that, as with his lectures, he almost entirely passed over the history books of Samuel, Kings and Chronicles, as well as Ruth and Esther.

Within that pattern, though, there are substantial differences. The Psalms were the source of 8 per cent of his sermons in Alloa, more than doubling to 17 per cent in Tyninghame. Isaiah featured in 7 per cent of his sermons in Dundas, dropping to 3.5 per cent in Tyninghame. Jeremiah became his later prophet of choice in Tyninghame at 7.5 per cent, while Hosea dominated his thoughts in Dundas with 12 per cent of all sermons.

Turning to the New Testament, the differences are all the more striking. The gospels represent 16.5 per cent of the whole, with the Pauline epistles (and Hebrews) sitting at 41 per cent of all sermons. This disguises a dramatic change in practice between Alloa and Tyninghame, with the use of the gospels rising from 12 per cent to 26 per cent of all texts while use of the epistles halved from 53 per cent to 26 per cent. It is not entirely clear what was happening in his thought but perhaps he was first of all setting out the doctrinal framework of his faith from the epistles and subsequently expounding its application from the gospels.[29] Putting this in the context of other preachers, Archibald Lundie, successor to Douglas at Saltoun and the first Presbyterian minister there after the Revolution, preached from the gospels 27 per cent of the time in two sample years of 1700 and 1703 with the Pauline epistles accounting for 19 per cent. The difference is not so marked for New Testament preaching, but where Lundie differed from Turnbull was in a much heavier reliance in the Old Testament on the Psalms (33 per cent compared to Turnbull's 17 per cent) and an almost total disregard for the remainder (9 per cent). Saltoun was not very far from Tyninghame and the two men were on visiting terms, although not necessarily close friends.[30]

The differences between Turnbull's use of scripture in his three parishes are even more striking as we go down to individual book level. In Dundas, his 43 per cent epistle texts represent 23 per cent from First and Second Corinthians, 10 per cent from Hebrews, 8 per cent from Philemon and a mere 2 per cent from Romans. In Alloa, his 53 per cent epistle texts represent 22 per cent from Colossians, 12 per cent from Romans and 8 per cent from Hebrews, with the remaining 11 per cent showing a scattering from both Corinthians, Galatians and Titus. In Tyninghame, his 26 per cent epistle texts are made up of 7 per cent Hebrews and 6 per cent Titus, with Romans and the two Corinthians sharing 10 per cent.

Thessalonians, Timothy, Phillipians and Ephesians hardly ever figure in his weekly sermons, though they appear occasionally in sermons for public occasions. His sole sermons from Timothy, one from each epistle, were both preached at ordinations, for example, the latter using this highly apposite passage:

> I charge thee therefore before God, and the Lord Jesus Christ, who shall judge the quick and the dead at his appearing and his kingdom; Preach the word; be instant in season, out of season; reprove, rebuke, exhort with all longsuffering and doctrine.[31]

However, that 22 per cent of sermons preached in Alloa from Colossians constitutes an even more dramatic dominance when looked at chronologically, for it represents twenty-one sermons out of a total of fifty-eight in 1694, twenty-two out of fifty-one in 1695, and a startling thirty-two out of fifty-six in 1696, dropping to twenty-one out of seventy sermons preached in 1697. It is an outstanding concentration on one book, for over that four-year period 96 sermons out of 235 (41 per cent) came from that one book of Colossians. Turnbull presumably felt he had exhausted the topic, for in the following seven years he preached from it only three times, twice in 1702 and once in 1704. The lack of information as to Turnbull's reading allows no explanation of this. It is interesting, though, that the Episcopalian Archibald Douglas preached a series of fifteen sermons on Colossians from December 1686 to March 1687 in Saltoun.[32]

Sadly there is no evidence regarding Turnbull's emphasis on one book nor his later ignoring of it. The following year, 1698, saw him concentrate slightly on Romans, and subsequent years saw him switch to 1 Corinthians and Titus but never again with the concentration of effort that he expended on Colossians.

Leaving the epistles, Turnbull's treatment of the gospels also raises questions. The 12 per cent share at Dundas and at Alloa rose to 26 per cent at Tyninghame, but this also shows real changes in practice. Despite, or perhaps because of, his long lecture series on it, Luke barely figures as a source of sermons: twelve in 1697, ten in 1704 and a mere eight over the other fourteen years. Mark fares even worse: three in 1696, three in 1703 and six across all the other years.

Turnbull's gospel preaching was based almost entirely on Matthew (5.5 per cent of all sermons) and John (6.8 per cent). During the epistles-dominated years at Alloa, these figures dropped to 4 per cent and 3.4 per cent respectively, but his move to Tyninghame brought figures of over 9 per cent and over 10 per cent respectively. As noted, at the same time as his use of the epistles halved, his use of the gospels more than doubled. Like Turnbull, Lundie (at least in the two years sampled) concentrated on Matthew and John for his sermons, to the complete exclusion of Luke and Mark. In Archibald Douglas's incumbency, the sample years also show a noted preference for the same two gospels.

What then can be learned from Turnbull's choice of gospel texts? As might be expected, the Christmas narrative, covered only briefly in lectures on Luke, is entirely missing, reflecting the Presbyterians' dislike of the 'Popish' festivals. Douglas, it may be noted, preached from a Nativity text on Christmas Day 1693; this may have been an innovation. Luke's version of the Nativity is ignored in Turnbull's sermons, while Matthew's is covered by only five sermons on the Annunciation, a series of four in Alloa in November 1690 and one in Fossoway for the ordination of a new kirk session the following year. There was also a single sermon on 'When Herod the king had heard these things, he was troubled, and all Jerusalem with him',[33] given as a visiting preacher, again in 1690.

At the other end of Christ's life, sermons on the trial and Crucifixion are entirely lacking, and again they are only briefly covered in two of the lectures on Luke's gospel. Two sermons delivered privately to the Earl of Haddington after a bereavement cover the burial, and a further two cover the women's discovery of the empty tomb in the Garden, all four taken from John.

In fact, there are many crucial parts of the gospel which were never covered at all. To take one example, the Sermon on the Mount (Matthew 5 and Luke 6) is entirely missing as sermon texts and while Luke 6 had four lectures devoted to it, Matthew 5 does not figure among the lectures. Taking this further, looking at the five major teaching passages in Matthew and cross-checking the equivalent passages from Mark and Luke, there are only three sermons, one from each evangelist, which are primarily based on Christ's major teaching (see Appendix 5). To some extent, as evidenced by those lectures on Luke's gospel which survive, this omission was covered by the lectures, but the essential brevity implied by covering a whole chapter in one or two lectures means that no concentrated treatment was possible. His lecture on Luke 14:15 and subsequent verses does explain the parable of the rich man's feast but in essentially superficial terms, albeit with a sideswipe against 'papists' who interpret one passage as an argument for 'converting people to Christ by fire and fagot'.[34]

So how did Turnbull select his texts? Sadly it is not possible to identify the influences which made him concentrate on the parts on which he based his series, although some were obviously core to his faith, as for example John 3:16, on which he preached over many weeks during the winter of 1699–1700. There is, however, no equivalent to the Norfolk rector whose collected sermons of 1700 contained such items as '*13 Heb. 4*; a discourse against fornication and adultery occasioned by yt great lewdness of yt kind in my parishes, especially in Hardwick'.[35]

It is, in fact, easier to surmise on the reasons for the breaks in the patterns. The diary only twice mentions reasons for discoursing on particular texts. In November 1703, he lectured on the Song of Solomon 2:14 onwards, and preached on Psalm 51:17 ('The sacrifices of God are a broken spirit: a broken and a contrite heart, O God, thou wilt not despise') 'on account of some dejected persons'.[36] Three months prior to that he had referred to the Countess of Haddington's circumstances leading him to a particular lecture topic (Job 29:1–3) and to articulate his practice in text choice: 'I think there is a special direction of God in leading ministers to these texts and subjects, where there is a waiting on him for that end; but it is best of all when the peoples or particular persons cases lead ministers to there [*sic*] text and subject.'[37]

It is possible to identify this 'leading' in several ways. Firstly there are the events of his own life described in his diary together with the external events also described there, and then there is the life of his parish as recorded in the session minutes. A more explicit 'leading' is of course found in the special services held for days of fasting and humiliation and days of thanksgiving.

A few examples will suffice. In April 1699 Turnbull heard that Tyninghame parish was preparing to call him: without telling his congregation what was afoot, he preached on 2 Samuel 22:31. ('As for God, his way is perfect; the word of the Lord is tried: he is a buckler to all them that trust in him.') He had used the same sermon text in April when he was distressed at some backsliding in the parish during his absence on health grounds, and again in February 1700 after the birth of his daughter.[38] Trust in God was clearly at the heart of his thinking. In October 1703, however, he was lamenting that his 'heart was dead within me' and felt that God was hiding from him; his next sermon was based on Psalm 48:3. ('God is known in her palaces for a refuge.')[39]

Turning to events as they affected his parish, in his first service in Alloa in 1690, which coincided with a fast day for the upcoming General Assembly, he had a message of reconciliation from Isaiah 1:18. ('Come now, and let us reason together, saith the Lord: though your sins be as scarlet, they shall be as white as snow: though they be red like crimson, they shall be as wool.')[40] Nine years later, for his farewell sermon, he chose Exodus 3:2. ('And the angel of the Lord appeared unto him in a flame of fire out of the midst of a bush: and he looked, and, behold, the bush burned with fire, and the bush was not consumed.')[41]

Fast days for the poor harvests of the 1690s (King William's 'ill years') were met with sermons from Psalm 59:15 ('Let them wander up and down for meat, and grudge if they be not satisfied') in August 1696, from Amos 4:6 ('And I also have given you cleanness of teeth in all your cities, and want of bread in all your places: yet have ye not returned unto me, saith the Lord') in January 1697 and from Jeremiah 14:7 ('O Lord, though our iniquities testify against us, do thou it for thy name's sake: for our backslidings are many: we have sinned against thee') in May 1698. Finally in November 1699, a thanksgiving for the harvest was felt to be in order when Turnbull, by then in East Lothian, preached from Joel 2:26–7 ('And ye shall eat in plenty, and be satisfied, and praise the name of the Lord your God, that hath dealt wondrously with you . . .').[42]

However, although some of these circumstances can be gleaned from Turnbull's diary, examination of the records of his kirk sessions gives a more consistent picture of his choice of texts. For example, on 10 July 1692, it was recorded in the minutes that 'Jainet Lindsay, fornicatrix with George Snadon is now dead not yet having satisfied the church'. That day Turnbull preached on Romans 6:7. ('For he that is dead is freed from sin.')[43] When people did 'satisfy the church' it was often, but not always, the occasion for a sermon outwith Turnbull's 'ordinary'. In March 1691, for instance, the absolution of Elizabeth Berrihill was marked not only with the remission of her fine due to poverty, but with a sermon on Acts 2:36. ('Therefore let all the house of Israel know assuredly, that God hath made the same Jesus, whom ye have crucified, both Lord and Christ.')[44] Similarly, January 1692 not only saw the absolution of Helen Marshall for her sin of fornication, but also the report of the death of Walter Richie, the man involved with her. The sermon that day was on Psalm 130:7. ('Let Israel hope in the Lord: for with the Lord there is mercy, and with him is plenteous redemption.')[45] The evidence is clear, then, that the events happening locally were used to trigger Turnbull's choice of text. Although it is unknown how Turnbull linked the texts to the occasion, he clearly broke his regular sequence and conformed to the accepted practice, as described by Walter Steuart of Pardovan in 1709, that 'the day being come, the minister is to preach a sermon suited to that occasion'.[46]

Departures from his ordinary seemed to have been a regular occurrence for Turnbull when dealing with the end point of discipline cases, but they were less so when a case was beginning, or when the series of public appearances was just starting. Here he seems simply to have continued his existing train of thought, only breaking it at the end of the process.

National events impinged too: fast day sermons were clearly marked off from the normal run and used, as already mentioned, a different repertoire of texts. Hosea was a particular favourite and appears on many occasions when fasts were called, but the Psalms too provided texts. An explosion at the powder works in Leith led him to Psalm 28:5 ('Because they regard not the works of the Lord, nor the operation of his hands, he shall destroy them, and not build them up'), while the failure of the Darien scheme led him to a text from Isaiah 1:5. ('Why should ye be stricken any more? ye will revolt more and more: the whole head is sick, and the whole heart faint.')[47] Turnbull's attendance at the rather fraught General Assembly of March 1703, where the church seemed under imminent threat from Catholicism, intruding episcopal clergy and abounding sin and profanity, and which was abruptly dissolved despite the protests of many ministers, led to a sermon on Proverbs 30:4 ('Who hath ascended up into heaven, or descended? ... who hath established all the ends of the earth? what is his name, and what is his son's name, if thou canst tell?'), a text that leads into an expression of trust in God's providence. It is a measure of Turnbull's disquietude with the national situation that he had previously used the same text for his first sermon after the death of his son a fortnight earlier.[48]

Of course, the passages used as header texts are not the only scripture found in Turnbull's sermons. The surviving dozen sermons provide evidence for this with both explicit quotation of other passages and implicit quotations without ascription. One of the sermons on Hosea 6:1, for example, quotes Genesis, Exodus, Isaiah and Matthew but Turnbull is not prone to stringing quotation after biblical quotation in the manner satirised in *The Scotch Presbyterian Eloquence Display'd*. It has to be admitted that occasionally he did indulge in the kind of language that the *Eloquence* referred to: 'oft-times stuffed with impertinent and base similies, and always with homely, coarse and ridiculous expressions, very unsuitable to the gravity and solemnity that becomes Divinity'.[49] In a sermon on Jeremiah 12:13 he referred to the Israelites having 'gone a-hooring from the Lord and worshipped other gods',[50] but this reflects the language elsewhere in Jeremiah even if it is always the noun that is used rather than the verb.

Over a period of sixteen years and a range of churches, it is not surprising that Turnbull's emphasis changed. The changing proportions of the sources of his texts has been mentioned, but within those texts it is possible to see a change (see Table 7.1). Although sin figured as strongly in the Tyninghame sermons, there is a dramatic change in the proportion of texts which specifically mention the themes of repentance and wrath between Alloa and Tyninghame. It is possible that because the latter had only 10 per cent of the population of Alloa, there were fewer penitents making their appearances before the congregation and hence it was a

Table 7.1 Word Counts in Turnbull's Header Texts

Word	Alloa texts	Tyninghame texts	Word	Alloa texts	Tyninghame texts
Anger	13	0	Mercy	21	3
Bless	2	4	Peace	15	5
Call	14	22	Praise	7	2
Compassion	10	0	Redemption	12	11
Covenant	6	13	Repentance	12	1
Cross/Crucify	16	3	Resurrection	3	6
Dead/Dying	52	10	Right/Righteous	30	19
Evil	7	7	Salvation/Sanctification/Save	15	17
Faith/Faithful	31	2	Saviour	0	3
Father	40	6	Servant/Serve	32	12
Forgive	9	2	Soul	18	9
Gospel	15	0	Spirit/Spiritual	23	6
Holy	17	5	Strength	10	11
Innocent	6	7	Thank/Thankful	18	0
Jesus	55	22	Trust/Truth	21	4
Joyfulness	5	0	Wicked	12	1
Know/Knowledge	42	8	Wise/Wisdom	18	6
Lord	143	56	Works	8	13
Love	18	14	Wrath	7	2
Lust	12	6	Zealous	1	5
Man/Men	63	46			

Source: Data collated from King James Version texts in 443 sermons preached in Alloa 1689–99 and 225 sermons preached in Tyninghame 1699–1704 by George Turnbull.

topic less immediate to Turnbull's hearers. It is also possible that the better harvests of the first years of the new century made for a less anxious population, although trade wars with England and the unfolding of the disaster that was the Darien scheme must still have had an impact on the parish. Alternatively, it shows a shift in Turnbull himself, settling into a more genteel ambience with a laird's family to whom his diary shows a much greater closeness than he ever had with the Earl of Mar and his family. A final possibility is that it shows a modernising away from the old styles, although this seems less likely in the light of his renewing the covenants for himself and his family in June 1700, again the following month and once more in June 1702.[51]

Whatever the reason, it is only within the context of Tyninghame that we find evidence of Turnbull's effect on his people. Within the diary he alludes to Communion seasons almost in revivalist terms. On 30 June 1701 'this was a sweet time of the gospel, and a good gathering of people. Lord follow it with lasting blessing', a sentiment repeated at several other sacraments.[52]

Only one external reference to Turnbull's preaching survives. The Edinburgh servant woman Elisabeth West, whose *Spiritual Exercises* gives a rare picture of the religion of ordinary people and especially of women, was twice at Tyninghame over the Communion season a few years after Turnbull's diary ends. Although on another visit to Tyninghame she was disappointed, her memoirs show the effect that Turnbull had on her:

Short while after this, I was for some time in the East Country, where the Lord dealt very graciously with my soul, and made over much of himself to me in that sweet duty of meditation ... On Sabbath our minister, Mr George Turnbull, had chosen that text, Psalm xix. 12. 'Who can understand his errors? Cleanse thou me from secret faults; and let them not have dominion over me.' When I heard these words read, I thought my heart cried out within me, that this is the very language and desire of my soul: and I must acknowledge, that I heard God's mind spoken from it to me.[53]

Comparison with Archibald Lundie's texts in Saltoun does show a general similarity in balance which is quite different from the balance used by Lundie's predecessor, Archibald Douglas. Equally, though, Douglas's use of his afternoon sermon apparently to expound in a similar way to Turnbull's early lectures suggests that the Episcopalian dislike of the 'lecture' may not be as absolute as has been thought. It is clear, though, that the survival of those early sermons and lectures of Turnbull, together with his listing of texts, deserves a more extended analysis than is practical in the context of this work.

Notes

1. Logan, *A Sermon Preached before His Grace James Duke of Queensberry*, p. 10.
2. See for example Glasgow University Library, MS Gen 938, which contains notes of 295 sermons by several dozen preachers between 1705 and 1723, at least two thirds of which were sacramental. Others were preached at ordinations or synods.
3. Macleod, *Scottish Theology in Relation to Church History since the Reformation*, p. 105.
4. McIntosh, 'Eighteenth-Century Evangelicalism', p. 84.
5. Little is known of the actual practice of psalm singing at this time, nor is there much information preserved about the content of prayers.
6. Turnbull, 'The Diary of George Turnbull', p. 385.
7. Calamy, *An Historical Account of My Own Life*, vol. 2, p. 177.
8. *A Directory for the Publique Worship of God*, pp. 38–9.
9. Raffe, 'Preaching, Reading, and Publishing the Word in Protestant Scotland', p. 322.
10. Act anent Lecturing: see 'Acts: 1694', in Church of Scotland, *Acts of the General Assembly of the Church of Scotland, 1638–1842*, pp. 235–45.
11. Boston, *Memoirs*, pp. 25, 46, 56, 62.
12. A few kirk session records of the time record the header texts of sermons; what makes Turnbull unusual is that the reader is able to follow his practice in different churches and circumstances.
13. NRS CH2/322/3.
14. Boston, *Memoirs*, p. 91.
15. Ibid., p. 116.
16. NRS CH12/21/7.
17. Turnbull, 'The Diary of George Turnbull', p. 347.

18. See for example 'Cameron's Preface, Lecture on Psalm 92 and Sermons on John 5.40', https://drmarkjardine.files.wordpress.com/2011/03/richard-cameron-hynds-bottom-sermons-11-july-1680.pdf (last accessed 12/2/2021).
19. Wodrow, *Life of James Wodrow A.M.*, pp. 242–5.
20. Ibid., p. 243.
21. Raffe, 'Preaching, Reading, and Publishing the Word in Protestant Scotland', p. 326.
22. NRS CH12/21/7, pp. 715–16.
23. Ibid., pp. 722–3.
24. Ibid., pp. 532–3.
25. NRS CH2/322/3 1686–96. Douglas was ordained to Saltoun and it remained in his charge through the Revolution period as a 'tolerated' Episcopal minister. He died in post in 1695. Information about his preaching is taken from the years 1686–8 and 1693 as sample years.
26. Curate, *The Scotch Presbyterian Eloquence Display'd*, p. 45.
27. This does not mean, however, that sermons were preached two and a half times each, for many of these were series where the theme was developed on one text over a period of weeks. Clearly there are some cases where sermons were repeated in a different church a week or two later, but these tended to be the exception and more common in his early ministry.
28. Boston, *Memoirs*, p. 93.
29. I am grateful to Professor David Bebbington for this suggestion.
30. Turnbull, 'The Diary of George Turnbull', p. 403.
31. 2 Timothy 4:1–2.
32. NRS CH2/322/3.
33. Matthew 2:3.
34. NRS CH12/21/7 Lecture on Luke 14:15ff.
35. Quoted in Chamberlain, 'Parish Preaching in the Long Eighteenth Century', p. 53.
36. Turnbull, 'The Diary of George Turnbull', p. 435.
37. Ibid., p. 420.
38. Ibid., pp. 381–2, 391.
39. Ibid., p. 435.
40. Ibid., p. 343. He had preached several times in Alloa prior to being called.
41. Ibid., p. 389.
42. Ibid., pp. 369, 371, 376, 389.
43. SCA CH2/942/6 10/7/1692; Turnbull, 'The Diary of George Turnbull', p. 353.
44. SCA CH2/942/6 29/3/1691; Turnbull, 'The Diary of George Turnbull', p. 344.
45. SCA CH2/942/6 24/1/1692; Turnbull, 'The Diary of George Turnbull', p. 335.
46. Steuart of Pardovan, *Collections and Observations Methodiz'd*, p. 241. Although this refers specifically to absolution after excommunication.
47. Turnbull, 'The Diary of George Turnbull', p. 393.
48. Ibid., pp. 429–30.
49. Curate, *The Scotch Presbyterian Eloquence Display'd*, p. 23.
50. NRS CH12/21/7 Sermon on Jer. 12:13.
51. Turnbull, 'The Diary of George Turnbull', p. 393.
52. Ibid., p. 403.
53. West, *Memoirs*, p. 124. On the second occasion, the preacher who left her less enthused is not named.

CHAPTER EIGHT

The Survival of Episcopacy

What then of the continuing remnant of the Episcopalians after Bishop Rose had made his position clear and the first flush of depositions had taken place? In looking at the Episcopalian history of the area, it would be all too easy to believe that the crisis hit in 1688 rather than 1689. The surviving records of Dunblane Diocesan Synod and the two episcopal presbyteries of Dunblane and Stirling all come to an abrupt end in 1688, as do the kirk session records of Dunblane. Most of the surviving kirk session records ended in 1689, with three continuing into 1690 and a sole survivor in 1691 (see Appendix 1).

One explanation for the earlier disappearance of the higher court records lies in the administrative habits of the clerks. Records for 1688 would not normally have been inscribed in the official record until they had passed the following meeting and it is not known whether there were later meetings of those courts whose minutes were unrecorded.

What is clear is that the administrative record of the Episcopalian faction is almost completely lacking after the re-establishment of Presbyterianism. Even where Episcopalian ministers remained in charge, the records are lost. With the exception of Logie and to a lesser extent Alloa, where there is an overlap of records for a few months until the Episcopalian ministers were deprived, there is no trace of how the survivors of the old regime administered their churches either as remaining parish ministers or as the incumbents of meeting-houses.

Of the four parishes which retained Episcopal ministry long-term after the Revolution,[1] none has surviving records prior to their acceptance of Presbyterian ministers. In the first instance, they do seem to have retained kirk sessions, even if the higher courts had disappeared. Evidence is limited, but in Bothkennar Church, where John Skinner remained until 1723, new Communion cups were presented to the church by 'the Minister and the Kirk Session' in 1690, and a new baptismal vessel followed in 1694 with the same inscription.[2] Skinner was obviously confident that he would remain in possession and that he had the administrative machinery to assist him. The evidence suggests that Alva, which flipped from Episcopalian to Presbyterian and back again before finally casting its lot with the Presbyterians, also had a kirk session that functioned throughout the whole period with a core of the same elders.[3]

A further complicating factor is the question of whether those who remained loyal to the episcopal regime were necessarily against William and vice versa. Tristram Clarke's analysis of post-Revolution Episcopalianism does identify Episcopalians whom he designates as 'Williamite' and indeed some of those ministered in the two presbyteries, but their views and actions remain shadowy, it only being known that they prayed for the new monarchs.[4] There is a little evidence locally to suggest that there were those of an episcopal hue prepared to throw in their lot with William, but equally few of the remainder took up arms against him in 1689, or against Queen Anne in 1708 (see Appendix 4). Parliamentary material clearly shows that many Jacobite sympathisers averse to the re-established Presbyterian regime were still expected to do their duty as commissioners of supply for the county administration.[5]

If some lairds' loyalties can be gauged fairly easily, it is much harder to come to any conclusion about the majority of the population. As already mentioned, historians differ considerably in their estimate of the relative strengths of the parties at the time of the Revolution. In the years following, the evidence becomes ever thinner. However, there are some signs, as for example the parish of Alva, which, as has been noted, changed hands more than once. When the case of the episcopal minister, William Lindsay, came before the Privy Council in 1696 he claimed that he had been invited back by the landowners and heritors. As previously discussed, however, this narrative can be put against the evidence of the weekly collections, which do not show popular support (see Appendix 3).

Whatever the level of local support, what Lindsay did not do was function within a structure. His elders seem to have continued, and the poor's fund continued to be distributed. Perhaps the session continued to deal with discipline as it always had. However, he had lost the discipline of the old episcopal presbytery and he never accepted its successor. By the time he resumed Alva's pulpit, he was isolated with, at best, only an informal grouping of local Episcopalian ministers for support. No evidence survives of any sense of control by a bishop or episcopal structure. Essentially what Alva had become was an independent congregational church, and it looks as though that held true for every continuing episcopal church within the bounds of the two presbyteries.

In neighbouring Logie, the demission of the Episcopalian incumbents was much less tidy. Almost alone among local parishes, Logie was subjected to a rabbling. The kirk session record, still episcopal, shows that George Schaw and his assistant/successor, his son-in-law William Elphinstone, were put out with a degree of violence in June of 1689. Elphinstone's account of his experience, written in the third person but subscribed by them both, is graphic, showing, as previously noted, that it was led by the women of the meeting-house congregation supported by soldiers of the Earl of Angus's Regiment. But this rabbling was not permanent; a few weeks later, in August, Schaw and Elphinstone were restored to their charge and continued for another few months, although it appears that Elphinstone at least was living in Stirling. Elphinstone himself was ambushed on the road the following year by members of the same group who had rabbled him and his life was saved only by the intervention of soldiers.[6] It is clear from this that, despite the animus against Elphinstone in particular, and the thriving nature of the meeting-house congregation, there must have been a core of powerful support for episcopacy in the parish for a year or two after the Revolution even if it is largely invisible in the records.

A more visible core of Episcopalian support can be seen in St Ninians, the large parish that essentially formed the hinterland of the Burgh of Stirling and had a complicated and intertwined relationship with the burgh. The deposition of the episcopal incumbent was relatively easily achieved, but unlike in Logie the pre-existing incumbent of the Presbyterian meeting-house was by no means acceptable to the majority of the local lairds. Patrick Couper's travails have been previously described; such was the strength of opinion against him that he was effectively driven out of the area and accepted transportation to Pittenweem in Fife. It is notable that the synod records show no attempt to fight against the situation in St Ninians, but perhaps the objectors' animosity was tempered by their declared willingness to accept any Presbyterian minister other than Couper. In the event, John Logan's translation to St Ninians seems to have met no opposition. His session was significantly different in composition from those of his predecessors in both camps, but William Livingston of Greenyards and John Forrest of Thirtieacres, who had both supported Couper, were active in their support, even if Greenyards was censured for non-attendance early in Logan's ministry. In some respects, opposition to Presbyterianism was subtle but so too was the new regime's attitude to supporters of the old. Where the Episcopalian lairds can be seen to be acting in co-operation with Logan is in the administration of the mortcloth, which was a separate institution in that parish. Here the records show clearly that Logan was sitting on a committee chaired by the Jacobite/Episcopalian laird of Torbrex.

Records do not show opposition by ordinary people in St Ninians to any extent, but the support of lairds such as Torbrex and Livilands meant that Episcopalian meeting-houses could survive and there was a clear network of episcopal clergy available to make use of them. Official activity against them waxed and waned according to the political climate of the time and whether civil authorities could be persuaded to take action. That, in its turn, presupposed that the civil authorities were not themselves sympathetic to the old regime. It is clear, for example, that the Stirlingshire justices of the peace in the 1690s still included some who were more sympathetic to episcopacy than to Presbyterianism.[7]

A contemporary account printed in 1908 from a manuscript (since lost) describes the situation from an Episcopalian point of view.[8] James Hunter, former episcopal minister of the 2nd Charge of Stirling, had certainly been active in the Stirling area from the Revolution; the account describes him as having a meeting-house in the home of Mr Murray of Livilands.[9] It then continues to describe a meeting-house erected near St Ninians

Church. This meeting-house was closed down periodically through the ensuing years, with alternative accommodation always being swiftly found through the support of lairds such as Murray of Polmaise and Paterson of Bannockburn.

If the landward areas showed a considerable degree of tacit toleration interrupted by occasional action, the situation in the Burgh of Stirling was more volatile. In 1703, Walter Stirling opened a meeting-house briefly in his own home and then in the home of Lady Balthayock.[10]

What the anonymous author does not mention is that a new meeting-house was opened in Stirling under the charge of Adam Peacock, pre-Revolution minister of Morebattle. James Hunter, as a locally known former minister of Stirling, may have been tolerated to a small degree, but Peacock was not and was arrested by a group, led by Bailie Allan, which marched on his meeting-house one Sunday. He fetched up in prison overnight, in response to which he took the burgh council to court but was unsuccessful in his suit.[11]

Peacock had his supporters, though: this incident happened shortly after the death of Robert Rule, elderly minister of the 1st Charge, and while the 2nd Charge was vacant due to the death of John Forrester. The arrest led to a tumult in the streets with six men, three fleshers, two weavers and a baker, charged that they had 'unwarrantably convocat with places in a most tumultuous manner absolutely refused and disobeyed the magistrates order, continued upon the streets in the backraw'. One of the six was Thomas Blackburn, a weaver, whose offence in cursing Rule, already quoted in Chapter 2, continued: he

> likeways express[ed] that those who took Mr Peacock to prison, these souls would be hurled to hell and that bubbly Baillie Allan behoved to be there amongst the rest and that Jock Presbyter [probably John Logan in St Ninians] would shyte his britches with many base and unworthy expressions unworthy to be rehearsed.[12]

Blackburn was fined £10. Another man, James Nairn, was charged:

> that whereas the reviling upon and reflecting against Magistrates is a crime of ane atrocious nature and severely punishable, yet nevertheless on 4 Sept last being Sunday the Magistrates and Council sent some few of their number to go to Mr Adam Peacock to dissuade him from preaching there the said defendant being standing on the street before several honest witnesses not only called the said persons sent by the said magistrates 'sons of whores' but likeways called the said magistrates themselves sons of whores.[13]

It is clear that Stirling was a divided town and that a good deal of sympathy still remained for the old regime.

Two other parishes within Stirlingshire require attention, each with different issues. Already referred to, Bothkennar, on the banks of the Forth, remained in the hands of John Skinner, an episcopal incumbent who had been presented to the parish in 1676 and survived many attempts to dislodge him, including an alternative kirk session as part of the campaign to replace him.[14]

Skinner was deposed in 1701, but restored again in 1703. He was finally deposed in the aftermath of the 1715 rising but a Presbyterian minister did not take charge of Bothkennar until 1721. Because there were so many processes against Skinner, his activities were documented and at the centre of them was a network of deposed episcopal ministers, acting all along the Forth from Falkirk to Stirling. Some of these had ministered locally. Paul Gellie was still holding on in Airth despite strong opposition from a more radical Presbyterianism than was found elsewhere in the area. Others also came into the area such as Robert Wright, former minister in Culross. Skinner was able to celebrate Communion in 1700. Whether this was the first time that the utensils bought a decade before had been used is not known. In this celebration, as was the habit of his Presbyterian counterparts, he was assisted by others of a similar theology. From the evidence of baptisms (see Table 6.1 above), and the communicants identified in the presbytery record, the support of the local landowners is clear.

It was not just the ecclesiastical irregularities that formed the evidence against these continuing incumbents. They were likely to be accused of drinking in taverns, drunkenness and swearing. One witness deponed that he had heard Gellie swear 'Goodfaith' and had seen him 'mistaken with drink'.[15] Such accusations, and worse, were part and parcel of most of the efforts to deprive incumbents and, according to Alasdair Raffe, show how the church courts were able to use grounds other than Jacobitism to attack the episcopal clergy.[16]

It would appear then that there were two Episcopalian networks within Stirling Presbytery's bounds but without evidence that they worked together. One was in Bothkennar, with John Skinner, Paul Gellie and Andrew Slirie involved, the other in Stirling itself and St Ninians, with James Hunter and Adam Peacock (see Appendix 4).

If these attempts to hold on were bold and well supported by the landowners in Stirling Presbytery, in the bounds of Dunblane the episcopal opposition seems to have been quieter in those parishes which had Presbyterian ministers. Evidence of opposition comes in two forms: in the frequency of irregular baptism or marriage and in the heritors' treatment of the minister. Neither may in themselves signify Episcopalian leanings, but it was well known that former episcopal clergy were available, either acting clandestinely in the local area or providing the service in Edinburgh, where provision of irregular marriages seems to have been a cottage industry.

James Wingate, the schoolmaster in Doune, seems to have acted as an agent for several ministers. In 1693 he was accused of allowing his schoolhouse to be used by William Wemyss, former minister of Lecropt, by Robert Stewart, the former minister of Balquhidder (who had joined

Dundee's rising in 1689) and by Robert Douglas (either the former Bishop of Dunblane or his son, former minister of Bothwell and librarian of the Leighton Library). Wingate was also accused of taking money to arrange marriages and provide testificats, and of preventing his pupils from hearing Presbyterian ministers. He was deposed from his various roles and barred from teaching.[17]

So far as the mistreatment of ministers by their heritors is concerned, obstruction over the provision of a manse was an obvious way in which unsympathetic heritors could make the life of any minister more difficult if they wished. The presbytery's sole weapon against this was the visitation. One in Gargunnock in 1693 found that one heritor, the Laird of Boquhan, was discouraging to the new minister, Robert Campbell, and disowned his ministry. A year later he had withdrawn from the congregation and the ministers of Dunblane and Alloa were sent to interview him.[18] A fresh visitation that year brought approval of the minister from the rest of the heritors, but Boquhan claimed that he had been misrepresented by Campbell and a fresh committee of two ministers and Lord Aberuchill was appointed to attempt a reconciliation. That this failed is shown by Campbell's asking to be made transportable so that he might be called to another parish. In response to this, John McLaren, the minister of Kippen, went to preach and interview the elders and heritors, while Campbell was sent to serve in the Perthshire parish of Rattray, for which the presbytery had been responsible. At the same time, he was considered for the vacant 2nd Charge of Stirling but finally stated categorically that the lack of an adequate manse in Gargunnock forced him to insist on being allowed to move. McLaren was once again sent to preach in Gargunnock and summon heritors, elders and heads of families to the presbytery in order to declare what they had to say against Campbell, but he came away without getting any satisfaction from the heritors regarding the lack of a manse. Campbell was declared transportable and took himself off to Galloway. McLaren himself was reported to be discouraged in his own parish. He left the area and his successor too complained of the lack of a manse several years later.[19]

Manses were a recurring theme in the rural parishes of Dunblane Presbytery and the recurring issues in Kincardine, Kippen, Logie, Kilmadock and Port of Menteith show clearly how unsympathetic (or impecunious) heritors could make life very difficult for their ministers. Meanwhile, as in Alva, episcopal former incumbents were always ready to take any opportunity to try to recover their positions. One of the reasons that Alloa was so keen to call John Logan from Kilmadock to succeed George Turnbull was that, as they reported to the General Assembly in 1703, 'the late prelatical incumbent resides there and celebrated sacrament last summer'.[20]

The legal circumstances of Episcopalian clergy changed regularly through the period, and this is reflected in the response from the Presbyterian courts. The early rabbling of the south-west was banned, and although an effort by the king to persuade the General Assembly to admit Episcopalians on their signing of a formula was rejected, the parliament of 1693 passed two acts which allowed them legally to remain provided they swore that William was king *de jure* as well as *de facto*. This and latter acts proved divisive for the Episcopalians, splitting them into two parties with differing political agendas.[21] The time allowed for qualifying by taking the oath was extended but it was used by the presbyteries to renew their efforts to prise remaining Episcopalians from their charges and a new generation of Presbyterians joined their colleagues in Stirling and Dunblane presbyteries.

The accession of Queen Anne changed the atmosphere. William had had a lurking liking for the Presbyterians, aided by his close relationship with William Carstares both in exile and in London. Queen Anne had no such ties and was receptive of the pleas of the disestablished, saying that provided they observed the law they should be allowed to worship in safety. Opposition to this being enshrined in law, however, meant that toleration was not yet a reality. Despite that, though, it meant that some attempted late depositions, such as that of John Skinner in Bothkennar failed, and the four Episcopalian parishes remained so until the ministers themselves died or decided to move on.

The continuing entwining of Episcopalianism and Jacobite politics prevailed through the first decade of the eighteenth century. As will be discussed in Chapter 11, petitions in opposition to the Union of the Parliaments were locally organised on partisan lines. The petition from Stirlingshire was clearly an Episcopal/Jacobite document that had no overlap in signatories with the more Presbyterian ones from the combined parishes of Airth, Larbert & Dunipace and Denny, from St Ninians and from Stirling itself.[22]

Opposition to William's and then to Anne's reigns finally led to the damp squib that was the 1708 Jacobite rebellion. This was a chance for the Episcopalian supporters of the Jacobean party to come out in arms to support their exiled king, by this stage James VII's son James VIII (at least to them). Five young men of the Stirlingshire gentry were among the few who showed any sign of supporting him. The five, scions of the Episcopalian landowners, were quickly arrested after the abortive coup. Removed to London, they were sent back to Scotland to be tried for treason, and much to the chagrin of Queen Anne, the case against them was found 'not proven'. It should be noted that the court only had the choice of 'proven' or 'not proven'. Despite several historians' statements that the verdict suggested they were guilty but had got away with it, a verdict of 'not proven' was the standard one of acquittal at that time. The real reason that no conviction ensued was that the legal authorities, particularly the Queen's advocate, Sir James Steuart of Goodtrees, had failed to summon the witnesses properly.

Official reaction to the 1708 events was wisely muted: it seemed to be recognised that making martyrs of the Jacobites would be counter-productive. Nonetheless action was taken against some of the Episcopalian ministers still around Stirling. In a sitting of the circuit court in Stirling in May 1709 more notable for the number of trials deserted for lack of 'probation' (that is, no evidence was presented by the prosecution), Andrew Slirie,[23] who had intruded in Falkirk, James Hunter, former minister of Stirling, and Walter Stirling, former minister of Baldernock, were all accused of intruding in St Ninians. Found guilty, they were to 'desist from the exercise of their ministerial function in tyme coming and while they do decline to qualify in terms of the law'. In addition, Hunter was ordered to remove himself from the parish.[24] This was not enough to silence him, though, for the following year Stirling Burgh Council was complaining of his irregularly baptising a child in the burgh and ordered him to desist on pain of banishment. Finally he moved to Edinburgh and took the oath allowing him to become a 'qualified' preacher and to minister in peace.[25] As it happens, another minister indicted at the same diet of the court was Henry Christie, deposed incumbent of Kinross in the neighbouring presbytery. Although it was not mentioned in the record of the case, and indeed, was probably still secret, Christie had been ordained one of the new generation of 'college bishops' (bishops without a specific see) just a month previously. Like Hunter, he was discharged from preaching and ordered to remove from the parish.

The indictment against Hunter establishes that he was exercising the full range of his ministry, including administering both the sacraments. By identifying the fathers of children whom he had baptised, it also shows that the local Episcopalians included the artisan class as well as the lairds. Among them were a flesher and a tailor in St Ninians and a surgeon apothecary in Stirling, but no real sanction was taken against anyone involved. This applies too to the 'host' of the meeting-house, who was also charged and tried:

> Mr Charles Bennet, of Livilands, Sheriff Depute of the shyre of Stirling indyted and accused of neglecting the orders of the privy Council as also her majestie's orders sent to him by her majestie's advocate by which he was commanded to seal up all meeting-houses kept by dissenting ministers not duly qualified within the bounds and notwithstanding of his being required under form of instrument . . . HM Advocat did try several times to the said Mr Charles Bennet particularly to seal up the meeting-house of one Mr James Hunter a disaffected preacher and also to discharge him and all disaffected preachers within his bounds as Mr Sliery and Mr Stirling, yet he disobeyed the same and furder when he took a bond and Caution of the said Mr Hunter he made a sham thereof and immediately did give up the bond to his fault to the cautioner, therein; for all which he ought to be deprived of his office and otherways punished with the pains of law.[26]

The advocate depute then drew back from asking for the full force of the law:

> And therefore the Lords Justiciary ordained that Mr Charles Bennet be more punctual in executing that office in the matter lybelled in

time coming ... Mr Charles Bennet report from time to time to the Lords of Justiciary or her Majestie's advocat his diligence in putting the laws in execution against such ministers as shall hereafter exercise their ministerial function contrair to the law.[27]

To modern eyes it seems extraordinary that someone in such a position as sheriff depute should essentially be let off from such a dereliction of his stated duty. Presumably again this was an attempt to defuse the situation by gentle handling, but it does demonstrate that the burden of the law was treated lightly by most of those involved in it. The judges involved in this particular case were James Erskine of Grange, brother of the Earl of Mar,[28] and Lord Tillicoultry, both of whom were active in the business of the Church of Scotland.

The sentence against Hunter does not seem to have had much effect. In August of 1709, his activities were also coming under the scrutiny of Stirling Burgh Council, which objected to his baptising the child of one of the burgesses.[29] He was forbidden from future activity on pain of imprisonment.

It was clear that governmentally, the tide was turning in the Episcopalians' favour. In 1709 an Edinburgh meeting-house incumbent, James Greenshields, appeared in front of the Presbytery of Edinburgh on account of his 'presuming without authority to exercise the office of the holy ministry on the Lord's Day'. He defended himself and then declined the jurisdiction of the presbytery. The case was then taken up by the burgh council as civil authority and he and several others (including Adam Peacock, who had moved from Stirling to Edinburgh) were imprisoned. Greenshields fought his case right up to the House of Lords, where, of course, English bishops sat and the Church of Scotland had the support only of those representative peers who had Presbyterian sympathies. Greenshields won his case and the way was open for others to follow his example and use the English prayer book in their services.[30]

The case raised questions both about the status of the established church and about those who did not wish to conform to it, and was followed in 1711 by the Scottish Episcopalians Act, which effectively allowed Episcopalian meeting-houses to be erected provided that the clergy had taken the oath of loyalty to Queen Anne.[31]

There was still a continuing tension between the two parties in Stirling which was not resolved before the rising of 1715. In 1712 came a series of 'humble addresses' to Queen Anne which thanked her for her role in promoting the peace which was to become enshrined in the Peace of Utrecht between 1712 and 1714. One presented by the Earl of Mar from the county in August 1712[32] was purely political, but in November a second one purporting to be from 'the Burgesses, freemen, and other considerable Inhabitants within your Majesty's antient and loyal borough of Sterling' was presented by the MP for Stirlingshire, Sir Hugh Paterson of Bannockburn, a lifelong Jacobite who had recently become Mar's brother-in-law.[33] That address offered appropriate praise for the truce which had recently been signed, but also thanked the Queen for the Act of Toleration and 'more especially for allowing the sons of the Church to officiate to us by the most Divine Worship of the Church of England'.[34] March 1713 brought a second address from the burgh which equally vocally praised Her Majesty for her 'repeated assurances to protect and maintain the Rights and Privileges of this national and legally established Church of Scotland'.[35] A fourth, religiously neutral, address was presented the following week from the justices of the peace of Stirlingshire.[36]

The reaction to these rival addresses shows how ingrained the split in both the Burgh and the County of Stirling had become. An article in a London newspaper, the *Post Boy*, attacked the two most recent addresses. It claimed that the justices' one was never officially passed and signed by only eight of the twenty-two justices, while that from the burgh was said to have been 'the address of the presbyterian teachers there and of the more illiterate and poorest mechanics of the town, whom they do influence'.[37] This was swiftly followed by a rebuttal in the opposing newspaper, the *Flying Post*, which defended the status of both addresses, and ascribed the *Post Boy* article to the pen of James Hunter, whose suspension for drunkenness by the episcopal Presbytery of Stirling in 1684 was lengthily alluded to. Paterson's original address, signed by 'any vagrant persons whatsoever, who could write and be perswaded to sign it', was backed by five men who had been magistrates before the Revolution and resigned because of embezzlement, one of whom, a former provost, had been expelled from Parliament 'on account of irreligious expressions'.[38] The whole episode, although out of the strict period of this book, shows how the divisions persisted and would continue to persist.

Mention of the English prayer book in the Episcopalian address provides a fragment of evidence for one aspect of Episcopalianism which is singularly hard to track in the records. What actually characterised their faith and their worship?

The pre-Revolution church was episcopal in its governance but was not substantially different in its theology or worship from its presbyterian predecessor. In worship, the pattern was broadly similar, with no fixed liturgy, extemporary prayer, the singing of psalms and a reliance on preaching the Word. Stylistically, sermons had changed under the influence of Robert Leighton, being more '"moderate" both in content and expression' as one historian put it.[39] Liturgically, the Lord's Prayer and the Doxology had been introduced, together with the Apostles' Creed at baptisms, while the lecture which preceded the sermon returned to being a reading of scripture rather than the discursive explanation which the Presbyterians employed and developed through the Restoration period.[40] Nonetheless, it was essentially plain, Protestant, even Puritan, worship with none of the vestments or ritual which might accompany Church of England episcopacy. In his thesis on Scottish Episcopalianism, Tristram Clarke ascribes some of the loss of lay support for episcopacy to the fact that most people were unaware of the subtle differences between the two regimes.[41]

Nothing describing local worship of the period has survived. Nor does the multitude of cases, civil and ecclesiastical, reflect any great theological difference. Perhaps the closest the ecclesiastical records get to theology is in 1695, when James Hunter appeared before the presbytery charged with a catalogue of misdeeds which included denying the Song of Solomon to be canonical and saying that a man of any persuasion might be saved. He rejected those charges, but they are indicative of the Episcopalian distrust of the Song of Solomon and of the Presbyterians' regard for it.[42]

Formal liturgy began to infiltrate the Episcopalian community from about 1690 in Aberdeen and Edinburgh,[43] and with a single recorded usage in Stirling in 1698, as mentioned,[44] it but made little headway until the new century dawned. Elgin had been among the first permanently to accept the English prayer book in 1703 but there is some evidence to suggest nationally that this was driven by lairds who had seen it in action in England and wished to conform, while their less-travelled fellow dissenters disliked the new 'foreign' forms. The spread was helped by large-scale donations of the English prayer book to selected areas of Scotland where episcopacy still had substantial support. There is no record of any coming into the Stirling and Dunblane bounds. The General Assembly thereafter started to make representations about 'innovations in worship', finally leading to the Greenshields case.

The Anglicisation of the landowners in religious matters was to become more marked as the century went on and increasing numbers of children were sent south for education. In 1709, Matthew Wallace, reporting on behalf of Dunblane Presbytery on two special collections that had been gathered, complained to the General Assembly that 'the country being very poor and few of the gentry coming to church here, they are afraid that what shall be gotten will be very inconsiderable'.[45] The Earl of Mar had always been ostensibly Presbyterian in his outlook, if not noticeably active in the promotion of it. His allegiance, however, began to slip and by 1712 he was attending the Episcopalian meeting-house in Stirling, presided over by the egregious, and now qualified by oath, Mr Hunter.[46] The occasion described may have been isolated, Mar being accompanied by several others of the peerage and attending in great state with two coaches pulled by six horses each, but even if it was an unusual visit, such a grand entrance to the town cannot but have been taken as a symbol of the growing ascendancy of the meeting-house.

Parallel with the growth of an Anglicised version of Scottish Episcopalianism came another development, the spread of Bourignonism and the 'French Prophets'.[47] Bourignonism was a phenomenon which swept parts of Europe briefly in the late seventeenth and early eighteenth centuries and found some reception in Scotland. It was sufficiently well known that it led the General Assembly to condemn the Prophets in 1701 and twice more before the end of the decade. It was associated with the activities and writing of Antoinette Bourignon. She had died in 1680 but a community of her followers, known as the Camisards, had grown up in the Cévennes before being scattered by the military action of Louis XIV. Three of the community fled to England, where they gained a following not only among the Huguenot exiles but among the English. Some of these English followers came to Scotland, where they were confusingly called the 'French Prophets' and caught the attention of George Garden, an Episcopalian minister in Aberdeenshire. The success of the movement owed much to its adoption by people from the Episcopalian landowning class, and it was particularly centred on Thomas Hope of Craighall in Fife. Some of its members took their prophecies around Scotland. In 1709, one of the leaders of the movement, Katherine Pringle, Lady Abden, a young widow, embarked on a tour preaching her vision. Between October and December, she and another 'prophet', James Cuninghame, were delivering her prophecies to private audiences and 'in publick' in both the Castle and later the Burgh of Stirling, before taking them to Glasgow.[48] From the pattern of their activities it can be taken for granted that the more receptive among their audiences would be found within the Episcopalian community, but it is a curious coincidence that they should be active in Stirling Castle the very month that a Presbyterian minister, Thomas Davidson, was ordained as the chaplain there.

There seems to be no record of how the people of Stirling received the Prophets. Their prophecies had been met with rioting elsewhere, to the extent that the English Presbyterian Edmund Calamy was threatened with violence in Aberdeen because he was wrongly associated with them.[49] In addition there is no record in burgh, presbytery or synod minutes of the Prophets' presence. The synod was far more interested in the irregularity of Davidson's ordination.[50]

Davidson was an appointment of the Earl of Mar, remaining at the castle until 1713. However, it was perhaps symbolic of Mar's increasing shift of allegiance towards the Episcopalian cause that the following year he was to present a Church of England cleric, Patrick Barclay, variously described as his chaplain and as minister of a meeting-house in Alloa, to be the new chaplain of Stirling Castle.[51]

Despite the tensions between the two parties, a degree of laissez-faire existed. Not every deprived Episcopalian cleric tried to intrude. George Brown, banished from Edinburgh in 1693, lived peaceably for five years in the Stirling area as a schoolmaster and mathematician with only a single brush with the kirk session of Stirling and without ever coming to the notice of the presbytery.[52] Meanwhile in Dunblane, Robert Douglas, son of the deprived bishop, and himself deprived of his parish of Bothwell, became librarian of the Leighton Library and served there for around fifty years. In his early years he fell under the discipline of the presbytery for irregularities, but thereafter there seems to have been no problem.[53] The names of the borrowers from the library show continuing Episcopalian interest. James Drummond and Charles Stirling of Kippendavie were known episcopal sympathisers. The most avid user was James Inglis, Episcopalian minister at Muthil in Perthshire, who remained in his parish for his whole life under the protection of the Murrays of Atholl. His particular interest was Spanish literature. The local deposed Episcopalian ministers do not appear in the register. It was not until 1705 that the local Presbyterian ministers are shown as borrowing: Hugh Walker (Lecropt), Michael Potter (Dunblane) and Alexander Douglas (Logie) from Dunblane Presbytery, together with John Logan, formerly of Kilmadock but by this time in Alloa, from Stirling Presbytery.[54]

It is all too easy consider Episcopalianism in eighteenth-century Lowland Scotland in terms of the influence of landowners such as the Earl of Mar or Sir Hugh Paterson of Bannockburn. That, however, is a feature of the survival of evidence. Yet sporadically through church and court records it can be seen that attachment to the old regime permeated all classes, albeit unquantifiably. The frequency of irregular marriage and baptism still showed attachment to the old ways even if many were using the ousted Episcopalians simply to avoid local embarrassment. The colourful abuse of Thomas Blackburn can be mirrored, if less colourfully in other sources. In 1699, for example, Janet Barron was accused in Clackmannan of:

> cursing the people of God in a malicious manner . . . Janet Young and Margaret Hardie witnesses declared they had heard her curse all the presbyterians and that she had seen a vision of their ruine and the like, but did not remember the particular expressions, they being about the change of government.[55]

Also in Clackmannan came the case of Allard Fithie, who, 'after hearing the curat of Dollar in July on horseback did ride violently after James Dove and beat him to the effusin of his blood'. That case was resolved amicably. Fithie was told to 'beg grace, to repent of all sin, and to live as becomes a Christian with his neighbours'. For his part, Dove was exhorted to pass by the offence and both of them were exhorted 'to live as becomes Christians for the time to come, and take the other by the hand before the Session and each to promise through the strength of God so to doe. Which they performed in face of the Session.'[56] Undoubtedly support for Presbyterian control of the Church of Scotland was not universal at any level of society but efforts were made to make the issue less confrontational.

Considering the attitudes, as far as can be gleaned from the evidence of the courts and of individuals, it seems clear that there was a *de facto* pluralism of belief in the area by 1710: attempts to remove Episcopalian worship had failed, and although the Presbyterians had control in all but two parishes, a parallel 'Episcopal' church was surviving and growing, albeit one with no apparent place for bishops. Beyond the chronological scope of this work, Episcopalianism in the Stirling area was reviving under the pro-Anglican rule of Queen Anne, but its ever-present shadow of Jacobitism led to its considerable eclipse in the area after the rising of 1715 and while it did not disappear thereafter, its character changed.

Notes

1. Bothkennar in Stirling Presbytery; Aberfoyle, Balquhidder and Callander in Dunblane Presbytery.
2. Burns, *Old Scottish Communion Plate*, p. 330.
3. SCA CH2/10/4.
4. Clarke, 'The Scottish Episcopalians, 1688–1720'; Clarke, 'The Williamite Episcopalians and the Glorious Revolution in Scotland'.
5. See for example RPS, Act anent the Supply of Eighteen Moneths' Cess upon the Land Rent (1696), www.rps.ac.uk 1696/9/53 (last accessed 15/2/2021).
6. NLS MS 7593/1–3.
7. Harrison, 'The Justices of the Peace for Stirlingshire, 1660-1706'.
8. 'Episcopacy in Stirling', pp. 213–29.
9. This appears to be conflation of two people, John Murray of Polmaise and Charles Bennet of Livilands.
10. Again Livilands is described as the property of Mr Murray, while the case of 1709 has it belonging to Charles Bennet. The situation is unclear. Balthayock is near Perth, and was in the hands of the Blair family. The source would seem to imply, though, that Lady Balthayock lived in the St Ninians area.
11. SCA B66/25/665.
12. SCA B66/25/779/1/18. I am grateful to John Harrison for drawing my attention to this item. This uproar seems to have happened on the day of Rule's funeral.
13. SCA B66/25/779/4 (unnumbered items).
14. Barclay, *Love, Intimacy and Power*, pp. 181–2, 189–90.
15. SCA CH2/722/8 21/3/1701.
16. Raffe, *Scotland in Revolution, 1685–1690*, p. 142.
17. SCA CH2/722/8 9/5/1693, 31/5/1693.
18. SCA CH2/722/8 13/7/1693, 9/5/1694.
19. SCA CH2/722/8 13/2/1696, 3/12/1696; SCA CH2/723/5 15/11/1698.
20. NRS CH1/2/4/11 1703–4.
21. Goldie, *A Short History of the Episcopal Church in Scotland*, p. 34.
22. NRS PA7/28/21; Bowie, *Addresses against Incorporating Union, 1706–07*, p. 115. Bowie sees this address as more accommodating to the church than its Angus counterpart (PA7/28/7); nonetheless the joint petition from the four parishes (PA7/28/49) and from St Ninians (PA7/28/80) are much more Presbyterian in tone.
23. Due to the vagaries of handwriting he is sometimes found as 'Hirie' rather than Slirie. I have preferred the *Fasti* usage.
24. NRS JC13/1 Journal book of the western district Oct. 1708 to May 1709, p. 168.
25. 'Episcopacy in Stirling', p. 227.
26. NRS JC13/1 Journal book of the western district Oct. 1708 to May 1709, p. 168.
27. Ibid.

28. Grange was a maverick figure whose later evangelical position belied his personal life. A useful summary of his career can be found in Coffey, 'Evangelical Revival in Enlightenment Britain'.
29. SCA SBC/11/5 23/8/1709.
30. James Greenshields, Clerk *v.* The Lord Provost and Magistrates of the City of Edinburgh, [1711] UKHL Robertson 12, available at www.casemine.com/judgement/uk/5a8ff8c360d03e7f57eccd21 (last accessed 15/2/2021).
31. An Act to prevent the disturbing those of the Episcopal Communion in Scotland in the Exercise of their Religious Worship and in the Use of the Liturgy of the Church of England and for repealing the Act passed in the Parliament of Scotland intituled Act against irregular Baptisms and Marriages, 10 Ann C. 10.
32. *London Gazette*, issue 5039, 2/8/1712, p. 1.
33. 'Paterson, Sir Hugh, 3rd Bt. (c.1685–1777), of Bannockburn House, St. Ninians, Stirling', History of Parliament, http://www.historyofparliamentonline.org/volume/1690-1715/member/paterson-sir-hugh-1685-1777 (last accessed 15/2/2021).
34. *London Gazette*, issue 5070, 18/11/1712, p. 1.
35. *London Gazette*, issue 5102, 10/3/1713, p. 1.
36. *London Gazette*, issue 5103, 14/3/1713, p. 1.
37. *Post Boy*, 19/3/1713.
38. *Flying Post*, 7/4/1713. The errant ex-provost was John Dick, expelled from Parliament in 1695, although his 'irreligious expressions' are not recorded.
39. Matheson, 'Preaching in the Churches of Scotland', p. 153.
40. But see previous chapter for Archibald Douglas's practice in Saltoun.
41. Clarke, 'The Scottish Episcopalians, 1688–1720', pp. 3–4.
42. SCA CH2/722/8 18/12/1695.
43. Goldie, *A Short History of the Episcopal Church in Scotland*, p. 39.
44. SCA CH2/1026/5 31/8/1698.
45. NRS CH1/2/30/3/283 Letter from Matthew Wallace to Moderator, 29/11/1709.
46. Clarke, 'The Scottish Episcopalians, 1688–1720', p. 360, quoting Bodl MS Ballard 36 fo.136r, Greenshields to Charlett.
47. Riordan, 'Mysticism and Prophecy in Early Eighteenth-Century Scotland'.
48. I am indebted to Michael Riordan for information about the Prophets' activities in Stirling. Some of the prophecies as delivered in Stirling can be found in Cuninghame and Mackenzie, *Warnings of the Eternal Spirit to the City of Glasgow*.
49. Calamy, *An Historical Account of My Own Life*, vol. 2, p. 197.
50. NRS CH2/449/5 11/4/1711.
51. Clarke, 'The Scottish Episcopalians, 1688–1720', p. 360, quoting Bodl MS Ballard 36, ff.136r & 170r. Barclay does not appear in Bertie, *Scottish Episcopal Clergy, 1689-2000*, and is otherwise unknown.
52. Clarke, 'The Scottish Episcopalians, 1688–1720', p. 482 n82.
53. SCA CH2/722/8 19/12/1694, 27/2/1695.
54. SCA CH2/101/9/2. A useful transcript of names compiled by Linda Chapman in 1999 is to be found at SCA CH2/101/9/1. This includes an index of borrowers but the identification of them is incomplete.
55. SCA CH2/1242/3.
56. SCA CH2/1242/3 23/12/1697, 10/2/1698.

CHAPTER NINE

Church Discipline and the Law

Church Discipline

True Discipline and Government, that which is conform to and founded upon the Word of God, is to be held fast.[1]

As that no Common-wealth can flourish, or long indure, without good lawes and sharpe execution of the same; so neither can the Kirk of God be brought to purity, neither yet retained in the same without the order of Ecclesiasticall Discipline, which stands in reproving and correcting of the faults, which the civill sword either doth neglect, or not punish: Blasphemie, adulterie, murder, perjurie, and other crimes capitall, worthy of death, ought not properly to fall under censure of the Kirk; because all such open transgressors of Gods lawes, ought to be taken away by the civill sword. But drunkenness, excesse, be it in apparel, or be it in eating and drinking, fornication, oppressing of the poore by exactions, deceiving of them in buying and selling by wrang met and measure, wanton words and licentious living tending to slander, doe openly appertaine to the kirk of God to punish them, as Gods word commands.[2]

The control which the church wielded over personal behaviour had been exerted, if somewhat less strenuously, by the pre-Reformation church. It was a noted and well-documented feature of the Protestant Scottish Church from early days, perhaps reaching its zenith shortly before Cromwell took control of Scotland. Reputedly discipline did not play as big a part in the episcopal church of Charles II and James VII; but the accuracy of this belief is a subject which would reward further study on a national basis. Discipline was certainly given considerable attention, and not just where the Sabbath observance laws were used to pursue Covenanters.

In St Ninians parish a Presbyterian session clerk indexed the volume of the session records which covered the final twenty-three years of Episcopalian administration and the first three years of Presbyterian. The former years included 125 cases of fornication and 41 of ante-nuptial fornication against twenty-four and four respectively in the latter period. Other offences show a similar pattern, as can be seen in Table 9.1. Whether the parish was less moral or more investigated in the later period is a question which must remain unanswered, but it is clear that both sessions paid considerable attention to the morals of their flocks.

Table 9.1 Discipline Cases in St Ninians Kirk Session Records, 1667–93

	Episcopal period		Presbyterian period	
	23 years	per year	3 years	per year
Adultery	13	0.57	3	1.00
Drunkenness	5	0.22	2	0.67
Fornication	125	5.43	24	8.00
Ante-nuptial fornication	41	1.78	4	1.33
Sabbath breaking	15	0.65	4	1.33
Scandals	23	1.00	3	1.00

Note: The latter part of this index covers only three years of Presbyterian control prior to the arrival of John Logan in 1694.
Source: CH2/337/2 pp. 417–72.

Some work has been done in the context of Dunblane parish by Bill Inglis,[3] and at a national level the work of Rosalind Mitchison and Leah Leneman covers the topic from 1660 onwards in two books,[4] while Alison Hanham's work on Cramond gives a concentrated study of one parish over a 200-year range.[5] There does seem to be a sense that the Revolution brought a new start to the exercise of church discipline if only because in most kirk sessions it was a new set of men who had taken up the task and they needed to set priorities and learn how to regulate their parishes.

The behaviour they were looking to control, together with a suitable division of responsibility between the courts of the church, was set out in the *First Book of Discipline* in 1560, one of the foundation documents of the reformed Church of Scotland. In general, kirk sessions were responsible for trying the more minor misdemeanours, with the more serious offences or the more recalcitrant of offenders being referred to the presbytery. One misdemeanour, dealt with at parish level, was profanation of the Lord's Day, which could encompass many activities which might be looked down upon on other days but sparked action on a Sunday or a fast day. These would include cursing and swearing, drunkenness, quarrelling and abusing family members, but also activities such as work which were encouraged on other days but not on Sundays.

Another problem dealt with in the kirk session was irregular marriage and baptism. Marriages and baptisms celebrated by people other than parish ministers had been deprecated under episcopal rule, when ousted Presbyterian clergy were the offenders. After 1690 deprived Episcopalian incumbents made what money they could from the Episcopalian faithful, and from not a few Presbyterian unfaithful. Such marriages and baptisms were recognised as legal though irregular, but those who were involved could expect to face the wrath of the kirk session in their home parish and probably a fine to pay for the benefit of the poor.

The major offence to occupy kirk sessions, though, tended to be fornication, ante-nuptial and otherwise, together with a vaguer charge of 'scandalous carriage'.[6] The offences which were referred to the presbytery included those mentioned where circumstances put them beyond the competence of the lower court. Both contumacy, where the accused persons refused to attend or refused the discipline of the session, and trilapse in fornication exacerbated the original offence and put the offenders into the ambit of the presbytery. Cases where the social standing of the offenders made the session less willing to consider their case also quickly made their way to the higher court. Other charges were automatically referred there: sexual ones such as adultery, incest, bestiality or homosexuality, and more rarely, infanticide and witchcraft.

Minor vestiges of pre-Christian belief might come under the kirk session, but any suspicion of witchcraft was dealt with by the presbytery and if deemed to be such, immediately transmitted to the civil authorities. In an area where Robert Kirk, one of the episcopal clergy, was deeply concerned with the otherworld, it is clear that those vestiges had significance.[7] Where the limits between those beliefs and witchcraft were set could be a matter for interpretation, though. In Clackmannan in 1702, one William Anderson of Sauchie confessed guilt in 'consulting a dumbie'. The kirk session thought it was a universal custom in and around Sauchie to consult mutes on account of a belief that they had second sight, and let him off with a sessional rebuke.[8] The only case actually referred to the presbytery was that of a group of people from Larbert, six women and a man, brought before Stirling Presbytery in May 1699 charged with 'turning the riddle', another divination practice. However, the presbytery was content to send them back to Larbert Kirk Session for a rebuke, for this too was not considered serious witchcraft.[9] In point of fact, neither Dunblane nor Stirling Presbytery saw any witchcraft cases after about 1660, despite the presence of ministers who had been or were to be involved in well-known cases in Renfrewshire and Fife. Cases of 'charming' and other pre-Christian practices were widespread and remained so but the accusation of witchcraft was more likely to bring the accuser rather than the accused to the attention of the courts.

If some offences were speedily transferred to the consideration of the presbytery, others were slower in their progress. Contumacy was necessarily one of the slower offences, dependent on a process of multiple citings. This could work through being told to appear, more formal summonses served by the session officer and finally public citations from the pulpit. Allowing for a significant number of excuses being given for non-attendance, the process could be strung out over several months.

Trilapse and quadrilapse in fornication and adultery tended to go to the higher court more quickly, although establishing the offence itself might take time. In these cases, the usual judgment of the presbytery was to remit the convicted offender back to the congregation for the appropriate number of appearances before it, but with the knowledge that civil penalties could follow and that the presbytery had the means to track miscreants.

The flight or non-availability of the accused was a perpetual issue. A significant number of alleged fathers were soldiers or, less commonly, vagrants. In the case of soldiers, efforts were made, sometimes successfully, to trace them through their units especially if they had been based locally for a time. Even if they had moved on, they often had not gone far. However, relocation to serve in the foreign wars made the problem greater. In some cases the alleged father absconded to join the army in Flanders, while the Darien scheme also drew young men in trouble to the ranks of its colonists.[10] They did not usually come back.

Flight was much less of an option for women. On the whole, if they left the area it was to move to neighbouring parishes, or to Edinburgh, as did many of the men. This led to continual requests either to Edinburgh Presbytery or to individual ministers for help in tracing persons of interest. Such requests were variable in their efficacy but some were traced and returned. Movement of people, particularly of servants, was supposed to be accompanied by testificats to confirm the good behaviour of migrants. They might also give evidence that previous issues had been dealt with and that satisfaction before the congregation had followed fornication. Arrival without such evidence meant that the person involved was unlikely to be admitted to Communion, and might indeed be expelled from the parish, especially if there was any issue suspected. Examples can be found in the session records of Clackmannan of actual expulsion, and also of forged testificats to try to convince the session of respectability.[11]

Adultery, of course, was always looked upon as heinous, although it is interesting to note that persistent, and especially promiscuous, fornication drew similar punishments in the ecclesiastical courts, although not in the civil ones. Of the other major sexual issues, those associated with homosexuality do not appear in the record for the two presbyteries at all, but incest and bestiality do occasionally. The two cases of bestiality which find their way into the record were both referred from the kirk session of St Ninians, one in 1706 and the other in 1709. In the former, James Gillespie, the son of a soldier, was referred to the presbytery meeting of 3 July 1706. By that stage he had gone away and no real effort seems to have been made to retrieve him. The witnesses were said to be abroad and in October, remarkably swiftly, it has to be said, the process was sisted (halted) on account of the 'slenderness of the evidence'. 'Discovery was left to the providence of God.'[12]

The second case involved one David Dinn, who sought permission to marry in November 1708. This was passed to the presbytery and in January of 1709 it was further referred to the synod, with his minister appointed to produce the report (in which appointment he was dilatory). The case was referred yet further to the General Assembly and the final ecclesiastical outcome is unknown. In both cases the unwillingness of the presbytery to act is evident, but the situation was further complicated by the fact that Dinn had been cited to a circuit court meeting in October of 1708 on a charge of bestiality and the case deserted with no evidence being presented. This must have made further action by the church courts difficult.[13]

Incest too was only claimed in a few cases, but with two distinct types, the consenting and the abusive. In June 1707, Agnes Graham confessed to an irregular marriage with James Smith. Irregular because conducted by a deposed Episcopalian, Archibald McLachlan, it was made even more so by the fact that Smith was her late husband's grandnephew, and therefore within the forbidden degrees at that time. Smith, a slater, appeared before Dunblane Presbytery in the November and also confessed. The case went to the synod, with Smith being declared contumacious in the midst of it. The two were forbidden from cohabiting on pain of excommunication and ordered to appear before the congregation of Kilmadock in sackcloth for removing the scandal. Graham's response to this was to say that she did not recognise the marriage as discharged (banned) by the law of God and so would not be convinced of the unlawfulness of it. At this the synod decided to move on with the sentence of excommunication and told the presbytery so to proceed.[14] At the same time, however, the Presbytery of Dunblane had sought advice from Sir James Steuart of Goodtrees, the Lord Advocate. There is no explanation of why Goodtrees referred to Agnes Graham as Hadden:

> Some tyme agoe my advice was asked anent the marriadge betwixt on James Smith and Agnes Hadden which was alledged to be insestuous because the said James Smith was grand-nephew to the said Agnes her former husband and I then answered that a nephew or grand-nephew was the same thing and seeing she could not be lawfully married to her husband's nephew no more could she be lawfully married to his grand-nephew.
>
> I perceive since that tyme your presbiterie is not only going to declare the marriadge incestuous but to enjoyne the persons to make publick repentance in sackcloath Under the pain of excommunication and that this is heavyly taken for besydes that the parties married ignorantly and innocently the woman has five children to her former husband and is presentlie with chylde to this present husband. I know they married disorderly without proclaimation qch makes it all the worse, but all things considered I would have the presbyterie to reprove them for the sin of their marriadge and bring them to a sense of the unlawfulness of it , and to enjoyn them for hereafter to seperat and not to cohabit as man and wife which I suppose they will observe and for farder censur since the thing was don innocently and ignorantly . . . I think they should leave the rest to the civall magistrate and I write this to you because I see the poor woman is greatly concerned and that ye are several that have confessions upon her soe that if you fairly seperat them for hereafter I would again entreat you to forbear farder censure and above all that of excommunication which is not lyke in this caice to be edifying. Sir this is the advice offer to you and your presbitrie and from Your most humble servant, James Steuart.[15]

This seems to have been a rare instance, and no other examples of legal advice by Goodtrees to presbyteries seem to have survived, but local elder Sir Colin Campbell, Lord Aberuchill, was regularly asked for advice in legal matters.

If that case seems to present two consenting adults at odds with the law, other incest cases savour more of family abuse. The unnamed daughter of Edward Wilson in Glendevon bore a child of which her father was accused of being the father. As the father had disappeared, little could be done other than make arrangements to baptise the child.[16]

Levels of Punishment and Resolution

The actual process of punishment was variable, and sometimes not clear from the record. The records refer to people 'entering the pillar', 'on the pillar', 'in the place of repentance' and 'on the black stool'. Sometimes a sackcloth gown was specifically added to the sentence, which seems to imply that not all offenders were expected to be so garbed. It is no coincidence that one of the early acts of the kirk session of Port of Menteith after the arrival of their new minister in 1697 was to purchase a new sackcloth gown at a cost of £2 9s. and 'a new ladder to the pillar' at 7s. A new 'transportable' seat for scandalous persons to appear publicly upon was built in 1703 at a cost of 25s.[17]

Stephen Davies's thesis 'Law and Order in Stirlingshire, 1637–1747' provides a very detailed breakdown of discipline cases in the historical county.[18] In his analysis he shows the wide variety of punishments for various offences although he does not attempt to break the figures down by either period or parish.

Thus there was a sliding range of punishments available for the discouragement of wrongdoing. The actual level of punishment would depend on the perpetrators' attitudes and perceived penitence. It might also depend on their individual circumstances, with a prominent citizen, or indeed a vulnerable person, being less likely to incur the full public ordeal. At the most trivial level an admonition might be enough, with a 'sessional rebuke' as a rather more formal action, often accompanied by the statement that repetition of the offence would lead to a more severe punishment. Not every kirk session recorded its sessional rebukes, but Clackmannan used them widely, especially for minor public order offences such as quarrelling, swearing or slander.

Clackmannan had a particular penchant for quarrelling and cursing, or perhaps for recording it, and it is clear that the session there felt it had an important role to play in preserving the peace of the community. A further example from Clackmannan also shows how the sessional rebuke was used if it was felt that a public penance would cause more harm than good. Thomas Hall was cited on the grounds of having hit some children on a Sunday when they were among his peas and stealing them. He acknowledged guilt, craved forgiveness and promised amendment: 'The session fearing the greater profanation of the Lord's Day by wicked children to go out among his and other folks' peas, if he should be brought to public, thought fit to give him a sessional rebuke and exhortation.'[19] Hall too was told that a repetition would lead to a public appearance.

The next step up tended to be appearance before the congregation. Most commonly this was used for cases of fornication. Davies's figures for 'fornication' show that 1,317 out of 1,951 recorded cases led to three Sabbaths' appearance before the congregation. Twenty-four had a mere single appearance, while 170 led to six or more appearances. Thirteen were purged by oath.[20] A total of six appearances was normal for a relapse and a variable number for adultery. The kirk session of Stirling was particularly firm and might insist on twenty-six, a half-year's sentence of appearances, for an adulterer.

The ritual of such an appearance must have been part of the punishment for the penitent in many cases. This can be confirmed from the record of another adulterer, Agnes Cousine, who approached the kirk session of Clackmannan in these terms in 1698. She,

> desiring to speak with them was called, & being asked what she had to say to the session, replyed that she humbly craved the session would take her case to their consideration, who, tho she hath been guiltie of gross adultery, through which she hath given offence to God & his people, and she now been nigh a year upon her publick repentance before the congregation in sackcloth, by which & the straitning circumstances of the time, her body is brought very low, therefore she humbly begs if their godly wisdom shall think fit, they would absolve her, nevertheless she is willing to refer her case to the session's determination.[21]

Practice varied between churches as to whether it was thought appropriate that the penitents should appear before the congregation together or consecutively, although this could also depend on the availability of the penitents. An errant mother might be permitted to delay appearance until a week or two after the birth, a father, particularly one who had denied involvement, might do his penance long after the mother had been absolved. In the case of ante-nuptial fornication, it was usual for the couple to make their appearance together, but in other cases the process for the one would be finished before the other made their appearance.

The actual appearance might then follow its own ritual. Detailed examples are rare, but the appearance of John Pirie and Agnes Rob before the congregation of St Ninians in December 1700 was ordered as follows:

> The which day the presbyterie considering that John Pirie and Agnes Rob were appointed to satisfie as Adulterers and execution of summons against them being returned. The sd Agnes was called who compeared and was appointed to stand at the church door of St Ninians in sack-

cloath the next Lord's day from the ringing of the second bell until the ringing of the third bell, and immediately thereafter to go through the congregation unto the public place of repentance and there to stand until she be rebuked and so make her appearance after this manner from Sabbath to Sabbath untill she be absolved.[22]

Pirie by this stage had fled and a bond given on his behalf for 500 merks was considered forfeit.

The kirk session did not have the authority to act independently in deciding that there had been enough appearances. It had to refer back to the presbytery, which would involve the pannel (defendant) appearing there. The presbytery would then decide that a final appearance followed by public absolution was in order and that would be the end of the process.

Such appearances depended on the co-operation of the penitent. It was not unknown for the object of the penance to take the occasion lightly. Again in Clackmannan, whose records are a fruitful source of the more eccentric manifestations of session business, John Hall made his disdain for the proceedings evident. He was said to have invited two young men to go along with him to the pillar to keep him company there. He denied he had engaged them but they sat with him 'on the black stool'. He had a further three appearances added on to the two he had made, while his two friends received sessional rebukes and were told the incident would be revisited if they transgressed again.

One matter which gave sessions particular difficulties was when the person summoned to appear was one of the local landowners, possibly landlord or employer to some of the session members. Sometimes the session would simply refer the matter to presbytery at an early stage, but sometimes it would take it on itself.

Port of Menteith parish was largely under the control of members of the Graham family, although there were many other Grahams who filled more modest roles. Eleven per cent of the heads of families recorded in the hearth tax records were called Graham. Of thirty cases of fornication or adultery dealt with by the session between 1697 and 1701, eleven involved a man called Graham and three involved a woman called Graham. One of these cases involved Walter Graham of Gartur, who was accused of fathering a child on his servant, Margaret Tailor. The session approached the matter cautiously. Rather than the normal procedure of summoning him, the minister was despatched to interview the laird. He acknowledged his child, but asked that he might do his penance not in the place of repentance, but in the front of the church sitting in an armchair because of his poor health. Further delays took place, again on health grounds, but two years later he was summoned again for a 'flagrant case of fornication with Isobel McLauran'. Again it was up to the minister to converse with him since he was reported to be dying. He finally paid a fine for the benefit of the poor, well in excess of the going rate, but he died before he could make his appearance.[23]

Other lairds were equally problematic. Sir John Schaw of Sauchie had already been dealt with by the then episcopal kirk session of Clackmannan in the 1680s, but David Bruce, laird of Clackmannan, whose child's baptism has previously been mentioned, took matters a stage further. The origins of the saga lie in a period from which Clackmannan church records have failed to survive. Unusually, in this case the reasons for non-survival are clear: the laird had abstracted them from the clerk's house and burned them, an action which he admitted but never paid any penalty for.[24] It is known, however, that Clackmannan was divorced on the grounds of adultery in 1694, there being three co-respondents.[25] Thereafter the Presbytery of Stirling was involved firstly for a case of fornication with Agnes Cousine (presumably a different one from the one noted above, but not necessarily). He was then charged with cohabiting with another of the three, Elizabeth Bruce, to whom he claimed to be married. As the law did not allow the guilty party in a divorce suit to marry the co-respondent, neither the church nor the law recognised the marriage. Clackmannan was also, incidentally, a party in a bond issued by Stirling Parish Church which he proved unable to repay. His refusal to give up his 'pretended lady', as the records refer to her, led ultimately to the excommunication of both of them.

Clackmannan's case takes up many pages in the records; he was adept at what some clerks called 'juggling' with the court. As a result his excommunication took many years, but also had its own ritual, involving public prayer for the people involved and intimations in all the neighbouring parishes. Excommunication was a seriously awkward position for those who remained locally as normal social intercourse was cut off and only those interactions required for purchasing necessities were allowed.

Another source of problems for a kirk session was its own servants. Port of Menteith had particular trials. The session wanted to reappoint the session officer who had served under the previous incumbent. This may have been a mistake. John Battieson was initially unwilling to serve as that meant taking an oath, which he was unwilling to do, but as the heritors wished for his continuation, he complied at a salary of £4 per year. In 1699 he was rebuked by the session for his negligence in failing to summon one of the many misbehaving Grahams. Worse was to come for the next year he was suspended for assisting the session clerk, precentor and schoolmaster John Gray to abduct Jean Mackieson from her brother's house.[26] Battieson's defence was that the lady was a willing accomplice, but nevertheless he was suspended from office and the matter referred to the presbytery, which ordered his appearance before the congregation and then permitted his reinstatement to his post on condition of retaking the oath '*de fideli*'. He was deposed from office again in 1703 on the grounds of extreme drunkenness coming back from the market in Doune and because he had ordered his servant and a boy to deliver summonses for him.[27] Meanwhile Gray was permanently deprived of his office.[28] The case does seem to have been one of elopement rather than abduction for he married the lady in question shortly after. James Hardie, Gray's replacement in all three roles, had been schoolmaster in Buchlyvie prior to appointment. He too was ultimately deposed in 1719 for a long litany of shortcomings including not filling in the session minute book for seven years.[29]

Elders too sometimes found themselves cited before their colleagues. Gabriel Ranken of Orchardhead was perhaps a special case in Bothkennar, but Bailie John Burd in Stirling and Robert Kemp in Airth both found themselves in trouble. The Airth case was more serious and in the absence of a parish minister was swiftly referred to the presbytery. As part of the presbytery's attention to a very divided parish in 1693, several ministers were conducting worship, receiving fairly discourteous treatment. The precentor, John Lamb, complained to the presbytery about his treatment by elders, with another man, Robert Cook, also asking that the presbytery should look into 'scandals'. When George Turnbull, minister of Alloa, was sent to investigate, as he reported, he appointed Lamb to precent as usual.

> [Lamb] accordingly having given out the line of the psalm, Robert Kemp, one of the elders, did officiously in a disorderly and irregular manner take upon him to raise the same sitting on his bottom to the opposing of the publick worship of God to the derision of the ungodly.[30]

Kemp, who was also under investigation for some unspecified 'gross scandals', was suspended from the eldership. Further trouble surrounded Kemp when Turnbull again preached in Airth in May of the following year and 'mett with some opposition on Mr Mair's account'.[31] Kemp was one of several elders alleged to be leading the abuse and was reported to the justices of the peace. The presbytery, for its part, asked the justices in question, the lairds of Thirtieacres and Greenyards, to be 'tender' with the men. Both Thirtieacres and Greenyards, as has been noted, were elders in St Ninians and long-term supporters of Presbyterianism locally while Thirtieacres himself had been censured by St Ninians session for his infrequent attendance.

In the general run of discipline cases, the session had the option of imposing fines on the perpetrators of the commoner offences, fornication, swearing and breach of the Sabbath. Mention has already been made of the substantial payment in Port by the laird of Gartur, but the normal level of fine for fornication tended to be around £4, substantially less than the potential civil law penalty, and usually earmarked for the support of the poor. Evidence for imposition of this is sketchy and irregular. The account books for Port show a number of payments, but not enough to suggest a universal imposition. However, in Port it was fairly common practice for the man to be fined £4 and the woman £2, and in several cases it was noted that the man had paid both. In Tulliallan and Clackmannan, on the other hand, both parties were generally fined £4 and there is no evidence of the man paying both. The situations were perhaps different in Port, where there was a preponderance of cases of the man being of a higher socio-economic class than the servant whom he had made pregnant. Also in Port, if the father was of a significantly higher status a higher amount might be levied.[32]

It would appear, although it was rarely stated, that fines were not imposed on those who could not afford to pay them. Where the income for fines is detailed, as in Port, there are simply not enough entries to suggest that they were universally enforced. In Port there is also a question of whether parish relief was in fact paid out to the women while they were still under scandal. Several names both of fornicators and of adulterers appear as recipients, but unfortunately it is not clear whether these were the same people or simply people of the same name.

There was more to submission to session discipline than just appearance in front of the session or congregation. Every parent wanted their child baptised, preferably as soon as possible. Some 'fornicators' took the step of using a deposed preacher, thereby incurring further disciplinary action, and others petitioned the kirk session to allow the child to be baptised. If the scandal was not yet satisfied, the parents would have to provide someone who would offer a bond against non-completion of the penalty, and also an external sponsor. William McFarlane in Port, who had appeared on two fornication charges in 1707, found himself with two children to have baptised the following year so a double baptism was celebrated in May 1708. 'Robert son to Wm & Margaret McFarlanes begotten without the bond of marriage; & Mary daughter to the said Wm Mcfarlane in Over Ardvickar and Lillias Taylour, all begotten in fornication; and held up by James McFarlane in Grameston.'[33] William and Margaret (who had been his servant) were only allowed to marry on condition that she moved out of his household prior to the wedding.[34] What Lillias Taylour thought is not recorded.

Once satisfaction for the scandal had been given, the miscreant would be rebuked and dismissed with an absolution for the offence. (The normal phraseology was '*x* appeared *pro 3tio*, absolved and dismissed'.) On the odd occasions when the appearances had been made but the session was unconvinced of the genuineness of the penitence, absolution might not be given, but further action stopped. Absolution, however, brought finality to the matter unless the penitent reoffended.

Not all discipline cases were proven and completed, though. Sometimes evidence was not forthcoming, or the two parties gave varying accounts of the matter. In such a case, an oath of exculpation might be offered by the party claiming to be innocent or it might be offered to them. The process for this was also charged with what was effectively a ritual. The significance of this would be spelled out in detail and one of the ministers appointed to compose it. At a following meeting of the session, the oath would be read to the person and he or she would be invited to go away and think about what they were doing. Finally, if they still were adamant in claiming innocence, they would be invited to swear the oath in front of the congregation. An example from an Episcopalian meeting-house in 1714 outlines the preamble to such an oath taken before the congregation, and there is no reason to think that it would be different in a Presbyterian congregation. Amid several similar paragraphs comes this:

> Sir as you know it is my duty to require you to ponder that no arts will be able to cover and palliate a conscience that is truly guilty in the sight of God. That no worldly shame is to be laid in the balance with the horror, the dreadful shame and confusion in when the prevaricative sinner shall stand before God to whom all things are naked and open, in an assembly that will be infinitely more solemn. The presence of angels and men when God shall bring every work into judgement with every secret thing whether it be good or whether it be evil.
>
> You are to ponder the words you have heard discoursed of he that covereth his sins shall not prosper, but whoso confesseth and forsaketh shall find mercy.[35]

The oath itself was in a similar vein. This is an example from 1695 in Dunblane:

> I after serious and due consideration of the majesty and justice of the great and eternal God who will not suffer any sin to be hid much less the taking of his glorious and blessed name in vain, do call this great and dreadful god, the searcher of the secrets of all hearts to witness of the truth of this my following deposition wherein I swear by the terrible and dreadful name of the eternal god as I shall be judged at the last and most solemn day of accounts, that I never at any time or in any place had carnal dealing or copulation with H And if this day I swear falsely do here before the people of the Lord in this congregation renounce my interest in Christ Jesus and that salvation purchased by him for sinners and any right in heaven or eternal happiness; wishing that all the plagues and judgements threatened and pronounced in the word of God contained in the scriptures of the old and new testaments against the breaking of the Law of God may be inflicted upon me in this life and that I may be an object of eternal wrath and vengeance in hell for the life to come if this be not the truth that I have sworn.[36]

For anyone who was actually innocent, the whole process must have been a daunting ordeal, possibly worse than that gone through by those pleading guilty to the offence. It is clear from the records that many did baulk at taking the oath and pled guilty. Many more men than women seem to have taken the oath, although it was certainly offered and administered to women.

One problem that arose was when the session or the presbytery decided that the prospective swearer of the oath did not have the mental or moral capacity and therefore should not take it.[37] When the oath had been taken, that was considered to be the end of the matter, and even if it contradicted the evidence given by the other party, no further action seems to have been taken against the person swearing.

Church Discipline and the Civil Law

Among the issues to affect the way that the church dealt with disciplinary matters was the place of the civil authorities in supporting the church courts, or otherwise, and the boundaries between ecclesiastical concerns and the law of the land. In the period under consideration, the application of secular law nationally was fragmented, imposed by acts of the two Parliaments (Scottish until 1707, British thereafter) and acts of the Privy Council. In the early months of the Revolution, the Privy Council was critical in establishing a firm base for the Presbyterianism which was to prevail and a number of acts made the position clear, both in the sense of establishing Presbyterian power and in establishing its limits. In addition, the Privy Council had always acted as a court to try individual cases and this continued.

In the actual administration of the law, it was only at the highest levels of the Privy Council and the Court of Justiciary that justice was centrally administered. In the landward counties and stewartries,[38] justice was the responsibility of largely hereditary sheriffs with sheriffs depute appointed by them to act on their behalf. Which laws to impose and how was largely left to the choice of the most powerful and their political stance at the time.

Justice in the royal burghs was administered by the town magistrates, the elected bailies. Their administration of justice would depend on its perceived utility to the prosperity of the town, or on their individual points of view; bailies would always be of the merchant class within a royal burgh and elected for a limited period. Smaller burghs, the burghs of regality and barony, might also have bailies, or a single bailie, but these would be appointed by and responsible to the landowner. Meanwhile there were also justices of the peace, who held courts to deal with minor matters, and they took on a greater importance after the Union of the Parliaments.

At a lower level still there might be constables and other officers to act on behalf of the bailies in the same way as session officers and presbytery officers acted on behalf of those courts. Finally, commissary courts, based locally in Stirling and Dunblane, had been ecclesiastical courts before the Reformation, but since then had been entirely secular institutions dealing with matrimonial and testamentary matters.

These legal arrangements were not static, and changed over the period. To put it simplistically, the Privy Council's interest in matters ecclesiastical was to change in its direction as its authority became more stable and it became less interested in the support of Presbyterianism. It finally met its demise as a collateral effect of the Union of the Parliaments. The post-Union Parliament would also pass acts which radically changed the dominant position of the church. By 1711, civil authorities were expressly forbidden to take action against Episcopalian meeting-houses, but civil support for other ecclesiastical cases also became rarer at the same time.[39]

Within the local areas, all these institutions and functionaries had their influence. Where they were appointed by the local magnates, sheriffs depute and stewards depute reflected the standpoint and priorities of their superiors. As a result, they could be less than helpful to parishes and presbyteries. Trying to dislodge one Magdalene Younger from cohabiting with her employer and banish her from Clackmannan, the kirk session was rebuffed in July 1699 by the sheriff depute, who told it that it was an affair purely ecclesiastical and therefore not competent for him to meddle with.[40] Thereafter Clackmannan session asked the minister of Alloa to take it to the bailie of the Regality of Alloa, who was more sympathetic. The same situation was echoed in St Ninians, where lack of co-operation from the sheriff depute was circumvented by referring matters to the Stirling Burgh courts, which were firmly Presbyterian in sympathy. The fragmented nature of legal governance allowed a pragmatic approach to parish and legal boundaries.

In Larbert, attempts began to eject their schoolmaster, John Carruthers, on the grounds of drunkenness, cursing, sloth and negligence in June 1695, when he was deposed. By December of the following year the presbytery was still trying to dislodge him and decided to enlist the sheriff depute's help. Carruthers was still there in June 1697 and his ejection still in the hands of the sheriff depute.[41]

A similar story unfolded in Dollar under a different sheriff depute. Robert Ritchie had been appointed as schoolmaster by some of the heritors despite the presbytery wishing to appoint another man. The presbytery had previously examined Ritchie for a different post and found him unsuitable. Ritchie had been discharged but remained in possession of school and schoolhouse. Application to the sheriff depute was swiftly refused and in November 1699, Harie Robine, minister of Alva, was instructed to escalate the matter to the sheriff principal. A year later Ritchie was still there, and by this stage the presbytery resorted to asking a judge of the Court of Session to add his weight. He declined too and it was not until the main heritor of Dollar, the non-resident Earl of Argyll,[42] was contacted that the Commissary of Stirling promised to take action in April 1701.[43]

In another case brought before the sheriff clerk at the same time, he was reported to have said that he could only fine people whom the presbytery referred to him, not force them to appear before the presbytery. However, some pressure could be brought on the sheriffs by referring cases to the King's advocate, who could then oblige them to summon contumacious witnesses.[44]

In contrast, after the Presbyterian faction obtained control of the council, the Burgh Court of Stirling seems to have been both willing and prompt in taking a hand on behalf of both kirk session and presbytery, probably because there was always at least one bailie sitting on the kirk session and sometimes also in the presbytery. In this case the recalcitrant Sabbath breakers were swiftly consigned to the tolbooth by bailie John Allan, although they were soon released.[45] More draconian still, as described in Chapter 8, the same bailie arrested Adam Peacock, a deprived Episcopalian minister, in 1703. Although the church was not involved in his arrest, the presbytery wrote to the Privy Council to complain of Peacock's intrusion.[46]

Although the arrest of Peacock was carried out by bailie Allan in person, where the civil authorities were involved, enforcement might devolve on to local constables or officers. In one such case,

> David Reid, weaver in toun, had been drunk and late at night . . . he went to John Stuart's and there under night pronounced with great oaths that the said John was obligded to him for his being in toun so long and that he would suffer him to abide no longer, the said David cited, compeared, and being charged with his guilt alleged that what he did to John Stuart was but part of his dutie as a constable and that he had a commission to put him out of toun, which if they would not allow, he should desist; The session considering that he was a constable appointed to give him a sessional rebuke and admonition to behave himself more Christianly in his office with certification that pretext should not shelter him if he should be found again guiltie of the like scandal and that he should be made an example to the parish.[47]

It must have created a certain amount of amusement as well as embarrassment that Reid was expelling John Stuart at the behest of the kirk session.

At the heart of this relationship between church and the law lay a tension as to which had the authority. By statute law, many of the cases that came before the ecclesiastical courts could also have legitimately come before the civil ones. These included the profanation of the Sabbath and fornication, but also the more serious matters of incest, adultery, infanticide and witchcraft.

There were certainly cases where civil and ecclesiastical courts were played off against each other. Dunblane Commissary Court was particularly prone to this. The case of Helen Corsar, a married woman accused of 'carnal dealings' with James Moir, shows the issue. As a means of subverting the Presbytery of Dunblane, Moir took it as a slander case to the commissary court and then refused to accept witnesses in the church courts because of the civil case. The presbytery finally consulted Lord Aberuchill, a judge and one of its occasional elders. He warned the commissary court that it was acting outwith its authority, but at the same time advised the presbytery to drop the case. The fact that the commissary court had apparently jailed an unidentified member of the presbytery from Kilmadock suggests that relationships were problematic.[48]

Another example which seems to show civil courts being used as a weapon was the citing of bailie John Don in Stirling for blasphemy in October 1708. The nub of the case was Don's profanity against a merchant in the town: 'God Almighty never thought it worth his while to sully his fingers in making the like of Robert Simson.'[49]

This should clearly have been a matter for Stirling Kirk Session as an instance of profanity, but taking it to the circuit court as blasphemy changed it to a potentially capital offence and Don's advocate made that point to the court. In the event, the court agreed, Don apologised for his actions and that was an end to it, but by bypassing the church courts the affair suggests a malicious intent by the pursuer. The incident was part of an ongoing feud between the men, who had previously appeared in the burgh court for challenging each other to a duel.[50]

It is clear, though, that the Union of Parliaments brought substantial changes to the legal situation. Queen Anne's Act for the Queen's Most Gracious and General Free Pardon[51] was intended to clear the air after the 1708 abortive Jacobite rising and generally let the courts take a fresh start in dealing with crime. The pardon extended to those being tried for a huge variety of offences, and specifically excluded others, mainly the most serious. In terms of those which the church also dealt with, incest and rape remained civil crimes, adultery and fornication did not. While the pardon did not decriminalise the behaviour and was perhaps intended as a one-off action, the resultant wholesale pardoning of those arraigned sent a clear message that the state was not to be concerned in such matters. The circuit court sitting in Perth in May of 1709 under the judges Gilbert Eliot of Minto and James Erskine of Grange reinforced this by pardoning no fewer than 325 people charged with fornication and adultery from the shires of Perth, Fife and Angus in one morning. In a paper dealing with this sitting of the court, Brian Levack comments that the prosecution of these crimes had been more a revenue-raising exercise than a moral campaign.[52] As well as dealing with the sexual crimes, however, the court also released without trial two of the 'Pittenweem witches' previously released and then rearrested, and also the minister of Blackford in the Presbytery of Auchterarder, who had been arrested for riot. This action in 1709, though, was not the whole story, for the sitting of the court in October 1708 in Stirling had already shown the way the wind was blowing. At that sitting, the Queen's advocate consistently failed to offer any evidence in adultery case after adultery case, with the pannels being told they would not be tried again in the future.[53]

In the last tranche of divorce cases in the Glasgow diet of the circuit court before it abrogated its authority, Margaret Rob in Blantyre (Lanarkshire) was sentenced to a day or two in the tolbooth of Glasgow before being led through the streets of the city with a notice on front and back describing her as an adulteress and put in the jougs[54] for two hours. Thereafter she was judicially passed back to the church courts 'and this to be but [without] prejudice of her satisfying the church for the scandal conform to the order and discipline thereof'.[55] This changed without explanation by the time the court sat in Stirling later in the month.

The record of the Stirling diet of the court suggests that the responsibility for the desertion of cases lay with a decision of the Queen's advocate, James Steuart. In one instance it would appear that the judges were not aware of what was happening. When the case was called, the court was challenged by George Erskine, factor for the Earl of Mar, who claimed that it should be held before the Regality Court of Alloa. The judges decided that the case should lie in their own hands, with Erskine allowed to sit with them but not to vote. The case was then promptly deserted with no 'probation' being offered.[56] In a further irony, one of the judges involved was James Erskine of Grange, Mar's brother. The case does suggest, though, that there was an agenda of taking cases away from the local courts.

In the other exceptional case, Elizabeth McKarter (her name is variously spelled in the records) was among those whose adultery proceedings had been dismissed. She had led Logie Kirk Session and Dunblane Presbytery in a long dance over her adultery with the laird of McNaghten in Logie parish in 1706 and would probably have been on the way to excommunication had she been resident locally. After an appearance before Logie congregation, and many non-appearances, the presbytery had referred her back to Kilsyth parish, where she lived. By late 1708 she had been widowed and married the laird. This in itself was technically illegal as they were both adulterers,[57] but the circuit court recognised them as married. Later in the diet McNaghten was also summoned, and in this case remanded for a few days before his case was also deserted, so it is clear that the judges expected to have a case to consider.[58] McNaghten must have felt himself doubly fortunate for as well as the original adultery with McKarter, he had been found guilty of a further offence of fornication (not described as adultery) since marrying her in Kilsyth.[59]

The actions of the judges and the Queen's advocate, if not the text of the act, make it clear that they took the view that specifically moral offences were not the business of the court and that the civil courts were not to be used to reinforce the ecclesiastical ones. On the sheer practicality of dealing with the case list of October 1708 in Stirling, or even more so, that in Perth in May 1709, it seems highly unlikely that the circuit court judges could ever have been expected to deal with such a volume of business. The correspondence of Lord Grange with his brother shows that the judges themselves felt they were being taken advantage of and not given adequate recompense for their work.[60]

This left the courts still with infanticide, incest, rape and sodomy to deal with, and Levack makes the point that rape was seen as a less serious crime than the others and that in the case of family abuse, an incest charge might be made against both parties with the woman being acquitted and the man convicted, in order to subject him to a more severe penalty.[61] Levack links this episode with a more general point about the decreasing reliance on scripture to define and identify crimes which took place throughout Europe at this time. In this reading the collapse of the blasphemy case against bailie Don in October 1708, in which the judges accepted Don's advocate's view about the proportionality of a possible death penalty for an incident of simple profanity, can certainly be seen as a modernising and secularising of the law. Despite this distancing of the secular courts from the ecclesiastical ones, it was not universal, and as late as 1709 Matthew Wallace, then moderator of Dunblane Presbytery, was able to report to the Commission of Assembly that 'as to the articles anent immorality, they as occasion requires make application to the magistrate for his concurrence and he hath hitherto readily granted the same'.[62]

Meanwhile, Queen Anne's actions in recognising the Scottish Episcopalians as having a legal right to existence, albeit under certain conditions, reduced the established church's ability to pursue those who underwent irregular marriage at the hands of outed episcopal ministers, or who had their children baptised by them.

Parallel to the law's backing away from ecclesiastical offences, a movement emanating from England began to make its presence felt. 'Societies for the reformation of manners' began to appear from the beginning of the century with a non-institutional but religious basis, although with some churchmen involved. This did mean that the societies were not answerable to the court of the church and were therefore regarded with a degree of suspicion. In England, they had had significant input from dissenters. However, in Scotland support for the Revolution Settlement was embedded in the movement and it was essentially Presbyterian. In fact one of the spurs for David Home of Crossrig in his setting up a society in Edinburgh was his view that the national church was not doing enough to counter the profanity, drunkenness and suchlike misdemeanours which were then prevalent there. As a visitor to Edinburgh, Daniel Defoe joined the movement and reported on his experiences but left, criticising both its efficacy and its double standards:[63]

> It is unreasonable and unjust, an injury to the common people, and a dishonour to the gentry, and nobility to make laws, acts of Parliament, proclamations, declarations, city laws or burgh-laws against vice and immorality, while you execute the laws upon the poor, mean, and common people only, and yourselves go unpunished in the open commission of the same.[64]

The church at large was asked to consider the place of the societies. At the behest of the synod, the presbyteries of Dunblane and Stirling were ordered to consider the matter in 1703. In March of the following year they dismissed it as 'impracticable'.[65] Church reaction was uniformly cool and the societies themselves were of very limited impact.

These changes in legal practice after the Union show that the first decade of the eighteenth century was gradually seeing an erosion in the legal basis for the seventeenth-century 'godly commonwealth' which the post-Revolution church had sought to reimpose. That erosion was followed in 1711–12 by the Toleration Act and then the reintroduction of patronage by the Patronage Act, but in many ways these acts were reflecting a plurality of religious views which already existed in the area. Although there were still efforts to control behaviour as part of the church's role in the country, John Logan's 'True Discipline and Government, that which is conform to and founded upon the Word of God' looked much less secure than it had when he was ordained in 1694.[66]

Notes

1. Logan, *A Sermon Preached before His Grace James Duke of Queensberry*, p. 10.
2. Church of Scotland, *The First and Second Booke of Discipline*, p. 54, 'The seventh head of ecclesiasticall discipline'.
3. Inglis, 'The Impact of Episcopacy and Presbyterianism'.
4. Leneman and Mitchison, *Sin in the City*; Mitchison and Leneman, *Girls in Trouble*.
5. Hanham, *The Sinners of Cramond*.
6. Mitchison and Leneman, *Girls in Trouble*, p. 91.
7. Kirk, *The Secret Commonwealth of Elves, Fauns and Fairies*.
8. SCA CH2/1242/3 20/1/1702.
9. SCA CH2/722/8 23/5/1699.
10. See for example SCA CH2/722/8 26/5/1698, 28/7/1697.
11. SCA CH2/1242/3 8/12/1700.
12. SCA CH2/722/9 2/10/1706.
13. SCA CH2/337/4/1 11/11/1708; SCA CH2/722/9 12/1/1709; NRS JC13/1 p. 75.
14. SCA CH2/723/5 29/4/1707, 24/6/1707, 16/9/1707.
15. NRS GD112/39/212/8 James Steuart to the moderator of the Presbytery of Dunblane, 6/2/1708.
16. SCA CH2/722/8 25/10/1693.
17. SCA CH2/1300/1 19/11/1697, 10/12/1703.
18. This includes several parishes outwith the bounds of either presbytery and likewise omits all the parishes in the two presbyteries which were in Clackmannanshire or Perthshire. It also omits the Burgh of Stirling in some of the discussion.
19. SCA CH2/1242/3 2/10/1698.
20. Davies, 'Law and Order in Stirlingshire, 1637–1747', p. 104.
21. SCA CH2/1242/3 20/6/1698.
22. SCA CH2/722/8 11/12/1700.
23. SCA CH2/1300/1 21/12/1698 and onwards.
24. SCA CH2/1242/3 2/8/1696.
25. NRS CC8/6/62 Process of Divorce: Lady Margaret Mackenzie *v.* David Bruce.
26. SCA CH2/1300/1 28/2/1697, 14/7/1700, 25/8/1700, 3/11/1700.

27. SCA CH2/1300/1 20/12/1707, 15/2/1708.
28. SCA CH2/723/5 20/8/1700.
29. SCA CH2/1300/1 9/10/1719. He was charged with 'supine negligence', 'palpable disobedience', 'scandalous covetousness' and making the congregation a laughing stock through his inability to lead the singing.
30. SCA CH2/722/8 20/12/1693. This is also evidence of the congregation being expected to stand to sing psalms.
31. Turnbull, 'The Diary of George Turnbull', p. 360.
32. SCA CH2/1300/1 pp. 224–8.
33. NRS OPR 388/10 9/5/1708.
34. SCA CH2/1300/1 9/11/1707.
35. NLS MS 7591/4.
36. SCA CH2/723/5 2/5/1699.
37. SCA CH2/722/9 27/12/1704, 24/4/1706.
38. The stewartry of Menteith, which covered the western part of Stirlingshire and parts of Perthshire, was one of six stewartries in Scotland. They had similar scope to counties but were held on a hereditary basis.
39. Scottish Episcopalians Act 1711, 10 Ann c. 10, pp. 557ff.
40. SCA CH2/1242/3 17/7/1699.
41. SCA CH2/722/8 26/6/1695, 2/12/1696, 19/5/1697.
42. The Earldom of Argyll was elevated to a dukedom in June 1701.
43. SCA CH2/722/8 1/11/1699, 2/4/1701.
44. SCA CH2/722/8 7/5/1701.
45. SCA CH2/1026/5 16/3/1699.
46. SCA CH2/722/8 20/10/1703.
47. SCA CH2/1242/3 22/11/1699.
48. SCA CH2/723/5 13/1/1702, 24/2/1702.
49. NRS JC13/1 p. 57, 20/10/1708.
50. SCA B66/25/779/1/5/66 11/3/1706.
51. An Act for the Queen's Most Gracious, General and Free Pardon 1708, 7 Ann c. 22, pp. 95ff.
52. Levack, 'The Prosecution of Sexual Crimes in Early Eighteenth-Century Scotland', p. 175.
53. NRS JC13/1 pp. 58ff.
54. An iron collar placed round the neck. Examples can still be seen outside some churches of the period.
55. NRS JC13/1 p. 36, 11/10/1708.
56. NRS JC13/1 22/10/1708.
57. Scots law allowed the remarriage of the guilty party in adultery but not to the person with whom they had been adulterous.
58. NRS JC13/1 p. 81, 25/10/1708.
59. NRS CH2/216/1 29/8/1708.
60. NRS GD124/15/768/3 29/1/1708; NRS GD124/15/768/11 3/8/1708; NRS GD124/15/768/17 4/10/1708; NRS GD124/15/768/31 25/12/1708.
61. Levack, 'The Prosecution of Sexual Crimes in Early Eighteenth-Century Scotland', p. 189.
62. NRS CH1/2/30/3/283.
63. Nathan Gray, preamble to Crossrig, 'A Narrative of the Rise, Progress and Success of the Societies of Edinburgh for Reformation of Manners'.

64. Quoted in Burch, 'Defoe and the Edinburgh Society for the Reformation of Manners'.
65. SCA CH2/723/5 2/2/1703, 7/3/1704.
66. Logan, *A Sermon Preached before His Grace James Duke of Queensberry*, p. 10.

CHAPTER TEN

Dunblane's Highland Parishes

Scotland north of the Tay, and to some extent north of the Forth, was seen as a particular problem by the church nationally, largely because of its attachment to Episcopalianism and indeed Catholicism. It proved difficult to establish Presbyterian influence both in the English-speaking north-east and in the Gaelic-speaking west and north-west, with the exception of Campbell-governed Argyll. The events in the north after the accession of William show that the new regime was weak both politically and ecclesiastically. Recognising this, one of the earliest initiatives by the General Assembly was the setting up of the Commission for the North and its equivalent for the South in 1690. Its remit was 'to cognosce, determine, and finally decide, in planting of vacant churches, constituting elderships, and trying and purging out all insufficient, negligent, scandalous, and erroneous ministers, conform to the particular instructions given them thereanent'.[1]

Like all commissions of the General Assembly, the commissions for the South and for the North were made up of ministers and elders from the previous General Assembly. They were commissioned to visit those areas and try to promote Presbyterianism, encourage conformity by previous episcopal incumbents to the new regime or, failing that, collect evidence against those who would not conform. The earliest commissions lacked a definite set of rules to determine whether episcopal incumbents should be accepted by the new establishment. For the Privy Council, failure to pray for the new monarchs was taken as a clear sign of hostility to the new regime; moreover a new criterion was set up in 1693 requiring potential conformists to subscribe to the Oath of Allegiance and accept publicly that William and Mary were monarchs not just *de facto*, which many could accept, but *de jure*. This was a concept which stuck in the throats of many Episcopalian ministers and provided a touchstone by which they could be judged acceptable or not, at the same time creating a significant rift in the ranks of the Episcopalian clergy.[2]

So far as the presbyteries of Dunblane and Stirling were concerned, there were several distinct aspects to the problem. On the one hand they were expected to contribute manpower to the work of the Commission for the North, and on the other, Dunblane Presbytery had Highland parishes and was itself in need of Gaelic-speaking ministers. A third factor, which grew in significance throughout the period, was that of the national attitude to Highland education and the steps taken to promote it.

Several of the ministers had to undertake lengthy journeys to the north as members of the Commission; meanwhile probationers, particularly those who did not look as though they were likely to receive a call speedily, might be allocated to the north for a year or more. On top of this, the periodic absence of ministers as commissioners for the North put a strain on the presbytery, for there was a need for the absent ministers' pulpits to be filled.

George Turnbull, minister of Alloa, was among the first to go. The intention was that presbyteries in the south should furnish ministers proportionately to their numbers to go north for three months on a rolling programme. After three weeks' notice of the task, Turnbull left home on 12 June 1694, returning on 31 August. Sadly, although Turnbull gave his itinerary in his diary, he furnished no details of his activities. His route took in both Angus and Aberdeenshire and then went on to Inverness where he spent two Sundays.[3] It would appear that the Commission did not meet with complete co-operation from the civil authorities, with a 'protestation' being raised in August regarding the production of witnesses.[4] In 1697, Robert Gourlaw, minister of Tillicoultry, took his turn, with Turnbull looking after his parish in return for Gourlaw's cover in 1694. Gourlaw told his kirk session that he was deputed to go to supply Caithness, Sutherland and Ross for three months, starting out on 1 March. He encouraged his session to be diligent and, unusually, asked them to send an elder to the presbytery each month in his absence to make sure that the church was supplied with preaching and that the poor were looked after.[5] John Watson, minister of Denny, followed Gourlaw later in the year. Watson and Gourlaw then collaborated in making a case to the General Assembly at the end of 1697 that there were not the vacancies needing to be supplied in the north. This must have been a remarkable piece of special pleading but sadly it has not survived.[6]

The disjunction of Dunblane Presbytery from the combined Presbytery of Stirling and Dunblane in 1698 led, as has been noted, to a protest by Alexander Douglas, minister of Logie. It was, perhaps, something of a statement that he should almost immediately volunteer to go for some months to the Commission for the North. Was he making the point that the disjunction had been because the charges in Dunblane were filled and that they could therefore take on the task of covering his parish instead of supplying Stirling churches as had happened before? Be that as it may, Douglas went north for several months, thus saving him from the early meetings of a body of which he disapproved.

The process continued for a number of years, with Hugh Whyte in Larbert & Dunipace serving his stint in 1700. In this case, a call ensued a year later inviting Whyte to become minister of the Highland parish of Kinnaird. The presbytery declined to sustain the call, and the case went to the General Assembly before he was confirmed as staying in Larbert, with the case still rumbling on in 1705.[7]

It might be said that the Commission for the North failed. Its impact was such that it does not even merit a mention in Douglas Ansdell's *The People of the Great Faith*. John MacInnes gives it rather more credit, finding its measures 'effective enough' but lacking the resources to provide pastoral care in all parishes.[8] However, although it took the close governmental control over the area in the aftermath of the 1715 Jacobite Rising to bring it about, the Highlands did largely become Presbyterian later in the eighteenth century.[9]

As well as drafting in ordained ministers for periods of three months, the Commission targeted probationers. Gaelic-speaking probationers were given no choice. Such was the desperation for their skills that it was very unlikely that any Gaelic-speaking probationer would be allowed to accept a call in a non-Gaelic charge. Even when that did provide potential ministers, they were not always what was sought. John McKillican, son of the minister of Alness, but educated in the south and licensed by the Presbytery of Dalkeith in 1696, found himself undergoing trials in Tain in 1701 where his theology was very thoroughly disapproved of by the Presbytery of Ross, so that he was not ordained until nineteen years later.[10] It was recognised, though, that a certain standard of Gaelic was requisite. In 1709, another probationer, John Mushet from the Presbytery of Argyll, asked to be deferred for a year in being sent to the north on account of his inadequacies in Gaelic. His appeal succeeded, though his later fate is unknown. Speaking on his behalf, his presbytery made the case for delay:

> He has no dexteritie as yet in that language, he never preached, lectured, prayed in public or secret, nor craved a blessing nor returned thanks in that language. He can speak something of the language but not pronounce well yet ... if the Lord please to spare him we doubt not but that in a little tyme he might marrie, baptise and pray with a dying person and discourse a little in secret with such as laboured under cares, so that in the meantime we hope you will excuse him till November next that he may improve himself in the language somewhat more.[11]

Other probationers too were targeted. Thomas Boston, newly licensed and looking for a call in the Borders, was told that he was to go to the north in April 1698 although, because a call to him was believed to be in preparation, he was not sent.[12] In 1698 the General Assembly had enacted that twelve ministers in the south together with four probationers should be appointed to charges in Angus and the Mearns, two areas where the people were still firmly attached to episcopacy. A further sixteen probationers were to be appointed to other charges in the north. In December Boston, by then in the Presbytery of Stirling, was told that he was to be one of the four. John Forrester, minister of the 2nd Charge in Stirling, encouraged him to go but clearly Boston was almost panic-stricken: 'I told them I could not go, in respect of the state of my health ... withal the weather was bad, and I had not money sufficient for the purpose. By this I judged that Providence did not call me to that removal.'[13]

The threat remained in his mind for several years, and 'threat' was how he regarded it. He worried whether his aversion to the idea of a mission in the north might affect the way he preached to the people of Dollar, whose minister he thought he might become.[14] In March he thought he was free of the threat, but it lay in the back of his mind all of 1699. Ironically, John Gray, the minister who was called to the parish of Dollar, thus triggering Boston's permanent move to the Borders, was sent north for a month in 1702.

With Stirling's position as the 'Gateway to the Highlands' and as a crucial crossing point for people and goods going north and south, there was usually a significant number of Highlanders in and around the burgh. In 1682 the Privy Council noted the pressures which large number of 'strangers from the highlands' put on the burgh in terms of both the crime they committed and the burden their children put on poor relief, especially in times of dearth.[15] It was, however, an English-speaking town and the outlying parishes which fell within the bounds of Stirling Presbytery apparently had no substantial Gaelic-speaking communities.

Without Gaelic speakers in numbers sufficient to warrant a Gaelic-speaking minister, Stirling Presbytery was only a contributor to the scheme in the north, although it did profit from legislation which used vacant stipends to pay probationers in parishes north of the Forth at a rate of 18 merks (£12 Scots) per Sabbath (see Chapter 3). This made providing pulpit supply that bit more attractive in the Clackmannanshire parishes of Clackmannan, Dollar and Alva.

The Presbytery of Dunblane, however, was a different matter and had a problem which its southern neighbour did not. In 1698, a visitor to the area had recorded five Gaelic-speaking parishes in the area as 'Aberfoill, Callender, Kilmadock, Port and Balquhiddar'.[16] Alexander Graham of Duchray, writing descriptions of the parishes to the north of the Forth in 1724, said of the parishes of 'Ballwhidder, Callander and Aberfoyle' that 'all the inhabitants use the Irish language' while in Port of Menteith, his own home parish, 'the Inhabitants of the most part of this paroch use the Irish language'.[17] A hundred years later Gaelic was still in use in some parts of Kilmadock, although its minister who contributed to the *Old Statistical Account* took a poor view of the quality of the language spoken there.[18]

That said, however, nowhere in the presbytery records of Dunblane is there any hint that Gaelic was to be found in use in either Port or Kilmadock, although the latter was regarded with some suspicion on account of the Jacobite leanings of some of its heritors and inhabitants. This led to the parish of Kilmadock's asking to be considered a priority when it came to opposing the departure of John Logan to Alloa in 1703. In its counter-petition placed before the General Assembly, Stirling Presbytery, anxious to fill the vacancy at Alloa, gave Kilmadock short shrift:

The Parish of Kilmadock is not of that importance and in that circumstances that were reported. Albeit it lies on the borders and frontiers of the highlands yet there are several of the parishes lying on the same frontiers some higher, such as Port and the Parish of Arochar which are also planted as Presbyterian.[19]

There is some evidence, though, in the General Assembly papers of 1704 of the situation, at least in Port of Menteith. A paper (now lost) which had been tabled against the idea of providing a Bible translated into Gaelic was answered by the anonymous 'An answer to the objection against making the Bible in Irish as being prejudicial to the design of extirpating the Irish Language out of the Highlands of Scotland'. In the course of discussing the strategy for educating the Gaelic-speaking population the author comments:

> In several parishes in the borders of the highlands there remains still some corners where the inhabitants goe to have their children baptised and to hear sermons in adjacent parishes where they preach in Irish because they understand not those who preach in English which plainly shows that the English Language doth not so much prevail over the Irish as some would make the world believe.[20]

The author then notes: 'In the parishes of Drimen, Port . . . in Perthshire. From whence it may appear what multitudes there may be in other parishes bordering on the highlands who don't understand sermons in English &c.'

In the light of this it seems curious that there was apparently no effort to recruit a Gaelic speaker for Port of Menteith in 1697 and there is no suggestion that Arthur Forbes, its minister after 1697, could speak Gaelic. But this seems to be clear evidence that the parish was not adequately providing gospel teaching for many of the inhabitants. Yet while Gaelic surnames proliferate in the kirk session records, nowhere is it suggested that Gaelic was even found, let alone dominant, in the parish.[21] The session records do, however, show practices which set it apart from the Lowland parishes of the presbytery. One of the issues which periodically turned up in discipline cases was 'charming' and the use of particular gestures at weddings. In 1705, Christian McKoskrich was reported to have used charms and incantations and circular motions at her marriage. She admitted the charge but said she saw no sin in it. She was rebuked in front of the congregation.[22] On the issue of 'superstitious customs', Michael Potter (the elder) wrote to the Commission of Assembly in 1706:

> As to the state of the highland congregations in our bounds they are all plagued with intruders and notwithstanding of all endeavours used we have gotten none of them as yet planted and throw [through] want of the Gospel amongst them several heathenish and superstitious customes abound. But for the growth of popery we can perceive little thereof.[23]

Two years later, Matthew Wallace's report to the Commission also stated: 'As to what was recommended ... for suppressing of pagan and popish superstitious customs, though we cannot say they are wholly rooted out here, yet through the blessing of God on the ministry of the gospel, they are so far abolished that we know no publick prejudice thereby.'[24] It is almost as though the presbytery was in denial of the Gaelic issue existing at all, while the survival of the old practices was seen as tiresome but insignificant.

Each of the other three Gaelic-speaking parishes, Aberfoyle, Callander and Balquhidder, had its own narrative in its relationship to the post-1690 Presbytery of Dunblane. Prior to the Revolution, Aberfoyle was in the charge of Robert Kirk, who was the son of a previous minister and had been born in the parish. Before returning to his birthplace he had been minister of Balquhidder. His Gaelic credentials were impeccable; as a folklorist, he wrote a work on the supernatural world which was published over a century after his death, as *The Secret Commonwealth of Elves, Fauns and Fairies*, and is now regarded as a minor classic. More importantly to his own day, he published the metrical Psalms in Scottish Gaelic and also an edition of the Irish Gaelic Bible of William Bedell with classical Irish conventions removed and the Irish font converted to a Roman one. Published in 1690, this was used in Scotland until James Stuart's native Scots Gaelic Bible became available in 1766.[25] Kirk died in 1692, allegedly kidnapped by the fairies. Although the abduction is unconfirmed, as a local legend it adds to the picture of the survival of pre-Christian folk belief. Kirk had apparently acted as clerk to the presbytery prior to the Revolution, for his widow was pursued for the return of presbytery records, handing over what she had in 1701.[26]

Kirk's position as an Episcopalian 'curate' had been unchallenged and his successor had the distinction of being the last patron-appointed Episcopalian parish minister in Scotland to remain in his charge. William Fisher was presented by the fourteen-year-old 4th Marquess of Montrose[27] in 1696 and remained in place until his death in 1732 despite the efforts of Dunblane Presbytery to depose him. Fisher's tenure was dependent on the support of his patron, who defended him because he had been instrumental in helping to protect the Presbyterian Sir John Maxwell of Pollock in Covenanting times. Fisher seems never to have caused much concern to the presbytery by acting outwith his own parish. On his arrival in 1696 he had been variously summoned to face the presbytery by the beadles of Port of Menteith and Kippen, but had simply ignored the summonses. Subsequent efforts by the presbytery to depose him in 1699 and 1701 were fairly half-hearted and completely unsuccessful.[28] Further communication with the Duke of Montrose followed in 1708.[29]

George Turnbull found himself in Aberfoyle in the spring of 1699. He was not on church business, but rather 'Providence in ane unexpected manner sent me up hither for my milke, in the midst of my barbarous and dissaffected neighbours, I looked to god . . .' Turnbull, suffering severely from gout, had been sent there in the hope that a diet of goats' milk might bring relief. His early suspicion of his neighbours quickly turned to an appreciation of their hospitality, initially qualified – 'the people rude and ignorant, but not unkind aftar the highland way' – but by the end of his five-week stay, he was 'giving thanks for all kindnesses I mett from all hands; for my safty and all'. His verdict on the people of Aberfoyle? 'The people of abrfoyll not untractable people, there psent minister silly. O that god show them mercy.'[30]

If William Fisher was 'silly', his colleagues in Balquhidder and Callander were seen as much more of a problem. James Menzies, Episcopalian incumbent in Callander since 1667, was officially deposed in 1689 but sat tight amid various attempts to dislodge him, even surviving the normally effective 'putting to the horn'. Although summoned to the presbytery several times over the years, he ignored every summons, his only co-operation being his assurance in 1701 that he did not have the Dunblane Presbytery minutes as Robert Kirk's widow thought he might.[31] As one of several deposed ministers who celebrated irregular baptisms, his was a destabilising influence in the parishes roundabout as he 'intruded' in Kincardine and Kilmadock. Nonetheless he held on in Callander until 1716 despite being referred to the King's advocate in 1702 and despite the arrival of a Presbyterian minister in 1709. The support of the local heritors was his greatest protection throughout the period.

If the heritors were important in Callander, the chief heritor was paramount in Balquhidder. The Marquess of Atholl had been a Jacobite in 1689, although wisely retiring to Bath for his health before he could be asked to support Viscount Dundee. Briefly imprisoned in the aftermath of Dundee's rising, thereafter he concentrated on his estates rather than becoming embroiled in politics. He left the politics to his son, the Earl of Tullibardine, who succeeded him in 1703, becoming 1st Duke of Atholl later the same year. Balquhidder was a small and isolated part of the Atholl patrimony, apparently used largely for hunting, and there is little evidence that the marquess visited, but his stewards did and both he and his son did take an interest.

The initial situation is unclear. Robert Stewart had been presented to the parish by the marquess in 1686; he followed Viscount Dundee in 1689 and was promptly deprived by the Privy Council. The *Fasti*, however, has William Campbell intruded into the parish sometime in 1687 and he it was who held it as an Episcopalian until 1710.[32] Campbell, alone of the local Episcopalian ministers, petitioned to join Dunblane Presbytery in February 1697.[33] Initially, the presbytery sent two ministers to talk to the parishioners and hear Campbell preach. At the same time, the two ministers identified a potential Presbyterian kirk session and went to examine sixteen candidates, ten of whom were ordained in June of 1697. By this time, Campbell had become the subject of complaints. Further detail was not forthcoming as the complainants were not in the area, although the presbytery officer came back with some written statements. Campbell was barred from officiating in the parish in late July until the matter could be investigated. At the same time, the presbytery sent John Logan (St Ninians) to Edinburgh to speak to the Earl of Tullibardine.

Meanwhile the presbytery started to cite witnesses, seven in all, including the Laird of Edinample and his tutor.[34] Five of the witnesses duly appeared three weeks later. At least one of them was a Gaelic speaker requiring an interpreter. The charges were varied and serious. Patrick Campbell, Edinample's tutor, accused William Campbell of violence towards a woman in the company of known thieves, Donald Ban and John McIntyre; two others accused him of speaking openly against Presbyterian government; another accused him of financial irregularity; and two more had been asked by him or the local schoolmaster to sign a call to the parish. Next month more witnesses attended and the evidence of Campbell's soliciting a call mounted up; he was cited to attend with his paper.[35] Matters then seemed to rest for a year, by which time Dunblane Presbytery was functioning on its own.

Thomas Buchanan (Tulliallan) was thrice appointed by the presbytery to go to preach in Balquhidder and find out the condition of the parish. He failed to do so. Finally, in December 1698 he promised to go the following spring as it was too difficult to travel there in winter. In February of 1699 he was told to go in March without fail as the road was reported passable. By the beginning of April, Buchanan was able to report that he had been and found that the parish was keen to be rid of Campbell, with one of the heritors, Sir Colin Campbell of Ardkinglas, offering help to find Gaelic-speaking supply. Whether as the result of this or not, one Alexander Shaw, a Gaelic-speaking probationer, came to the presbytery's attention and steps were taken to assess his potential. Robert Gourlaw was then appointed to preach in May, and like Buchanan, failed to do so. When Gourlaw did attend, he was refused access to the church but found that Campbell was holding a service in his house. Others followed equally ineffectively, Matthew Wallace, Arthur Forbes and finally Hugh Walker in September, who did succeed in serving the summons, although without effect. Campbell was then summoned to the synod as contumacious.[36]

The wheels turned, but they turned slowly. By summer of 1700, Matthew Wallace had preached in Balquhidder and found some of the elders were wanting to resolve the matter with a new minister. This was followed by a formal request from the kirk session and Tullibardine was informed of how matters stood. Unfortunately from the presbytery's point of view, Tullibardine had taken offence and ordered the church door to be barred to the presbytery's preacher. Later he was asked to allow a Gaelic-speaking probationer to preach, which he did, even coming to hear him in the October. Edinample approved of Shaw and a call was said to have been drawn up for him to become the minister, subject to approval from

Tullibardine. No response came and Shaw continued to supply Balquhidder for a further year, with Andrew Ure also taking his turn through 1701 and John Robertson, another Gaelic speaker, taking over in 1702. The situation remained in stalemate. At various times the probationers were forced to preach in the churchyard, while if a non-Gaelic-speaking minister came, he did not preach at all as there was no one to listen to him preach in English outside. Campbell retained access to the church and made sure he concealed himself in the pulpit prior to the first bell being rung. When the visiting minister entered at his due time, Campbell would pop up in the pulpit ready to preach. From three centuries' distance this seems a moment of comedy, but it is unclear whether anyone saw the humour at the time.[37]

Finally in October of 1703, Tullibardine, by then Duke of Atholl, promised to support any Gaelic speaker who was acceptable to the people, at which point he would remove Campbell.[38] By this stage, the three probationers had been settled elsewhere. Shaw had been ordained to Edenkillie in Forres in 1702, where he remained until 1753. Robertson was sent to the north by the General Assembly; attempts to persuade Atholl to permit his settlement in Balquhidder on his return failed and he settled in Lairg. Ure remained closer at hand in Muckhart in the Presbytery of Auchterarder.

The presbytery's attention then shifted away from probationers to Robert McFarland, minister of a Gaelic congregation in Arrocher who was said to be disenchanted with his current charge. Unfortunately for the plan, McFarland was sent off to the Presbytery of Ross for four months. By November 1704, Atholl had been visited in person by two ministers from Dunblane Presbytery but was unwilling to allow the settlement of McFarland without hearing him. Arrangements were duly made, but McFarland made the crucial mistake of failing to visit the duke to pay his respects. Again one of the ministers was detailed to visit the duke, who said he was sympathetic but would not endorse McFarland without meeting him. That hurdle too was crossed and approval was forthcoming, but conditional on the parish showing a desire for his settlement. The parish did not.[39] The same week as this was reported to the presbytery, McFarland was inducted to the parish of Fintry in Dumbarton Presbytery.

The evidence from the records of the Atholl estate clearly show that there was a body of tenants content to continue with Campbell, possibly even a majority. Nominally Presbyterian, Atholl does not seem to have had any doctrinaire loyalty to the cause and made it quite clear that he would support the local people's choice and neither seek to impose his own choice nor suffer the presbytery to impose its choice.[40] As early as 1693, he had written to his wife suggesting that Presbyterians should be more tolerant of Episcopalian ministers because they would strengthen them against the dangers of 'popery'.[41] A letter from the duchess, herself a much more convinced Presbyterian than her husband, blamed the presbytery's actions for the lost opportunity in Balquhidder.[42] Atholl himself claimed always to have allowed the planting of Presbyterian ministers in his lands.

He was, however, put under more pressure by the Presbytery of Perth than by that of Dunblane, and found himself under competing pressure from the church and his wife on one hand and his far more episcopally minded family on the other. In 1706, Atholl was still trying to protect his Episcopalian ministers from attacks from the Presbytery of Perth, writing to the Earl of Mar seeking his support:

> I have always allowed the churches where I am concerned when they were vacant to be planted by Presbeterian ministers; but have also thought it just and reasonable to preserve those of the Episcopal ministers who are good men in the churches they possess. There are yett five of these remaining in Atholl; three of them were in before the Revolution, and has preached in theire churches ever since. The other two have been in several yeares before King William's death, tho' not admitted by the Presbetery. And now during her Majesteis reigne they doe expect her protection, which I humbly desire for them if her Majestie think fit.[43]

A report by Matthew Wallace to the General Assembly in 1708 on the topic of schools in Highland parishes sums up the situation:

> There are 12 parishes in the presbytery of which 9 are legally settled and the other three are Irish congregations in which there is no access on account of the episcopal intruders and the unsuccessfulness of any endeavours to get any of them planted with Presbyterian ministers . . .
>
> As to the three Irish congregations to which the Presbyterie hath no access . . . The Queen is patron of one of these paroches [i.e. Callander] and such as nearest the Court and can make the best hand there still procures gifts and promises of the vacant stipend long ere the terms of payment. The Duke of Atholl and Marquess of Montrose are patrons of the other two [i.e. Balquhidder and Aberfoyle] with whom this presbyterie could never prevail to get anything done effectually for the good of these paroches.[44]

It is perhaps reading too much into this response of Wallace to the Commission to see a degree of impatience with the two peers and the advisors of the Queen, yet things were on the move and the following year both Callander and Balquhidder saw the induction of Presbyterians, even if John McCallum, minister of Comrie, had to wait over a year between call and settlement in Callander and thereafter still had to cope with his predecessor remaining active in the parish.

In Balquhidder the situation was different. Atholl's appointee, William Campbell, removed right out of the area to Glenorchy, where he served as assistant until 1728 and incumbent until his death in 1731. The mechanism was unclear, but the arrival in Dunblane Presbytery of James Robertson, a Gaelic-speaking probationer, seems to have been the catalyst. Coming with excellent testimonials from John McCallum, still in Comrie, and from the University of Aberdeen,[45] Robertson was promptly sent off to take on pulpit supply in Balquhidder. He was evidently acceptable, for he was soon summoned to Blair Atholl to meet the duke, who seems to have approved:

> Mr Walker reported that according to appointment we went with Mr Robertson to Blair of Atholl and attended his grace the Duke of Atholl, who, upon presenting him the presbyteries letter was pleased to express his willingness that the paroch of Balquhidder be planted with a good man and desired he might signifie so much to the presbyterie in his name.[46]

Robertson was invited to remain in Blair Atholl for a few days and the presbytery wisely decided to wait until his return before prosecuting any further action. Perhaps it was wary of the duke's previous prickliness. A further month passed without any message from the duke and Thomas Buchanan was despatched to deliver another letter from the Presbytery to him. Finally, yet another month later, a letter was delivered from the duke

> in which his Grace having signified his approbation of Mr Robertson and satisfaction that the Presbyterie should proceed in the legal and orderly way to his settlement in the paroch of Balquhidder. They saw it necessary to return answear to his Grace rendring him the presbyteries most hearty and humble thanks for this favour and entreating his Grace would signify his pleasure anent a day for the heretors, elders and others concernd in that paroch to meet for drawing up & subscribing a call which they did accordingly and appointed their brother Thomas Buchanan to go and present the letter to the Duke.[47]

In the event, Buchanan was ill and sent the letter instead, but a suitable reply was received which allowed them to proceed. Carrying on with a kid-glove approach, various ministers were deputed to visit the other heritors and 'signify' how acceptable Robertson was and how the duke had expressed his approval to them.

Finally on 10 November, not only was John McCallum inducted to Callander, but later in the same meeting, reports were received from all those who had been visiting the heritors of Balquhidder. The presbytery was pleased with the great harmony which followed Atholl's approval of James Robertson. A formal call came from the elders and heads of families and he was duly ordained and inducted in March 1710.

The Balquhidder saga reflects how, despite the theoretical power of heritors, elders and heads of families, the church in post-Revolution Scotland was still heavily dependent on the previous patron, particularly when they were the dominant heritor. Despite the theoretical loss of the right to present, some patrons had never, in fact, lost it.

Nationally, two more initiatives were aimed at propagating Presbyterian influence in the Highlands. They were the institution of libraries in Highland parishes and the promotion of schools through the foundation of the Society in Scotland for the Propagation of Christian Knowledge (SSPCK), founded in 1709.

In the former case, the Presbytery of Dunblane was considered Highland and presented with two libraries, the Leighton Library in Dunblane itself also being considered in the equation. Much of the financing of these libraries came from south of the border, and much of the record is concerned with administrative accounts of them and not their efficacy in promoting the reading of scripture and the religious education of the people. The moderator of the Commission of Assembly, George Meldrum, wrote to each presbytery involved:

> Some charitable persons in England having sent several libraries for the use of the nation, the Commission appointed for distribution thereof have allowed your presbytery one of these libraries, and you are desired to empower a person to receive the same from the agent for the Kirk, to give receipt and thereupon the books will be sent to you and the expenses of carriage paid here. You shall have sent also a true catalogue of these books in the library with a printed copie of rules concerning the preservation thereof. So soon as these books come to your hand it is desired that there will be a particular receipt returned to the agent, subscribed by the moderator and clerk to your presbytery, and therein to give an account how these sent agree with the catalogue. This library being appointed for the use of your presbytery, you will take care the same be fixed where the design thereof be best obtained and send an account of the place to the commission. Seeing strangers have begun it is hoped members of Presbytery will not only contribute themselves but also deal with others to help to augment the said library, seeing it is a charitable design and may be of use to themselves and posterity.[48]

To this came back reply from the moderator of Dunblane Presbytery:

> And as to the libraries, we received two parochial in two boxes marked Dunblane No. 35 & 36 whereof that marked No. 35 contained 28 books and 6 small treatises and that marked No. 36 – 38 books and 17 small treatises according to the catalogue contained in each box excepting one small treatise in which was wanting in the box marked No. 36 . . . These libraries were received Apryll last day 23 and they are yett lying in the Minister's house of Dunblane until we consider where to dispose of them.[49]

Nothing is recorded about the impact of these libraries locally.

As for the other scheme to 'civilise' the Highlands, the planting of schools, this was a theoretical imperative of the church anyway, by the early years of the new century, external forces promoted schemes more energetically. This led to the foundation of the SSPCK. While it had considerable impact both in Scotland and abroad, its activities lie outwith the timescale of this study, but the early promotion of it does fall within the period. The SSPCK was set up to provide schools in rural northern Scotland with the religious motive of securing Presbyterianism there, and the political one of ensuring the Protestant succession: 'Through inculcating and reinforcing Presbyterian beliefs and forms of worship among children, it was believed that Highland communities would be won over to the post-Revolution political and religious establishment, and would become integrated, industrious, and loyal subjects of the British state and Empire.'[50]

Allied to this movement was also one to promote the use of 'Irish' Bibles and catechisms by donation. This was a scheme in which Robert Kirk, Episcopalian minister of Aberfoyle, had been involved before his death.

By its very title, the paper 'An answer to the objection against making the Bible in Irish as being prejudicial to the design of extirpating the Irish Language out of the Highlands of Scotland' asserts that the lost paper to which it was a response assumed that it would be beneficial to wipe out the use of Gaelic. 'An answer' challenges that ambition and suggests that notwithstanding that purpose, the progress of Presbyterianism against creeping Catholicism would be better served by promoting the use of vernacular Bibles among an admittedly largely illiterate Gaelic-speaking population.[51] The author of 'An answer' takes a fairly pragmatic stance over the Gaelic language, believing 'first that the extirpation of the Irish language out of the highlands of Scotland [is] not possible in this age and 2ndly that it is not probable to be effected in succeeding ages'. He believed that not one in a hundred children went to school in the Highlands, and those that did learn English still spoke Gaelic to the other children, and observed, 'The highlanders as much as any people are very much in love with their own ancient language.' In any case,

> it is next to impossible to get the other sort of schools settled in the manner as is necessary for reaching all the children in that country (to say nothing of aged persons) to speak the English language and therefore to supersede the necessity of teaching to read the Irish bibles.
>
> About half the ministers in the highlands preach only in Irish which shows that there is little or no English understood in their parishes, and where they preach one half of the day English, it is many places of very little use to the generality of the people . . . As to the women and children, scarce 1 of 20 can speak English throughout the highlands . . .
>
> The scriptures are the weapons of our Christian Warfare shall we unmercifully deprive our brethren of that which [they] have so great a need of . . .
>
> How just a prejudice against the papists is their hindering the people from reading Holy Scriptures. They hide that light under a bushel which God hath appointed to be set on a candlestick.

For the author of the paper, the argument in favour of circulating Gaelic Bibles was unassailable. But from a Church of Scotland point of view the involvement of Episcopalians, Scottish or English, did taint the project and there was a mixed response to it. In that same letter of Forbes as moderator of Dunblane Presbytery, already quoted in the context of the libraries, he wrote:

> We received your letter dated 19th of Apryll last in Presbytery. Be pleased to know that as for the Irish Bibles and Catechisms sent down to be distributed among the highland congregations in regard we had no access at the time to any of the Irish congregations within our bounds, none of them come into our hands. Only we understand that some of them were sent into those parishes though the exact number, notwithstanding of the pains we have been at to inform ourselves, we have not as yet learned.[52]

The early years of the SSPCK were marked by increasing pressure on individual parishes to support it. Matthew Wallace, by this stage moderator of Presbytery, wrote in 1709: 'As to the propagating of Christian knowledge, they have appointed their brethren to cause collect in their respective parishes for that effort according to the Act of assembly thereanent. But as for procuring subscriptions their bounds are in such circumstances that they have little hope of success.' And in the context of collections for a different cause, he went on: 'The country being very poor and few of the gentry coming to church here, they are afraid that what shall be gotten will be very inconsiderable.'[53]

In Dunblane Presbytery, the Kirk Session of Port of Menteith made it clear to the minister that if he wanted the contributions collected, he should do it himself:

> This day the Act of the Assemblie for Propagating Christian Knowledge in the Highlands & islands of Scotland was read from the pulpit and the people warned to provide something for promoting and furthering such a good and pious work. And that the minister was to gather the said collection in his ordinar course of visitation of families within the parish.[54]

The 1708 minutes of Stirling Presbytery are full of references to the collection of contributions and the unwillingness of some parishes, notably Stirling itself, to co-operate. At the very end of the minute book used from 1701 to 1712 is a list of the amounts subscribed to the SSPCK by six of the parishes. It is a sign of how seriously the SSPCK was taken as a weapon against the spread of Catholicism that the St Ninians contributors include several well-known Episcopalian lairds such as Paterson of Bannockburn and Murray of Polmaise, while most surprising of all, the steadfastly Episcopalian parish of Bothkennar even has its (rather small) contribution noted, including £12 18s. from the minister.[55]

The attitudes of Dunblane and Stirling presbyteries, and perhaps the wider church, to the challenges presented by the Highlands give the impression of being somewhat detached. When it was not actively pursuing a settlement in the three Episcopalian parishes, Dunblane gives the impression of ignoring them. There was a real sense in which the Highland aspects of the parishioners of Port and Kilmadock were ignored and no concession made to their Gaelic heritage. For Stirling the Highlanders were also seen only as an issue grudgingly addressed. Memories of the Highland Host in 1678 were not so distant, and the depredations of cattle thieves only too frequent. But perhaps these local attitudes echo the attitudes of the church throughout Lowland Scotland.

Notes

1. Commission for Visitations on the North Side of Tay: see 'Acts: 1690', in Church of Scotland, *Acts of the General Assembly of the Church of Scotland, 1638–1842*, pp. 221–35.
2. MacInnes, *The Evangelical Movement in the Highlands of Scotland, 1688 to 1800*, p. 16.
3. Turnbull, 'The Diary of George Turnbull', pp. 360–61; SCA CH2/722/8 23/5/1694. Turnbull's absence is not noted in the Alloa Kirk Session minutes.
4. NRS CH1/2/2/1/29.
5. SCA CH2/726/1 25/2/1697; SCA CH2/722/8 10/3/1697.
6. SCA CH2/722/8 10/4/1697.
7. NRS CH1/2/22/3/215–19 1701-3; NRS CH1/2/23/3/215; CH1/2/24/2/2/71–114.
8. MacInnes, *The Evangelical Movement in the Highlands of Scotland, 1688 to 1800*, pp. 16–18.
9. A more sanguine view of the Commission's work can be found in Maclean, 'Scottish Calvinism Resurgent Especially in the North'.
10. Maclean, 'The Presbytery of Ross and Sutherland, 1693–1700', p. 260.
11. NRS CH1/2/30/3/292.
12. Boston, *Memoirs*, p. 40.
13. Ibid., pp. 46–7.
14. Ibid., p. 55.
15. RPCS, vol. 7, pp. 264–5.
16. Withers, *Gaelic in Scotland, 1698–1981*, p. 52, quoted in McNiven, 'Gaelic Place-Names and the Social History of Gaelic Speakers in Medieval Menteith'.
17. Graham of Duchray, 'Description of Six Parishes in Perthshire, 1724'.
18. Macgibbon, 'Parish of Kilmadock or Doune'.
19. NRS CH1/2/23/2/173 Petition of Presbytery of Stirling re Alloa to the General Assembly 1703.
20. NRS CH1/2/24/1/2/66–8 An answer to the objection against making the Bible in Irish as being prejudicial to the design of extirpating the Irish Language out of the Highlands of Scotland.
21. The matter did, however, surface during a disputed settlement in 1724–6 when the ability of one candidate to speak Gaelic was a crucial factor. See Withers, 'Gaelic-Speaking in a Highland Parish'.
22. SCA CH2/1300/1 9/12/1705, 16/12/1705.
23. NRS CH1/2/25/3/247 23/7/1706.

24. NRS CH1/2/27/3/246 1/3/1708.
25. Meek, *The Scottish Highlands*, pp. 18–19.
26. SCA CH2/723/5 14/1/1701.
27. 1st Duke of Montrose from 1707.
28. SCA CH2/722/8 2/12/1696, 30/12/1696, 24/2/1697; SCA CH2/723/5 19/12/1699 etc.
29. NRS CH1/2/27/4/256 Commission to Duke of Montrose anent parish of Aberfoyle 1708.
30. Turnbull, 'The Diary of George Turnbull', pp. 383–4.
31. SCA CH2/723/5 4/2/1701.
32. *Fasti Ecclesiae Scoticanae*, vol. 4, p. 337.
33. SCA CH2/722/8 24/2/1697.
34. SCA CH2/722/8 28/7/1697.
35. SCA CH2/722/8 18/8/1697, 18/9/1697, 8/10/1697, 30/10/1697.
36. SCA CH2/723/5 27/9/1698, 14/2/1699, 4/4/1699, 2/5/1699, 17/9/1699, 8/10/1699.
37. SCA CH2/723/5 25/6/1700, 23/7/1700, 20/8/1700, 22/10/1700, 26/11/1701, 26/5/1702, 15/12/1702, 4/5/1703, 25/5/1703, 29/6/1703.
38. SCA CH2/723/5 26/10/1703.
39. SCA CH2/723/5 26/10/1703, 15/8/1704, 30/10/1704, 28/11/1704, 26/12/1704, 1/2/1705, 4/4/1705, 13/6/1705.
40. Atholl Muniments, Box 45/5/37. I am grateful to the archivist for drawing my attention to these.
41. Cowmeadow, 'In Sum What Have I Don for God or My Soule This Day?', pp. 15–16.
42. Atholl Muniments, Box 45/5/91.
43. NRS GD124/15/410 Atholl to Mar 31/5/1706.
44. NRS CH1/2/27/3/246 Wallace in name of Presbytery of Dunblane to Moderator, 1/3/1708.
45. SCA CH2/723/6 5/7/1709.
46. SCA CH2/723/6 30/8/1709.
47. SCA CH2/723/6 25/10/1709.
48. NRS CH1/2/25/3/244 Meldrum to presbyteries, anent highland libraries, 5/7/1706.
49. NRS CH1/2/25/3/247 Forbes to Meldrum, 23/7/1706.
50. Kelly, 'The Mission at Home'.
51. NRS CH1/2/24/1/2/66–8 An answer to the objection against making the Bible in Irish as being prejudicial to the design of extirpating the Irish Language out of the Highlands of Scotland.
52. NRS CH1/2/25/3/247 23/7/1706.
53. NRS CH1/2/30/3/283 Wallace to Moderator, 29/11/1709.
54. SCA CH2/1300/1 14/5/1710.
55. SCA CH2/722/9, pp. 353–4.

CHAPTER ELEVEN

The Church and the Union of Parliaments

I may likewise take Occasion to exhort this Church and the Members thereof especially such as are hearing me this day, to hold fast sound doctrine, pure worship, true and excellent Government, and to follow all prudential methods for preventing invasion thereupon by Adversaries.[1]

The sermon which John Logan, minister of Alloa, preached to the commissioners of the Scottish Parliament in 1706 and which has been a *leitmotif* throughout this work holds a plea to his hearers to recognise that their duty was to safeguard both church and nation. This was indeed a recurring theme in the church's consideration of the Union of the Parliaments as it made its way through the legislative process. If 1689 had been one critical point in Scotland's history, so too was 1707 with the union of Scotland's Parliament with that of England, a pivotal point in the history of the nation and potentially of the church.

Union of the Parliaments had been mooted intermittently ever since the Union of the Crowns in 1603. James VI and Oliver Cromwell had had their own plans which did not reach permanent fruition,[2] but William II had also begun looking towards a union by the time he died, and Queen Anne had made it an early priority after William's death.[3]

The new queen's ambitions did not meet with any great enthusiasm from either side. Early discussions took place and the records show the extent of England's indifference to the project. Meeting after meeting was cancelled as inquorate when England's commissioners failed to attend. The main driver for the attempt on both sides was to make the Protestant succession secure. This was seen as urgent because the English Act of Settlement of 1701 and Scotland's statement in the Claim of Right of 1689 had left the possibility that different monarchs could succeed to the two thrones on the death of Anne, especially if none of Anne's children survived her.[4]

The role of the church in the union process has been widely examined. There are several monographs devoted to it and countless papers cover most aspects. The ecclesiastical aspect hinged on the place of Presbyterianism as the established governance of the Church of Scotland. As Alasdair Raffe has shown, the threat was interpreted differently by different groups. Those most influenced by the Covenants were convinced that an incorporating union was contrary to the two Covenants and hence to the law of Scotland; even the most moderate of Presbyterians saw the place of bishops in the House of Lords and therefore with legislative authority over Scotland as anathema.[5] Karin Bowie and Jeffrey Stephen present the picture nationally, and, not surprisingly, the emphasis is on Edinburgh and on the concerted resistance in the west.[6] Taking a more detailed approach, Bowie's edition of the *Addresses against Incorporating Union, 1706–07* provides a complete text of all the petitions with a degree of analysis of the signatories which highlights some of the issues in considering the people who signed them and the relationship of the texts to each other.

As many of the petitions emanated from 'parishes', there is some question as to whether such petitions had ecclesiastical impetus or simply were from the parish as a geographical area. The existence of specific ecclesiastical petitions from the Commission of Assembly and from three presbyteries perhaps leads to an assumption that the parish petitions were ecclesiastical too, an assumption that Stephen is at pains to discount.[7] The intention of this chapter is not to revisit the core narrative, but to examine in detail the elements of the debate which relate to the presbyteries of Stirling and Dunblane.

Several of the major participants in the process had links to the area. The Earl of Mar, with his ancestral home in Alloa Tower, was the major landowner in Alloa parish, in Stirling Presbytery's bounds, and hereditary governor of Stirling Castle; the Duke of Atholl, a major opponent, was a heritor in several of the northern parishes of Dunblane Presbytery; and the Duke of Argyll was a heritor in Dollar. Out of power, but with considerable influence against the treaty, was Lieutenant-Colonel John Erskine of Carnock, a heritor in Stirling and elsewhere, provost of Stirling, leader in the Convention of Royal Burghs and former lieutenant-governor of Stirling Castle. Meanwhile his successor in Stirling Castle and parliamentary commissioner for Stirling Burgh, the other Lieutenant-Colonel John Erskine, was active on the pro-treaty side.

The Articles of Union were published in October 1706, having been negotiated in secret and kept so until the Scottish Parliament convened on 3 October. Their imminence was expected, and the very fact of their secrecy was in itself an encouragement to speculation and suspicion. Even prior to publication of the Articles, pamphlets had been published in opposition, especially to the concept of an 'incorporating union'[8] where Scotland would only ever send a small minority of MPs and peers to a very much larger Parliament whose interests were not necessarily the interests of Scotland.

Two months earlier, at the end of August, John Logan, minister of Alloa, had written to Mar on his way home from London, giving a report of local feelings. He reported on the general aversion felt for an incorporating union, however favourable the terms. This aversion he identified as coming from the 'different principles of the Jacobites and the true revolutionists'.[9]

There seems little doubt that the people of Scotland did not want the Union of the Parliaments. One of the commissioners, John Clerk of Penicuik, described in rather hurt terms the response to their efforts:

> The Commissioners, on their return to Scotland, fancied to themselves that as they had been doing great service to their Country in the matter of the Union, so they would be acceptable to all ranks and degrees of people, but after the Articles of the Union were published by order of Parliament, such comments were made upon them, by those of the adverse party, that the Mob was almost universally set against them.
>
> Under these hardships and misrepresentations the Articles of the Union were introduced into the Parliament of Scotland. The bulk of the nation seemed altogether averse to them . . .[10]

The Edinburgh servant Elisabeth West put into words her abhorrence of the proposed union in no uncertain terms based both on a distrust of England and on her fears for her religion:

> And should we again join in a confederacy with such a deceitful and cunning people, who would, if it lay in their power, ruin all their neighbour nations, to advance their own interest? But that which most troubled me, was, that this union of theirs would prove a snare to our covenanted church of Scotland; for they that would ruin our state, would also ruin our church.[11]

Immediately after publication of the articles, the Commission of Assembly sent an address, the first of four, to Parliament. Described by the emphatically pro-union journalist and spy Daniel Defoe as 'moderate and well temper'd',[12] it was put together by those ministers and elders who attended the Commission on 11 October. Such was the lay make-up of the General Assembly and its executive 'Commission' that the elders included many who were closely involved in Parliament including three of the Queen's officers. Judging from the memoirs of one of the ministers present, John Bell, the first draft simply gave the church's consent to an incorporating union, but determined opposition to the union from two ministers led to an attempt to ask Parliament to announce a national fast. Defoe thought this was in order to persuade people 'to fast all over the Kingdom and therein to give the ministers occasion to pray and preach against it, and as soon as that is done tumultuous addresses are preparing in several parts of the country'.[13]

In the event, this was defeated amid a debate which threatened to bring the whole church into danger 'by an open rupture'. A much less effective, largely unannounced day of fasting and prayer was held in Edinburgh. Other presbyteries were invited to hold their own if they so wished.[14] In the case of the Presbytery of Dunblane, individual parish fasts were ordered for 6 November and there was also a day of prayer set aside for the ministers on 28 October, five to meet in Logie and four in Kippen. However, two were absent at the Commission of Assembly and others for unspecified reasons.[15] Reporting of the fasts in parishes is limited.

The Commission's address to Parliament was but the first of eighty-five representing 123 different bodies ranging from individual parishes to the Darien Company. It was read to Parliament on 17 October, giving hope to the supporters of union that if the church was already acquiescent, the treaty would be quietly passed.[16] Defoe certainly thought that the ministers had been appeased:

> But the prudence of the Ministers prevented all this designed mischief; and though the [fast] day was, as I have said, observed with great solemnity and affection, yet it was to their great disappointment, that the Ministers generally, as well those who were against the Union, as those who were for it, in their respective parishes, applied themselves only summarily to the substance, nay, to the very words of the Assembly's, viz. 'That all the determinations of the Estates of Parliament, with respect to an Union with England, might be influenced and directed by Divine Wisdom, to the glory of God, the good of religion, and particularly of the Church of Scotland.'[17]

Despite this, or perhaps because of this, the people of Edinburgh gave vent to their feelings by rioting in the days following the fast. Again to quote Defoe:

> This was the unhappy divided condition of this people, at the beginning of the treaty. The division was so general that it spread through every part; the gentry were divided; the common people divided; nay the very Ministers were divided; Parliament, Assembly, court, city, counties, towns, nay almost every family were divided; and, as the event began to be feared on every side, people stood strangely doubtful of one another.[18]

In that context then, further rioting began to be reported in various parts of Scotland, particularly in the south and west.

The Earl of Mar had been instrumental in calling John Logan from Kilmadock in Dunblane Presbytery to Alloa. By this time, he was also secretary of state for Scotland and a leading promoter of the union. It cannot have been a coincidence that when Logan attended the Commission of Assembly in late October 1706, he was invited to preach in front of the Queen's high commissioner and the commissioners to the Scottish Parliament. Daniel Defoe was not impressed, he reported to his employer, Robert Harley:

> The Mob you have heard of are affrighted with the loss of the Scots Crown – and the parsons Maliciously Humour it, and a Country parson who preach't yesterday at the high Kirk before the Commissioner took

this Text, 'Behold I Come quickly. Hold fast that which thou hast; let no man take thy Crown.' He pretended not to mean an Earthly Crown but made his Wholl sermon a bald allegory against the Union. I confess I had patience to hear him but to an Exceeding Mortification.[19]

Logan's sermon was published shortly afterwards, with his own justification for the publication: 'There being different commentaries and glosses put upon this following sermon after the preaching thereof the author was prevailed with (at the desire of friends) to allow the printing and exposing thereof in the same popular dress it was delivered in.'[20] There is perhaps an air of defensiveness in this, an effort to distance himself from the political interpretations of his words. Reading Logan's sermon, it is hard to see from the written word just what Defoe was complaining about. Logan took his text from Revelation 3:11, and followed a conventional sermon plan, although his twice commenting on a lack of time may imply that he had been given a time limit. The core of the sermon was the concept of the 'crown' as being the privileges and future of the church and of Christians. Therefore, the duty of Christians, especially commissioners to Parliament, was to make sure that the 'crown' of the church's status in the kingdom would be protected. Logan's central statement, baldly put to Queensberry and the commissioners, was this:

> Now as it's the concern of all to hold fast, to (I must presume in all humility to say) of [sic] the High Court, of Parliament in a more peculiar manner this day. To discourse on the holding fast of the civil privileges of this land, it being somewhat alien both from my text and my office, I shall forbear it at the time, specially when inclination leads me to hope that the wise notable and worthie patriots in this august assembly will contribute every way for the honour and interest of their nation.
>
> But as to our church priviledges, and present settlement, it dependeth upon them to see the preservation thereof and the rather, that our gracious Queen hath given repeated assurances of her stated resolution to maintain and protect the samen, and now intirly commited to this parliament for doing what may be necessary for the future security thereof, against all incroachments whatsoever.[21]

He then went on to ask his listeners to consider specific points: the difficulties with which these privileges had been obtained, the soundness and purity of Scottish church doctrine, the certainty of Christ's calling to account and the unhappiness of the land prior to the 'late happy revolution'. He finished:

> All of which I hope, will influence your Grace and Lordships to do your utmost for the standing settlement of peace and truth amongst us, and for securing them against the incursions of enemies, and attempts of ill desiring men, as ye would not displease a Holy God, part with the

purchase of blood, lose your ornament and glory, create for yourselves danger against the day of the Lord, and involve this poor nation in new confusions.[22]

Given that Logan was Mar's own parish minister, appointed with the agreement and approval of Mar, it seems unlikely that he would have wanted to be seen preaching directly against the union, nor would Mar have allowed him to preach in Edinburgh if he thought there was a danger of it. As already noted, Logan himself had been in correspondence with Mar earlier in the summer about the union and was later to report on Stirling Presbytery's reactions.

Logan's view, given in his letter to Mar in August and echoed in his sermon in October, was that the ministry of the national church had been silent on the matter of union and were unwilling to interfere as ministers in civil matters, even though as men and subjects they were equally concerned in the 'resignation of the sovereignty'. While he commented on the Commission of Assembly's efforts to maintain neutrality by their refusal to call for a national fast, he also asserted that the members of the Commission whom he had spoken to were uniformly against the incorporating union and indeed saw it as sinful and of dangerous consequence as contradictory to the covenants against prelacy in the 'three dominions'. What they were particularly worried about was the possibility of the union parliament, heavily weighted in favour of England, changing the fundamentals of the Scottish constitution without consent. His purpose in writing to Mar was therefore to urge him to protect Scotland, and particularly the Scottish church, against possible future infringements.

Logan was writing personally, not on behalf of Stirling Presbytery, and finished his letter with the statement that the local ministers, the 'ministers in this country have been wise and prudent and never done anything in the matter, but prayed to God for Divine conduct to those that had the management therof among their hands'.[23]

It is therefore open to argument that either Defoe misunderstood Logan's stance or he misrepresented it. It may be, however, that others misunderstood it too, but it seems unlikely that Logan would step far from the line taken by one who was his patron in all but name.

Defoe's complaint about Logan's sermon ties it to the rioting in Edinburgh that week, but the same week also brought the first of the localised addresses against the union. The 1st and 2nd of November brought eight addresses from six counties, and another three from burghs and parishes. One thing that perturbed Defoe was the fact that activists from both ends of the political spectrum were united against the union. He saw the addresses coming in, and thought he saw a pattern in them:

> Addresses are delivered in from several places and more preparing, but tis observed the addresses discover a fraud which shows the party here at their shifts. The addresses are found in the cant of the old

times, deploring the misery of Scotland for want of a further reformation and the security of the church and the Lord's covenanted people, but when the names come to be examined they are all signed by known Jacobites and Episcopal men.[24]

One of these county addresses was that of Stirlingshire, together with three from Perthshire. Stirlingshire's was signed largely by landed proprietors, but with an addition of a considerable number 'of the middling sort' from the burgh of Falkirk. The 323 signatories did indeed include a considerable number of those known to support both Jacobitism and the old Episcopalian establishment. Murrays, Patersons and Stirlings were among the first signatories but others from throughout the county reflected other views. Perhaps mirroring its more mixed constituency of signatories, it still acknowledged the danger to the established church inherent in an incorporating union while some of the other addresses with predominately Jacobite signatories ignored that issue.[25]

From a local perspective, the shire address was followed six days later by one of the earliest of the parish addresses, that of Tulliallan, now in Fife, then in Perthshire, but in the Presbytery of Dunblane and not far from Logan's Alloa. Tulliallan's approach, unlike Stirlingshire's, not only stressed the threat to the church, 'having a direct tendency to the subverting of Presbyterian Government now settled amongst us by the thrice happy Revolution',[26] but explicitly mentioned the Covenants while offering the signatories' lives to protect the nation from pretenders.

There is a tendency in all these addresses for the first signatories to be men of high status and the sponsors of the document. In the case of Tulliallan, this does not seem to include the minister or the elders. They signed but they did not add the descriptor of 'elder' when signing on their own behalf, and the three elders who attested the marks of the illiterate, Thomas Primrose, Walter Steuart and George Ramsay, are well down the list of signatories, as is Thomas Buchanan, who also did not identify himself a minister.[27] Tulliallan had a civil identity as a parish, to the extent of having its own bailie, John Crockatt, who was also a leading elder. Crockatt, one of three John Crockatts who signed the address, was one of the top row of signatories. But this is one of the petitions where the 'parish' identity may represent the community rather than the church as chief promoter.[28]

The address had 211 signatories, with the elders who attested the marks identified as such, and this shows at least tacit approval by the kirk session. The fact that there were 211 male signatories shows substantial support in a population of 1,300, which equates to 368 adult males.[29] However, the session minutes of Tulliallan show no mention of any decision to send an address against the union.

Two days prior to this address being presented, the Convention of Royal Burghs had presented its address. Naturally this was concerned with the commercial aspects of union with England, but did not neglect to ask protection for 'the true reformed religion and church government as by law established'.[30] Aside from Stirling's place among the royal burghs, what gives this address particular local significance is that it was drafted by John Erskine of Carnock, provost of Stirling, confirming his eminence in the anti-union camp. As referred to earlier, Erskine was a prominent supporter of the Presbyterian cause. A former Covenanter, as an elder in Stirling Kirk Session while depute-governor of Stirling Castle, he had been a leading layman in the church locally.

Opinions at the time differed as to the representative status of this petition. The burghs themselves voted twenty-four to twenty in favour of sending it. But the pro-union commentators at the time were at pains to point out that those who voted for the address were the poorest burghs, with the more prosperous and higher tax-paying burghs being in support of the union. In the nature of things, the burghs represented primarily the concerns of merchants. There is no doubt that the commercial interests of Glasgow and Edinburgh in particular were desperate for trading disadvantages to be removed; however, it is equally clear that in some of the smaller burghs, no commercial advantage was expected from union, and English taxes were seen as a real threat.[31]

A fortnight after the Convention sent in its address, Erskine was involved in another address, or indeed probably two. The Royal Burgh of Stirling sent in its views; on the same day the Royal Burgh and parish of Culross did likewise. Since Erskine was provost of one and was a landowner and heritor in the other, he signed both and may have drafted both.

Within Stirling itself there was substantial resistance to the treaty, even if the parliamentary commissioner, the other Lieutenant-Colonel John Erskine, was consistently in favour of it. The burgh council agreed to draw up and send an address against the union to Parliament on 16 November. The same meeting

> appointes intimation imediatelie to be made by tuck of drum to the Act for being haill inhabitantis within this burgh and territories thairof, betuixt sixtie and sixtine yearis, to be in readines with their swords and gunnis at their respective officeris quarteris, upon Monday next be nyne aclock in the morning, under the penaltie of 5 lib.[32]

Although the council minutes do not make the connection, Defoe did:

> Col. Areskin is highly blamed even by his own friends for his imprudences, who being Provost of Stirling drew out the militia to sign an Address, and with his sword drawn in one hand, and his pen in the other signed it, and made the rest do so also, with some very indecent expressions which in any Government but one so mild and forbearing as this would have been otherwise resented; but he is a malcontent and declining in his fortunes, though otherwise a very honest man.[33]

Unusually, the position of provost of Stirling was largely honorary. He did not chair the council; that was formally the prerogative of the dean of the guildry, who was not a signatory to the address.[34] While the provost had a vote, he was not expected to be present regularly and so Erskine's intervention was unconventional. The protest was duly signed by 564 names, including fourteen of the twenty-one councillors. Even allowing for Erskine's gambit of persuading the militia to sign *en masse*, Stirling's signatories made up a significant proportion of adult males in the burgh. The two ministers of the town, James Brisbane and the newly inducted John McAla, were not among the signatories but several of the Stirling Kirk Session can be identified, including bailies and James Forrester of Logie, an advocate in the burgh but also a heritor in Logie parish.[35]

Stirling's protest concentrated on commercial aspects of the union, as might be expected, but the religious issues were not ignored. Parliament was asked 'That ye will soe setle the state of this Natione as the hopes and attempts of all Papish pretenders whatsomever may be for ever defeat; That ye will mantaine and support the true reformed Protestant religione, the Government of this National Church, As now by law established.'[36] The action of sending an address to Parliament was not enough, though, and on 4 December the inhabitants of Stirling, or some of them, rioted and burned the Articles of Union at the market cross.[37] The burgh council immediately moved to defuse the situation with actions including writing to both John Erskines, the provost and the town's commissioner to Parliament.[38] The minute did not mention names, but a letter written to the Earl of Mar by Captain Holburn, who was stationed in Stirling Castle, plainly identifies the ringleader as the burgh's former treasurer Patrick Stevenson. Holburn was instructed to take action against Stevenson, but although his arrest was ordered, no trace can be found of the action. Holburn also commented on the convenient absence of Bailie John Allan, captain of the Town Guard. Bailie Allan, however, was to be found dispensing justice as a magistrate in the burgh court the very next day.[39] His name, like Patrick Stevenson's, is also prominent on the burgh's address.

One of the factors in considering any riot in Stirling was the influence of the castle, an influence which potentially acted in two directions. On the one hand the economic influence on the burgh by way of contracts was considerable; on the other, the soldiers in the castle were always available to deal with the periodic riots and disturbances which punctuated burgh life. Additionally, at various times, troops might be billeted out in the community; a troop was based in the suburb of St Ninians in late 1704, for example. This would not be seen as a benefit to the community. There was therefore considerable reason for the burgh council to play down its involvement in active opposition to the treaty even if it felt the need to oppose it formally.

The following week, St Ninians followed suit. Its address to Parliament, purportedly from 'the heritors and other inhabitants of the parish', shows no sign of church sponsorship while resolutely supporting the concerns of the church nationally. Despite being led by the heritors, there is no sign of the names of the Jacobite sympathisers among the heritors who had led the address from the county.[40]

On 3 December 1706, the Presbytery of Dunblane commissioned Thomas Buchanan to deliver its address to the Queen's commissioner.[41] It was signed by twelve men, the nine constituent ministers of the presbytery and three elders. The one minister missing from the meeting which decided to send the address was one of the signatories, and so the decision was unanimous. The three elders were John Crockat, John Henderson and Thomas Prymrose.[42] Curiously, none of them had been present at the meeting. Prymrose had last attended the presbytery two years previously and Crockat only slightly more recently, in February 1705, and so the question arises of how they were able to sign the address. For two of them, Crockat and Prymrose, the answer is simple: they were elders at Tulliallan, where Buchanan was the minister.[43] The third signatory, Henderson, was an elder in Logie.[44] It is perhaps significant that Logie and Tulliallan were the two parishes of the presbytery which sent in their own address about the projected union to Parliament.

Defoe named Michael Potter, minister of Dunblane, as the chief instigator of this address, being an old Covenanter.[45] There is no other evidence to confirm this. The address itself was a model of restraint compared to those of Hamilton and Lanark presbyteries. Almost apologetic in tone, it acknowledged full agreement with the various 'addresses and representations' which the Commission of Assembly had composed and then continued: 'Tho it may appear unnecessar, that we should give Your Grace and the Honourable Estates of Parliament any trouble this way, yet from a sense of duty . . .' This duty was to God, to the Queen, to the Queen's commissioner and to the Estates of Parliament, and was specifically aimed at the religious implications of a full union, seen as 'fatal consequences to our sacred and religious concerns'. The itemised concerns were 'ecclesiastical persons being legislators in the Commonwealth, the setting up of Publick Mass and English Ceremonies, the illegal and disorderly practices of episcopal clergy and the hopes of a popish successor to the crown'.[46] The address therefore asked Queensberry and the Estates to 'be tender of the peace and quiet of this church and nation, and settle the Protestant line; and do nothing that may be prejudicial to the National Church in any of its Religious or Sacred interests'. There was a clear worry that the union could lead to unacceptable changes in the religious landscape.

In contrast, the Presbytery of Lanark took a much more robust line despite saying it was not against the union in principle:

> Only as Ministers SCOTSMEN, and subjects of the Free and Independent Kingdom, We cannot but wish and pray, that our Civil Government may be rectified, . . . Our Monarchy may be regulated and

limited, without being suppressed: Our Parliament may be secured from English influence, without being extinguished and the just rights and Liberties of the Nation, as to laws, trade and all other concerns may be asserted.[47]

Lanark's address was drafted by John Bannatyne and signed by, among others, Thomas Linning, a former Cameronian. Defoe's letters refer to them as 'two firebrands and who merit to be marked as incendiaries'.[48]

It would seem that Dunblane's acquiescence in the Act of Union had been achieved by the passing of the Act for Securing of the Protestant Religion and Presbyterian Church Government in the early months of 1707.[49] This act, approved by Queen Anne, seemed to give the Presbyterians all they wanted, with the exception of the removal of the prospects of laws governing Scotland in the future being enacted by a House of Lords which contained English bishops. Putting those provisions in a separate act allowed the Scottish commissioners agreeing the Treaty of Union not to have any detailed statement about religion in the treaty itself, but only this rather anodyne passage:

> And likewise, her majesty, with advice and consent of the estates of parliament, resolving to establish the Protestant religion and Presbyterian church government within this kingdom, has passed in this session of parliament an act entitled, *Act for securing of the Protestant Religion and Presbyterian Church Government*, which, by the tenor thereof, is appointed to be inserted in any act ratifying the treaty and expressly declared to be a fundamental and essential condition of the said treaty or union in all time coming.[50]

This helped prevent a backlash from the English commissioners, who were very wary of anything about the rights of Presbyterians appearing in the act. The same day as Buchanan delivered Dunblane's address, that of Logie, the second of the presbytery's addressing parishes, was also presented, as was a joint address from four of Stirling Presbytery's parishes.[51]

Jeffrey Stephen argues that there is no evidence to suggest the national church was involved in 'an official capacity' in the production of parish addresses, saying that the lack of involvement of presbyteries other than Dunblane, Lanark and Hamilton was the reason for the numbers being so low elsewhere in the country. In so far as there was no guidance from the Commission to the lower courts, he is correct, but the Commission's multiple addresses do show that the church was responding nationally, leaving it to individual localities to decide on a local response. Local evidence for action is mixed or lacking; the addresses of Tulliallan and St Ninians suggest secular impetus but have identifiable church signatories. On the other hand, the address from Logie suggests that the church took the lead. The total number of signatories, representing 61 per cent of the adult male population, was the highest in the area.[52] This might in itself suggest that the driver was local feeling as the proportion is so much higher than in those Lanarkshire parishes where a more organised approach was taken (see Table 11.1).[53]

Last of the local addresses to be presented, and one of the last nationally, was that of Clackmannan in Stirling Presbytery,[54] signed on 19 and 20 December and presented on the 26th. At face value it supports Stephen's view: only the minister, the first signatory and the schoolmaster are identified. However, the session record shows the appointment to the treasurer 'also to give fourteen pound and a groat which is the value of a guinea to my Lord Register with the address subscribed by the Parish and sent to the Parliament against the Union that is under their consideration at this time'.[55] The names of the elders are spread through the signatures and not designated as elders but, although the schoolmaster/session clerk did sign it, a comparison between the writing of the address and the session minute book shows that the clerk was not responsible for scribing the address as the clerks were in some of the western parishes.[56] Additionally, church involvement is clear, with John Logan able to tell the Earl of Mar on 23 December, prior to the address's submission:

> Though I need not trouble your Lop with the occurences here, yet I thought it convenient to inform you that much of the heat about and clamour against the Union in this Country is abated. And that notwithstanding (as I was informed in Saturday's night) ane address was framed for the Parish of Clackmannan the last week against ane incorporating union and signed by the minister elders and all the heads of families which I doubt not ye will have before you very soon.[57]

If Dunblane Presbytery's approach to Queensberry and to Parliament was low-key, that of its sister presbytery in Stirling was even more so and also too late. In the same letter, Logan describes the belated efforts:

> I cannot omit to acquaint your Lop also that the presbytery has met over and again on the same point of Addressing and on Wednesday last I did expostulate at them for laying that designe aside from several topics and urged the inconvenience thereof at this juncture upon all which they delayed the further consideration thereof till Thursday next at which tyme I am hopeful to have the concurrence of some other Brethren that seem to join with me thereon to obtain a total diversion.[58]

This is one of the very few occasions on which any external evidence of the workings of the presbytery is available; and raises an interesting question. 'Wednesday last's' meeting was otherwise unrecorded; the minutes of the meeting of 4 December end with an adjournment until 8 January, the meeting which Logan anticipated. Not only that, but Logan was absent from the meeting of 4 December, so there seems to have been at least one (and possibly more) unrecorded, unconstituted meeting of the ministers of Stirling Presbytery without the presence of elders.

Table 11.1 Local Petitions against the Union of Parliaments, 1706

NRS reference		Number of signatories	Estimated adult male population	Percentage signing	Church led	Minister signed	Elders identified
PA7/20/49	Dunblane Presbytery	12	n/a	100%	Yes	Yes	Yes
PA7/28/21	Stirlingshire	323	n/a	n/a	No	No	No
PA7/28/48	Stirling	564	1,100	51%	No	No	Some
PA7/28/49	Airth, Larbert, Dunipace and Denny parishes	572	1,551	37%	No	No	Yes
PA7/28/61	Clackmannan parish	309	533	58%	Yes	Yes	Some
PA7/28/75	Logie parish	335	553	61%	Yes	Yes	Yes
PA7/28/80	St Ninians parish	566	1,807	31%	No	No	No
PA7/28/83	Tulliallan parish	211	362	58%	No	Yes	Yes

Note: Adult male population estimated at 48% of the adult population, itself estimated at 58% of the overall population, in Webster's census of 1755.

Source: Numbers of signatories taken from Bowie (ed.), *Addresses against Incorporating Union, 1706–07.*

Another of the ministers, Harie Robine in Alva, wrote up his own importance in a begging letter to the Earl of Mar two years later. He wrote that he had made himself unpopular among his fellow ministers: 'For indeed, my Lord, I have opposed my brethren ... as particularly when they were going to address the late parliament against the Union, I did by argument and otherwayes, effectually crush it after they had mett three times only for that effect.'[59] It is a reminder that church records do not necessarily tell the whole story. Logan is clear in his view that opposition has become much less active and in his encouragement to Mar contradicts Defoe's view of him as a parson 'maliciously humouring' the mob.

In the event, Stirling Presbytery drew back from sending an address to Parliament at that late stage and like others simply made an approach to the Commission of Assembly, broadly supporting it and asking it to continue trying to protect Presbyterian polity. The reasons for this rather muted approach are several and probably lie in the civil politics of the time and in the differing attitudes of town and country. The three parliamentary commissioners from Stirlingshire,[60] only two of whom lived in the Stirling Presbytery bounds, were uniformly against the union, but were part of the Jacobite party and were identifiably against the Presbyterian establishment in the church. The commissioner for the burgh was for the union, while the Earl of Mar wielded considerable influence.

Unlike the addresses submitted to Parliament, Stirling's address to the Commission of the General Assembly has not been published, so it is perhaps worthwhile to quote it at length so as to complete the survey of local reaction to the union:

> We have judged it our indispensable dutie to signify to you Our very dear brethren our deep concern therein and as upon the one and we doe heartily bliss God for what ye have done in giving such a testimonie for God conform to our Covenanted principles with which doe concur and cheerfullie homologate, so we entreat that ye would faithfully go on in growing the Covenanted work of Reformation, as being now planted by the Assembly upon the watch tower of this Church, not that we doubt your vigilance and carefulness; but when all is in hazard we are afraid all the securitie that can be had will not be of great avail upon such ane union; yet we humbly suggest that if ye think fit, we may insist for the securitie of the liberties and privileges of this Church, as particular as possible. We will not take upon us to condescend upon particulars to you who no doubt understands them better than we, yet we cannot but suggest that a secureing of our Gen. Ass., that none should represent our sovereign therein but a peer of the realm that owns the Government now established by Law would be desireable. That none might enjoy places of trust but they who are in the Communion of the Church and that a particular way be descended upon for preventing ane imposition of ensnaring oaths upon persons

in our communion, that a way may be found out for the churches corresponding with the state fasts and thanksgivings. We need not represent what danger of a toleration will be to this church when in the view of this shere there are alreddie such disorders much abounding and we but represent in a business of this concern, that the mind of the Church of Scotland ought to be heard with respect to her present Claim for her own securitie, and at least we think that the Commission should know the minds of the respective presbyteries in this matter when in business of far less moment also will remit to presbyteries for their judgements, and that it will be to a prejudice to this Church if she be not consulted with respect to her purity.

The Presbterie considering that the present juncture of affairs does call the lovers of Zion's good to meet often together and join in prayer to God. They appoint that they meet tomorrow for the reason foresaid.[61]

The last sentence of the first paragraph seems to have an implied criticism of the Commission of Assembly, that it was ignoring the concerns of individual presbyteries when matters of less import were sent down for consultation, and that even in the central belt of Scotland, presbyteries might feel remote from and ignored by those in power over the church. Both Dunblane and Stirling presbyteries spent part of their first meetings of 1707 considering letters from the Commission about such topics as profanity, atheistic writing, episcopal ministers, witchcraft, idolatrous practices, seeking contributions to a fund to send probationers to the north and the sending in of lists of 'papists'.[62]

At the 8 January meeting, a letter was read to the presbytery, as it had been to every other in the land, from the Commission of Assembly desiring 'presbyteries to use endeavours for suppressing tumults ariseing at the seeming success of the business of ane union between Scotland and England'.[63] The following week, the Commission of Assembly submitted its fourth address to Parliament, expressing its concern that a united parliament, heavily weighted towards England, might take it on itself to legislate for the Church of Scotland. It was read to Parliament. The Union of the Parliaments went ahead, voted through in Scotland on 14 January 1707, although with that separate act guaranteeing the right of Presbyterianism passed on 16 January.

Despite the fundamental changes to the governance of the nation in 1707, there was no immediate discontinuity in the life of the church. Nonetheless it has to be said that many of the Presbyterians' fears for the Church of Scotland were justified. Toleration of Episcopalian dissenters became enshrined in law, the Episcopalian prayer book came into use openly among them, and 1712 brought the Church Patronage (Scotland) Act, restoring the right of presentation to the patrons who had lost it in 1690. Complained about by the General Assembly for decades afterwards, this act laid the foundations for the multiple secessions within the Church of Scotland which occurred from 1733 to 1843, with the right of patronage not disappearing until 1874.

Notes

1. Logan, *A Sermon Preached before His Grace James Duke of Queensberry*, p. 11.
2. Lynch, *Scotland*, pp. 310–11, 317.
3. Fry, *The Union*, p. 56; Bowie, *Scottish Public Opinion and the Anglo-Scottish Union, 1699–1707*, p. 73.
4. Stephen, *Scottish Presbyterians and the Act of Union 1707*, p. 21.
5. Raffe, *The Culture of Controversy*, pp. 87–8.
6. Bowie, *Scottish Public Opinion and the Anglo-Scottish Union, 1699–1707*; Stephen, *Scottish Presbyterians and the Act of Union 1707*.
7. Stephen, *Scottish Presbyterians and the Act of Union 1707*, p. 112.
8. As distinct from a 'federal union', which would allow the Scottish Parliament to retain its identity and Scotland to have some sort of decision-making powers on its own affairs.
9. NRS GD124/15/457/1 Logan to Mar, 27/8/1706.
10. Clerk, *Memoirs of the Life of Sir John Clerk of Penicuik*, p. 64.
11. West, *Memoirs*, p. 146.
12. Bowie (ed.), *Addresses against Incorporating Union, 1706–07*, p. 37.
13. HMC, 'The Manuscripts of His Grace the Duke of Portland', vol. 4, p. 343.
14. Bell, 'The Most Memorable Passages of the Life and Times of Mr J.B.'; Fry, *The Union*, p. 204.
15. SCA CH2/723/5 28/10/1706.
16. Bowie (ed.), *Addresses against Incorporating Union, 1706–07*, pp. 16–17.
17. Defoe, *The History of the Union of Great Britain*, pp. 235–6.
18. Ibid., p. 243.
19. Daniel Defoe to Robert Harley, 4/11/1706, available at Electronic Enlightenment, https://doi.org/10.13051/ee:doc/defodaOU0010132b1c (last accessed 17/2/2021).
20. Logan, *A Sermon Preached before His Grace James Duke of Queensberry*, p. 2.
21. Ibid., p. 2.
22. Ibid., p. 13.
23. NRS GD124/15/457/1.
24. HMC, 'The Manuscripts of His Grace the Duke of Portland', vol. 4, p. 345.
25. Bowie (ed.), *Addresses against Incorporating Union, 1706–07*, p. 115.
26. Ibid., p. 215; NRS PA7/28/83.
27. Buchanan's signature is sufficiently unlike that on the Dunblane Presbytery address to raise some doubt as to its identity. Its placing with those of the kirk session suggests it may have been written 'on his behalf' but if with his permission it should have been attested as such.
28. Bowie (ed.), *Addresses against Incorporating Union, 1706–07*, pp. 216–17; NRS PA7/28/83.
29. Only men signed the petitions. The figures are estimated from Webster's census of 1755, assuming a population of 42 per cent under the age of eighteen and a male percentage of 48 per cent (Kyd, *Scottish Population Statistics*, p. 46). The percentages are estimated from Flinn (ed.), *Scottish Population History*, pp. 257

(age groups), 283 (gender). While accurate figures and demographic proportions cannot be ascertained for the first decade of the eighteenth century it can be assumed that in the absence of a major demographic event they serve as indicative figures.
30. Bowie (ed.), *Addresses against Incorporating Union, 1706–07*, p. 68.
31. Defoe, *The History of the Union of Great Britain*, p. 245.
32. Stirling Burgh Council, *Extracts of the Records of the Royal Burgh of Stirling*, A.D. *1667–1752*, p. 109; NRS PA7/28/48; Bowie (ed.), *Addresses against Incorporating Union, 1706–07*, pp. 166–7.
33. Daniel Defoe to Robert Harley, 3/12/1706, available at Electronic Enlightenment, https://doi.org/10.13051/ee:doc/defodaOU0010152a1c (last accessed 17/2/2021).
34. 'Setts of the Royal Burghs of Scotland', p. 167.
35. NRS PA7/28/48; Bowie (ed.), *Addresses against Incorporating Union, 1706–07*, pp. 166–7.
36. Ibid. (both sources).
37. NRS GD124/15/478/2 Finlaysone to Erskine 5/12/1706.
38. Stirling Burgh Council, *Extracts of the Records of the Royal Burgh of Stirling*, A.D. *1667–1752*, p. 110. The potential for confusion of the two John Erskines is considerable.
39. NRS GD124/15/478 Holburn and Erskine correspondence 4–13/12/1706; SCA B66/25/779.
40. Bowie (ed.), *Addresses against Incorporating Union, 1706–07*, p. 212.
41. SCA CH2/723/5 3/12/1706.
42. NRS PA7/20/49, also printed as *To his Grace, Her Majesties High Commissioner and the Right Honourable Estates of Parliament, the Humble Address of the Presbytry of Dumblane.*
43. NRS CH2/710/2.
44. Logie Kirk Session's minutes are missing for this period.
45. Quoted in Bowie, *Scottish Public Opinion and the Anglo-Scottish Union, 1699–1707*, p. 113.
46. NRS PA7/20/49.
47. NRS PA7/20/28; Bowie (ed.), *Addresses against Incorporating Union, 1706–07*, pp. 272–4.
48. HMC, 'The Manuscripts of His Grace the Duke of Portland', vol. 4, p. 353.
49. RPS, Act for Securing of the Protestant Religion and Presbyterian Church Government (1707), https://www.rps.ac.uk/trans/1706/10/251 (last accessed 18/2/2021).
50. RPS, Act Ratifying and Approving the Treaty of Union of the Two Kingdoms of Scotland and England (1707), https://www.rps.ac.uk/trans/1706/10/257 (last accessed 18/2/2021).
51. NRS PA7/28/75; NRS PA7/28/49. Although having separate kirk sessions, Larbert and Dunipace formed a joint charge served by the same minister.
52. In the context of discussing the identity of the third elder signing Dunblane's address, it is worth noting that Logie's 335 signatories on NRS PA/28/75 include eight by the name of James Henderson and five by the name of John Henderson as well as sundry Georges and Williams of the Henderson family. Identity of individuals is of necessity speculative.

53. The parish of Hamilton, for example, hotbed of resistance, only managed a 27 per cent signatory rate, Biggar 47 per cent. Bowie (ed.), *Addresses against Incorporating Union, 1706–07*, pp. 243, 259.
54. NRS PA7/28/61; Bowie (ed.), *Addresses against Incorporating Union, 1706–07*, p. 199.
55. SCA CH2/1242/3/167 24/12/1706.
56. For example Lesmahagow. See Bowie (ed.), *Addresses against Incorporating Union, 1706–07*, pp. 234–5.
57. NRS GD124/15/457/2 Logan to Mar, 23/12/1706.
58. Ibid.
59. NRS GD124/15/922 Robine to Mar, 29/11/1708.
60. John Graham of Killearn, James Graham of Buchlyvie and Robert Rollo of Powhouse.
61. SCA CH2/722/9 8/1/1707.
62. Ibid.; SCA CH2/723/5 7/1/1707.
63. SCA CH2/722/9 8/1/1707.

CONCLUSION

The New Ecclesiastical Regime

The letter previously quoted from Christian Russell in Stirling to her uncle in Rotterdam in October 1690 expresses something of the uncertainty faced by the population of central Scotland after the Revolution.[1] In theory, matters had been settled by then. James had been deposed, William and Mary proclaimed as joint monarchs, the Jacobites defeated and Presbyterianism established as the form of governance for the Church of Scotland, the General Assembly had sat, and the antediluvians had been restored to their old pulpits. And yet the pious and Presbyterian Christian Russell was filled with apprehension.

The purpose of this study has been to examine how events developed within the context of the church over the twenty years after William's accession within a restricted area of Scotland. Even after the forces loyal to James VII had been defeated at the Haughs of Cromdale, there was still the fear (or hope, depending on point of view) that the reign of William and Mary was but a temporary interruption in the dynastic progression, and a very real apprehension that armed strife was never far from breaking out. Locally this was emphasised by the divisions within Stirling Burgh and by the large number of minor lairds who remained loyal to the old regime. The constant presence of troops in the area, whether in Stirling Castle or elsewhere, kept the government visible, but the real power in the country as a whole lay in the hands of a small number of nobles whose commitment was largely to their own interests.

After several abortive attempts, Scotland was again racked by open strife twenty-five years later in the 1715 Jacobite Rising, and the matter was not finally settled for a further three decades, but the happenings of those first two decades after the deposition of James VII were crucial in forming the future path of the church both locally and in the wider nation.

Within that context, the restoration of Presbyterianism was accompanied by risk. In the area of this study, the Toleration had brought in a means by which support for Presbyterianism could be shown openly and three meeting-houses provided a nucleus for the restored Presbytery. The exclusion of any who were not approved by the old Presbyterian clergy from attending the first General Assembly led to charges that it was not representative. While historians have debated how much popular backing Presbyterianism had, the evidence of St Ninians and Logie meeting-houses in particular, and the indirect evidence of Alva, shows that there was considerable support. On the other hand, events in Stirling itself show the support was far from unanimous. Some historians have been keen to suggest that much of the 'rabbling' of the episcopal clergy was done by firebrands coming into parishes rather than by parishioners. It is undoubtedly true that the late rabbling of John Monro in Stirling in 1694[2] and the earlier rabbling of George Schaw and William Elphinstone in Logie were accompanied by visiting soldiery, and it is equally true that those concerned returned to their pulpits after a few weeks, albeit temporarily, but it is also true that the evidence shows that the women of Logie needed no encouragement to play a full part in the proceedings.[3]

Perhaps the clearest indication of the public mood in one parish at least can be seen in the financial giving in Alva parish, detailed in Appendix 3. The drop in giving in Alva when the Presbyterian meeting-house in Logie, opened in 1688, the increase on the return of Richard Howieson in 1690, the dramatic drop again when the Episcopalian Lindsay returned in 1692 and another increase on the restoration of Presbyterian control all give a clear view that in one parish anyway, there was a strong support for Presbyterianism. Alongside that, though, can be put the continuity of the eldership of Alva apparently collecting for the poor of the parish and serving their kirk regardless of who was in the pulpit.

But if there was considerable support for the Presbyterian cause locally, it was counter-balanced by the continuing of an unquantifiable number who remained aligned to the old regime. Most easily seen in the actions of heritors and the influential, a sub-culture of resistance by ordinary people can also be glimpsed through the incidents recorded in burgh court records and session minutes. These show a lively opposition to Presbyterianism through flyting and abuse, through irregular marriages and baptisms and simply through absence at the ordinances.

Presbyterianism re-established as the governance of the national church depended on the availability of Presbyterian ministers. Locally the numbers increased slowly as parish after parish came under Presbyterian governance (see Table 1.1). The ministers came in by their several routes – returning antediluvian, meeting-house preacher, newly ordained, drawn in from other charges – all enabled to function largely by the actions of the Privy Council. Some of those ministers who came into the area moved on quickly, others remained for many decades.

There was no long-term influence from the antediluvians locally. All those reappointed to their old parishes quickly moved on. Robert Rule, coming back at a later stage having been restored to Kirkcaldy, seems to have been more symbolic than influential. The ministers whose first charges had been early meeting-houses, whether in the area or not, were perhaps of more importance: the elder Michael Potter in Dunblane was accused of fomenting some of the opposition to the union and others like Alexander Douglas and George Turnbull had longer periods of involvement, but the overall impression is that those ordained in the 1690s very quickly had more influence than their older brethren.

The nature of church records does not allow of much evidence of parties and splits within presbytery, but traces can be seen. Alexander Douglas (Logie) showed his displeasure at the disjunction of Dunblane and Stirling presbyteries. Thomas Boston's experiences when contemplating a ministry in Dollar show that John Forrester (Stirling) and possibly Robert Gourlaw (Tillicoultry) were not in favour of ministers seen as too 'severe'. Thomas Buchanan (Tulliallan) complained of his treatment by the moderator over his call to Kilmadock; John Logan (St Ninians) and Harie Robine (Alva) allude to the arguments over the union among the clergy in letters to the Earl of Mar. Several protested over the ordination of Thomas Davidson as chaplain to Stirling Castle. Clearly there were disagreements and probably parties and factions within the presbyteries, but by papering over the undoubted cracks the two bodies in Stirling and Dunblane were able to function as united.

There was a constant supply of men eager to take on the role of ministry. Calling an ordained minister to a charge was a long process, sometimes years in length, while ordaining a probationer could be swift and, unless the Duke of Atholl was involved, relatively pain-free. The converse of that, though, was that the life of the probationer was difficult, submitting to trials of his learning and orthodoxy, supplying pulpits constantly all over the presbytery bounds with scant and tardy recompense and in the knowledge that he might have to start the process all over again in a new presbytery if no parish called him. However, the perceived need of some parishes for a minister of known worth and experience led to constant tensions between parishes and presbyteries, with 'the greater good of the church' being a mantra that was always capable of being quoted in support of either party.

Beyond presbytery level, at synod level, a fresh tension was evident. The cost in time to attend and the distances involved combined to make each diet of the synod very different in its membership from half-year to half-year. The evidence is that the meetings' deliberations were heavily influenced by their location and that co-operation between presbyteries was not always the first imperative. In dealings with the General Assembly and its Commission too, there is also evidence to suggest the individual presbyteries and parishes sometimes felt cut off from the decision-making process.

At the local level, changing to a Presbyterian regime was dependent on the attitudes of the heritors. Even when the heritors did allow a Presbyterian settlement, their goodwill was crucial to the effectiveness of the minister; the evidence shows that patronage may have been abolished, but the influence of the patron remained considerable. Ministers called without the consent of the heritors rarely lasted long, and most of the new men were only called with the consent of the old patron of the parish.

The church did not operate in a vacuum, however; if the heritors and former patrons had a part to play, so did other structures of local society. At a local level, secular power could be a major factor in religious strife. The Royal Burgh of Stirling had suffered substantial division and rioting during the time of James Guthrie; the parish church still showed the result in the wall that split the two factions. Under episcopal rule too, there had been some factionalism. The junior minister, James Hunter, had been deposed for drunkenness in 1684, but the ramifications of the resulting quarrel with John Monro, minister of the 1st Charge, were still reverberating in print in 1713,[4] and it is surely no coincidence that Hunter was pursued by the Privy Council in the first sweep of episcopal ministers while Monro retained his pulpit for four years more. Hunter remained firmly in the Episcopalian resistance, appearing through the courts over the following two decades, while Monro faded from the narrative. But it also is noticeable that Hunter, alone of the local Episcopalian ministers, was arraigned on theological grounds, accused of denying the canonical nature of the Song of Solomon, a charge which he denied.

Mixed in all of this was a power struggle within the burgh council. Manifested in part by the controversy over whether Stirling Kirk Session should be chosen by the council and whether there should be elders elected from Stirling Castle, it was only resolved when the old council was put out in its entirety by the Privy Council, a new sett for the council laid down and a new group of councillors, all from the Presbyterian party, elected. Thereafter the council kept the town Presbyterian, but there is plenty of evidence of dissenters. This influence of the burgh council on church matters, while echoing that of Guthrie's day, also presaged events of the 1730s when Stirling was at the centre of the Secession under the ministry of Ebenezer Erskine.[5] The dividing line between religion and town politics was always narrow in the Royal Burgh.

With the gradual placing of Presbyterian ministers in the parishes the numbers of Episcopalian ones declined correspondingly, but if some of the Presbyterian clergy battled with the enmity of their heritors, some of the Episcopalian clergy retained a degree of support that allowed them to survive, or indeed be newly placed in a parish in defiance of the wishes of the presbytery. Clearly this was entirely in the hands of the landowners; the Marquess of Montrose and Duke of Atholl showed that in Aberfoyle and Balquhidder. There is little, if any, evidence of a theological reason. Montrose's placing of William Fisher in Aberfoyle was a response to his sheltering of Covenanters in the past; Atholl's support of William Campbell was based on a belief that he was acceptable to the people and Atholl himself, with a much more doctrinaire wife to influence him, espoused the Presbyterian cause nationally. Equally the Earl of Mar's initial support of Presbyterianism was probably influential in making sure Alloa was Presbyterian from an early point. The fragmented nature of power in some other parishes, particularly St Ninians, made for a more confused situation but what is evident is that to a great extent, it was the individuals involved and personal relationships rather than a doctrinaire attachment to a theological position that led to the Episcopalian clergy initially remaining in post.

On paper, one of the most obvious differences between pre- and post-Revolution church governance lay in the role of the elder. In episcopal times, it was limited entirely to the kirk session; thereafter elders had, once again, a role to play in the higher courts. The nature of the eldership had changed between the two regimes; although there were exceptions, most, though not all, elders after 1690 were newly ordained and generally of a lower social standing than their predecessors. It is also notable that some landowners with a strong prior background in conventicling, such as Lord Cardross and James Ure of Shirgarton, played no part in church affairs locally.

In practice, however, the restored right of elders to sit in the higher courts of the church does not seem to have been highly valued. Attendance at presbyteries was poor, at synods poorer, and when elders did attend, they were usually of higher rank and had little to do with the day-to-day work of the kirk session to which they belonged. Most of the elders were also side-lined from much of the work of these courts. Except where they had particular skills and influences, like Sir Colin Campbell of Aberuchill, they are largely invisible in the record other than in surveying ground at visitations. It is perhaps symbolic of their lack of importance in the higher courts that there is never any mention of their absence nor any apology recorded, while ministers were expected to tender excuses and were liable for practical censure if the excuses were not adequate. It is also significant that there is evidence of deliberate exclusion of elders during the union debate.

Within the kirk session, elders' roles remained as they had always been; the maintenance of discipline, the honest distribution of poor relief and the seemly administration of the sacraments. In addition, they had the role of acting with the heritors and male heads of families in calling a minister. Despite changes in their social status, this seems to be the only significant difference in how the kirk sessions functioned before and after the re-establishment of Presbyterianism. So far as discipline was concerned, while Bill Inglis has drawn attention to differences in Dunblane,[6] and while the index to cases in the St Ninians minutes shows differences in numbers and in emphasis,[7] the overall intention of maintaining a godly people remained the same. The offences considered varied widely from session to session; equally varied was the approach to penitents and the punishment meted out by the sessions. It is not possible to gauge to what extent this reflected the ministers' views and to what extent the elders', but numbers of appearances before the congregation and differences in financial penalties and in how such penalties varied between men and women were clearly governed by local practice rather than by any concerted approach even at presbytery level, let alone nationally. In one sense this finding contradicts Alistair Mutch's statement that 'Scottish practices favoured a systematic form of authority based on detailed record keeping'[8] although perhaps it is only the 'systematic' which is in doubt. However non-uniform the authority was, it was always based on the records of the institution and every attempt was made to establish the continuity of the record through the passing of time.

In the celebration of the sacraments it is evident that both presbyteries found the reluctance of ministers to hold Communion services frustrating. Although the Register of the Privy Council shows how the failure of some episcopal incumbents to celebrate Communion over many years was seen as a major sign of negligence, some were holding Communion celebrations right up until the Revolution and some of the evidence led against those seen as intruders after the Revolution was the celebration of both sacraments in Bothkennar and St Ninians. It is equally evident that the lack of Communion services was an issue for some Presbyterian ministers. The reasons for delay were twofold: the minister wanted to be sure that he knew his people and that the people were sufficiently versed in the catechism to be worthy of the privilege. The celebration itself was considered on several levels. The care taken to orchestrate the occasion in Stirling shows it almost as performance, but equally the deeply personal responses by people such as Boston and George Turnbull, Elisabeth West and Elizabeth Cairns show how it fed into a piety which was a precursor to evangelicalism and revivalism.[9] The sacrament of baptism, on the other hand, still showed the feeling of need for every child to be baptised as part of the nation's membership of the church universal. At the same time, perhaps because it was almost universal it received less attention in the records and perhaps had less impact on the people.

Although the consideration of preaching has been limited to a brief consideration of what can be gleaned from Turnbull's diary and from a volume of sermons from early in his incumbency in Alloa, most chapters have been headed by quotations from a single published sermon by his successor, John Logan. Logan's sermon, being for a particular occasion and context, is not typical, but it lays out his view of the mutual relationship of church and state and the state's responsibility to uphold the church. Turnbull's selection of texts cannot be taken as typical either, without a wider comparison with other preachers, but it shows how the circumstances of his charges affected his choice.

Every minister was different and it not possible to generalise from one individual's usage to say this was the pattern. It is generally recognised that this period in the church's life was not noted for its theological insights or its preaching. J. R. McIntosh comments: 'One of the striking features of evangelical publication in the eighteenth century is the relative sparsity of theological work. Apart from the notable figure of Thomas Boston there are only about eight writers who made a contribution of any great substance to theological publication.'[10] Such comparisons as have been made, with the Episcopalian Archibald Douglas and the Presbyterian Archibald Lundie, both in Saltoun in East Lothian, suggest that Turnbull's use of the lecture was not so very far different from the afternoon sermons of the former. Although Douglas was very different in his concentration on the gospels, Lundie's themes were, as might be expected, closer in emphasis to those of Turnbull.

Leaving aside the question of governance, prior to the Revolution the theology of Scots, whether in the establishment or on the hillsides, while always showing a spectrum of belief, was Calvinist in nature. The development of the lecture by field preachers into something more than the reading of a scripture passage became a difference between Presbyterian and Episcopalian preachers as time went on, but essentially the two parties worshipped the same God in much the same way. Alasdair Raffe draws attention to the way that Episcopalian theology changed in its emphasis, with changes accelerating after the Revolution and the loss of power. At the root the differences were firstly in the Episcopalians' acceptance of the rule of civil authority over the church as against the partnership of two parallel authorities sought by the Presbyterians, and secondly in the Presbyterian disdain for any differences in rank and authority between ministers. Ironically, in the functioning of Episcopalian incumbents through the post-Revolution period, one aspect that seems entirely missing is any sense of episcopal authority over them, but instead a growing awareness of a 'new' style of worship in the development of liturgy. Contrariwise, it was the civil authorities' initial backing of Presbyterianism tempered by a later moderating influence that made Presbyterian re-establishment viable.

While the post-Revolution Episcopalians developed their liturgy, at the other end of the theological spectrum there seems to have remained an almost invisible hankering for 'non-institutional' Presbyterian worship. The controversy surrounding George Mair in Airth and his association with John Hepburn[11] is evidence for this, as are also the memoirs of Elizabeth Cairns, initially in Blackford but later in Stirling, showing a strongly committed adherence to the Presbyterian theology of the conventicles. There is also evidence for dissenters of a Presbyterian mindset in the baptismal register of John Macmillan[12] and in the much later existence of praying societies who contacted Ebenezer Erskine for preaching in Kilmadock after the Secession.[13]

Historians belonging to dissenting Presbyterian traditions have claimed that the Church of Scotland lost its way very quickly after the Revolution Settlement because of the influence of earlier conformists percolating into and controlling the trajectory of the church away from the practices and views of the pre-Revolution Presbyterians. There is no evidence of this within the two presbyteries; no Episcopalian incumbents played any part in Presbyterian governance, and only one applied to be admitted to the joint presbytery and was rejected.[14] Those Episcopalian clergy who retained their pulpits did so in isolation and had no influence on the rest of the church locally.

Although it is easy to link the survival of Episcopalianism with the influence of Jacobite lairds, this is partly a feature of the nature of surviving evidence. However, alongside people like Paterson of Bannockburn, Stirling of Keir and later the Earl of Mar on the national stage, a substantial cast of Episcopalian sympathisers makes its appearance in local court records, civil and ecclesiastical, with irregular marriage and baptism, riot and affray, the use of 'Presbyterian' as a term of abuse showing that Episcopalian sympathies were not limited to the landowning classes. The relationship between the two polities was also affected by the civil law. Episcopalian sympathisers who held certain offices such as commissary or sheriff depute were as influential in baulking Presbyterian control as a Presbyterian burgh court was in promoting it. To some extent this situation changed after the union when the civil courts stepped back from matters which they considered ecclesiastical and declined to use their power to enforce the decisions of kirk sessions, thus weakening the power of the church. This change further opened the door for those who did not accept the new settlement to worship in an alternative manner, provided they accepted Queen Anne as legitimate monarch. The evidence is clearly there to suggest that by the end of the period under consideration the area was religiously pluralist with two parallel churches in existence.

Situated as they were on the verge of the Highlands, the two presbyteries were firmly Lowland in their outlook. Highland influence on Stirling was only in as much as the burgh and its suburbs were the normal route for traffic to and from the north and thus had a transient connection This does not seem to have affected the church to any great extent. Dunblane, on the other hand, with Gaelic dominant in three Episcopalian and two Presbyterian parishes, was a different matter. After regular failures to bring Balquhidder into the Presbyterian fold, it and Callander quietly conformed right at the end of the period of study with the settling of Gaelic-speaking Presbyterian ministers. For those Gaelic-speaking parishes it seems clear that any worship in Gaelic was preferable to any worship in English and this led to the continuation of Episcopalian clergy. The experiences of ministers and probationers sent to Balquhidder is ample evidence of that, and yet there seems to have been no recorded public desire for Gaelic preaching in Port of Menteith or Kilmadock prior to the disputed settlement in the former in 1725, just the quiet comment that the Gaelic speakers go elsewhere to worship.[15] Through the whole period there is a real feeling that the Highland aspects of those two parishes were simply ignored and no concession made to those parishioners who might not have been able to understand the ministers. At a period when the education of the Highlands was beginning to take prominence in the mind of the nation, the overwhelming impression left by the two presbyteries is that they were not too interested.

The major topic which occupied the minds of the two presbyteries and their inhabitants towards the end of the period under consideration was the Union of the Parliaments. The attitude of the people to the Union of the Parliaments seems to have been largely hostile throughout the country, except for those who saw the opportunities in trade and the possible benefits of tapping English markets. The most vocal opposition in the country was from the south-west and Lanarkshire, but the area of this study showed considerable opposition too. The large number of petitions against the union show the depth of feeling in the two presbytery areas. This opposition was shared, but not co-operatively, by Episcopalians and Presbyterians, as evidenced by the Stirlingshire petition of the former and by parish and presbytery petitions of the latter, signed by elders and to a lesser extent by ministers. Just what the church's formal role was is not always clear. Some of the many petitions were clearly instigated by the church, other petitions emanated from individual parishes but with an element of doubt as to whether the local kirk session was involved, others such as the Stirling burgh petition clearly were supported by individual elders.

Jeffrey Stephen rejects the idea that the church was 'the bulwark of the opposition', 'played an important role in articulating anti-union feeling' or was the 'greatest threat to union'.[16] This rejection seems to over-simplify the case. The churches' involvement in opposition as represented by the petitions shows clearly that whether or not individual kirk sessions instigated them, and some certainly did, they were heavily represented among the signatories of the others. Equally it is true that the church nationally tried to stem public disorder although there is no evidence of this in Stirling or Dunblane. There is evidence, though, that the churches were not united: for example, the letters of John Logan (Alloa) and Harie Robine (Alva) and the sermon which Logan preached in Edinburgh show that individual ministers were in favour of the act with safeguards. Thus formal Presbyterian opposition and concerns seem largely to have been neutralised by the separate act giving security to the Church of Scotland, and this was instrumental in the ultimate passage of the union, leading, as Stephen has pointed out, to the charge that the church put its own priorities before the need of the nation.[17]

Queen Anne's commitment to preserving Presbyterianism in Scotland was not strong. Her agenda of encouraging toleration of such Episcopalian clergy as were prepared to pray for her weakened both the monolithic structure of Presbyterianism and enthusiasm for the Union. By subjecting Scots to a House of Lords which included bishops she made sure that cases involving religious matters were not treated with any sympathy towards Presbyterianism. But by the end of this period of study there are signs that even those of the gentry who had embraced Presbyterianism were finding the blandishments of a less severe creed tempting, evidenced particularly in the support of Mar for the almost invisible meeting-house in Alloa and for the more obvious one in Stirling.

There must be a strong suspicion that only the Episcopalians' strong attachment to the cause of Jacobitism prevented them from becoming a much more powerful force in the nation. But even without this, Anne's insistence on restoring the rights of patrons in appointing ministers in 1712 was probably the most effectively divisive act in the history of the relationship between civil and ecclesiastical governments, and therefore in the ensuing history of the church.

Every parish, every presbytery in every age has its own character, its own travails, its own issues and challenges, and yet taking these two presbyteries as a whole, they show signs of almost all the issues which exercised the mind of the national church in the period. The weighting might change between the deeply Presbyterian parishes of the south-west or the stubbornly Episcopalian parishes of the north-east, and yet the presbyteries of Stirling and Dunblane had the same issues to face on a parochial scale in Airth and Bothkennar respectively. The difficulties of propagating a faith from the south to the Highlands, areas which shared neither language nor culture but only a deep mutual suspicion, were shown in the Highland parishes of Dunblane. The challenges and opportunities of reconciling church interests with the power of a royal burgh were as evident in the relationship with Stirling Burgh as they might be in Glasgow or Edinburgh, just on a smaller scale.

But overarching all the local concerns, issues and problems, the two presbyteries and their constituent parishes, like their equivalents through the land, used the two decades which followed the Williamite Revolution to lay the basis of the Church of Scotland. It is slightly ironic that although they had the early opportunity to recruit to their bounds the outstanding preachers and theologians of the new generation in Thomas Boston, John Willison and Thomas Halyburton, each of them was to plough his furrow elsewhere. Despite those lost opportunities and despite division, schism, reunion and the odd theological heresy, some of which was to emanate from their bounds, the two presbyteries of Stirling and Dunblane helped mould the national church locally for the next three centuries.

Writing about an earlier period, Margo Todd referred to 'the diversity that received protestantism in sixteenth century Scotland – Gaelic and Scots, rural and urban, elite and unlearned, male and female, pious and worldly – together with the amalgam of tradition and innovation that so remarkably joined them in a visible, covenanted protestant identity'.[18] This applies as much to the later period and restricted area under consideration here. The different interest groups still survived and indeed still do, and the 'amalgam of tradition and innovation' is still a characteristic of the national character, even if the concept of 'covenanted protestant' is rather less obvious. In their approach to re-establishing Presbyterianism to the people within Stirling and Dunblane presbytery bounds, the two presbyteries can be seen as a microcosm of the nation as a whole.

Notes

1. NRS RH15/106/709/10, Christian Russell to Andrew Russell, 13/10/1690.
2. 'Episcopacy in Stirling', pp. 219–20.
3. NLS MS 7593/1–3.

4. *Flying Post*, 7/4/1713.
5. Muirhead, 'Religion, Politics and Society in Stirling during the Ministry of Ebenezer Erskine'.
6. Inglis, 'The Impact of Episcopacy and Presbyterianism, Before and After 1690, on One Parish'.
7. SCA CH2/337/2 pp. 206–32.
8. Mutch, *Religion and National Identity*, p. xv.
9. Spurlock, 'Boundaries of Scottish Reformed Orthodoxy, 1560–1700', p. 372.
10. McIntosh, 'Eighteenth-Century Evangelicalism', p. 84.
11. SCA CH2/722/8 30/12/1696.
12. Macmillan, *Register of the Rev. John Macmillan*.
13. There does not, however, seem to be evidence for their existence in the area during the period under consideration.
14. SCA CH2/722/8 23/9/1696, 24/2/1697.
15. NRS CH1/2/24/1/2/66–8 An answer to the objection against making the Bible in Irish as being prejudicial to the design of extirpating the Irish Language out of the Highlands of Scotland.
16. Stephen, *Scottish Presbyterians and the Act of Union 1707*, p. 232.
17. Ibid., p. 235.
18. Todd, *The Culture of Protestantism in Early Modern Scotland*, p. 412.

Appendices

Appendix 1: Survival of Church Records, 1688–1710

	1688	1689	1691	1692	1693	1694	1695	1696	1697	1698	1699	1700	1701	1702	1703	1704	1705	1706	1707	1708	1709	1710
Synod																						
Perth & Stirling				P	P	P	P	P	P	P	P	P	P	P	P	P	P	P	P	P	P	P
Presbyteries																						
Dunblane	E				P	P	P	P	P	P	P	P	P	P	P	P	P	P	P	P	P	P
Stirling												P	P	P	P	P	P	P	P	P	P	P
Dunblane Presbytery Session Records																						
Aberfoyle																						
Balquhidder																						P
Callander																						
Dunblane				P	P	P	P	P	P	P	P	P	P	P	P	P	P	P	P	P	P	P
Kilmadock				P	P											P	P	P	P	P	P	
Kincardine																						
Kippen																						
Lecropt																						
Logie	E	E																				
Logie	P	P	P	P	P	P	P	P	P	P	P											
Port									P	P	P	P	P	P	P	P	P	P	P	P	P	P
Tillicoultry				P	P	P	P	P	P	P	P	P										
Tulliallan	E	E	E	P	P	P	P	P	P	P	P	P	P	P	P	P	P	P	P	P	P	P
Stirling Presbytery Session Records																						
Airth																						
Alloa	E	P	P	P	P	P	P	P	P	P	P	P	P	P	P	P	P	P	P	P	P	P
Alva	E	E																				
Alva (accounts)	E	E	P	P	E	E	E	P	P	P	P	P	P	P	P	P	P	P	P	P	P	P
Bothkennar																						
Clackmannan	E	E							P	P	P	P	P	P	P	P	P	P	P	P	P	P
Denny																						
Dollar															P	P	P	P	P	P	P	P
Gargunnock											P	P	P	P	P	P	P	P	P	P	P	P
Larbert & Dunipace																						
St Ninians	P	P	P	P	P	P	P	P	P	P	P	P	P	P	P	P	P	P	P	P	P	P
Stirling					P	P	P	P	P	P	P											

Episcopal Records E | Presbyterian Records P | No surviving records

Appendix 2: Parish Statistics

		Hearth tax 1691–5: no. of hearths (Source 1)	Population, 1755 (Source 2)
Presbyteries			
	Dunblane	3,522	19,228
	Stirling	5,627	26,179
Dunblane parishes			
	Aberfoyle	101	895
	Balquhidder	241	1,586
	Callander	281	1,737
	Dunblane	672	2,728
	Kilmadock	619	2,730
	Kincardine	190	1,248
	Kippen	289	1,799
	Lecropt	103	577
	Logie	332	1,985
	Port of Menteith	295	1,865
	Tillicoultry	137	757
	Tulliallan	262	1,321
Stirling parishes			
	Airth	620	2,316
	Alloa	558	5,814
	Alva	120	436
	Bothkennar	128	529
	Clackmannan	479	1,913
	Denny	260	1,392
	Dollar	115	517
	Gargunnock	220	956
	Larbert & Dunipace	412	1,864
	St Ninians	1,377	6,491
	Stirling	1,338	3,951

Source 1: NRS E69/6/1

Source 2: Alexander Webster's 1755 census; see Kyd (ed.), *Scottish Population Statistics*.

Note 1: No. of hearths excludes those listed as too poor to pay.

Note 2: No. of hearths for Tulliallan is low due to figures being conflated with those of Culross.

Note 3: Kippen, Lecropt and Logie straddle county boundaries and hence the figures are an aggregate.

Note 4: It is not clear whether the population figures for Dunipace are included in Larbert or Denny.

Appendix 3: The Evidence from Alva's Collections, 1687–1700

With a fifty-year coverage, Alva's financial accounts from 1667 to 1717 (SCA CH2/10/4) provide a useful guide to the fluctuating state of the collections at morning worship. They not only list the amount garnered Sunday by Sunday, but note, for the most part, which elder was responsible.

Prior to 1689, the episcopal incumbent was William Lindsay, but the opening of the Presbyterian meeting-house in the neighbouring parish of Logie in August 1688 saw an immediate drop in collections, implying that a substantial number had deserted the parish church for the Presbyterians. The collections recovered, and more, as soon as Richard Howieson, the previous Presbyterian minister, was reintroduced to Alva in April 1689. His departure in the autumn of 1691 led to a two-month hiatus and then the return of Lindsay, apparently at the behest of the heritors. The evidence of the collections shows, however, that local support for Lindsay had dwindled substantially. The identification of the elders also ceased during this period, only to reappear when Stirling Presbytery reasserted control in September 1695 and further elders were added to the rota. The collections received a further boost in 1699 when a new Presbyterian minister, Harie Robine, was finally settled there.

It should be noted that the figures do not take into account the many occasions when there was no collection taken, but there is no evidence to show that a gap one week was made up for a greater figure when next there was a service.

Evidence from baptisms in Alva through the period is less clear-cut, with a fairly steady figure through the decade of change increasing sharply only when Robine was settled.

The numbered columns on the chart represent these significant points:

1. The planting of a Presbyterian meeting-house in the neighbouring parish of Logie.
2. The departure of Episcopalian William Lindsay and return of Presbyterian Richard Howieson.
3. The departure of Howieson and return of Lindsay.
4. The second departure of Lindsay, the parish coming under presbytery control but with no settled minister.
5. The ordination and settlement of Harie Robine.

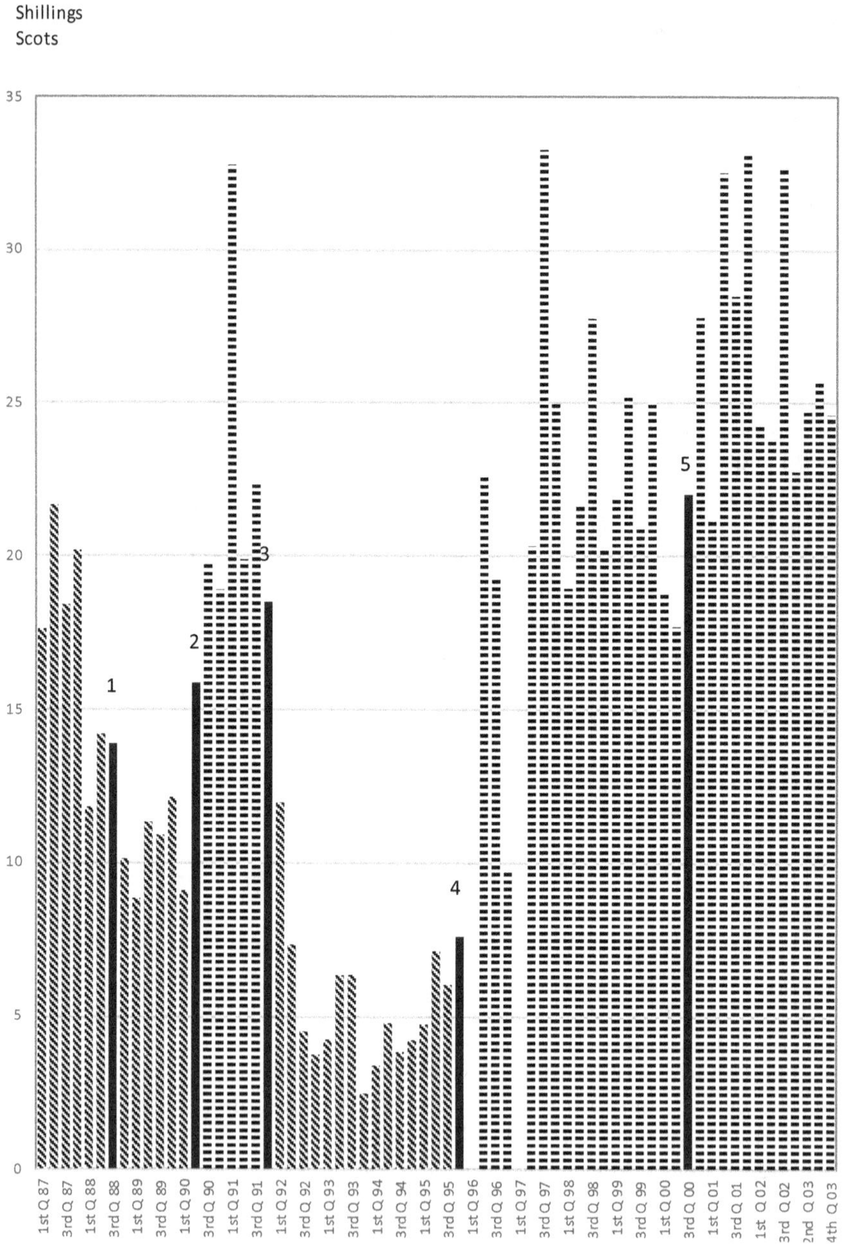

Alva average collections January 1687–December 1700

Appendix 4: The Post-Revolution Careers of Local Episcopal Ministers

	Name	Deprived	Left charge	Impact on presbytery	Later years
Dunblane Presbytery					
Bishop of Dunblane	Robert Douglas	1689	1689		Retired to Dundee
Aberfoyle	Robert Kirk		Died 1692		
Aberfoyle (2)	William Fisher		Died 1732	Minor complaint	The last Episcopalian parish minister in Scotland.
Balquhidder	Robert Stewart	15/8/1689	1689	Irregular baptism 1693	Jacobite at Killiecrankie
Balquhidder (2)	William Campbell		1710	Continuous irritation	Served at Glenorchy
Callander	James Menzies	3/10/1689	1716	Frequent intrusion 1699	
Dunblane	Gaspar Kellie	1689	1689–92		Meeting-house in Edinburgh
Kilmadock	David Drummond	26/9/1689	1689–93	Irregular marriage; retained records and utensils	
Kincardine in Menteith	John Cameron	29/8/1689	1689–95		Died Edinburgh 1719
Kippen	Robert Young	3/10/1689		Retained records until 1701	Edinburgh
Lecropt	William Wemyss	Deprived		Irregular marriages in 1693	Died 1705
Logie	George Schaw*	27/7/1689	1691	Possessed manse till 1693, dispute till 1702	
Logie (2)	William Elphinstone	after 11/5/1690			Longforgan 1709
Port of Menteith	Patrick Bell	3/10/1689			Retired to his estate
Tillicoultry	Alexander Keith*		1688		Moved to Orkney
Tulliallan	Alexander Williamson	25/8/1689	1690		Died Edinburgh 1701
Stirling Presbytery					
Airth	Paul Gellie	4/9/1689		Constant irritation till 1703	Resident Edinburgh 1707
Alloa	James Wright	3/9/1689		Assisted at Communion in Bothkennar 1701	
Alva	William Lindsay	Retired 25/5/1690	1696	Returned to charge 1692–6	
Bothkennar	John Skinner	10/4/1701 but reponed	1717	Irregular marriages etc. all through	
Clackmannan	Daniel Urquhart*	about 1696		Retained records and utensils	
Denny	John Wingate	4/9/1689	1691	Attended to give evidence	Died Edinburgh 1712
Dollar	George Monro*	1698	1698	Given financial assistance after he demitted	'Insufferably poor'
Gargunnock	John Edmonstone	3/10/1689			Died 1693
Larbert & Dunipace	Alexander Sutherland	1689	1689		Meeting-house in Edinburgh
St Ninians	James Forsyth	4/11/1690	1690	Son became Presbyterian minister	
Stirling (1st Charge)	John Monro*		Demitted 1693		
Stirling (2nd Charge)	James Hunter	1689		Meeting-house in St Ninians, irregular marriages etc. up to 1703	Lived in Edinburgh & Musselburgh
Other Episcopalian clergy who 'intruded' locally					
Kilmaurs or Dryfesdale	George Brown	Previously deprived		Administered sacraments and used English liturgy 1698	
Bothwell	Robert Douglas (younger)	Previously deprived		Disorderly preaching	Librarian of Leighton Library until death in 1746
Tarbet	Archibald McLachlan	Previously deprived		Iregular marriage	
Cumbernauld	Gilbert Muschet	Previously deprived		Irregular marriages in 1698 & 1706	
Morebattle	Adam Peacock	Previously deprived		Meeting-house in St Ninians 1703	
Dalry	Andrew Slirie	Previously deprived		Intruded in Falkirk, Irregular communion and baptisms in Bothkennar	

*These five ministers were among eight co-signatories of a letter to clergy in Edinburgh implying a willingness to work under the new regime. NRS CH12/12/467 25/5/1690.

Appendix 5: Distribution of George Turnbull's Header Texts as a Settled Minister

Book	All sermons	Dundas 1688–9	Alloa 1689–99	Tyninghame 1699–1704	Fasts 1688–1704	Communion 1688–1704
Genesis	1.2%	1.7%	1.4%			3.6%
Exodus	1.4%		0.9%	4.9%	2.4%	1.8%
Leviticus						
Numbers						
Deuteronomy	0.2%		0.2%		2.4%	
Joshua	0.8%	1.7%	0.5%		4.8%	1.8%
Judges	0.1%			0.4%		
Ruth						
1 Samuel	0.2%			0.4%	2.4%	
2 Samuel	1.2%		2.3%			3.6%
1 Kings						
2 Kings						
1 Chronicles						
2 Chronicles						
Ezra						
Nehemiah						
Esther						
Job	1.3%		0.9%	1.3%	9.5%	3.6%
Psalms	11.6%	10.0%	7.9%	16.8%	28.6%	16.1%
Proverbs	1.1%		0.7%	1.8%	2.4%	
Ecclesiastes	0.4%		0.5%	0.9%		
Song of Solomon	0.2%					3.6%
Isaiah	5.1%	6.7%	4.1%	3.5%		
Jeremiah	3.9%		2.7%	7.5%	2.4%	7.1%
Lamentations	0.3%		0.5%	0.4%	4.8%	
Ezekiel	0.4%	1.7%	0.2%	0.4%	7.1%	
Daniel						
Hosea	2.9%	11.7%	2.9%	0.9%	21.4%	
Joel	0.1%			0.4%	2.4%	
Amos	0.1%		0.2%		2.4%	
Obadiah						
Jonah	0.5%		0.2%			
Micah	0.2%					
Nahum	0.1%	1.7%				
Habakkuk						
Zephaniah						
Haggai	0.1%		0.2%			
Zechariah	0.8%		1.6%		2.4%	
Malachi	0.3%		0.5%	0.4%		

Appendix 5 (*continued*)

Book	All sermons	Dundas 1688–9	Alloa 1689–99	Tyninghame 1699–1704	Fasts 1688–1704	Communion 1688–1704
Matthew	5.4%	3.3%	4.1%	9.3%		
Mark	1.2%		1.4%	1.3%	2.4%	
Luke	3.1%	1.7%	3.2%	5.3%		10.7%
John	6.8%	6.7%	3.4%	10.2%		8.9%
Acts	2.7%		3.4%	3.1%		
Romans	7.6%	1.7%	12.2%	4.4%		1.8%
1 Corinthians	4.1%		4.5%	3.5%	2.4%	7.1%
2 Corinthians	3.4%	23.3%	1.8%	2.2%		1.8%
Galatians	0.9%		1.1%	0.4%		
Ephesians	1.0%		0.2%	1.3%		3.6%
Philippians	0.4%		0.2%			
Colossians	10.6%		21.9%	0.4%		
1 Thessalonians	0.1%		0.2%			
2 Thessalonians						
1 Timothy	0.1%					
2 Timothy	0.1%					
Titus	2.7%		2.3%	6.2%		1.8%
Philemon	0.6%	8.3%				
Hebrews	8.8%	10.0%	8.1%	7.1%		12.5%
James	0.7%		0.7%	0.4%		1.8%
1 Peter	1.3%			2.2%		7.1%
2 Peter	0.6%		1.1%			
1 John						
2 John						
3 John						
Jude	1.0%	10.0%	0.2%			1.8%
Revelation	1.8%		1.6%	2.2%		
Summary: Old Testament						
Pentateuch	2.9%	1.7%	2.5%	4.9%	4.8%	5.4%
History	3.7%	1.7%	3.6%	2.2%	16.7%	8.9%
Poetry	13.3%	10.0%	9.0%	19.5%	31.0%	19.6%
Major Prophets	9.7%	8.3%	7.5%	11.9%	14.3%	7.1%
Minor Prophets	5.2%	13.3%	5.7%	1.8%	28.6%	
Summary: New Testament						
Gospels	16.5%	11.7%	12.0%	26.1%	2.4%	19.6%
Acts	2.7%		3.4%	3.1%		
Pauline Epistles	40.6%	43.3%	52.7%	25.7%	2.4%	28.6%
General Epistles	3.7%	10.0%	2.0%	2.7%		10.7%
Revelation	1.8%		1.6%	2.2%		

Note: This analyis excludes sermons as a visiting preacher.
Source: Turnbull, 'The Diary of George Turnbull'.

Bibliography

PRIMARY SOURCES

1) Manuscript Sources

Records of Church Courts

GENERAL ASSEMBLY PAPERS
All in National Records of Scotland (NRS)
CH1/2/1/1–2   Overtures for making the liberty practicable July 1687.
CH1/2/1/46   Case of James Forsyth, minister at St Ninians 1690.
CH1/2/2/1/29   Protestation of committee against sheriff depute of Aberdeen 18/8/1694.
CH1/2/3/4/317–24   Call of Alexander Hamilton from Airth to Stirling 1702–3.
CH1/2/4/1/1–15   Call of John Logan from Kilmadock to Alloa.
CH1/2/4/1/75–88   Petitions and other papers in connection with the call of Mr Alex. Hamilton, minister at Airth, to the Parish Church of Stirling.
CH1/2/4/1/89–91   Call of James Brisbane from Kilmacolm to Stirling.
CH1/2/5/1/70–83   Papers regarding disputed calls of Thomas Buchanan to Culross and Kilmadock.
CH1/2/5/2/99–111   Petitions etc. regarding the proposed translation of Mr Hugh Whyte from Larbert and Dunipace to Kinnaird.
CH1/2/22/3/215–19   Call of Hugh Whyte from Lerbur [*sic*] to Kinnaird 1701–3.
CH1/2/23/2/173   Petition of Presbytery of Stirling re Alloa to the General Assembly 1703.
CH1/2/23/3/207–21   Call of Hugh White from Larbert to Kinnaird.
CH1/2/24/1/2/66–8   An answer to the objection against making the Bible in Irish as being prejudicial to the design of extirpating the Irish Language out of the Highlands of Scotland.
CH1/2/24/2/2/71–114   Case of Hugh White, unwillingly transported to Kinnaird from Larbert and Dunipace 1704–5.
CH1/2/25/3/244   Letter from George Meldrum to presbyteries, anent highland libraries 5/7/1706.
CH1/2/25/3/247   Arthur Forbes to George Meldrum 23/7/1706.
CH1/2/27/3/246   Letter from Matthew Wallace in name of presbytery

of Dunblane, to Moderator, answering Commission's questions on schools, growth of popery etc. Kincardine 1/3/1708.
CH1/2/30/3/283 Letter from Matthew Wallace to Moderator, answering Assembly's queries. Dunblane 29/11/1709.
CH1/2/30/3/292–3 Letter from presbytery of Argyll to Moderator, anent John Muschet, probationer, who has been requested to repair north 30/3/1708.

SYNOD, PRESBYTERY AND KIRK SESSION RECORDS
National Records of Scotland (NRS) or Stirling Council Archives (SCA)
NRS CH2/449/3   Synod of Perth & Stirling   1691–1707
NRS CH2/449/4   Synod of Perth & Stirling   1691–5
NRS CH2/449/5   Synod of Perth & Stirling   1708–14
NRS CH2/710/1   Tulliallan Kirk Session   1673–1701
NRS CH2/710/2   Tulliallan Kirk Session   1692–1715
SCA CH2/10/1   Alva Kirk Session (Episcopal)   1681–90
SCA CH2/10/4   Alva Kirk Session (Accounts)   1660–1717
SCA CH2/101/2   Dunblane Kirk Session   1692–1714
SCA CH2/101/9/1   Dunblane Kirk Session   1699–1745 (Transcription of Leighton Library catalogue and borrowers)
SCA CH2/101/9/2   Dunblane Kirk Session   1700–1766
SCA CH2/101/13   Dunblane Kirk Session (Accounts)   1707–35
SCA CH2/212/2   Kilmadock Kirk Session   1704–9 (Includes 19th-century transcription of 1693–4)
SCA CH2/337/2   St Ninians Kirk Session   1667–1705
SCA CH2/337/4/1   St Ninians Kirk Session   1695–1712
SCA CH2/469/1   Balquhidder Kirk Session   1710–24
SCA CH2/722/8   Presbytery of Stirling   1693–1701
SCA CH2/722/9   Presbytery of Stirling   1701–12
SCA CH2/723/5   Presbytery of Dunblane   1698–1709
SCA CH2/723/6   Presbytery of Dunblane   1709–16
SCA CH2/723/41   Presbytery of Dunblane   1690–1929 (Presbytery subscriptions to the Westminster Confession)
SCA CH2/726/1   Tillicoultry Kirk Session   1623–1766 (Includes accounts)
SCA CH2/763/1   Dollar Kirk Session   1702–10
SCA CH2/763/7   Dollar Kirk Session (Accounts)   1699–1733
SCA CH2/942/6   Alloa Kirk Session   1664–1709
SCA CH2/942/7   Alloa Kirk Session   1706
SCA CH2/942/8   Alloa Kirk Session   1706–8
SCA CH2/942/9   Alloa Kirk Session   1708–20
SCA CH2/1001/1   Logie Kirk Session   1688–1700
SCA CH2/1001/7   Logie Kirk Session (Episcopal)   1686–90
SCA CH2/1001/39   Logie Kirk Session (Accounts)   1689–1726 (Not digitised)
SCA CH2/1026/5   Stirling Kirk Session   1695–1701

SCA CH2/1121/3   Gargunnock Kirk Session   1698–1740
SCA CH2/1242/2   Clackmannan Kirk Session (Episcopal)   1673–90
SCA CH2/1242/3   Clackmannan Kirk Session   1696–1715
SCA CH2/1300/1   Port of Menteith Kirk Session   1697–1723 (Includes accounts)

OTHER CHURCH RECORDS
NRS CH2/163/1   Presbytery of Kinross: Fossoway   1706–37
NRS CH2/216/1   Presbytery of Glasgow: Kilsyth   1690–1713
NRS CH2/242/6   Presbytery of Linlithgow   1676–88
NRS CH2/242/7   Presbytery of Linlithgow   1687–94
NRS CH2/322/3   Presbytery of Haddington: Saltoun   1685–1713
NRS CH2/359/3   Presbytery of Dunbar: Tyninghame   1699–1760
NRS CH2/464/1   Synod of Glasgow and Ayr (Clydesdale)   1687–1704
NRS CH2/546/4   Presbytery of Dumbarton   1689–95

With a single exception, noted above, synod, presbytery and kirk session records have been digitised and are consultable both in the National Records of Scotland (NRS) and in certain local authority archives, including Stirling Council Archives (SCA). The originals of those held in Stirling can also be consulted; those held in the NRS can only be consulted in digital form. In April 2021 it was announced that these records are available on the ScotlandsPeople website (https://www.scotlandspeople.gov.uk).

National Records of Scotland

EDINBURGH COMMISSARY COURT
CC8/6/62   Process of Divorce: Lady Margaret Mackenzie *v.* David Bruce.

RECORDS OF THE EPISCOPAL CHURCH
CH12/12/263   Copy of 'A letter from a gentleman in Scotland to his friend at London', dated at Edinburgh, 12 & 19/3/1713.
CH12/12/467   Letter from eight Episcopal clergy in and near Stirling, at Stirling, to clergy meeting at Edinburgh.
CH12/12/472   Letter from W. Bennet of Livilands [*sic*] to unidentified recipient, 27/4/1713.
CH12/21/7   Sermons by Mr George Campbell and Mr George Turnbull.

COURT OF SESSION PAPERS
CS140/244   Turnbull *v.* Parish of Dalmeny 1709.

HEARTH TAX RECORDS 1691–5
E69/6   Clackmannanshire 1694.
E69/19/1   The presbyteries of Dunblane and Auchterarder and parishes of Culross and Tulliallan 1694.
E69/22   Stirlingshire 1694.
Available online at ScotlandsPlaces, https://scotlandsplaces.gov.uk/digital-volumes/historical-tax-rolls/hearth-tax-records-1691-1695

PAPERS OF THE LESLIE FAMILY
GD26/9/104   Charles Erskine to Lord Melville? 15/6/1689.

PAPERS OF THE CAMPBELL FAMILY, EARLS OF BREADALBANE
GD112/39/212/8   James Steuart, Edinburgh, to the moderator of the Presbytery of Dunblane 6/2/1708.

MAR & KELLY MUNIMENTS
GD124/15/410   Atholl to Mar 31/5/1706.
GD124/15/457/1–2   John Logan to Mar 27/8/1706, 23/12/1706.
GD124/15/474   Letter to George [Erskine] from Mar 16/11/1706.
GD124/15/478/1–2   Holburn to Lt-Col Erskine 4/12/1706.
GD124/15/478/2   Magistrates of Stirling to Lt-Col. Erskine.
GD124/15/552/4   to Lord Grange from Mary, Countess of Mar 3/6/1707.
GD124/15/753/1–3   John Logan to Mar.
GD124/15/768/3, 11, 17, 31   Lord Grange to Mar 1708–9.
GD124/15/771/1   to Lord Grange from Mary, Countess of Mar 19/1/1708.
GD124/15/870/29   David Erskine to Mar 29/1/1709.
GD124/15/922   Harie Robine to Mar 29/11/1708.
GD124/15/970/1   to Lord Grange from Lt-Col. Erskine Nov. 1709.
GD124/15/985/1–2   Col. Erskine to Grange Jul./Aug. 1710.

WEST CIRCUIT COURT OF JUSTICIARY
JC13/1   Journal book of the western district Oct. 1708–May 1709.

OLD PARISH REGISTERS
OPR 331/10/6   Balquhidder 1696.
OPR 388/9   Port of Menteith 1708.
OPR 397/10   Tulliallan.
OPR 465/20/37   Alloa 1696.
OPR 465/20/49   Alloa 1698.
OPR 467/10/15   Dollar 1707.
OPR 469/10/345   Airth 1696.
OPR 470/10/164   Alva 1709.
OPR 490/20/299   Stirling 1702.
OPR 490/20/331   Stirling 1702.
Available online at ScotlandsPeople, https://www.scotlandspeople.gov.uk

SUPPLEMENTARY PARLIAMENTARY PAPERS
(petitions regarding the Union of the Parliaments 1706)
PA7/20/18   Convention of Royal Burghs.
PA7/20/28   Lanark Presbytery.
PA7/20/49   Dunblane Presbytery.
PA7/28/21   Stirlingshire.
PA7/28/48   Stirling.
PA7/28/49   Airth, Larbert, Dunipace and Denny parishes.
PA7/28/61   Clackmannan parish.

PA7/28/75   Logie parish.
PA7/28/80   St Ninians parish.
PA7/28/83   Tulliallan parish.

LETTERS TO ANDREW RUSSELL, MERCHANT IN ROTTERDAM
RH15/106/709/4, 10.

Other Manuscript Sources
(Several not inspected personally)

ABERDEEN UNIVERSITY LIBRARY
MS 3245/2   Notes by Thomas Boston of Ettrick on his and other ministers' sermons.

ATHOLL MUNIMENTS
Atholl Muniments, Boxes 45/5/37, 45/5/91.
I am grateful to the archivist for drawing my attention to these.

GLASGOW UNIVERSITY LIBRARY
MS Gen 342   Volume of homilies by various Glasgow University students of James Wodrow 1701–7.
MS Gen 938   Volume of sermons 1705–23.

NATIONAL LIBRARY OF SCOTLAND
NLS MS 5770   Sermon notebook 1688.
NLS MS 7593/1–3   Rabbling at Logie.
NLS MS 7593/4–5   Discipline case at Burntisland.
NLS Wod. Qu.LXXIII fo. 50–51   Mair to Douglas 2/2/1694.

OXFORD UNIVERSITY BODLEIAN LIBRARY
Bodl MS Ballard 36 fo.136r   Greenshields to Charlett.

STIRLING COUNCIL ARCHIVES
B66/25/665   Extract decreet of absolvitor in action at instance of Mr Adam Peacock, minister of the gospel, against the magistrates, town councillors and keepers of the tolbooth of Stirling seeking damages for alleged wrongful imprisonment for preaching in a meeting-house in the Backraw while uncertificated and deposed by the church 5/1/1704.
B66/25/779/1/5/66   11/3/1706.
B66/25/779/1/18.
B66/25/779/4.
SBC/11/5   Burgh minutes 23/8/1709.

2) Printed Sources

Newspapers
Flying Post
London Gazette
Post Boy

Other Sources

Atholl, John, 7th Duke, *Chronicles of the Atholl and Tullibardine Families*, Vols 1–2 (Edinburgh, privately printed, 1908).

Bell, John, 'The Most Memorable Passages of the Life and Times of Mr J.B. Written by Himself', in *Miscellany of the Scottish History Society, Vol. XIV* (Woodbridge, Scottish History Society, 2013), pp. 139–228.

Blackwell, Thomas, *Methodus evangelica: or, a modest essay upon the true scriptural-rational way of preaching the Gospel* (London, 1712).

Boston, Thomas, *Memoirs of the Life, Times and Writings of the Reverend and Learned Thomas Boston* (Edinburgh, Oliphant Anderson & Ferrier, [1776] 1899).

Bowie, Karin (ed.), *Addresses against Incorporating Union, 1706–07* (Woodbridge, Scottish History Society, 2018).

Brisbane, James, *A sermon preached at Denny in the shire of Stirling; on Monday the 11th. August 1718* (Edinburgh, 1719).

By the King a proclamation: James R. the Seventh . . . Whereas by our royal proclamation of the date the 12 day of February 1686/7 . . . (Edinburgh, 1687).

Cairns, Elizabeth, *Memoirs of the Life of Elizabeth Cairns, Written by Herself Some Years before Her Death* (Glasgow, 1762).

Calamy, Edmund, *An Historical Account of My Own Life*, 2 vols (London, Henry Colburn & Richard Bentley, 1829).

Chamberlayne, John, *Magnae Britanniae notitia; or, the present state of Great Britain, with divers remarks upon the ancient state thereof*, 22nd ed. (London, 1708).

Church of Scotland, *The Acts of the General Assemblies of the Church of Scotland from the year 1638 to the year 1649 . . . to which are now added . . . the Acts of the General Assembly, 1690* (Edinburgh, 1692).

Church of Scotland, *Acts of the General Assembly of the Church of Scotland, 1638–1842* (Edinburgh, Edinburgh Printing & Publishing Co., 1843). Also online at https://www.british-history.ac.uk/church-scotland-records/acts/1638-1842/

Church of Scotland, *The First and Second Booke of Discipline, together with some Acts of the Generall Assemblies . . .* (Amsterdam, 1621).

Clerk of Penicuik, Sir John, *History of the Union of Scotland and England* (Edinburgh, Scottish History Society, 1993).

Clerk of Penicuik, Sir John, *Memoirs of the Life of Sir John Clerk of Penicuik, Baronet . . . Extracted by Himself from His Own Journals, 1678–1753* (Edinburgh, Scottish History Society, 1892).

Cook, W. B. and David B. Morris (eds), *The Stirling Guildry Book: Extracts from the Records of the Merchant Guild of Stirling, A.D. 1592–1846* (Stirling, Glasgow, Stirlingshire and Sons of the Rock Society, 1916).

Cooke, John, *The preacher's assistant, (after the manner of Mr Letsome) containing a series of the texts of sermons and discourses published either singly, or in volumes . . .* (Oxford, 1783).

Crossrigg, David Home, Lord, 'A Narrative of the Rise, Progress and Success of the Societies of Edinburgh for Reformation of Manners', in *Miscellany of the Scottish History Society No. XIV* (Woodbridge, Scottish History Society, 2013) pp. 111–39.

Cuninghame, James and Margaret Mackenzie, *Warnings of the Eternal Spirit to the City of Glasgow, in Scotland*... (London, 1711).

Curate, Jacob, *The Scotch Presbyterian eloquence display'd; or, the foolishness of their teaching discovered from their books, sermons, and prayers*... (London, 1693).

Defoe, Daniel, *A collection of original papers and material transactions, concerning the late great affair of the union between England and Scotland* (London, 1712).

Defoe, Daniel, *The History of the Union of Great Britain* (London, 1709).

Defoe, Daniel, *Presbyterian persecution examined: with an essay on the nature and necessity of toleration in Scotland* (Edinburgh, 1707).

A Directory for the Publique Worship of God throughout the Three Kingdoms of England, Scotland, and Ireland (the *Westminster Directory*) (London, 1651).

Douglas, Robert, Bishop of Dunblane, 'An Account of the Foundation of the Leightonian Library', in Sir W. Scott, D. Laing and T. Thomson (eds), *The Bannatyne Miscellany, Vol. III* (Edinburgh, Bannatyne Club, 1855), pp. 227–64.

'Episcopacy in Stirling', in William Harvey (ed.), *The Stirling Repository* (Stirling, 1908), pp. 213–37.

Erskine of Carnock, John, *Journal of the Hon. John Erskine of Carnock, 1683–1687* (Edinburgh, Scottish History Society, 1893).

Extracts from the Records of the Convention of the Royal Burghs of Scotland, 1677–1711 (Edinburgh, William Paterson, 1880).

Fountainhall, John Lauder, Lord, *The decisions of the Lords of Council and Session from June 6th, 1678, to July 30th, 1712*, 4 vols (Edinburgh, 1759).

Fraser, James, *Memoirs of the life of the Very Rev. Mr James Fraser, of Brae, Minister of the Gospel at Culross* (Inverness, 1890).

Graham of Duchray, Alexander, 'Description of Kippen Paroch, Buchanan, ... and Gargunnock, in Stirlingshire, ... 1724', in Walter MacFarlane, *Geographical Collections Relating to Scotland Made by Walter MacFarlane (MacFarlane's Collections), Vol. I* (Edinburgh, Scottish History Society, 1906), pp. 344–51.

Graham of Duchray, Alexander, 'Description of Six Parishes in Perthshire 1724', in Walter MacFarlane, *Geographical Collections Relating to Scotland Made by Walter MacFarlane (MacFarlane's Collections), Vol. I* (Edinburgh, Scottish History Society, 1906), pp. 334–43.

Halyburton, Thomas, *An abstract of the life and death of the reverend learned and pious Mr Tho. Halyburton, MA, Professor of Divinity at the University of St Andrews* (London, 1739).

Hamiltoun, Alexander, *A sermon explaining the life of faith: preached in the city of Edinburgh, by a minister of known learning, piety and integrity* (Edinburgh, 1705).
Historical Manuscripts Commission, 'The Manuscripts of His Grace the Duke of Buccleuch and Queensberry Preserved at Drumlanrig Castle', C. 8553, 1897.
Historical Manuscripts Commission, 'The Manuscripts of His Grace the Duke of Portland, Preserved at Welbeck Abbey, Vol. IV', C. 8497, 1897.
Historical Manuscripts Commission, 'Report on the Manuscripts of the Earl of Mar and Kellie Preserved at Alloa House, N.B.', Cd. 2190, 1904.
The humble address of the ministers and elders of the Provincial Synod of Perth and Stirling, met at Stirling the 13th of April 1708, presented to Her Majesty by the Rt Hon. the Earl of Mar (Edinburgh, 1708).
Kirk, James (ed.), *Stirling Presbytery Records, 1581–1587* (Edinburgh, Scottish History Society, 1981).
Kirk, Robert, *The Secret Commonwealth of Elves, Fauns and Fairies* (Edinburgh, 1815).
Kirkton, James, *The secret and true history of the Church of Scotland, from the Restoration to the year 1678* (Edinburgh, John Ballantyne, 1817).
Kyd, James Gray (ed.), *Scottish Population Statistics, Including Webster's 'Analysis of Population 1755'* (Edinburgh, Scottish History Society, 1952).
Laick, William, *The Scots episcopal innocence; or, the juggling of that party with the late King, his present Majesty, the Church of England, and the Church of Scotland, demonstrated* (London, 1694).
Lenman, Bruce P. and John S. Gibson (eds), *The Jacobite Threat: Rebellion and Conspiracy, 1688–1759* (Edinburgh, Scottish Academic Press, 1990).
'Letters Relating to the Leightonian Library, Dunblane, 1703–1710', in Sir W. Scott, D. Laing and T. Thomson (eds), *Bannatyne Miscellany, Vol. III* (Edinburgh, Bannatyne Club, 1855), pp. 265–72.
Lockhart, George, *Letters of George Lockhart of Carnwath, 1698–1732* (Edinburgh, Scottish History Society, 1989).
Logan, John, *A sermon preached before His Grace James Duke of Queensberry, Her Majesties High Commissioner: and the Honourable Estates of Parliament, in the New-Church of Edinburgh, upon the 27 of October 1706* (Edinburgh, 1706).
McCormick, Joseph, *State-papers and letters addressed to William Carstares, to which is prefixed a life of Mr Carstares* (Edinburgh, 1774).
MacFarlane, Walter, *Geographical Collections Relating to Scotland Made by Walter MacFarlane, Vol. I* (Edinburgh, Scottish History Society, 1906).
Macmillan, John, *Register of the Rev. John Macmillan: being a record of marriages and baptisms solemnised by him among the Cameronian Societies* (Edinburgh, 1908).
Morer, Thomas, *A short account of Scotland: being a description of the nature of that kingdom, and what the constitution of it is in church and state . . .* (London, B. Bragg, 1706).

Mullan, David George, *Narratives of the Religious Self in Early-Modern Scotland* (Farnham, Ashgate, 2010).
Mullan, David George (ed.), *Protestant Piety in Early-Modern Scotland: Letters, Lives and Covenants, 1650–1712* (Edinburgh, Scottish History Society, 2008).
Mullan, David George (ed.), *Women's Life Writing in Early Modern Scotland: Writing the Evangelical Self, c.1670–c.1730* (Aldershot, Ashgate, 2003).
Paton, V. A. Noël (ed.), 'Masterton Papers, 1660–1719', in *Miscellany of the Scottish History Society, Vol. I* (Edinburgh, Scottish History Society, 1893), pp. 449–96.
Register of the Diocesan Synod of Dunblane, 1662–1688 (Edinburgh, William Blackwood, 1877).
The Register of the Privy Council of Scotland, 3rd Series, 16 vols (Edinburgh, 1908–70).
'Register of the Provincial Synod of Glasgow and Air, A.D. 1687–A.D. 1690', in *Miscellany of the Maitland Club, Vol. IV, Part I* (Maitland Club, 1847), pp. 209–92.
Rule, Gilbert, *A second vindication of the Church of Scotland: being an answer to five pamphlets . . .* (Edinburgh, 1691).
Sage, John, *The case of the present afflicted clergy in Scotland truly represented to which is added for probation the attestation of many unexceptionable witnesses to every particular, and all the publick acts and proclamations of the convention and Parliament relating to the clergy* (London, 1690).
Sage, John, *The fundamental charter of Presbytery as it hath been lately established in the kingdom of Scotland: examin'd and disprov'd by the history, records, and publick transactions of our nation* (London, 1695).
The Scotish [sic] Inquisition; or a short account of the proceedings of the Scotish Privy Counsel, Justiciary Court, and those commissionated by them . . . (London, 1689).
'Setts of the Royal Burghs of Scotland', in *Miscellany of the Scottish Burgh Records Society* (Edinburgh, Scottish Burgh Records Society, 1881), pp. 159–295.
A short account of the proceedings of the criminal-court, at Edinburgh, in Scotland: at the tryal of James Stirling, of Keir, Archibald Seton of Touch etc. (Edinburgh, 1709).
Spalding, John, *Synaxis sacra; or, a collection of sermons preached at several communions . . .* (Edinburgh, 1703).
The Statutes of the Realm . . . from Original Records and Authentic Manuscripts . . . 1101–1713, 11 vols (London, 1810–28).
Stephen, William (ed.), *Register of the Consultations of the Ministers of Edinburgh and Some Other Brethren of the Ministry, Vol. I* (Edinburgh, Scottish History Society, 1921).
Steuart of Pardovan, Walter, *Collections and observations methodiz'd concerning the worship, discipline and government of the Church of Scotland* (Edinburgh, 1709).

Stirling, William MacGregor, *Notes, Historical and Descriptive, on the Priory of Inchmahome* . . . (Edinburgh, 1815).
Stirling Burgh Council, *Extracts of the Records of the Royal Burgh of Stirling, A.D. 1667–1752* (Glasgow, Glasgow, Stirlingshire and Sons of the Rock Society, 1889).
To His Grace, His Majesties High Commissioner and the Right Honourable the Estates of Parliament, the humble address of the Presbyterian ministers and professors of the Church of Scotland (Edinburgh, 1689).
To the King's Most Excellent Majesty, James the VII, the Humble Address of the Presbyterian Ministers in his Majesties Kingdom of Scotland (Edinburgh, 1687).
To the King's Most Excellent Majesty, the Humble address of the cittizens and inhabitants that are of the Presbyterian Perswasion in the City of Edinburgh and the Cannongate (Edinburgh, 1687).
To the Queen's Most Excellent Majestie, the humble address and supplication of the suffering episcopal clergy in the kingdom of Scotland, whose names and designations are underwritten (Edinburgh, 1703).
Turnbull, George, 'The Diary of George Turnbull, Minister of Alloa and Tyninghame, 1657–1704', in *Miscellany of the Scottish History Society, Vol. I* (Edinburgh, Scottish History Society, 1893), pp. 293–445.
Ure, James, 'Narrative of the rising suppressed at Bothwell Bridge; written by James Ure of Shargarton: with notices of the writer', in William Veitch and George Brysson, *Memoirs of Mr William Veitch, and George Brysson, written by themselves, with other narratives illustrative of the history of Scotland* . . . (Edinburgh, William Blackwood, 1825), pp. 433–83.
Veitch, William and George Brysson, *Memoirs of Mr William Veitch, and George Brysson, written by themselves, with other narratives illustrative of the history of Scotland* . . . (Edinburgh, William Blackwood, 1825).
Webster, Alexander, 'Webster's Census', in James Gray Kyd (ed.), *Scottish Population Statistics, Including Webster's 'Analysis of Population 1755'* (Edinburgh, Scottish History Society, 1952), pp. 1–92.
West, Elisabeth, *Memoirs, or spiritual exercises of Elisabeth West: written by her own hand* (Glasgow, 1766).
William II of Scotland (III of England), *His Majesties most gracious letter to the Parliament of Scotland* (Edinburgh, 1693).
Williamson, David, *A sermon preached in Edinburgh at the opening of the General Assembly of this National Church of Scotland* (Edinburgh, 1703).
Wodrow, Robert, *Analecta; or, Materials for a History of Remarkable Providences*, 4 vols (Edinburgh, Maitland Club, 1842–3).
Wodrow, Robert, *The Correspondence of the Rev. Robert Wodrow, Minister of Eastwood* . . ., 3 vols (Edinburgh, Wodrow Society, 1842–3).
Wodrow, Robert, *The History of the Sufferings of the Church of Scotland: From the Restauration to the Revolution*, 2 vols (Edinburgh, 1721).
Wodrow, Robert, *Life of James Wodrow A.M.* (Edinburgh, William Blackwood, 1828).

Websites

'Acts of the General Assembly of the Church of Scotland, 1638–1842', British History Online, https://www.british-history.ac.uk/church-scotland-records/acts/1638-1842/

Casemine, www.casemine.com/

Electronic Enlightenment: Letters & Lives Online, http://e-enlightenment.com/

Jardine's Book of Martyrs, https://drmarkjardine.wordpress.com/about/

Legislation.gov.uk, https://www.legislation.gov.uk/

'Members, 1690–1715', History of Parliament Online, https://www.historyofparliamentonline.org/research/members/members-1690-1715

Records of the Parliaments of Scotland to 1707 (RPS), www.rps.ac.uk

ScotlandsPeople, https://www.scotlandspeople.gov.uk/

ScotlandsPlaces, https://scotlandsplaces.gov.uk/

SECONDARY SOURCES

Ahnert, Thomas, *The Moral Culture of the Scottish Enlightenment, 1690–1805* (New Haven, Yale University Press, 2015).

Allan, David, 'Reconciliation and Retirement in the Restoration Scottish Church: The Neo-Stoicism of Robert Leighton', *Journal of Ecclesiastical History*, 50(2) (1999), pp. 251–78.

Anderson, Rosalind, *The Jacobite Rising of 1715 and the Murray Family: Brothers in Arms* (Barnsley, Pen & Sword History, 2020).

Ansdell, Douglas, *The People of the Great Faith: The Highland Church, 1690–1900* (Stornoway, Acair, 1998).

Apetrei, Sarah and Hannah Smith, *Religion and Women in Britain, c.1660–1760* (Farnham, Ashgate, 2014).

Atkinson, Justine, 'The Society in Scotland for Propagating Christian Knowledge: Establishing Identity under the Union, 1709–1715', MA thesis, University of Newcastle, 2011.

Barclay, Katie, *Love, Intimacy and Power: Marriage and Patriarchy in Scotland, 1650–1850* (Manchester, Manchester University Press, 2014).

Begg, Tom, *The Kingdom of Kippen* (Edinburgh, John Donald, 2000).

Bertie, David, *Scottish Episcopal Clergy, 1689–2000* (Edinburgh, T. & T. Clark, 2000).

Beveridge, David, *Between the Ochils and Forth: A Description, Topographical and Historical, of the Country between Stirling Bridge and Aberdour* (Edinburgh, William Blackwood, 1888).

Beveridge, David, *Culross and Tulliallan; or, Perthshire on Forth* (Edinburgh, William Blackwood, 1885).

Blaikie, William Garden, *The Preachers of Scotland, from the Sixth to the Nineteenth Century* (Edinburgh, T. & T. Clark, 1888).

Bowie, Karin, 'Public Opinion, Popular Politics and the Union of 1707', *Scottish Historical Review*, 82(2) (2003), pp. 226–60.

Bowie, Karin, *Scottish Public Opinion and the Anglo-Scottish Union, 1699–1707* (Woodbridge, Boydell Press, 2007).
Brown, John, *Gospel Truth Accurately Stated and Illustrated* (Glasgow, Blackie, 1831).
Brown, S. J. and Christopher Whatley (eds), *Scottish Historical Review*, 87(2), supplementary issue: 'Union of 1707' (2008).
Burch, Charles Eaton, 'Defoe and the Edinburgh Society for the Reformation of Manners', *Review of English Studies*, 16(3), (1940), pp. 306–12.
Burleigh, John H. S., *A Church History of Scotland* (London, Oxford University Press, 1960).
Burns, Thomas, *Old Scottish Communion Plate* (Edinburgh, R. & R. Clark, 1892).
Cage, R. A., *The Scottish Poor Law, 1745–1845* (Edinburgh, Scottish Academic Press, 1981).
Cameron, George G., *The Scots Kirk in London* (Oxford, Becket, 1979).
Chamberlain, Jeffrey S., 'Parish Preaching in the Long Eighteenth Century', in Keith A. Francis and William Gibson (eds), *Oxford Handbook of the British Sermon, 1689–1901* (Oxford, Oxford University Press, 2012), pp. 47–63.
Chambers, Robert (ed.), *A Biographical Dictionary of Eminent Scotsmen*, 9 vols (Glasgow, Blackie, 1855).
Chambers, Robert, *History of the Rebellions in Scotland: Under the Viscount of Dundee, and the Earl of Mar, in 1689 and 1715* (London, Constable, 1829).
Clarke, Tristram N., 'The Scottish Episcopalians, 1688–1720', PhD thesis, University of Edinburgh, 1982.
Clarke, Tristram N., 'The Williamite Episcopalians and the Glorious Revolution in Scotland', *Records of the Scottish Church History Society*, 24 (1990), pp. 33–51.
Coffey, John, 'Evangelical Revival in Enlightenment Britain: James Erskine of Grange and the Pietist Turn', in Anthony R. Cross, Peter J. Morden and Ian M. Randall (eds), *Pathways and Patterns in History: Essays on Baptists, Evangelicals and the Modern World in Honour of David Bebbington* (London, Spurgeon's College, 2015), pp. 187–214.
Cowmeadow, Nicola, '"In Sum What Have I Don for God or My Soule This Day?" The Religious Writing of Katherine, first Duchess of Atholl (1662–1707)', *Journal of Scottish Historical Studies*, 34(1) (2014), pp. 1–19.
Cross, Anthony R., Peter J. Morden and Ian M. Randall (eds), *Pathways and Patterns in History: Essays on Baptists, Evangelicals and the Modern World in Honour of David Bebbington* (London, Spurgeon's College, 2015).
Cullen, Karen J., *Famine in Scotland: The 'Ill Years' of the 1690s* (Edinburgh, Edinburgh University Press, 2010).
Cullen, Karen J., Christopher A. Whatley and Mary Young, 'King William's Ill Years: New Evidence on the Impact of Scarcity and Harvest Failure

during the Crisis of the 1690s on Tayside', *Scottish Historical Review*, 85(2) (2006), pp. 250–76.

Davies, Stephen J., 'Law and Order in Stirlingshire, 1637–1747', PhD thesis, University of St Andrews, 1984.

Devine, Thomas M. (ed.), *Conflict and Stability in Scottish Society, 1700–1850* (Edinburgh, John Donald, 1990).

Donaldson, Gordon, *The Faith of the Scots* (London, B. T. Batsford, 1990).

Drummond, Andrew L. and James Bulloch, *The Scottish Church, 1688–1843: The Age of the Moderates* (Edinburgh, Saint Andrew Press, 1973).

Dunlop, A. Ian, *William Carstares and the Kirk by Law Established* (Edinburgh, Saint Andrew Press, 1967).

Edwards, Roger, 'Terror and Intrigue: The Secret Life of Glasgow's Episcopalians, 1689–1733', *Records of the Scottish Church History Society*, 40 (2010), pp. 31–68.

Fasti Ecclesiae Scoticanae: The Succession of Ministers in the Church of Scotland from the Reformation, new ed., 11 vols (Edinburgh, various publishers, 1915–2000).

Ferguson, William and Gordon Donaldson, *Scotland, 1689 to the Present* (Edinburgh, Mercat Press, 1978).

Fergusson, David and Mark W. Elliott (eds), *The History of Scottish Theology, Vol. I: Celtic Origins to Reformed Orthodoxy* (Oxford, Oxford University Press, 2019).

Fergusson, David and Mark W. Elliott (eds), *The History of Scottish Theology, Vol. II: The Early Enlightenment to the Late Victorian Era* (Oxford, Oxford University Press, 2019).

Fergusson, R. Menzies, 'Episcopal Intruders in the Presbytery of Dunblane', in W. B. Cook (ed.), *The Stirling Antiquary: Reprinted from 'The Stirling Sentinel', Vol. IV: 1903–1906* (Stirling, Cook & Wylie, 1908), pp. 175–81.

Fergusson, R. Menzies, *Logie: A Parish History*, 2 vols (Paisley, Gardner, 1905).

Flinn, Michael W. (ed.), *Scottish Population History: From the 17th Century to the 1930s* (Cambridge, Cambridge University Press, 1977).

Forrester, Duncan B. and Douglas M. Murray (eds), *Studies in the History of Worship in Scotland* (Edinburgh, T. & T. Clark, 1984).

Foster, Walter Ronald, *Bishop and Presbytery: The Church of Scotland, 1661–1688* (London, SPCK, 1958).

Foyster, Elizabeth and Christopher A. Whatley (eds), *A History of Everyday Life in Scotland, 1600 to 1800* (Edinburgh, Edinburgh University Press, 2010).

Frace, Ryan K., 'Religious Toleration in the Wake of Revolution: Scotland on the Eve of Enlightenment (1688–1710s)', *History*, 93(311) (2008), pp. 355–75.

Francis, Keith A. and William Gibson (eds), *Oxford Handbook of the British Sermon, 1689–1901* (Oxford, Oxford University Press, 2012).

Fry, Michael, *The Union: England, Scotland and the Treaty of 1707* (Edinburgh, Birlinn, 2006).
Gardner, Ginny, *The Scottish Exile Community in the Netherlands, 1660–1690: 'Shaken Together in the Bag of Affliction'* (East Linton, Tuckwell, 2004).
Goldie, Frederick, *A Short History of the Episcopal Church in Scotland from the Revolution to the Present Time* (London, SPCK, 1951).
Goodare, Julian, *The Scottish Witch-Hunt in Context* (Manchester, Manchester University Press, 2002).
Goodare, Julian (ed.), *Scottish Witches and Witch-Hunters* (New York, Palgrave Macmillan, 2013).
Gordon, George and Brian Dicks (eds), *Scottish Urban History* (Aberdeen, Aberdeen University Press, 1983).
Graham, Michael F., T*he Blasphemies of Thomas Aikenhead: Boundaries of Belief on the Eve of the Enlightenment* (Edinburgh, Edinburgh University Press, 2013).
Gray, Nathan Philip, '"A Publick Benefite to the Nation": The Charitable and Religious Origins of the SSPCK, 1690–1715', PhD thesis, University of Glasgow, 2011.
Gregory, Jeremy (ed.), *The Oxford History of Anglicanism, Vol. II: Establishment and Empire, 1662–1829* (Oxford, Oxford University Press, 2017).
Gribben, Crawford, 'Preaching the Scottish Reformation, 1560–1707', in Peter McCullough, Hugh Adlington and Emma Rhatigan (eds), *The Oxford Handbook of the Early Modern Sermon* (Oxford, Oxford University Press, 2011), pp. 271–86.
Hanham, Alison, *The Sinners of Cramond: The Struggle to Impose Godly Behaviour on a Scottish Community, 1651–1851* (Edinburgh, John Donald, 2005).
Harrison, John G., 'The Hearth Tax and the Population of Stirling in 1691', *Forth Naturalist and Historian*, 10 (1986), pp. 89–110.
Harrison, John G., 'The Justices of the Peace of Stirlingshire, 1660–1706', *Scottish Archives*, 12 (2006), pp. 42–52.
Henderson, G. D., *The Scottish Ruling Elder* (London, J. Clarke, 1935).
Henderson, Lizanne, *Witchcraft and Folk Belief in the Age of Enlightenment: Scotland, 1670–1740* (Basingstoke, Palgrave Macmillan, 2016).
Inglis, Bill, 'The Impact of Episcopacy and Presbyterianism, Before and After 1690, on One Parish: A Case Study of Dunblane Kirk Session Minutes', *Records of the Scottish Church History Society*, 33 (2003), pp. 35–61.
Inglis, Bill, *A Scottish Town: Dunblane, 1560–1919* (Stirling, Jamieson & Munro, 2016).
Johnston, Samuel H. F., *The History of the Cameronians (Scottish Rifles), 26th and 90th, Vol. I: 1689–1910* (Aldershot, Gale & Polden, 1957).
Kelly, Jamie, 'The Mission at Home: The Origins and Development of the Society in Scotland for Propagating Christian Knowledge, 1709–1767', *eSharp*, 24 (2016), article 5.

Kennedy, Allan, 'Managing the Early Modern Periphery: Highland Policy and the Highland Judicial Commission, c.1692–c.1705', *Scottish Historical Review*, 96(1) (2017), pp. 32–60.

Killeen, Kevin, Helen Smith and Rachel Willie (eds), *The Oxford Handbook of the Bible in Early Modern England, c. 1530–1700* (Oxford, Oxford University Press, 2015).

Kirk, James (ed.), *The Church in the Highlands* (Edinburgh, Scottish Church History Society, 1998).

Kirk, James (ed.), *The Scottish Churches and the Union Parliament, 1707–1999* (Edinburgh, Scottish Church History Society, 2001).

Leneman, Leah, *Alienated Affections: The Scottish Experience of Divorce and Separation, 1684–1830* (Edinburgh, Edinburgh University Press, 1998).

Leneman, Leah, *Living in Atholl: A Social History of the Estates, 1685–1785* (Edinburgh, Edinburgh University Press, 1986).

Leneman, Leah and Rosalind Mitchison, *Sin in the City: Sexuality and Social Control in Urban Scotland, 1660–1780* (Edinburgh, Scottish Cultural Press, 1998).

Lenman, Bruce, *The Jacobite Risings in Britain, 1689–1746* (London, Eyre Methuen, 1980).

Levack, Brian P., 'The Prosecution of Sexual Crimes in Early Eighteenth-Century Scotland', *Scottish Historical Review*, 89(2) (2010), pp. 172–93.

Levack, Brian P., *Witch-Hunting in Scotland: Law, Politics and Religion* (New York, Routledge, 2008).

Lynch, Michael, *Scotland, a New History* (London, Pimlico, 1992).

McCallum, John, *Poor Relief and the Church in Scotland, 1560–1650* (Edinburgh, Edinburgh University Press, 2018).

McCullough, Peter E., Hugh Adlington and Emma Rhatigan (eds), *The Oxford Handbook of the Early Modern Sermon* (Oxford, Oxford University Press, 2011).

Macgibbon, Alexander, 'Parish of Kilmadock or Doune', in *The Statistical Account of Scotland* (Edinburgh, William Creech, 1798), vol. 20, p. 40, https://stataccscot.edina.ac.uk:443/link/osa-vol20-p40-parish-perth-kilmadock.

Macinnes, Allan I., 'William of Orange – "Disaster for Scotland"?', in Esther Mijers and David Onnekink (eds), *Redefining William II: The Impact of the King-Stadholder in International Context* (Abingdon, Routledge, [2007] 2016), pp. 201–26.

MacInnes, John, *The Evangelical Movement in the Highlands of Scotland, 1688 to 1800* (Aberdeen, Aberdeen University Press, 1951).

McIntosh, John, 'Eighteenth-Century Evangelicalism', in David Fergusson and Mark W. Elliott (eds), *The History of Scottish Theology, Vol. II: The Early Enlightenment to the Late Victorian Era* (Oxford, Oxford University Press, 2019), pp. 84–97.

McIntyre, J. W., *Early Episcopalians of Stirling: being an historical account of the Scottish Episcopal Church in Stirling from Reformation times until 1845* (Stirling, J. W. McIntyre, 1997).
McLachlan, Hugh V. (ed.), *The Kirk, Satan and Salem: A History of the Witches of Renfrewshire* (Glasgow, Grimsay Press, 2006).
MacLean, Colin and Kenneth Veitch (eds), *Scottish Life and Society: A Compendium of Scottish Ethnology, Vol. XII: Religion* (Edinburgh, John Donald, 2006).
Maclean, Donald, 'The Presbytery of Ross and Sutherland, 1693–1700', *Records of the Scottish Church History Society*, 5(3) (1935), pp. 251–61.
Maclean, Donald, 'Scottish Calvinism Resurgent Especially in the North', *Evangelical Quarterly*, 6(2) (1934), pp. 169–87.
Macleod, John, *Scottish Theology in Relation to Church History since the Reformation* (Edinburgh, Free Church of Scotland, 1943).
McNiven, Peter Edward, 'Gaelic Place-Names and the Social History of Gaelic Speakers in Medieval Menteith', PhD thesis, University of Glasgow, 2011.
Mann, Alastair J., 'Inglorious Revolution: Administrative Muddle and Constitutional Change in the Scottish Parliament of William and Mary', *Parliamentary History*, 22(2) (2003), pp. 121–44.
Mann, Alastair J., *James VII: Duke and King of Scots* (Edinburgh, John Donald, 2014).
Marshall, Gordon, *Presbyteries and Profits: Calvinism and the Development of Capitalism in Scotland, 1560–1707* (Oxford, Clarendon Press, 1980).
Marshall, James Scott, *The Church in the Midst: South Leith Parish Church through Five Centuries* (Edinburgh, Edina Press, 1983).
Marshall, James Scott, *North Leith Parish Church: The First 500 Years* (Edinburgh, Saint Andrew Press, 1993).
Marshall, Rosalind K., *Virgins and Viragos: A History of Women in Scotland from 1080 to 1980* (London, Collins, 1983).
Matheson, Ann, 'Preaching in the Churches of Scotland', in Keith A. Francis and William Gibson (eds), *Oxford Handbook of the British Sermon, 1689–1901* (Oxford, Oxford University Press, 2012), pp. 152–69.
Meek, Donald E., *The Scottish Highlands: The Churches and Gaelic Culture* (Geneva, World Council of Churches, 1996).
Meiklejohn, William, *Thomas Buchanan, minister of Tulliallan, 1692–1710* (Tulliallan, 1987?).
'The Ministers of Kincardine-in-Menteith', in W. B. Cook (ed.), *The Stirling Antiquary: Reprinted from 'The Stirling Sentinel', Vol. I: 1888–1893* (Stirling, Cook & Wylie, 1893), pp. 140–44.
Mitchison, Rosalind, *The Old Poor Law in Scotland: The Experience of Poverty, 1574–1845* (Edinburgh, Edinburgh University Press, 2000).
Mitchison, Rosalind and Leah Leneman, *Girls in Trouble: Sexuality and Social Control in Rural Scotland, 1660–1780* (Edinburgh, Scottish Cultural Press, 1998).

Muirhead, Andrew T. N., 'Eighteenth Century Occasions: Communion Services in Georgian Stirlingshire', *Forth Naturalist & Historian*, 15 (1992), pp. 87–98.

Muirhead, Andrew T. N., 'The Presbytery of Dunblane and the Treaty of Union', *Journal of the Society of Friends of Dunblane Cathedral*, 23(1) (2018), pp. 2–12.

Muirhead, Andrew T. N., *Reformation, Dissent and Diversity: The Story of Scotland's Churches, 1560–1960* (London, Bloomsbury T. & T. Clark, 2015).

Muirhead, Andrew T. N., 'Religion, Politics and Society in Stirling during the Ministry of Ebenezer Erskine', MLitt thesis, University of Stirling, 1983).

Muirhead, Andrew T. N., 'A Secession Congregation in Its Community: The Stirling Congregation of the Rev. Ebenezer Erskine, 1731–1754', *Records of the Scottish Church History Society*, 22(3) (1986), pp. 211–33.

Mutch, Alistair, 'Management Practice and Kirk Sessions: An Exploration of the Scottish Contribution to Management', *Journal of Scottish Historical Studies*, 24(1) (2004), pp. 1–19.

Mutch, Alistair, *Religion and National Identity: Governing Scottish Presbyterianism in the Eighteenth Century* (Edinburgh, Edinburgh University Press, 2015).

Mutch, Alistair, '"To Bring the Work to Greater Perfection": Systematising Governance in the Church of Scotland, 1696–1800', *Scottish Historical Review*, 93(2) (2014), pp. 240–61.

Onnekink, David, 'The Earl of Portland and Scotland (1689–1699): A Re-evaluation of Williamite Policy', *Scottish Historical Review*, 85(2) (2006), pp. 231–49.

Patrick, Derek J., 'The Kirk, Parliament and the Union, 1706–7', *Scottish Historical Review*, 87 (2), supplementary issue: 'Union of 1707' (2008), pp. 94–115.

Primrose, James, *Strathbrock: Or the History and Antiquities of the Parish of Uphall* (Edinburgh, Andrew Elliot, 1898).

Raffe, Alasdair, *The Culture of Controversy: Religious Arguments in Scotland, 1660–1714* (Woodbridge, Boydell Press, 2012).

Raffe, Alasdair, 'Female Authority and Lay Activism in Scottish Presbyterianism, 1660–1740', in Sarah Apetrei and Hannah Smith (eds), *Religion and Women in Britain, c.1660–1760* (Farnham, Ashgate, 2014).

Raffe, Alasdair, 'Preaching, Reading, and Publishing the Word in Protestant Scotland', in Kevin Killeen, Helen Smith and Rachel Willie (eds), *The Oxford Handbook of the Bible in Early Modern England, c.1530–1700* (Oxford, Oxford University Press, 2015), pp. 317–31.

Raffe, Alasdair, 'Presbyterians and Episcopalians: The Formation of Confessional Cultures in Scotland, 1660–1715', *English Historical Review*, 125(514) (2010), pp. 570–98.

Raffe, Alasdair, 'Scotland', in Jeremy Gregory (ed.), *The Oxford History of Anglicanism, Vol. II: Establishment and Empire, 1662–1829* (Oxford, Oxford University Press, 2017), pp. 150–59.

Raffe, Alasdair, *Scotland in Revolution, 1685–1690* (Edinburgh, Edinburgh University Press, 2018).

Riordan, Michael B., 'Mysticism and Prophecy in Early Eighteenth-Century Scotland', *Scottish Historical Review* 98 (Supplement) (2019), pp. 333–60.

Robertson, John (ed.), *A Union for Empire: Political Thought and the British Union of 1707* (Cambridge, Cambridge University Press, 1995).

Schmidt, Leigh Eric, *Holy Fairs: Scotland and the Making of American Revivalism* (Grand Rapids, MI, W. B. Eerdmans, 2001).

Shirra, James, *Nips and Rips No. 1*. Manuscript notebook of transcriptions of historical articles c.1863, held in Stirling Central Library.

Shukman, Ann M., 'The Fall of Episcopacy in Scotland, 1688–1691', PhD thesis, University of Glasgow, 2012.

Smout, T. C., *A History of the Scottish People, 1560–1830* (London, Collins, 1969).

Somerset, Douglas W. B., 'Notes on Some Scottish Covenanters and Ultra-Covenanters of the Eighteenth Century, Part I', *Scottish Reformation Society Historical Journal*, 6 (2016), pp. 87–130.

Somerset, Douglas W. B., 'Walter Ker and the "Sweet Singers"', *Scottish Reformation Society Historical Journal*, 2 (2012), pp. 85–108.

Spurlock, R. Scott, 'Boundaries of Scottish Reformed Orthodoxy, 1560–1700', in David Fergusson and Mark W. Elliott (eds), *The History of Scottish Theology, Vol. I: Celtic Origins to Reformed Orthodoxy* (Oxford, Oxford University Press, 2019), pp. 359–76.

Stephen, Jeffrey, *Defending the Revolution: The Church of Scotland, 1689–1716* (Farnham, Ashgate, 2013).

Stephen, Jeffrey, 'Defending the Revolution: The Church of Scotland and the Scottish Parliament, 1689–95', *Scottish Historical Review*, 89(1) (2010), pp. 19–53.

Stephen, Jeffrey, *Scottish Presbyterians and the Act of Union 1707* (Edinburgh, Edinburgh University Press, 2007).

Steuart, Katherine, *By Allan Water: The True Story of an Old House* (London, Methuen, 1903).

Stewart, Ralph, 'The Scottish Presbyterian Eloquence', *Restoration: Studies in English Literary Culture, 1660–1700*, 27(1) (2003), pp. 39–49.

Strong, Rowan, 'Episcopalian Theology, 1689–c.1900', in David Fergusson and Mark W. Elliott (eds), *The History of Scottish Theology, Vol. II: From the Early Enlightenment to the Late Victorian Era* (Oxford, Oxford University Press, 2019), pp. 265–83.

Strong, Rowan, *Episcopalianism in Nineteenth-Century Scotland: Religious Responses to a Modernizing Society* (Oxford, Oxford University Press, 2002).

Taylor, Nicholas, 'Liturgy and Liturgical Method in the Scottish Episcopal Church', in *Records of the Scottish Church History Society*, 47 (2018), pp. 143–53.
Todd, Margo, *The Culture of Protestantism in Early Modern Scotland* (New Haven, Yale University Press, 2002).
Wallace, Valerie, 'Presbyterian Moral Economy: The Covenanting Tradition and Popular Protest in Lowland Scotland, 1707–c.1746', *Scottish Historical Review*, 89(1) (2010), pp. 54–72.
Whatley, Christopher A. and Derek J. Patrick, *The Scots and the Union* (Edinburgh, Edinburgh University Press, 2006).
Whetstone, Ann E., *Scottish County Government in the Eighteenth and Nineteenth Centuries* (Edinburgh, John Donald, 1981).
Whitley, Laurence A. B., *A Great Grievance: Ecclesiastical Lay Patronage in Scotland until 1750* (Eugene, OR, Wipf & Stock, 2013).
Whytock, Jack C., *'An Educated Clergy': Scottish Theological Education and Training in Kirk and Secession, 1560–1850* (Milton Keynes, Paternoster Press, 2007).
Withers, Charles W. J., *Gaelic in Scotland, 1698–1981: The Geographical History of a Language* (Edinburgh, John Donald, 1984).
Withers, Charles W. J., 'Gaelic-Speaking in a Highland Parish: Port of Menteith, 1724–1725', *Scottish Geographical Magazine*, 98(1) (1982), pp. 16–23.
Withers, Charles W. J., 'A Geography of Language: Gaelic-Speaking in Perthshire, 1698–1879', *Transactions of the Institute of British Geographers*, 8(2) (1983), pp. 125–42.
Woodruff, Stephen A., 'The Pastoral Ministry in the Church of Scotland in the 18th Century, with Special Reference to Thomas Boston, John Willison and John Erskine', PhD thesis, University of Edinburgh, 1965.
Wright, David F., Ian Campbell and John C. L. Gibson, *The Bible in Scottish Life and Literature* (Edinburgh, Saint Andrew Press, 1988).

Websites

Ecclegen: Ministers of the Free Church of Scotland 1843–1900, https://www.ecclegen.com (linked index to the *Fasti* and other biographical sources for the Presbyterian ministry of Scotland).

Index

Abden, Katherine Pringle, Lady, preaching in Stirling, 154
Aberfoyle, 25, 103, 156n, 184–5, 188, 216
  Gaelic, 182, 184–5, 191
Aberuchill, Sir Colin Campbell, Lord Aberuchill, 77, 84, 87, 89, 94, 148, 163, 172, 217
Act of Settlement (England 1701), 195
Addresses against Union, 196, 201–6, 221
  table, 207
Airth, 58, 60–1, 66, 123, 124, 167, 222
  abuse of Presbyterian ministers, 123
  Kirk Session, 83–4
  laird of, 54
  support for George Mair, 53–4
  vacancy, 54
Alexander, James (baker in Dunblane), 113
Allan, John, Bailie, 111, 172, 203
Alloa, 3, 60
  collections, 97
  Communion services, 43
  Episcopalianism, 148, 154, 221
  Kirk Session records, 143
  Parish Church, 35, 62, 79, 129
  poor relief, 100
  regality court, 171, 174
  town constable, 172
Alva, 144, 214, 182
  account books, 29, 58
  baptismal records, 119
  collections, 22, 57–8, 96, 213, 227–8
  heritors, 104
  Kirk Session, 26, 40, 89–91, 143
  Parish Church, 26–7, 57
  poor relief, 99, 102
  support for Presbyterianism, 17

Anne, Queen, 144, 149, 151, 156, 175, 188, 195, 220–1
antediluvians (reinstated former Presbyterian ministers), 7, 9n, 36–9, 59, 82, 214
Argyll, Earl of, 54, 171
Atholl
  James Murray, Duke of, 25, 55–6, 85–8, 103, 189, 196, 216
  Katherine, Duchess of, 187
Auchterarder Presbytery, 8, 12

Balquhidder, 55–6, 59, 103, 185–9, 216, 220
  baptismal records, 121
  Episcopalianism, 25
  Gaelic language, 182
  Presbyterianism, 28
Balthayock, Margaret (Blair), Lady, 146
Bannockburn, Presbyterian meeting-house see St Ninians
baptism, 53, 119–25, 218
  irregular, 123, 150, 159
  numbers, 120, 124
  of children 'born under scandal', 123
Barclay, George (minister of Gargunnock), 33, 35
Barclay, Patrick, appointed to Stirling Castle as chaplain, 154
Bargarran witch trials, 66
Barrier Act, 1697, 77
Bass Rock, 34
Battieson, John (Session Officer of Port of Menteith), suspension, 166
Bell, John (minister of Haddington), 197
Bennet, Charles, of Livilands, 150–1
Bible, Gaelic, 183–4, 191–2
  texts used by George Turnbull, 129–46

bishops, 5, 10–11, 221
Blackburn, Thomas (weaver in Stirling), 43, 146, 155
Blackford, 115
Blair, John (minister of Bothkennar), 40–1
Boquhan, laird of, 148
Boston, Thomas (minister of Simprin, later Ettrick), 3, 47, 49–51, 53–5, 57–9, 101, 116, 129, 130–1, 134, 215, 218
  as preacher, 128
  Communion services, 114
  fear of the Highlands, 181–2
Bothkennar, 146–7, 222
  Communion services, 147, 218
  Kirk Session, 143
  Parish Church, 27, 143
  Presbyterian Kirk Session, 93
  Presbyterianism, 28
  support for SSPCK, 192
Bothwell Bridge, battle, 14
Bourignonism, 153–4
Brisbane, James (minister of Stirling), 65–6, 118, 203
Brisbane, Matthew (physician in Glasgow), 66
Broich, laird of, in debt to Stirling Kirk Session, 99
Brown, George (former episcopal incumbent of Stranraer) celebrates Communion, 110, 154
Brown, John (secession minister of Whitburn), 118
Brown, Thomas, in Ferrytown, 49
Bruce, David, of Clackmannan, 99, 123, 166
Buchanan, Thomas (minister of Tulliallan), 46, 52, 54, 63–5, 67, 73, 90, 117, 122, 186, 189, 201, 204
Burd, John, Bailie, 91–2, 110–11, 167
Burntisland, Episcopalian meeting-house, 169

Cairns, Elizabeth, 115, 218
Calamy, Edmund (English Presbyterian minister), 129, 154
call to the ministry, 46–8
Callander, 182, 184–5, 188–9, 220

Episcopalianism, 25
  Gaelic language, 182, 185
Cameron, Richard (field preacher), 131
Cameronians see Regiments, Earl of Angus's Regiment
Campbell, Sir Colin, of Aberuchill see Aberruchill, Sir Colin Campbell
Campbell, Elspet, in Logie, 21–2
Campbell, George (minister of Kilmadock), 52
Campbell, Robert (minister of Gargunnock), 61, 148
Campbell, William (episcopal minister of Balquhidder), 25, 55, 185–6, 188, 216
Cardross, Henry Erskine, Lord, 23–4, 33, 35, 87, 217
Cargill, Donald (covenanting field preacher), 14
Carruthers, John (schoolmaster in Larbert), 171
Carstares, William, 3, 149
Catholicism, 137
chaplains, as source of potential ministers, 51
Charles II, King, 7, 11, 15, 38, 73
Christie, Henry (episcopal minister of Kinross), 150
Chrystie, John, Bailie, role in Communion service, 111
Chrystie, John (elder in Stirling), cited for non-attendance, 92
church furnishings, 104
church law and procedure, 94
Church of England, liturgy, 110
Circuit Court, 149, 161, 173–4
Clackmannan, 49–50, 58, 75, 79, 182
  baptismal records, 121
  discipline cases, 155, 160–1, 163–5, 167, 171
  Kirk Session, 54, 206
  laird of see Bruce, David
  loss of records, 119, 166
  opposition to Parliamentary Union, 206
  Parish Church, 27, 54, 79
Clackmannanshire, assessed for support for Stirling Castle, 21

Claim of Right, 19, 195
Clerk, Sir John, of Penicuik, 93, 197
Clerk, Sophia, 93
Clow, John (student), 52
coinage, bad money, 99–100
collections, 80, 97, 107n
Collector of Vacant Stipends, 58
Colliers, involvement in affairs of Tulliallan, 65
Commissary courts, 170–3
Commission for the North, 43, 58, 73, 83–4, 179–81
Commission for the South, 83, 179
Commission of Assembly, 63, 73, 83–4, 183, 198, 208–9
and Parliamentary Union, 196–7
Communion services, 43, 78, 102, 109–18, 140–1, 148
collections, 101
economic factors, 116
Episcopalian, 109–10, 147, 150, 218
failure to celebrate, 109
fencing the table, 117
preaching, 116–17
preparation for, 102, 111–13
reconciliation, 113, 117
role of elders, 95
tokens, 111, 114
utensils, Bothkennar, 111, 143, 147
Convention of Estates, 19–20
Convention of Royal Burghs, 17–18, 201–2
Cornton, laird of, episcopal elder in St Ninians, 90
Couper, Patrick (minister at St Ninians), 33, 60, 89–90, 104, 145
Cousine, Agnes, in Clackmannan, 164, 166
covenanters, influence on later kirk sessions, 88
poor relief, 101
Covenants, 195–6, 201
Cramond, parish, 159
Crighton, William (minister in Falkirk), 32, 53
Cunningham, James, preaching in Stirling, 154
Cunninghame, William, of Boquhan (heritor in Gargunnock), 24

Dalmeny, Presbyterian meeting-house, 35
Darien Scheme, 103, 139–40, 161
Davidson, Thomas (chaplain in Stirling Castle), 154, 215
deacons, 95
deaf-mutes, divination, 160
Defoe, Daniel, 175, 197–202, 204–5, 208
Denny, Kirk Session, 7
Dick, Quintin, in Ayrshire, 32
Dinn, David, in St Ninians, 161
Directory for the Publick Worship of God, 129
discipline cases, 158–78, 217
absolution, 125, 138, 165, 168
adultery, 53, 122–3, 137, 159–61, 164, 172–5, 177n
and preaching, 137–9
antenuptial fornication, 81–2, 158
appearance before the congregation, 164
bestiality, 161
blasphemy, 124, 173, 175
breach of Sabbath, 102, 163–4
charming, 160
contumacy, 124, 160
drunkenness, 24, 110, 113, 147, 152, 159, 166, 171, 175, 216
excommunication, 162, 166, 174
fines, 167–8, 171
flight of the accused, 160–1
fornication, 123–4, 137–8, 158–60, 164–8
incest, 161–2
oath of exculpation, 168–70
reconciliation, 113, 138, 155
referral to Presbytery, 159–60
role of elders, 95
sabbath breach, 159, 167
scandalous carriage, 159
sessional rebukes, 124, 128, 160, 163–5, 172
wife-beating, 91–2
Dollar, 155, 171, 182, 196, 215
collections, 57–8
Parish Church, 27, 54–5, 79, 82
Don, James, Bailie, 111, 173, 175

Douglas, Alexander (minister of Logie), 6, 21, 34, 43, 52, 112–13, 117, 180, 214–15
Douglas, Archibald (episcopal minister of Saltoun), preaching, 133, 135–6, 141
Douglas, Robert (father or son), conducting irregular marriages, 148
Douglas, Robert (librarian of Leighton Library), 27, 154
Douglas, Robert, Bishop of Dunblane, 27
Doune, 21, 147
Dow, Henry, of Wester Polder, 88
Dumbarton, Presbytery, 46
Dunblane, 1, 21, 60
 baptismal records, 121
 Bishop of, 11, 27
 Commissary Court, 172–3
 discipline cases, 159, 217
 Kirk Session, 87, 89, 143
 oath of exculpation, 169
Dunblane Diocesan Synod, 3, 109, 143
Dunblane Presbytery, 5–6, 50–2, 58, 71–2, 190, 222
 after restoration of episcopacy, 12
 and Parliamentary Union, 196
 and Presbytery of Stirling, 83
 attendance, 72–3
 day of fasting, 197–8
 Gaelic speaking parishes, 179, 182
 moderatorial elections, 74–5
 records, 2–3, 185
 resists Logan's call to Alloa, 62–3
 post-Restoration deprivations, 12
 vacancy in Kilmadock, 63
 visitations, 78–9, 148
 witnesses from Balquhidder attending, 186
Duncanson, John (elder in Alva), 90, 102
Dundee, James Graham, of Claverhouse, Viscount, 19–20, 22
Dunipace, parish *see* Larbert & Dunipace
Dunkeld, battle of, 22

Edinburgh, anti-James riots, 18
 Bishop of, 27
 Communion services, 110
Edmonstone, John (episcopal incumbent of Gargunnock), 24
education for the ministry, 47–50
elders, attendance at meetings, 84
 excluded from Presbytery discussions, 206
 means of electing, 89
 non-attendance at early meetings of higher courts, 39
 qualifications, 92–3
 role, 87, 95–6, 106, 217
Eliot, Gilbert, of Minto, 173
Elphinstone, William (episcopal assistant minister of Logie), 21–3, 144–5
Episcopalians, 219–20
 legal right to existence, 175
 meeting-houses, 145–6
 numbers of, 214
 post-Revolution, 103, 143–57, 229
 support for SSPCK, 192
 theology, 219
 worship, 152
Erskine, Sir Charles, of Alva, 22
Erskine, Christian, Lady, wife of Sir Charles E. of Alva, 29
Erskine, Ebenezer (minister of Stirling), 118, 216, 219
Erskine, George, factor to the Earl of Mar, 174
Erskine, Henry, Lord Cardross *see* Cardross, Henry, Lord
Erskine, James, of Grange (circuit court judge), 151, 173
Erskine, Sir John, of Alva, 104, 122
Erskine, Lt-Col John (variously Lt-Governor of Stirling Castle, Provost of Stirling, later 'of Carnock'), 14, 23–4, 35, 47–8, 84, 91–2, 99, 101, 111, 196, 202–3
Erskine, Lt-Col John (The 'White Colonel', variously Lt-Governor of Stirling Castle, Provost of Stirling), 23, 91, 196, 202
Erskine, Ralph (minister of Dunfermline), 118

excommunication, 162, 166, 174
exercise and addition, 52–77

famine, 97, 101, 104–5, 138–9
  effect on birth rate, 120–2
Ferguson, Patrick, in Glenogle, 121
field preaching, 38, 219
First and second books of discipline, 158–9
Fisher, William (episcopal minister of Aberfoyle), 184–5, 216
Fithie, Allard, in Clackmannan, 155
Forbes, Arthur (minister of Port of Menteith), 73, 75, 101–2, 117
  Communion services, 110, 117
  lack of Gaelic language, 183
Forrest, John, of Thirtieacres, 33, 89, 145, 167
Forrest, John (minister of Tulliallan), 13, 40–1, 67
Forrester, James, of Logie, 6–7, 92, 111
Forrester, John (minister of Stirling), 61, 66, 111, 146, 181, 215
Forrester, Thomas (minister of Kincardine), 40
Forrester, Thomas (minister of Alva), 40–1, 44
Forsyth, James (episcopal minister of St Ninians), 89
Fossoway, 72, 81
Fraser, James (minister of Culross), 53
'French Prophets', 153–4

Gaelic, 3–4, 25, 55, 58, 179, 181, 191–2, 220
Gaelic speakers, difficulty of receiving the Gospel in English, 183
Garden, George (episcopal minister in Aberdeen), 154
Gargunnock, inadequacy of manse, 148
  Presbyterian meeting-house, 17, 24, 32
Geddes, John (probationer), 81–3, 86n
Gellie, Paul (episcopal minister of Airth), 24, 147
General Assembly, 73, 76, 77, 83–4, 161, 209
  of 1690, 36–9
  of 1693, 53
  of 1697, 94, 180
  of 1703, 148

General meetings of Presbyterians, 36, 39
Gibbites, 53
Glasgow & Ayr, Synod of, 39, 41, 83
Glass, Adam (minister of Aberlady), 67, 117
Glendevon, 72
Glentirran, Presbyterian meeting-house *see* Gargunnock
Gourlaw, Robert (minister of Tillicoultry), 35–6, 63, 78–9, 110, 122, 180, 186, 215
Gourley, Robert, of Kepdarroch (heritor in Gargunnock), 24
Graham, Agnes, in Kilmadock, 162
Graham, Alexander, of Duchray, 182
Graham, Walter, of Gartur, 165–6, 168
Graham family, extramarital fecundity, 165–6
Grahams, representation on Port of Menteith Kirk Session, 87
Gray, John (schoolmaster, precentor and session clerk of Port of Menteith), 166–7
Gray, John (minister of Dollar), 9n, 54–5, 57–8, 182
Greenshields, James (episcopal minister in Edinburgh), 151
Guild, John (presbytery officer of Dunblane), 63–4
Guthrie, James (minister of Stirling), 11–12, 40, 42

Haddington
  Earl of, 136
  Countess of, 137
Haldane, Mungo, in Dykehead of Cardross, 124
Halyburton, Thomas (minister of Ceres), 3, 47, 50–1, 128
Hamilton, Alexander (minister of Airth and later Stirling), 46, 60–1, 66–7, 75, 118
Hamilton, Alexander (minister of Dalmeny), 35
Hardie, James (schoolmaster, precentor and session clerk of Port of Menteith), 99–100, 104, 167, 177n

Harley, Robert, 198
Haughs of Cromdale, battle, 23
hearth tax, 226
Hebronites, 53
Henderson, John (elder in Logie), 113
Hepburn, John (deposed minister of Urr), 53, 123
heritors, 36, 78, 103, 148, 153, 215
  obstruction by, 56, 60
  responsibilities, 98, 103–4
  with Jacobite sympathies, 56
Highland Host 1678, 13–14
Highlands, 179–80, 192–3, 220–1
Hog, Thomas (minister of Larbert), 40
Holburn, Captain, in Stirling Castle, 203
holy fairs, 109, 113, 117–18
Home, David, of Crossrig, 175
Hope, Thomas, of Craighall, 154
House of Lords, 221
Howieson, Richard (minister of Alva), 13, 26–7, 29, 40, 90–1, 102, 125n, 227–8
  removal of presbytery records, 8, 42
humble addresses to Queen Anne, 151–2
Hunter, James (episcopal minister of Stirling), 13, 21, 24, 145–7, 150, 152–3, 216
Hunter, Thomas, probationer, 58

incest, 174
indulgences, 13
Inglis, James (episcopal minister of Muthil), 154
irregular baptisms *see* Baptism, irregular
irregular marriages *see* marriage, irregular or clandestine

Jacobite rising
  of 1708, 149
  of 1715, 181, 213
Jacobitism, 144, 219
James VI, King, 10, 195
James VII, King, 7, 15–18, 20, 73, 213
James 'VIII' (The Old Pretender), 149
Justices of the Peace, 145, 167

Kemp, Robert (elder in Airth), 167
Kennedy, Hugh, of Shalloch (provost of Stirling), 16, 19–20
Kennet, Clackmannan, 49–50
Killiecrankie, battle of, 22
'Killing Times', 14
Kilmacolm, resistance to transportation of James Brisbane, 65–6
Kilmadock, 52, 54, 58, 63–5, 148, 162, 185, 220
  baptisms, 119, 121, 124
  Gaelic language, 25, 182–3
Kincardine, 124, 148, 185
Kincardine on Forth *see* Tulliallan Parish
king's curates, 13, 38
Kinnaird, 180
Kippen, 20, 56, 79, 124
  inhabitants protecting Convention of Estates, 20
Kirk, Robert (episcopal minister of Aberfoyle), 25, 160, 184–5, 191
kirk sessions, 12, 76–7, 89, 100, 143, 217
  records, 76, 94
Kirkton, James (historian and minister), 41–2
Koenigsburg, Protestant church, collection for, 80

Lamb, John (precentor in Airth), 167
Larbert and Dunipace, 78, 83–4, 160, 171
lecturing, 128–31, 141, 218
Leighton, Robert (Bishop of Dunblane, later Archbishop of Glasgow), 11–12, 129, 152
Leighton Library, 23, 27, 154–5, 190
Leith, South Leith meeting-house, 110
libraries, in Highland parishes, 189–91
Lindsay, William (episcopal minister of Alva), 26–7, 40, 90–1, 104, 144, 227–8
Linlithgow, Presbytery of, 32
liturgy, 151–2, 219
Livingstone, William, of Greenyards (elder in St Ninians), 33, 89–90, 145, 167

Logan, John (successively minister of Kilmadock and Alloa), 52, 60–3, 67, 75, 128, 148, 155, 158, 182, 196, 198–200, 206, 221
  sermon to Parliament 1706, 1–3, 10, 71, 109, 176, 195, 218
Logan, John (successively minister of Lecropt and St Ninians), 60, 63, 67, 75, 90, 145–6, 186, 215
Logie, 6, 34, 117
  baptisms, 124
  Communion services, 112–13
  discipline cases, 174
  Episcopalians reoccupy parish church, 23
  inadequacy of manse, 56, 148
  Kirk Session, continuing membership of pre-Revolution elders, 89
  opposition to Parliamentary union, 204–5
  Presbyterian meeting-house, 17, 21, 26, 32, 213, 227–8
  rabbling of episcopal ministers, 21–3, 144
  records, 143
Lord Advocate *see* Steuart, Sir James, of Goodtrees
Lundie, Alexander (minister of Saltoun), 135–6, 141, 218

McAla, John (minister of Stirling), 203
McAlpine family, representation on Port of Menteith Kirk Session, 88
McCallum, John (minister of Callander), 188–9
McEchny, James (schoolmaster of Dunblane), 76
McFarland, Robert (minister of Arrocher), 187
McKarter, Elizabeth, 174
McKillicen, John (probationer), 181
McLaren, John (minister of Kippen), 118, 148
McLaurin, Isobel, 165
McMillan, John (deposed minister of Balmaghie), 123–4, 219
McNaghten, laird of, 174

Mair, George (probationer), 52–4, 60, 123, 219
manses, inadequacy of, 34, 52, 54, 56, 59–60, 65, 148
Mar, John Erskine, Earl of, 51, 63, 82, 103, 151, 155, 188, 206, 215, 221
  and Episcopalianism, 153
  debt to Stirling Kirk Session, 98–9
  support for Parliamentary Union, 196, 198–200
Mar, Marie, Dowager Countess of, 131
marriage, irregular or clandestine, 123
Marrow Controversy, 68n, 118
Mary II, Queen, 1, 23
Masterton, Francis, 97, 101
Meldrum, George (minister in Edinburgh), 190
Menzies, James (episcopal minister of Callander), 185
Millar, James, in debt to Stirling Kirk Session, 98–9
ministers, as 'property' of their parish, 65
  recruitment, 214
Mitchell, James (minister of Auchterarder), 56
moderators, as chair of church courts, 73–4
  elections, 74
Monro, Capt George, of Auchenbowie, 23
Monro, George (episcopal minister of Dollar), 27
Monro, John (episcopal minister of Stirling), 21, 23–5, 27, 42, 214, 216
Montrose, James Graham, Marquess of (later Duke), 103, 184, 188, 216
Montrose, Communion services, 112
Morer, Thomas, 46
Mores, Patrick (elder in Alva), 90
mortcloths, 97, 100, 104, 145
Murray, John, of Polmaise, 146, 192
Mushet, John (probationer), 181

Nairn, James, in Stirling, 146
Napier, Francis, of Craigannet (provost of Stirling), 66, 111
Napier, John, of Merchiston, 66
National Covenant (1638), 10, 25

Naughty, Mr (deposed episcopal minister), 123
Netherlands, exiles, 34, 36–8, 47, 91
Newcastle, Presbyterian church, 80

Oath of Allegiance and Assurance, 52–3, 179
  of exculpation, 168–70
Orr, Alexander (minister of Beith), 61

Pardovan's Collections, 59, 94–5, 105, 138
parish records, importance of, 7
Parliament of Scotland, 19–20, 149, 195, 208
  of the United Kingdom, 151, 176, 209
Paterson, Sir Hugh, of Bannockburn, 146, 151, 155, 192, 219
patronage, 54, 103, 209–10, 221
Peacock, Adam (episcopal minister of Morebattle), 146–7, 152, 172
penance, 164–5
Perth and Stirling, Synod of, 39, 44, 80–1, 84, 215
poor relief, 91, 96–8, 105
population statistics, 226
Port of Menteith, 76, 148
  accounts, 96, 101
  baptisms, 124, 168
  Communion services, 102, 110, 117
  discipline cases, 163, 165–8
  famine, 97, 99
  Gaelic language, 25, 124, 220
  heritors, 104–5
  Kirk Session, 87–8, 192
  parody of baptism, 124
  poor relief, 99–101
Potter, Michael (minister of Dunblane), 32, 34, 56, 73, 75, 155, 183, 204, 214
Potter, Michael (yngr) (minister of Kippen), 52, 56, 75, 79
praying societies, 219
preaching, 128–46, 218–19
pre-Christian belief, 160
presbyteries, 12, 77–9, 84
  records, 76, 94

presbytery clerk, 75, 100
  officer, 76, 100
privy censure, 79
Privy Council, 42, 170, 172, 179, 182, 185, 216, 218, 234
  and composition of Stirling Kirk Session, 91
probationers, 39, 49–52, 56–7, 77, 180, 215
  payment of, 58–9, 182
Protesters (Presbyterian party in mid-17th century), 11, 36–8, 42
pulpit supply, 77

Queensberry, Duke of, attitude to Catholicism, 15

rabbling, 18, 41, 214
Ramsay, Thomas (minister of Cadder), 61
Ranken, Gabriel, of Orchardhead (elder in Bothkennar), 93, 167
records, record-keeping, 8, 217–18
  survival, 2–3, 143, 225
Regiments
  Earl of Angus's (Cameronians), 18–22, 144
  Earl of Leven's, 20
  Lord Kenmure's, 21
Reid, David (town constable in Alloa), 172
Reid, William (student), 51
Renwick, James, 16
repentance, place of, 163, 165
Resolutioners (Presbyterian party in mid-17th century), 11, 36–8
revivalism, 119, 140, 218
Ritchie, Robert (schoolmaster in Dollar), 171
Robertson, James (minister of Balquhidder), 188–9
Robertson, John (probationer), 55, 187
Robine, Harie (minister of Alva), 57, 82, 90, 122, 171, 208, 215, 221, 227–8
Rose, Alexander (Bishop of Edinburgh), 5, 19, 143
Rose, Alexander (chaplain in Alva), 122

Rule, Gilbert (Principal of Edinburgh University), 3, 43–4
Rule, Robert (minister of Stirling), 40, 42–3, 61–2, 73–4, 99, 125n
  and communion services, 111, 114
  death, 146
  first incumbency in Stirling, 11
Russell, Andrew, in Rotterdam, 41
Russell, Christian, 27, 213

sackcloth gown, 100, 163–5
Sage, John (historian and Episcopalian polemicist), 24, 113–14
St Ninians, 28, 33, 79, 90, 104, 192, 203
  and Parliamentary Union, 203–4
  attendance at church, 79
  baptisms, 119–20
  Communion services, 118, 218
  discipline cases, 158–9, 161, 164–5, 217
  Episcopalian meeting-house, 145, 150
  Episcopalians, 150
  heritors, 33, 60, 104
  Kirk Session, 89–90
  Presbyterian meeting-house, 17, 32, 60, 89, 213
  penitents, 164–5
Saltoun, Parish Church, 130
Sands, Robert (elder in Port of Menteith), 102
Sauchenford, proposed erection of new parish and church, 79
Schaw, George (episcopal minister of Logie), 27, 34, 109, 144, 214
  rabbled, 21–3
Schaw, Henry (episcopal minister of Logie), 6
Schaw, Sir John, of Sauchie, 166
Schools, in Highland parishes, 190–1
Scotch Presbyterian Eloquence Display'd, 36, 41–3, 134, 139
sermons, 1, 128–46
services, format, 128–9
session clerks, fees, 100
session officers, fees, 100
Sharp, James (Archbishop of St Andrews), 11–12, 14

Shaw, Alexander, probationer, 55, 186–7
Sheriffmuir, battle of, 96
sheriffs depute, 170–2, 220
Simpson, Patrick, author of *'Scriptural Songs'*, 43
Simson, James (minister of Airth), 12, 40
Skinner, John (episcopal minister of Airth), 27, 143, 147, 149
Slirie, Andrew (episcopal minister of Falkirk), 147, 150
Smith, James, in Kilmadock, 162
Societies for the Reformation of Manners, 175
Society in Scotland for Propagating Christian Knowledge (SSPCK), 191–2
Solemn League and Covenant (1643), 10–11, 25
Song of Solomon, 126n, 216
Spalding, John (minister of Dundee), 117
Spence, William (minister of Glendevon, later Fossoway), 40–2, 44, 82–3
SSPCK *see* Society in Scotland for Propagating Christian Knowledge
Steuart, Sir James, of Goodtrees (Lord Advocate), 92, 149, 162–3, 173–4
Steuart, Sir Walter, of Pardovan, 59, 94–6
Stevenson, Patrick (elder in Stirling), 111, 203
Stewart, James (miller in Bridge of Allan), 6
Stewart, Robert (episcopal minister of Balquhidder), 25, 147, 185
Stewart, Robert (minister of Gargunnock), 60
Stirling, 18–19, 21, 203
  as port, 3
  Episcopalian meeting-house, 146, 153
  Episcopalians, 150, 152
  famine, 97–9
Stirling Castle, 3, 17, 20, 85, 91, 154, 203, 213, 215

Stirling Parish Church, 11, 21, 61, 65–6, 150
  baptism records, 119, 121, 150
  Communion services, 110
  discipline cases, 164
  Kirk Session, 89–91, 98–9, 216
Stirling Presbytery, 40, 50–1, 53, 62, 71–2, 179, 192, 222
  and Parliamentary Union, 196, 206, 208–9
  and Presbytery of Dunblane, 23, 83
  attendance, 72–3
  deprivations, 12
  discipline cases, 167
  Gaelic language, 182
  joint with Dunblane, 8, 34, 39–40, 44, 46
  moderatorial elections, 74–5
  records, 2–3, 8
  visitations, 79
Stirling Royal Burgh, 20, 28, 66, 92, 125n, 213, 215–16, 222
  Burgh Council, 21, 61, 66, 85, 90–1, 146, 216
  Burgh Court, 146, 150, 172, 220
  Cowane's Hospital, 91, 98
  elections, 16–17
  Incorporated Trades, 92
  Merchant Guildry, 92
  opposition to Parliamentary Union, 202
  proclamation of accession, 20
  relationship with Parish Church, 90–1
  Spittal's Hospital, 98
  Tolbooth, 91
Stirling, Charles, of Kippendavie, 155
Stirling, James, of Keir, 219–20
Stirling, Walter (episcopal minister of Baldernock), 146, 150
Stirlingshire, assessed for support for Stirling Castle, 21
students, 51, 77
Sutherland, Alexander (episcopal minister of Larbert), 25

Tests, applied in Stirling, 14–15, 89
testificats, 84, 161

Tillicoultry, baptisms, 121
  Communion services, 78, 95, 110
  deacons, 95
  visitation, 78–9, 110
Tillicoultry, Sir Robert Stewart, Lord (circuit court judge), 151
Todd, Thomas, chaplain to Earl of Mar, 51
Toleration (1687), 10, 15, 213
  Queen Anne's, 152, 209
Torbrex, laird of (episcopal elder in St Ninians), 90, 145
Torwood, 14
Traill, Ensign James, (elder in Stirling), 35, 84, 91–2, 111
Traill, Robert (minister in London), 35
transportation of ministers, 59, 62
trials for licence, 46, 52, 54
Tulliallan, 28–9, 79, 84
  and Parliamentary Union, 201, 204–5
  baptisms, 29
  famine, 98
  fines, 167
  poor relief, 99–101
  records, 97
  robust usage of Presbytery Officer, 63–5
Tullibardine, Marquess of see Atholl, Duke of
Turkish pirates, collection for victims, 80
Turnbull, George (minister of Alloa and later Tyninghame), 34, 43, 47, 54, 75, 167, 180, 214, 218
  children, 122
  Communion services, 110, 114–18
  diary, 4, 35, 129
  effect on listeners, 140–1
  health, 73, 184–5
  lecturing, 130–4
  licensing and ordination, 48
  preaching, 97, 129–46, 218–19, 230–1
  transportation to Tyninghame, 62–3, 105
  visit to Aberfoyle, 184–5
turning the riddle, divination, 160
Tyninghame, communion services, 115, 130

Union of Parliaments, 4–5, 80, 149, 196, 201–206, 220–1
    table of addresses, 207
United Societies, 53
Ure family, representation on Port of Menteith Kirk Session, 88
Ure, Andrew, probationer, Gaelic speaker supplying Balquhidder, 187
Ure, James, of Shirgarton, 14, 20, 24, 217
Urquhart, William (episcopal minister) of Clackmannan, 27
Utrecht, university of, 48

voting procedures, 82

Walker, Hugh (minister of Lecropt), 75, 155
Wallace, Matthew (minister of Kincardine), 153, 175, 184, 186, 188, 192
    as Presbytery Clerk, 76
Warden, John (minister of Gargunnock), 69n, 75, 118
Wardon, Adam (schoolmaster of Larbert), Presbytery Clerk, 75–6
Watson, John (minister of Denny), 35–6, 43, 123, 180
Webster, Alexander, census, 114, 210–11n, 226
weekday services, poor attendance, 78–9
Wemyss, William (episcopal minister of Lecropt), 147

West, Elisabeth, 109–10, 114–15, 128, 140, 218
    and Parliamentary Union, 197
Westminster Confession, 25
Whyte, Hugh (minister of Larbert & Dunipace), 35, 78, 122–3, 180
    Presbytery Clerk, 74, 76
William II (III of England), King, 1–2, 5, 17–18, 23, 144, 149, 195, 213
    and General Assembly, (1690), 25–6
    proclaimed at Stirling Cross, 20
Williamson, David (minister of Edinburgh West Kirk), 87
Willison, James (elder in Stirling), 111
Willison, John (minister of Brechin), 15, 47, 128
Wilson, Edward, in Glendevon, 163
Wingate, James (schoolmaster in Doune), 123, 147–8
witchcraft, 66, 160
Wodrow, James (professor in Glasgow University), 44, 49–50, 131–2
Wodrow, Robert (historian and minister of Eastwood), 32, 36–7, 49, 68n
women, as patrons, 107n
Wright, Robert (episcopal minister of Kinross), 147
Wylie, John (minister of Clackmannan), 75, 122

Young, Alexander (elder in Alva), 90, 102
Young, Robert (episcopal minister of Kippen), 24

EU representative:
Easy Access System Europe
Mustamäe tee 50, 10621 Tallinn, Estonia
Gpsr.requests@easproject.com

www.ingramcontent.com/pod-product-compliance
Lightning Source LLC
Chambersburg PA
CBHW052048220426
43663CB00012B/2480